STATES AND NATIONS, POWER AND CIVILITY

Hallsian Perspectives

States and Nations, Power and Civility

Hallsian Perspectives

EDITED BY
FRANCESCO DUINA

UNIVERSITY OF TORONTO PRESS
Toronto Buffalo London

Toronto Buffalo London
utorontopress.com

ISBN 978-1-4875-0237-9

Library and Archives Canada Cataloguing in Publication

States and nations, power and civility : Hallsian perspectives / edited by Francesco Duina.

Includes bibliographical references and index.
ISBN 978-1-4875-0237-9 (cloth)

1. Courtesy – Political aspects. 2. Nationalism. 3. Power (Social science). I. Duina, Francesco G., 1969–, editor

BJ1533.C9S73 2019 177'.1 C2018-904144-7

University of Toronto Press acknowledges the financial assistance to its publishing program of the Canada Council for the Arts and the Ontario Arts Council, an agency of the Government of Ontario.

Canada Council for the Arts
Conseil des Arts du Canada

Funded by the Government of Canada
Financé par le gouvernement du Canada
Canada

Contents

Part Two: International and Comparative Contexts

Acknowledgments

This volume focuses on the nature and preservation of civility in and between nation-states and, going back in time, empires. The chapters are wide reaching in geographical and historical terms. Analytically, however, they share a commitment to the "Hallsian" paradigm: the rich and sophisticated ideas put forth over the last four decades by John A. Hall – the James McGill Professor of Comparative Historical Sociology at McGill University. We are grateful to John for offering comments and insights on the overall direction of the volume and on specific chapters. We are also thankful for his willingness to provide a concluding chapter reflecting on the key theoretical points and empirical findings.

Early drafts of several chapters were presented at the Canadian Sociological Association's annual conference in Toronto in May 2017. Led by Matthew Lange, the Comparative and Historical Research Cluster hosted a regular session on the influence of the Hallsian paradigm on a variety of sociological areas of study – from nationalism to religion to historical comparative methods. In keeping with the volume's focus, our attention went especially to civility. Yesim Bayar, Joe Bryant, Matthew Lange, and I participated; John, also present, shared his own thoughts. The event attracted a very attentive and large audience. When the floor opened for discussion, a lively Q&A exchange helped us collect further thoughts and ideas for the volume. We are grateful to have had such a stimulating opportunity to discuss our plans for the project.

Bates College offered financial support as part of a Faculty Development Grant I secured for 2016 and 2017. Some of the funds were used to pay a brilliant undergraduate, Zeke Smith, to review every chapter, format the volume, and offer feedback on the clarity of the arguments being articulated. I am thankful to both Bates and Zeke for their help.

A special thanks goes to Douglas Hildebrand, who, as acquisition editor for the social sciences at the University of Toronto Press until summer 2017, expressed interest in the project early on, offered valuable guidance at key moments in the volume's development, attended the session at the Canadian Sociological Association, and met with me at the American Sociological Association's annual conferences in Chicago (2015), Seattle (2016), and Montreal (2017) to discuss the volume and offer advice. He helped immensely to define both the vision and the scope of the contributions.

Three anonymous reviewers shared their positive assessments of the volume along with suggestions for sharpening certain ideas and passages. We took their comments to heart and sought to address them. We did so with the help of Jodi Lewchuk, a seasoned editor with a keen sense of the academic publishing industry, who took over the project in late 2017. I am very grateful to the reviewers and Jodi for helping us finalize the intellectual reach and quality of the writing, to Terry Teskey for her outstanding copy-editing, and to Janice Evans for her editorial assistance.

This volume reflects the work of many people. Responsibility for any errors rests, however, with me.

Francesco Duina
June 2018
Cumberland, Maine

STATES AND NATIONS, POWER AND CIVILITY

Hallsian Perspectives

Introduction: Vulnerable Civility

FRANCESCO DUINA

> In a fundamental sense nationalism stands opposed to the very base of civility: it seeks unity, in contrast to civility's desire to manage diversity.
>
> Hall (2013, 7)

Western politicians have long believed that modern, democratic nation-states protect and advance civility – understood, at the simplest level, as the tolerance for diversity. This has been a cornerstone of US and European foreign policy, whether in Myanmar, China, Russia, the Korean peninsula, Cuba, Iraq, or any other part of the world (Huber 2015; Smith 2012). It has also been a basic assumption of much of the research on democratization. Scholars believe that countries transitioning from repressive regimes towards modern democracies experience, almost by definition, an opening up of "civil society": non-governmental associations, an independent media, and a spectrum of interest groups establish themselves and voice new perspectives (Beichelt et al. 2014; Tilly 2000).

Non-governmental organizations intent on promoting democracy in African, Asian, and Middle Eastern countries have subscribed to a similar view. Democratic nation-states protect freedom of expression, women's rights, religious freedom, and other principles and practices closely associated with the tolerance of diversity (Mendelson and Glenn 2002). Something similar can be said of many international governmental organizations, such as the European Union or the United Nations (Huber 2015; Mansfield and Pevehouse 2008; Pevehouse 2002): believing that democratic nation-states offer the best space for civility to flourish, they have discouraged other types of political arrangements and funnelled resources towards what they view as a superior model of political organization.

The concern with the promotion of civility – or the more general concept of civil society – is easy to understand. Civility is the opposite of abusive behaviour: in a "civilized" society, individuals have the most room to exercise their faculties. Like-minded people are permitted to form associations for the articulation and promotion of their interests. Religious, political, sexual, artistic, and cultural freedoms are protected, provided, as civility would have it, that those do not infringe on the freedom of others. Civility is also seen as essential to capitalism: the latter relies on individual initiative, the principle of private property, and reliable social peace. It follows that civility is related to wealth creation, technological progress, and other forms of progress. We encounter writings on the importance and merits of civility from Aristotle onwards (Peck 2002), with perhaps the most original articulations expressed during the Enlightenment in Europe, by thinkers such as John Locke, Immanuel Kant, and Adam Smith.

There are certainly good reasons to think that modern democratic nation-states do in fact promote civility. Democracy is rooted in liberalism, and liberalism is closely related to civility. Modern democratic nation-states have done more than any other type of political regime to support and protect civil life. History has shown that dictatorships, communist regimes, empires of various sorts, and other sorts of political orders stifle alternative mindsets, dissent, and the plurality of perspectives. There are obvious connections between democracy, modern nation-states, and civility.

But matters may not be so straightforward. Nation-states, including democratic ones, inevitably embody power, and do so in multiple and often subtle ways (Mann 2012). Power is found in the coercive nature of state policies across numerous areas, from education to the economy. National life presumes acceptance, by its members, of some degree of cultural homogeneity, and therefore at least some rejection of "others" (Gellner 1983; Greenfeld 2016). It is predicated on autonomy from foreign intrusion and thus on suspicion of alien elements found within. Power is present in the structuring of political and social life – for instance, in the rules that define elections or parties' participation in law-making. At a more basic level, states have a monopoly over the legitimate use of violence: weapons and the presumed right to use them are concentrated in their hands. Indeed, the formation of nation-states in the first instance involves, in different ways depending on the specific case, major assertions of power, whether through wars (revolutionary, civil, for independence, etc.), new social contracts bestowing transfers of authority to various branches of government, or other means.

Power, then, is concentrated in nation-states. Perhaps more precisely put, nation-states serve as containers for the accumulation of power. This is so both when it comes to the "nation" and to the "state." Because of this, nation-states – even democratic ones – always present a potential, if not real, threat to civil society or, more fundamentally, to civility in society. To ignore or underestimate this potentiality reflects an inaccurate understanding of the nature of nation-states and is, in practical terms, very risky. In many countries, state officials owe their allegiances to different sectarian or ethnic groups. This creates the possibility for domestic conflict and, in the worst cases, civil war. Economic inequality or racial tensions, in turn, can easily generate dissent, and state actors can overstep their boundaries in response (Lange 2011, 2013). Indeed, in historical terms, the very process of nation-state–building in every continent – that is, the crafting of a single national identity matched by corresponding institution-building – required (and requires, to the extent that nation-building is currently taking place in various parts of the world) some degree of forceful co-optation of the young (for instance, by requiring compulsory primary education and the teaching of a national language, or by compulsory military service), minorities, and other segments of the populace.

There is, in turn, always the possibility that inclusive arrangements falter and open the gate to more authoritarian ones. The Weimar Republic in Germany's interwar years serves as a primary example, and events in Turkey in recent years serve as a second. Faced with pressures (economic, ideological, ethnic, etc.), nation-states, even tolerant ones, can quickly become intolerant: when they do so, they engage in submission, repression, and the violation of rights. The potential is ever present.

Similar observations can be made with regard to the international arena. We are often reminded that war seldom happens between democratic nation-states. Yet it would be erroneous to assume that civility is bound to define the relationship between nation-states, even democratic ones. There is plenty of room for tensions and for the usurpation of basic principles of sovereignty, human rights, and freedom. History is replete with examples.

The United States' interventions in democratically elected regimes in Latin America, Africa, and other parts of the world during and after the Cold War offer powerful illustrations (Cox, Lynch, and Bouchet 2013, 1). It is also clearly the case that democratic nation-states regularly intervene, with power, in non-democratic ones – sometimes, it turns out, in the name of civility itself.

None of this is to suggest that modern nation-states inevitably usurp their powers. On the contrary, when we consider alternative forms of political organization, such as empires, modern nation-states can be reasonably viewed as being especially respectful of civility in society. They clearly encourage it, with many positive consequences for the unfolding of everyday life but also for economic, scientific, artistic, and other kinds of achievements. The point, rather, is to appreciate the power inherent in modern nation-states, democratic or not, on the one hand, and the *delicate relationship* that these states, by necessity, have with civility in society – at both the domestic and international levels.

With this in mind, this volume aims to identify explicitly and then explore in detail the complex and profoundly consequential relationship between nation-states, and specifically the powers that rest within them, *and* civility. What kinds of power do nation-states embody? What is civility? What tensions exist between the two? And what should be done to successfully manage the delicate relationship between civility and nation-states? These are challenging and significant questions. They deserve, as a whole, extensive systematic investigation.

The focus is on both democratic and non-democratic nation-states: we are interested in the "nation-state" as a historically distinct type of political organization – one that sets it apart from alternatives such as empires, tribes, or city-states. This is because we live in a world of nation-states and, therefore, it is in this context that we must think about civility. Globalization has certainly not equated to the end of the nation-state, as many scholars predicted (Held 2005; Ohmae 1995). If we are concerned about civility – its existence, protection, and flourishing – in the contemporary world, we would do well to begin with the recognition that the building blocks of today's world order are nation-states generally – many democratic, but also many not.

This volume brings together twelve distinguished sociologists, political scientists, and historians from North America, Europe, and China to explore conceptually and empirically the relationship between nation-states, as loci of power, and civility. The first group of chapters considers dynamics at the domestic levels; the second group examines dynamics at the international dimension. The analyses cover a wide range of geographies – the Balkans, the United States, Germany, Turkey, China, the global South, and more – and of time periods. Some chapters consider democratic states; others turn their attention to countries in transition or more authoritarian ones. The last two chapters consider, by way of comparison, pre-modern empires (themselves types of "states") across the globe. All seek to shed light on the delicate relationship between politics, power, and civility.

Guiding and structuring their investigations is the seminal work of John Hall – the James McGill Professor of Comparative Historical Sociology at McGill University. No contemporary social scientist has done more than Hall to identify and investigate the intricate relationships between nation-states, the power they hold, and civility. In fact, while the idea that nation-states embody power is not novel, the notion that such power – when properly understood – can undermine civility can be most directly linked to Hall's writings starting in the late 1970s. The appreciation of the problem requires a particular understanding of the nation-state and its power, of the nature of civility, and of the relationship between the two. It is predicated on an understanding of the multifaceted character of power in nation-states, and the complex, subtle, and numerous ways it can affect civility.

The authors of the chapters in this volume accordingly ground their investigations in Hall's work. That work provides both the initial inspiration for the chapters and the conceptual vocabulary and in many cases methodological tools for empirical enquiry. The results prove very rewarding. Hall's perspective allows the authors to extend their analyses to very different time periods, geographies, and dynamics. The empirical findings and conceptual conclusions "speak" to each other, and together paint a rich and detailed picture of the complex relationship between nations, states, power, and civility.

Given the above, the purpose of this introductory chapter is twofold. First, I identify the fundamental elements of the Hallsian paradigm: the core concepts, relationships, normative stances, and preferred methodological approaches. When properly elucidated, these reveal a number of fundamental assumptions about the nature of not only polities, power, and civility but also human beings, culture, and structures. Second, I offer a brief overview of the coming chapters.

The Hallsian Paradigm on Nations, States, Power, and Civility

Hall has dealt with the themes of nations, states, power, and civility in over twenty authored or edited volumes and nearly one hundred articles and chapters in edited volumes. The conceptual, geographical, and historical reaches of his work are formidable. He has, for instance, examined the formation of empires in ancient history, the religious and economic systems of pre-modern China and India, the emergence of nation-states in Europe in the last four centuries, wars across the world, globalization and contemporary national policy-making in Europe and North America, sociological theory, and much more. In those works he has laid out what we may call the *Hallsian paradigm*: a particular view of the world – of its political and cultural landscapes, the key forces that shape it, and the logic by which we should seek to investigate it.

Any effort to reduce Hall's thinking to a simple and cohesive paradigm is bound to be limited: some ideas will inevitably be left out. Yet, upon close analysis, certain fundamental points consistently present themselves throughout much of his writing. They cluster around four key themes, depicted in Figure A. We can analyse each element in turn and reflect, at the end, on Hall's methodological tendencies and his appreciation for complexity and ambiguity in social scientific analysis.

First, Hall sees *nation-states* as still the *building blocks* of the contemporary world. "We live," he writes with John Campbell, "in a world of states." "This," he continues, "denies outright the claim often made, by politicians as well as by academics, that states are losing their powers as economic interactions around the world increase in speed and intensity" (Campbell and Hall 2015a, 1). Indeed, Hall (2011, 17) observes, "it has been both necessary and easy to poke holes in extravagant claims suggesting that globalization has so undermined the power of the

Figure A Elements of the Hallsian Perspective

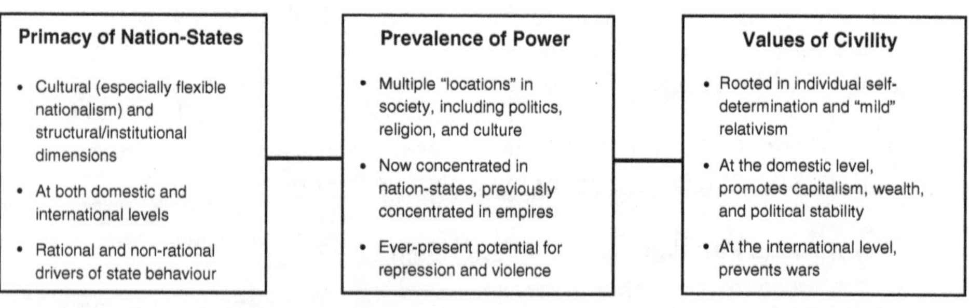

nation-state, either by hollowing it out both from above and below, that it has lost its place in the modern world." Nation-states began emerging in sixteenth- and seventeenth-century Europe and assumed their dominant position in the political order after the collapse of empires at the beginning of the twentieth century. Globalization may be happening, but states continue to determine the shape of our world and its future direction. They engage with, but are not overtaken by, global forces. For this reason, social scientific attention should continue to focus on their emergence, internal functioning, and relationships on the world stage.

The primacy of nation-states manifests itself on two broad fronts. The first is cultural. Hall rejects the view of globalization and world society theorists, such as Meyer (2007) or Soysal (1994), that there exist transnational values and blueprints (for instance around the environment or human rights) that dominate the aspirations and behaviours of individuals, governments, organizations, and groups. While some sort of international society – primarily inhabited by politicians, business people, and the rich who comprise the upper classes of society (Hall 2011, 24) – is certainly in place and while some countries (the United States above all, along with many Western countries, Japan, and parts of China) are especially influential over its direction (Campbell and Hall 2015a), the fact remains that nations retain a great amount of cultural content and significance. This is so even in the most integrated spaces in the world, such as the European Union, and in highly exposed countries, such as Denmark (Hall 2011, 23). Culture remains by and large national.

The point is made most forcefully with regard to national identity: nationalism remains the fundamental glue that holds countries together. Globalization has challenged nationalism, but the latter remains strong and adaptable. Hall (2011, 18) compares nationalism to Freud's characterization of the libido as "sticky, attaching itself to different desires and neuroses. This is how we should see nationalism, changing its character according to the forces with which it interacts." At most, globalization "has helped to remove some of the worst excesses of nationalism," but not its centrality to contemporary societies (25). Nationalism emerged in modern Europe alongside (and, as Gellner would have it, as a result of) industrialization (18), established itself with various degrees of intensity in much of the West (requiring among other things a fair amount of ethnic cleansing or homogenizing by various methods), took on different guises in Europe with tensions erupting during World War II, found significant expressions during the Cold War era and decolonization, and is now taking on new forms in the age of globalization.

Today, Hall writes, "nationalism still has the capacity to change its colours" (24).

There exist multiple types of nationalism. There are ethnic, civic, civil, and other varieties (Hall 2013, 88–90). Nationalism can vary in intensity as well. In some parts of Europe and perhaps selectively elsewhere, thanks in part to economic integration, milder versions are in place: some countries could be called "state-nations." Yet in other places, including some countries in the "advanced world," Hall (2011, 25) sees a "strand of nationalism" that is much more "nativist" in nature, with the potential for "substantial political bite." The Brexit vote in summer 2016 and Donald Trump's stunning victory in the American presidential election a few months later offer the most recent validations of this view. Variations are in place, but this should in no way be seen as a sign of nationalism's waning relevance. On the contrary, they represent vitality, adaptability, and continued significance.

The primacy of nation-states also concerns more structural and institutional dimensions: the "state," that is, continues to matter a great deal. Deepening economic ties may have blurred boundaries between countries, especially in the global North (and much less so elsewhere) (Hall 2011, 18–19), but these countries still require administrations, governments, courts, and legislative bodies. As a matter of fact, "there is every sign that many national groupings still seek their own state, in the advanced as well as in the developing world" (Hall 2011, 17). Thus, even in those countries that are the most exposed to the pressures of the international economy, national institutional arrangements endure and make a difference for how countries behave (Campbell and Hall 2015b). It might actually be precisely in those societies that one can hear calls "for a state to protect" the nation from foreign influences (Hall 2011, 24).

Hall extends his arguments about the primacy of nation-states to the international arena. Geopolitically, in some ways like a realist, Hall sees states as the primary players on the world stage. The relevance of entities like the United Nations or regional alliances is small. He is even sceptical of the real power of the European Union. Yet, unlike a realist, Hall recognizes that the power of states has as much to do with economic interests and rationality as with less calculable and measurable factors such as ideas, infrastructure, a desire to impress, leaders' personalities and insecurities, and more. The United States' invasion of Iraq under George W. Bush offers an example: "hubris" in American power and visions of democracy, coupled with a "personal desire of the younger Bush to complete the work of his father," "prevented sufficiently consequentialist thought" (Hall 2013, 120). States can thus be quite irrational (121–2). As such, they remind us of human beings themselves – sometimes reasonable, sometimes far less so. The result is that, rather than an anarchical space of atomistic countries looking to advance their own interests in the most effective way possible, the international sphere is more like a loose society of nation-states, engaged in "economic and military competitions," perennially changing and evolving, with interactions of various kinds shaping their behaviour (121–2).

The second element of the Hallsian paradigm is *power*. Power, primarily understood in the Weberian sense as a situation where someone is able to have someone else do something that they would not necessarily do on their own (Hall 1985, 22), comes in many forms: political, military, economic, ideational, and more. This means that power does not exist independently in society but is associated with, or found in, certain institutions (such as legal and administrative systems, policy legacies, and traditions), cultural dimensions (identities, values, religion), and even periods of time (including, crucially, the evolution of empires and their eventual decline, which led the way for the emergence of nation-states). It follows that power should also be seen as belonging to specific societal and historical contexts – a view consistent with Michael Mann's (a contributor to this volume) 1986 classic work on the matter. As Hall and Campbell (2015a, vii) put it, "we believe that power has economic, political, and ideological dimensions."

In contemporary times, for Hall (2013, 121) such "belonging" concerns, above all though not exclusively, the nation-state. "We live in a world of states," he observes, and this means that "power is accordingly at the center of our attention, both as it exists within and between states and as it has changed over time" (Campbell and Hall 2015a, vii). Simply put, nation-states wield enormous power: they are the loci of concentrations of power. And, moreover, "the powers of modern states have increased enormously since the seventeenth century," when states "did little for their societies" (3). Before nation-states, empires were the centres of power and, before and sometimes in tandem with empires, tribal and other smaller-scale forms of organizations enjoyed great power (Hall 2013, 21). This has now changed: "a proper understanding of our world must entail an analysis of power relations within and between states even in this era of economic globalization" (Campbell and Hall 2015a, 115).

And just as the "nation" refers to something cultural and ideological, and the "state" to something more tangible and physical, power finds itself above all expressed or operating within nations or between nations (but not above them) in a spectrum of guises. These include the military, the court systems, education, health care, and, of course, our values and ways of making sense of the world. Hall talks about the "huge infrastructures" of states as well as their abilities to affect every aspect of our daily lives: "we now look to our states to stop us smoking and to prevent violence in the most private places of our homes" (Campbell and Hall 2015a, 3). At the international level, wars are unfortunately all too frequent demonstrations of enormous state power (Hall 2013; Hall and Malešević 2013, 1), but so is the ability of dominant countries – the United States above all – to manipulate global norms, currency reserves and exchange rates, and the general direction of international politics (Campbell and Hall 2015a, chap. 6).

Importantly, while nation-states hold much power, Hall also feels that they do not control all of it. "It is in the rarest of circumstances," he notes, "that states have achieved their desires: that of being complete power containers" (2013, 121). A host of factors affect power in any given setting. "Economic interchange," for instance, "has made it harder for states to control economic processes" (121). The presence of a regional hegemon can limit the reach of other countries. Competing groups within society can challenge even authoritarian elites (124). Even the most brutal dictators, such as Hitler, cannot control the fates of their societies. Indeed, the same observation applies to empires. This is a function of the multiple types of power that exist and the fact that, ultimately, much of it is inherently not "controllable." Thus, some people, or groups of people, in a nation-state have more power than others. Religious orders, political parties, corporations, communities of experts, and so on all have power – but in different amounts and often of different types.

Balances of power can change, as well, over time in a single society and across societies. Hall's wide-ranging analyses of world religions and politics over the centuries – including imperial China, the classical period of Brahmans in India, Islam over the centuries, and Europe itself – are driven precisely by this flexible view of the nature of power (Hall 1985). Power in turn can lie dormant or suddenly be exercised. Peaceful social arrangements can quickly break down, and vicious war and destruction can ensue; after all, "human beings face a permanent political problem because they are all too capable of oppressing each other" (Hall 1987, 46). Tensions can be tamed and managed until an event occurs (from large-scale occurrences like the end of the Soviet Union to a terrorist attack) and then dramatic change takes place.

The third element of the Hallsian paradigm is *civility*. Civility here means above all the willingness to respect one another even when holding very divergent opinions. The "nature of civility," Hall (2013, 251) writes, "rests firmly on the presence of sufficient means for self-expression, as well as the ability to resist arbitrary subordination." The ground rules of behaviour – physical, verbal, and otherwise – must transcend substantive differences in viewpoints about the world. A commitment to a shared community of basic principles of interaction, in other words, defines the idea of civility. Civility is thus, above all, relational or procedural: it consists of guidelines for people to deal with each other. It is, in this regard, closely associated with European principles of liberalism, an ideology influencing much of Hall's writing.

As such, civility recognizes the importance of "individual self-determination" (Hall 2013, 12). Civility celebrates differences among persons: it ensures limits on intrusion in the private sphere of people. A society where civility is in place "is one in which individuals have the chance of at least trying to create their own selves." Uncivil societies, by contrast, can exert an "all powerful tyranny ... over every aspect of daily life, from clothing to the choice of a marriage partner to the details of belief" (21). Here, echoes of English liberalism in particular – with its belief in the value of the individual as something worth protecting and, ultimately, as the basis of any sound and realistic social contract – can be detected.

Hall adopts a clear normative stance towards civility: we should embrace it. There are several reasons for this. Human beings are always works in progress rather than finished products. Society must give its members the chance to develop, evolve, and refine themselves. Hall is suspicious of thinkers, like Sartre and Rousseau, who believe in the a priori existence of a "true" self that must simply be discovered. He views beliefs in a "real self" that is "always available" as "facile." Instead, siding more with symbolic interactionists such as Erving Goffman, Hall (2013, 151) feels that "social practices" that allow "people to establish identities of their own, at their own place" should be "welcomed." There is a self, to be sure, but it is bound to emerge over time, is always evolving, and often lacks complete coherence (2007, 232).

Civility should also be embraced because of its consequences for the life of nations. It is an essential ingredient in their success, and ultimately in good relationships among nations. Civility, after all, protects liberty, democratic principles, human rights, and individualism – that is, many key elements of liberalism itself. These, which are often described as the basis of "negative" liberties (in so far as they set limits around behaviour rather than describe substantively what to use freedom for), serve as foundations for good governance and ultimately wealth generation. As Hall (1987, 48) notes, "the modern, liberal conception of 'negative' liberty has a natural affinity with choice in the market." Authoritarian, theocratic, communist, and other such political regimes, by contrast, stifle prosperity. Any society will have its own tensions, but when conflict can be managed without violence it can be productive (Hall 2013, 3). Data on GDP figures per capita show this: liberal (i.e., civil) countries have historically become richer than illiberal ones. At the international level, civility in turn regulates potentially extremely destructive tensions and instead fosters useful cooperation.

Hall is accordingly prone to remind us that civility helps explain the ascendancy of the West from the fifteenth century on. Innovation and ingenuity, and hence capitalism, sprung in part from competition among fiefdoms and states, which was made possible by the absence of an overarching sovereign authority in Europe – by "a power vacuum" (Hall 1987, 55) – whether political or theocratic (unlike in other parts of the world at that time), and the move, by kings and feudal lords, to grant some degree of autonomy to their own towns and other entities (Hall 2013, 28). The latter amounted to the establishment of some civility within political units, where individuals were free to explore, examine, and advance their lot: "there was, in other words," Hall writes (1987, 55), "a type of laissez faire built into Europe as a whole, and there is a relationship between this and the creation of favourable climates for capitalists inside nations." Importantly, the existence of Christian norms and a "shared membership in a civilization" made it all easier. "Church, nobles, and townsmen" could now come together, and a "measure of internal decency" was ensured by fear of rival states (Hall 2013, 28–9). All this had earlier roots: "the origins of toleration of this sort," Hall notes, "lie within Europe. Perhaps its deepest roots result from the way in which the removal of the centralized authority of Rome places power in several sets of hands" (27). Indeed, there is even something about Christianity itself that limited its grip on the unfolding of everyday social and political life (27).

Accompanying the economic advantages of civility are political ones. Here Hall points to the work of Ralf Dahrendorf (1959) and Albert

Hirschman (1970) to argue that civility may have one very practical consequence: stability. Stifling dissent, Hall reasons, is very likely to lead to social unrest and revolutions: it can intensify conflict. But when disagreeing factions in society are allowed to voice their concerns, the chances for violent conflict to erupt diminish. As Hall (2013, 71) puts it, "political civility can defuse tensions throughout society, thereby creating fundamental political stability." Civility, then, can have "pacifying effects" (77), and examples of these can be seen throughout the globe, from India to Costa Rica. There is certainly something Machiavellian about this: the best way to stay in power is to allow for some dissent. Hall recognizes as much. Yet the more fundamental point concerns the maintenance of peace as, in general, a good in itself and certainly superior, in most cases, to violent alternatives. Differing viewpoints always exist in any given society. Suppression cannot be a long-term solution: it will lead to conflict. If peace is the desired outcome, civility is surely a vehicle for it.

On more philosophical terms, it is worth noting that Hall (2013, 2) feels that a commitment to civility reflects "a mild form of relativism." The principle of civility implies an agnostic position regarding what might be "good" and predilects instead the "right" way to treat one another, precisely as each of us goes about fulfilling or looking for our visions of the good. There is, he notes in his intellectual biography of Ernest Gellner, "the indisputable fact that significant areas of social life are best seen in relativist terms. Who indeed is to say that one form of dance is better than another?" (Hall 2010, 128). These principles of civility are therefore neither numerous nor overbearing: they simply prevent encroachment or intrusion. Yet they are nonetheless grounded in some notion of superiority: they are preferable to the alternatives. In this regard, Hall writes, civility cannot be thought of as a completely relativistic principle: it "does *not* entail absolute denial of all universal standards. How could it given that the ideal of civility considers the agreement to differ to have universal status!" (2013, 2; see also 1987, 2).

Such an understanding of civility is rooted in yet a deeper philosophical premise: an epistemological view that nothing can be known for certain. Hall spends considerable time, precisely when investigating the nature of civility, in examining the writings of thinkers such as David Hume, John Locke, and Friedrich Nietzsche to show that, ultimately, the most sensible position to adopt towards reality is not to dismiss it either as fully a mystery or as something we can know with absolute certainty. The correct perspective is somewhere in-between, and it follows, as Hall (2007, 242) memorably puts it, that "academics should resist being clearer than the truth." Indeed, he reminds us that even "predicting the past is hard," and that it is "mere foolishness to offer certainty about the future." Social and human lives are messy, partly penetrable and knowable but never transparent.

We can now identify the fourth – and most crucial for this volume – point of the Hallsian paradigm: successful countries in the contemporary world must *manage* the delicate and at times tense *relationship* between power and civility. Such management hinges on awareness of two closely related points. First, we must not hesitate to recognize that nation-states, even democratic ones, always present the potential for creating precisely the opposite effects of civility. Hall could not be clearer about this. Sometimes the culprit is the more cultural dimension of the nation-state – specifically, nationalism. As he, along with Malešević, writes:

> It is easy to see why nationalism is seen as likely to cause war once it gains salience in the historical record. If nationalism insists that one live with members of one's nation in a state free from alien rule, then avenues to violence open up immediately. Members of the nation left outside the state should be brought in and untrustworthy elements within expelled … Europe's hideous twentieth century makes it only too easy to recognize these forces, all capable of leading to organized brutality. (Hall and Malešević 2013, 1)

Nationalism, as a force of inclusion and assimilation, is very much a double-edged sword: it can unite – indeed, "it seeks unity" (Hall 2013, 7) – but, in so doing, it can be extremely divisive. Homogeneity tends to go hand in hand with nationalism (Hall 2006, 39). If some people can belong to the nation, others must be excluded, removed, or purged. Countries with balanced ethnic minorities are rare: in most cases, Hall reminds us, minorities comprise such a small percentage of the population as to be almost irrelevant. Thus, even "an advanced social democracy such as Denmark has enormous difficulty, both in welcoming those that its low birth rate necessitates and then including them within society, above all through intermarriage with native Danes" (Hall 2013, 251).

The power inherent in the more structural dimensions of the nation-state is similarly potentially dangerous. Large, organized armies of committed citizens are capable of massive atrocities. Bureaucracies facilitate in moral and practical terms the punishment of vast amounts of people. It follows that nation-states, even the most liberal ones, can generate large-scale violence, war, ethnic cleansing, economic hardships, and many more problems. This is true both internally and externally. All that is needed are the wrong sorts of ideas and fashions. Accordingly, when states "put ideological dreams into effect, they become the enemies of civility" (Hall 2013, 247). The same applies to cases where different national movements claim "the same piece of territory" and are backed, in so doing, "by powerful neighbouring states" (2006, 40). With these possibilities in mind, Hall describes with great horror both the civil conflicts in countries like Yugoslavia in the 1990s and the mass atrocities of World War II. Indeed, he sees the twentieth century overall as one of nations and great violence, of "horrors" that "reminded us of the benefits of civility" (2013, 250). The same applies to the start of the twenty-first century: Hall (2007, 243) describes as unprecedented in history the massive and "naked power" of the United States, and worries deeply about Russia's nuclear arsenal.

The second step is to see that power and civility need not stand in contradiction: they can be reconciled, with very positive implications for the quality of social life, economic productivity, individual creativity, and much more. As Hall puts it, "one should not surrender to pessimism" (Hall and Malešević 2013, 22). We find plenty of cases where power and civility are successfully coexisting, in Europe as well as Asia, Africa, and the Americas. This is the case even in very diverse societies. "Political loyalty," Hall thus notes, "in combination with the accommodation of ethnic, religious and linguistic differences seems to allow India to work" (Hall and Malešević 2013, 22; see also Hall 2011, 24). Switzerland offers another example (Campbell and Hall 2017). Indeed, it is interesting to note that in his classic 1985 piece on power and liberties, Hall recognizes that power may even be seen as a "capacity created by social agreement," so that rather than entailing the ability to force others to do something they otherwise would not, it can actually reflect the opposite (22–3).

For civility and power to coexist and even mutually benefit from each other, the right sort of state has to be in place. The very idea of "civil society," Hall (2013, 19) observes, is not "simply" a matter of "societal self-organization" but involves a healthy, carefully calibrated relationship between citizens and the "state." Without that, civility in society is hardly attainable. "Despotism is a danger," he writes, but "so too is anarchy." Those who call for a dismantling of the state are in fact deluded: they "overgeneralize on the basis of the pacific consensus that marks their social words" (20). That consensus involves a state that is tolerant and mindful of individual needs – even those needs that may be present when individuals form one ethnic group among other groups in a given state (69). The term "civil society," Hall argues, "should be reserved for social self-organization that cooperates with a responsible and responsive state" (21).

Key, then, is the presence of a state that is both competent and open to the needs of the people. For Hall, this means above all ensuring the presence of particular kinds of institutional and policy arrangements. Hall's most recent work on successful small European states – whether during the financial crisis of 2007–8 or at other points in time – offers specific insights into what those arrangements might be. The case of Denmark teaches us, for instance, of the merits of corporatist arrangements that encourage negotiation and learning, a focus on long-term collective goods, and a sense of social solidarity (Campbell and Hall 2006, 4, 41). The case of Switzerland, in turn, shows the benefits of very inclusive and representative institutional mechanisms: these have helped foster a very strong sense of national identity, even among very different ethnic groups, and trust in the public sphere (Campbell and Hall, 2017). These and many other cases represent specific embodiments of the broader principles of stable and reliable openness and communication, especially between the people and elites (Hall, 1996, 30–1), even when multiple ethnic groups are present in a country (Hall 2013, 68). "Allowing voice," in this context, is thus a central point, in line with Hirschman's recommendations (Hall 2013, 68).

Hall extends the underlying logic of this argument to the international sphere. Disagreement among powerful nations is possible and in fact inevitable. Realism should moreover be taken seriously and is in fact in good part accurate (Hall 1996, 31). But the presence of disagreement should never translate into repressive hegemonic arrangements or complete lack of coordination or cooperation. When thinking about the growing tensions between Europe and the United States after the invasion of Iraq by President George W. Bush and his pursuit of a neoconservative agenda in world affairs, Hall urged us to "reflect on the nature of civil society." "What really matters," he stressed, is the "*agreement* to differ. The Atlantic community would now be best served by a measure of separation in some areas so as to allow for greater harmony in others" (2007, 246). The goal should not be to expect full harmony but, rather, to allow those differences to exist while always submitting to certain basic principles of acceptable behaviour. More generally, Hall

(1996, 5) feels that the "international order is likely to be strengthened by the extensive sharing of norms and practices, that is, from the presence of international society." Briefly put, liberalism and realism can and should meet.

With this said, Hall of course recognizes the very real and frequent possibility that countries will not behave internally or externally in a civil manner: this is a simple historical fact. Moreover, even ideologies rooted in civility have, within themselves, the seeds of potential intolerance: this is because "those imagining themselves in possession of the truth can all too easily be disastrous makers of policy. The danger of self-righteousness is that it can lead to ruling others." It is also the case that at times those ideologies can be too tolerant, assume everyone thinks alike, and even "forget the importance of state power." All one needs to consider are the policies of appeasement towards Hitler (Hall 1996, 31). This means that Hall believes military interventions and wars can and in fact should happen in certain cases. His call for civility is, in other words, not based on an expectation of universal compliance. The objective is rather to underscore the possibility, need, and advantages of civility in political affairs. Loftier objectives might be possible but are probably not attainable. Civility offers a set of pragmatic principles that allow for flexibility and self-determination, while regulating the relationship between people and states.

The above reflections amount to only a broad description of the Hallsian paradigm. More elaboration is in order, and is something that the coming chapters accomplish to a good extent. We should nonetheless add here a few additional points. The Hallsian perspective advocates for certain *methods* for social scientific investigation over others. The preferred approach rests on concrete empirical, historical, and often comparative data, analysed with sociological lenses (i.e., with a predisposition to look for causal patterns over time and across cases, and with an appreciation for cultural and institutional factors as especially important). Heavily quantitative models, while often elegant, cannot capture reality. In-depth, theoretically informed but open-minded historical analysis can be very revealing.

The Hallsian perspective also calls for an appreciation of *complexity* and *ambiguity* in the social world. When it comes to nationalism, for instance, Hall insists, as already noted, that it "is best seen in plural rather than singular terms. As with religion, there are varieties of nationalist experience." He continues to stress that "ethnicity is by no means a simple matter," and there can be in a polity "multiple and at times complementary identities" (Hall and Malešević 2013, 11, 14). "Nationalism," he writes elsewhere, "is a liable force that can take different forms" (Hall 2013, 7). Power comes in many guises. Predictions are very hard to make. Change is ubiquitous and causal arguments should be contextualized and universal claims resisted. Structural and cultural variables both matter, and arguments categorically favouring one over the other are inaccurate. The world is messy, and while categorizations should be sought, definitional and conceptual flexibility are necessary. Indeed, civility itself calls for much tolerance, though always with some grounding in a few basic principles of behaviour. There is, in sum, a certain balance in the Hallsian paradigm.

The Chapters Ahead

The primary objective of the coming chapters is to leverage the Hallsian perspective to improve our understanding of the relationship between power, civility, nations, and states. Twelve distinguished sociologists, political scientists, and historians take part in this task. The chapters speak to each other on multiple levels – substantively, geographically, historically, and methodologically. The geographical scope covers the world – from individual countries (Turkey, China, Germany, the United States), to sets of countries, regions of the world, and the world at large.[1] The result improves our understanding of a host of current and past political, economic, and social events in the world.

The chapters in Part 1 focus on specific nation-states. The first two turn to the United States, the most powerful country on earth but currently also a major site of political and social tensions. John Campbell engages, in chapter 1, with Hall's view that social cohesion in the United States remains strong despite the rise of identity politics and other forces (Hall and Lindholm 1999). Cracks in that cohesion are becoming cleavages. Growing intolerance, the rise of right-wing populism as seen in the election of Donald Trump, widening inequalities, and political polarization threaten the very fabric of the nation. Civility, in the Hallsian sense, may be at risk in America – and Campbell gives us the analytical and empirical tools to assess this.

Civility in America is also of concern to Liliana Riga. In chapter 2, she sees it as central to the American social contract. Yet, with a historical eye, she points to the moral, social, and political costs paid for it. She

1 Note that the authors have used their own translations, rather than relying on previously translated versions, when quoting directly from foreign-language texts.

argues that American civility has been, above all, a white man's project. Blacks, in particular, have not simply been excluded from it but have been *used* to build a white sort of ethno-nationalism, replete with supporting social and economic policies. America could be more genuinely civil if it could face, and deal with, its appalling history of racial abuse. The election of Barak Obama to the presidency was an important step in the right direction. Riga warns, however, that, in keeping with Hall's view of historical change, steps forward in America's evolution have generally been followed by backward ones.

The next two chapters turn to another social and geopolitical hotspot: Turkey. With a complex and rich history at the crossroads of civilizations, and currently undergoing very challenging changes, the country is an exceptionally revealing case study to consider. In chapter 3, Yesim Bayar investigates why, despite considerable economic and educational progress, Turkey has struggled to achieve a modern – that is, mindful of minority rights and general civic liberties – sort of nationalism. Leveraging Hall's views of the difficulties associated with state-building after a nation is created, she finds in the early Republican period (1920–38) the foundations of a simultaneously assimilationist and exclusionary national vision. The key players, then and in later decades, were state and military elites. State structures and programs followed, but they were never embracing of "others" or of extended liberties. The relevance of Bayar's argument for understanding the current repressive situation in Turkey since the failed 2016 coup especially is considerable.

Yet, just as Turkey seems headed towards a reversal of democratic principles, Berna Turam observes in chapter 4 the rise of a "new urban civility." As the regime increases its repression, otherwise contested urban spaces have become "breathing spaces" for freedom. Here, at a very micro-level, secularists, pious Muslims, feminists, Kurdish nationalists, and others interact in public spaces such as markets, shops, campuses, and squares. Her ethnographic analysis applies the Hallsian concept of civility to hitherto unexamined spaces. Such "spatialization" proves rewarding for understanding both Turkey and the versatility – conceptual as well as methodological – of Hall's ideas.

In chapter 5, Frank Trentmann probes further into Hall's understanding of civility. The context is the refugee crisis in Germany after 1945, when many ethnic Germans moved to the war-ravaged country from other parts of Europe. They looked for practical help and inclusion into German society – that is, within their original ethnic group. Trentmann observes that Hall's notion of civility centres on a laissez-faire philosophy. But when food, shelter, and health care are lacking, should that notion not include more social action? Can we expand Hall's view of civility to include those more humanitarian dimensions? And how can we explain any observable variation in civility between the "host" Germans and those ethnic Germans coming into the country looking for help? The argument has considerable implications for our understanding of nationalism in times of internal crisis, the politics of empathy, and the dynamics of civility within the same ethnic group that, supposedly, makes up a nation.

Part 2 turns our attention to more comparative and international analyses. In chapter 6, Siniša Malešević builds on Hall's key insight that nationalism and imperialism may be more connected than is generally understood. Hall's point has been that nineteenth-century empires actually deepened their power over people by nationalizing them. Reversing that idea, Malešević argues that in some cases something rather different can happen: nations can deploy imperial and quasi-imperial designs to boost their nationalist legitimacy at home and standing abroad. The context of his analysis is the Balkans during the nineteenth century and early twentieth century. He focuses in particular on the Serbian and Bulgarian nationalist and quasi-imperial projects, and how both used the discourses and legacies of their respective medieval empires of Tsar Dušan (Serbia) and Simeon the Great (Bulgaria) to advance their nationalist programs.

In chapter 7, Michael Mann builds on decades of conversation with Hall over the nature of power in society. As is well known, Mann recognizes two primary forms of power: despotic and infrastructural. These can vary in strength, and in combination yield three types of regimes: democratic, autocratic, and authoritarian. Mann observes that Hall is normatively supportive of the democratic sorts. There, after all, is where civility can thrive. But Mann warns that democratic regimes – in Europe, North America, and elsewhere – are showing signs of weakness. Historically, they have been low in despotic power and high in infrastructural power. Contemporary trends show the former increasing and the latter decreasing. If true, such a trend presents serious problems for Hall's normative hopes for the world.

Power is also at the core of Lange's analysis. In chapter 8, he considers colonialism and the way European countries sought to limit nation-building in their territories. He draws on Hall's methodological inclinations to carefully combine historical and sociological analyses to question how in certain circumstances organized mass religion (and missionaries in particular) actually strengthened (rather than weakened, as is often depicted) anti-colonial sentiments and nationalistic violence. Lange helps us appreciate the different dynamics involved in the rise of nation-states in post-colonial settings. The empirical focus is on Burma. But Lange also considers Thailand, which was never colonized, to show how much more limited religion was in the crafting of that nation.

The next chapter turns to China in comparative perspective. Luyang Zhou focuses in chapter 9 on communist revolutions. He notes that the Chinese revolution was cast in nationalistic terms while its Russian counterpart – more closely following Marxist doctrine – made far more use of anti-nationalist ideology. Also consistent with Marxist thought, the Bolsheviks seized power through an urban coup and a relatively rapid civil war with the military playing a limited role. By contrast, the Chinese Communist Party fought mostly in the rural areas, and was embroiled in a twenty-eight-year-long military war. This, too, went against Marxist predictions. Why such differences? Zhou turns to the Hallsian perspective and identifies the importance of three factors: the pace of nationalization, the extent of political decency, and the character of military experiences. Zhou closes his chapter by elaborating on the implication of the two revolutions for the countries' trajectories to the present.

The two final substantive chapters concern ancient empires. As we think about nation-states, and the relationship between power and civility within and across them, useful lessons can be gathered from thinking about what came before those nation-states. This is certainly in line with the Hallsian paradigm. The focus is on the relationship between polity and religion. In chapter 10, Sun and Zhao identify in pre-modern empires important differences in one dimension of civility: religious toleration. They attribute the observable variation to more than monotheistic versus polytheistic orientations, as has been argued of the Roman Empire prior to and after its Christianization. Attention should go, instead, to two key variables: the extent to which the embraced religion/system of belief makes claims to exclusive access to the truth and, in parallel, its evangelical tendencies. Variations along those variables can help us make sense of religious tolerance in a great number of empires, from the Achaemenid (550–330 BCE) to the Mughal ones (1526–40, 1555–1857). The finding is consistent with many of the essential elements of the Hallsian paradigm and has potential ramifications for contemporary nation-states – or any other kind of polity – in so far as they belong to any given religious tradition.

Joseph Bryant proposes in chapter 11, in turn, that the religious conversions of two immensely powerful actors ("mega-actors") – the Christian one of Roman emperor Constantine (r. 306–37 CE) and the Buddhist one of King Ashoka of the Maurya dynasty (r. 268–232 BCE) – had very different long-term societal impacts. In the case of Constantine, it led to an enduring state-church alliance and the consolidation of a Christian civilization. In the case of Ashoka, despite his own efforts, it led to limited institutional and cultural change, and to eventual retreat as Brahmanical Hinduism gained prominence. Bryant seeks to explain those differences in terms of sociological factors – ranging from the structures of the societies in question to the modes of patronage and institutionalization. This is therefore a fully Hallsian analysis: powerful political figures can matter, but how they penetrate and organize societies varies greatly as a function of a wide-ranging set of societal variables.

Taken together, the chapters help us make sense of a world defined, as the Hallsian paradigm would have it, by the concentration of power in nations and states where civility can, under the right circumstances, temper individual and collective instincts and allow for the peaceful and productive unfolding of social life. This, of course, could easily be a multivolume exercise, and limitations of space constrain how much we can cover. The volume ends, however, with a treat: Hall closes these pages with his own reflections on the chapters. Have they correctly captured the fragility, merits, and limitations of civility in modern and earlier polities? Have the authors accurately understood and deployed, in their analyses, the Hallsian paradigm? Do their arguments offer opportunities for adjustments, revisions, or expansions? An already rich paradigm acquires further specifications and depth. Indeed, rather than an endpoint, Hall's piece should be seen as a launching pad for additional work on civility within and across polities, and the potential and limitations of the Hallsian paradigm to guide that work.

REFERENCES

Beichelt, Timm, Irene Hahn-Fuhr, Frank Schimmelfennig, and Susann Worschech, eds. 2014. *Civil Society and Democracy Promotion*. Houndmsill, Basingstoke, Hampshire: Palgrave Macmillan. https://doi.org/10.1057/9781137291097.

Campbell, John L., and John A. Hall. 2006. "The State of Denmark." In *National Identity and the Varieties of Capitalism: The Danish Experience*, edited

by John L. Campbell, John A. Hall, and Ove K. Pedersen, 3–49. Montreal: McGill-Queen's University Press.
– 2015a. *The World of States*. New York: Bloomsbury.
– 2015b. "Small States, Nationalism and Institutional Capacities: An Explanation of the Difference in Response of Ireland and Denmark to the Financial Crisis." *Archives Européennes de Sociologie* 56 (1): 143–74. https://doi.org/10.1017/S0003975615000077.
– 2017. *The Paradox of Vulnerability: States, Nationalism and the Financial Crisis*. Princeton: Princeton University Press.
Cox, Michael, Timothy J. Lynch, and Nicolas Bouchet. 2013. "Introduction: Presidents, American Democracy Promotion and World Order." In *US Foreign Policy and Democracy Promotion: From Theodore Roosevelt to Barack Obama*, edited by Michael Cox, Timothy J. Lynch, and Nicolas Bouchet, 1–12. New York: Routledge.
Dahrendorf, Ralf. 1959. *Class and Class Conflict in Industrial Society*. Stanford: Stanford University Press.
Gellner, Ernest. 1983. *Nations and Nationalism*. Ithaca: Cornell University Press.
Greenfeld, Liah. 2016. *Advanced Introduction to Nationalism*. Northampton: Edward Elgar.
Hall, John A. 1985. *Powers and Liberties: The Causes and Consequences of the Rise of the West*. Berkeley: University of California Press.
– 1987. *Liberalism: Politics, Ideology, and the Market*. Chapel Hill: University of North Carolina Press.
– 1996. *International Orders*. Cambridge: Polity Press.
– 2006. "Structural Approaches to Nations and Nationalism." In *The Sage Handbook of Nations and Nationalism*, edited by Gerard Delanty and Krishan Kumar, 33–43. London: Sage. https://doi.org/10.4135/9781848608061.n4.
– 2007. "Passions within Reason." In *The End of the West? Explaining the Deep Structure of the Transatlantic Order*, edited by Jeffrey Anderson, G. John Ikenberry, and Thomas Risse, 229–46. Ithaca: Cornell University Press.
– 2010. *Ernest Gellner: An Intellectual Biography*. New York: Verso.
– 2011. "Nationalism Might Change Its Character, Again." In *Nationalism and Globalisation: Conflicting or Contemporary?* edited by Daphne Halikiopoulou and Sofia Vasilopoulou, 17–26. New York: Routledge.
– 2013. *The Importance of Being Civil: The Struggle for Political Decency*. Princeton: Princeton University Press.
Hall, John A., and Charles Lindholm. 1999. *Is America Breaking Apart?* Princeton: Princeton University Press.
Hall, John A., and Siniša Malešević. 2013. "Introduction: War and Nationalism." In *Nationalism and War*, edited by John A. Hall and Siniša

Malešević, 1–28. Cambridge: Cambridge University Press. https://doi.org/10.1017/CBO9781139540964.001.

Held, David. 2005. "At the Global Crossroads: The End of the Washington Consensus and the Rise of Global Social Democracy?" *Globalizations* 2 (1): 95–113. https://doi.org/10.1080/14747730500085122.

Hirschman, Albert O. 1970. *Exit, Voice, and Loyalty: Responses to Decline in Firms, Organizations, and States*. Cambridge, MA: Harvard University Press.

Huber, Daniela. 2015. *Democracy Promotion and Foreign Policy: Identity and Interests in US, EU and Non-Western Democracies*. Houndmsill, Basingstoke, Hampshire: Palgrave Macmillan. https://doi.org/10.1057/9781137414472.

Lange, Matthew. 2011. "Social Welfare and Ethnic Warfare: Exploring the Impact of Education on Ethnic Violence." *Studies in Comparative International Development* 46 (4): 372–96. https://doi.org/10.1007/s12116-011-9095-y.

– 2013. "When Does Nationalism Turn Violent? A Comparative Analysis of Canada and Sri Lanka." In *Nationalism and War*, edited by John A. Hall and Siniša Malešević, 124–44. Cambridge: Cambridge University Press.

Mann, Michael. 1986. *A History of Power from the Beginning to AD 1760*, vol. 1: *The Sources of Social Power*. Cambridge: Cambridge University Press.

– 2012. *The Rise of Classes and Nation-States, 1760–1914*, vol. 2: *The Sources of Social Power*. Cambridge: Cambridge University Press.

Mansfield, Edward D., and Jon C. Pevehouse. 2008. "Democratization and the Varieties of International Organizations." *Journal of Conflict Resolution* 52 (2): 269–94. https://doi.org/10.1177/0022002707313691.

Mendelson, Sara E., and John K. Glenn, eds. 2002. *The Power and Limits of NGOs: A Critical Look at Building Democracy in Eastern Europe and Eurasia*. New York: Columbia University Press. https://doi.org/10.7312/mend12490.

Meyer, John W. 2007. "Globalization." *International Journal of Comparative Sociology* 48 (4): 261–73. https://doi.org/10.1177/0020715207079529.

Ohmae, Kenichi. 1995. *The End of the Nation-State: The Rise of Regional Economies*. New York: Free Press.

Peck, Dennis L. 2002. "Civility: A Contemporary Context for a Meaningful Historical Concept." *Sociological Inquiry* 72 (3): 358–75. https://doi.org/10.1111/1475-682X.00022.

Pevehouse, Jon C. 2002. "Democracy from the Outside-In? International Organizations and Democratization." *International Organization* 56 (3): 515–49. https://doi.org/10.1162/002081802760199872.

Smith, Tony. 2012. *America's Mission: The United States and the Worldwide Struggle for Democracy*. Princeton: Princeton University Press. https://doi.org/10.1515/9781400842025.

Soysal, Yasemin. 1994. *Limits of Citizenship: Migrants and Postnational Membership in Europe*. Chicago: University of Chicago Press.

Tilly, Charles. 2000. "Processes and Mechanisms of Democratization." *Sociological Theory* 18 (1): 1–16. https://doi.org/10.1111/0735-2751.00085.

PART ONE

National Contexts

1 Is America Breaking Apart? The Rise of Donald Trump

JOHN L. CAMPBELL

Conflicts and arguments over identity – particularly racial, ethnic, religious, regional, and class identities – became a hallmark of public, political, and academic discourse in the United States during the late twentieth century. Many thought that these culture wars signalled the breakdown of American society. America, it was believed, was devolving into isolated identity groups so obsessed with their particular interests as to jeopardize the collective moral identity required to hold this large and diverse nation together. John Hall and Charles Lindholm (1999) disagreed. They argued in their provocative book *Is America Breaking Apart?* that the culture wars were actually a sign of national strength and resilience. Why? First, conflicts over these issues can be a healthy and necessary prerequisite to compromise and consensus as long as they are not layered on top of one another. Second, underneath these conflicts lay a set of structures and shared values that fortified rather than destroyed national solidarity.

Much has happened in American society since they published their book, notably the election of Donald Trump to the presidency. And much of it raises questions about their view of America. I begin by reviewing the important details in their argument and then reflect on them in light of a variety of evidence. I argue that America may be closer to breaking apart now than they ever anticipated. In this chapter I thus join Liliana Riga, in her contribution to this volume, in taking a critical stance towards the largely positive account of America found in *Is America Breaking Apart?*[1] I also share the concern that Michael Mann

1 Much of the material in this chapter is drawn from Campbell (2018).

expresses in his chapter about the ongoing worrisome corrosion of democracy in the United States.

Mechanisms of National Solidarity

Hall and Lindholm (H&L) identified in their book a number of mechanisms – some structural, some cultural – that have served to unite the nation and that, in their view, would in all likelihood continue to do so. Consider structure first. Things like political checks and balances, a stable two-party system, and opportunities for upward mobility were particularly important. Of course, solidarity was not guaranteed. Early in America's history conflicts over regional autonomy, divergent cultural attitudes, modes of production, and the morality of slavery were gradually layered in ways that culminated in a vicious and protracted civil war that nearly destroyed the nation. Once this ended, however, the nation underwent a process of homogenization that led to unification and stability: migration of blacks from the south to the north; the industrialization of the south; diffusion of a common dialect of English across the country; and the extension of civil rights to blacks and women.

Furthermore, H&L argued that the formation of class solidarity and a socialist movement were muted due to the opportunities for upward mobility, the decentralization of politics in a federalist system, skill-based and other divisions within the labour movement, and the business community's ability to subvert unionization. As a result, Americans did not experience the class conflicts that many Europeans did. Similarly, the advent of civil rights legislation and the emergence of a suburbanized black middle class dampened – but certainly did not fully resolve – racial conflicts in the last third of the twentieth century. Moreover, once America finally extricated itself from the Vietnam War, the domestic conflicts over having troops in combat abroad disappeared. Finally, because the United States was by the late 1990s the world's economic and military hegemon, capable of deciding its own fate in an increasingly interdependent world, it was not subject to international pressures that might otherwise have undermined national solidarity. National unity and political and social stability followed accordingly.

Cultural factors contributed to solidarity and stability too. Indeed, according to H&L most Americans share a set of core values. This includes most African Americans even though they have been excluded historically in various ways. Immigrants to America have demonstrated time and again a capacity for pragmatically transforming themselves to conform to basic American values and aspirations in pursuit of the "American Dream." As such, Americans subscribe to a strong sense of anti-authoritarianism, individualism, and egalitarianism with an almost religious fervour that has tremendous cohesive force. This is because these values are so vague and nebulous that it is difficult for anyone to disagree with or debate them.

Especially important is the fact that, with the exception of African Americans, racial and ethnic groups in the United States are not "caged." That is, racial and ethnic identity is to a certain degree a matter of choice. People in America may hail from a particular racial or ethnic group but the degree to which they subscribe to the practices of that group is largely voluntary, much like membership in civic associations. The result historically has been the remarkable capacity of these groups to assimilate into American culture – a phenomenon perhaps best exemplified by rising rates of intermarriage. Remarkably, as noted, even though African Americans have been involuntarily caged within a negative racial category they too are often believers in core American values.

In sum, H&L concluded that for a variety of reasons the homogenizing powers of America are formidable. With the partial exception of African Americans, this has ensured that domestic conflicts remain relatively subdued and that national solidarity remains strong despite what the naysayers of the culture wars may have claimed. This is not to deny that racism, social inequality, or other social problems exist. They do. H&L's point was that they are masked and muted by the appearance of opportunity, equality, and cultural conformity. Hence, America is not in any danger of breaking apart.

A Reconsideration

What are we to make of this argument now, nearly two decades later? H&L wrote the book during a time of already rising political polarization in America. Conservative Republicans led by Newt Gingrich won control of the House of Representatives in 1994 for the first time in forty years, intending to push government in a much more conservative direction. They impeached but failed to convict President Bill Clinton with votes cast along party lines. They shut down the federal government twice during highly partisan budget confrontations between the Congress and White House. So, even as H&L were writing, signs were beginning to appear that something might be amiss with their argument.

Since the book's publication things have gotten much worse, to the point where America may be on the verge of breaking apart. To be clear, if by "breaking apart" we mean that the nation is poised for another civil war, which seems to be what H&L meant, then they have nothing to worry about – civil war is not in the cards. But if by "breaking apart" we mean things like a descent into dysfunctional government, growing racial and religious intolerance, and increasing class polarization, then we are beginning to see cracks in the American façade.

Since 1980 politics have become increasingly polarized and government has become largely dysfunctional at the national level. The ideological overlap between Republicans and Democrats has diminished significantly over the last twenty years. Today, 92 per cent of Republicans are to the right of the median Democrat, and 94 per cent of Democrats are to the left of the median Republican (Pew Research Center 2014). Moreover, partisan fights over the federal budget and debt ceiling have grown more acrimonious, as a full government shutdown happened again in 2013 on Obama's watch. Gridlock was not limited to budgetary issues. Senate Majority Leader Mitch McConnell vowed to neither meet with nor hold confirmation hearings on Obama's recent nominee, Merrick Garland, to fill a vacancy on the Supreme Court. McConnell has been a paragon of obstructionism ever since Obama won the presidency in 2008, when he promised to make him a one-term president and rallied his Republican troops to try to block as much legislation as possible coming from the congressional Democrats, not to mention many administrative and judicial nominations coming from the White House. Finally, and perhaps most telling, Donald Trump's victorious campaign for the presidency was the most vitriolic, racist, and xenophobic one we have seen since at least the 1960s and perhaps earlier.

Racial and religious intolerance has also reached high levels, undoubtedly aggravated by rising anti-Muslim sentiment in the wake of the 9/11 terrorist attacks in New York and Washington. From 2008 when Barack Obama was elected president through 2012, explicit anti-black attitudes among Americans increased from 48 per cent to 51 per cent. When measured by an implicit racial attitudes test, anti-black sentiments among Americans jumped from 49 per cent to 56 per cent. Anti-Hispanic attitudes were comparable – 52 per cent of non-Hispanic whites explicitly expressed anti-Hispanic attitudes, a figure that rose to 57 per cent in the implicit test. This reflected growing racial polarization within American society (Agiesta and Ross 2012). In many cities the police are far more likely to pull over, frisk, ticket, and/or arrest

African Americans and Hispanics than whites. For instance, between 2005 and mid-2008 roughly 80 per cent of the stops in New York City were of blacks and Latinos, which comprised only 25 and 28 per cent of the city population, respectively, whereas 10 per cent of the stops were of whites, which comprised 44 per cent of the city population (US Department of Justice 2014). Insofar as religious tolerance is concerned, the United States experienced a rise in social hostilities involving religion between 2007 and 2013. Although moderate during that time compared to all countries in the world, the Pew Research Center's Social Hostilities Index for the United States rose from 1.9 to 3.1, the third highest of the thirty-five countries in the Americas (Pew Research Center 2015, 58).

Finally, the possibility of class polarization has increased. Beginning in the 1970s median family income in the United States began to stagnate and has been essentially flat ever since. During the late 1960s and early 1970s average wages grew about 2.5 per cent annually. Since then, however, they have barely budged at all. Average family income grew between 1979 and 2007 by only 0.6 per cent for the middle fifth of the income distribution – the middle class – but by 1.5 per cent for the top fifth and even more for the top 5 per cent of the income distribution (Mishel et al. 2012, 27). Income inequality, already bigger than in most advanced countries, grew significantly. Between 1975 and 2010 the Gini coefficient, a standard inequality measure, increased steadily from about .301 to .365 (OECD 2011). Moreover, between 1980 and 2000 intergenerational mobility as measured by the correlation between parental income and sons' earnings declined significantly (Mishel et al. 2012, 34). In short, the rich got richer, the poor got poorer, and the middle was being slowly eviscerated.

None of this was good news for H&L's argument. Nor did it bode well for politics in the United States, which as we have just seen slipped ever closer to dysfunctional polarized gridlock.

The Roots of National Fragmentation

How did American things deteriorate to this point? To answer this question we need to see how trends in the economy, race relations, demography, and ideology converged historically on party politics, and how the 2008 financial crisis, Obama's election, and his health-care reform made it even worse.

Economy and Class

In the face of wage stagnation, in order to make ends meet, the average American family had to work more hours, with women often bearing a disproportionate share of that burden, and borrow more money. From 1973 to 2007 average household debt more than doubled from about 60 per cent to 138 per cent of disposable income, and then slipped a bit to 119 per cent by 2011 in the wake of the 2008 financial crisis and Great Recession (Mishel et al. 2012, 405; Schor 1992). All of this was necessary for the baby boom generation, born between 1946 and 1964, to maintain the same standard of living as their parents' generation. It is even harder for today's millennial generation. In short, Americans have had to run faster and faster just to stay in the same place. Some people have been unable to do so, which is why the middle class has been shrinking. Nowadays, American middle-class prosperity has become more of an illusion than a reality because it is based increasingly on overwork and debt (Leicht and Fitzgerald 2007). As noted, things were much better for people at the top of the income distribution. But why?

One reason had to do with policy decisions – a series of regressive tax and welfare reforms under both Republican and Democratic administrations. Another reason was that the economy was being restructured. Traditional US manufacturing jobs were moving from the northeast and upper midwest to the sunbelt in the south and southwest where unions were weaker or non-existent and wages and benefits were lower. Furthermore, since the early 1970s the United States had been losing its competitive advantage in both domestic and international markets – America's economic hegemony was eroding. Foreign firms were moving into the US market for automobiles, steel, consumer electronics, and many other products. And American jobs were either outsourced to foreign countries or eliminated entirely by technological improvements like computerization and robotics. Downsizing became the watchword for many US firms. Not everyone was hurt equally. As the shift from manufacturing to a more service-oriented economy proceeded, those who managed to get good educations or upgrade their skills, particularly in ways that made them technologically savvy, did alright. Those who did not fared worse (Bluestone and Harrison 1988; Danziger and Gottschalk 1997).

These shifts in class structure, income distribution, and the economy were important for three reasons that exacerbated political divisions. First, the poor, who tend to vote Democratic, are less likely to vote than the rich. As people slipped out of the middle class the aggregate profile of the voting public shifted in a more conservative direction. Second, attending to middle-class interests had helped anchor American politics in a relatively centrist position (Skocpol 2000). Once that anchor began to slip, Democrats and Republicans tended to drift farther apart. Third, the gender gap in politics grew. Women tend to vote more for Democrats while men tend to vote for Republicans. In presidential elections the gap first emerged in the early 1950s and grew through the mid-1980s, more or less levelling off after that. The gap stemmed largely from the rise in female labour force participation, because women who work or want to find work want more public services to help make this possible, such as child care, elder care, full-day kindergarten, public transportation, and the like. Insofar as families were under increasing economic pressure, women's labour force participation increased, thus exacerbating political polarization (Manza and Brooks 1998). The gender gap spiked following the Great Recession in the 2012 presidential election when women turned out in droves for Obama – the largest gender gap ever recorded by Gallup Polling since it began tracking the gap in 1952 (Jones 2012).

For H&L, opportunities for mobility, US economic hegemony, and beliefs in egalitarianism were all important supports for national solidarity in America. But all were eroding by the early twenty-first century.

Race Relations

The economic stories just told played out to a significant degree along racial lines. Blacks and Hispanics fared worse than whites. The ratio of black to white median wages barely budged between 1989 and 2011, when blacks on average earned only about 72 per cent of what whites earned. For Hispanics the ratio dropped from about 67 per cent to 64 per cent. By 2010 the poverty rates for blacks and Hispanics (23.3 and 22.4 per cent, respectively) were roughly two and a half times higher than for whites (Mishel et al. 2012, 233, 425). To be sure, particularly in the black community a bifurcation occurred along class lines. A black middle class emerged since the 1960s thanks to affirmative action legislation. But a black underclass persisted, characterized by high rates of female-headed households, out-of-wedlock births, joblessness, crime, drug abuse, and other social problems (Wilson 1980, 1990).

Contrary to conservative dogma that the persistence of the underclass was due to cultural decay in poor African American communities, most blacks living in these communities still subscribed to middle-class values, as H&L noted, including a desire for legitimate jobs and traditional family life. However, they recognized that their ability to achieve these things given the scarcity of economic opportunities was virtually nil. Opportunities for upward mobility were being seriously questioned (Wilson 1997, 2010).

But problems of race ran deeper than that. Republicans pioneered the so-called Southern Strategy in the 1960s and 1970s as a way to get white working-class voters from the south to abandon the Democratic Party and vote Republican. The strategy blamed wage stagnation and inflation on the growing tax burden shouldered by the white working class, which was necessary, it was said, to pay for the welfare programs that benefitted "other" people, which was code for people of colour. The strategy worked as the white working class grew sceptical of traditional Democratic Party social programs.[2] It worked and a significant part of the American working class began turning to the right. This contributed to political polarization insofar as it helped foster the rise of increasingly conservative Republican and Democratic politicians, particularly in the southern Bible Belt where the evangelical movement was gaining political traction. The layering of racial and class divisions was becoming more pronounced and politically polarized – just the sort of layering that H&L warned against. Racial antagonisms were later exacerbated by racist police practices, noted earlier, in poor urban communities that eventually triggered the Black Lives Matter movement in 2013.

Demographic Change

The rightward shift and polarization in American politics was also fuelled by demographic trends. First, as the generation of the Great Depression and its children died off, younger generations began to forget that social programs had been established to help ensure political stability during times of severe crisis. This contributed to the erosion of national unity and its replacement with more individualistic attitudes (Judt 2010). It was another reason why people became less willing to pay taxes to support social programs. Indeed, cutting taxes emerged as a hot political issue in the 1970s, led by Americans

2 George Wallace, a four-term governor of Alabama and a rabid segregationist, used the Southern Strategy too when he ran as an independent for the presidency.

for Tax Reform, an organization that pressed politicians during elections to sign a pledge not to raise any taxes (Edsall and Edsall 1992; Martin 2008).

Second, the population was aging. The problem was that private pensions began to disappear thanks to the decline of traditional manufacturing jobs. People had to learn to save for retirement, but not everyone did given wage stagnation and inflation. Between 1970 and 2004 net savings in the United States declined from about 8 per cent to 1 per cent annually as a percentage of gross national income (Leicht and Fitzgerald 2007, 58). Retired people were increasingly in danger of running out of money to sustain themselves through old age. And since they are generally on fixed incomes, they oppose tax increases and are therefore susceptible to conservative calls for tax cuts. Older Americans tend to be more conservative and Republican in orientation anyway, but this compounded the rightward shift in American politics, particularly as the large baby boom generation moved towards retirement. An intergenerational wedge – a new form of identity politics – was added to the already growing number of cleavages threatening American solidarity. As a result, politicians catered increasingly to the interests of the elderly as represented by the American Association of Retired Persons – one of the most powerful lobbies in Washington. With entitlement programs for the elderly off-limits politically, conservative calls for budget reductions focused more on programs for younger people. For instance, state and local government appropriations for public universities dropped steadily after 2000. To compensate, universities raised tuition and fees and in turn students took on debt that proved to be increasingly difficult to pay off later (College Board 2015a, 2015b; Kingkade 2012).

Third, demography intersected with racial politics. Thanks to immigration the Hispanic population grew significantly during the 1990s and 2000s and today constitutes 16 per cent of the population – a larger percentage than blacks. Republicans began worrying that the country's electoral base was shifting towards the Democrats, as most Hispanic immigrants and their children were relatively poor and uneducated and tended to vote for Democrats. Indeed, Obama won the presidency twice garnering a vast majority of the minority vote, including not only blacks but Hispanics. In response, Republicans in several states passed voter registration and other laws designed ostensibly to reduce voter fraud but that made it more difficult for poor minorities to vote. All of this further aggravated political polarization over race (Waldman 2016).

Ideology

Shifting ideologies also helped polarize US politics. As is well known, the embrace of neoliberalism by virtually all Republicans and some Democrats shifted the ideological terrain of policy debate to the right. This began in the late 1970s and accelerated thereafter. It was driven in part by Keynesianism's difficulty in explaining stagflation during the 1970s. But neoliberalism was also elevated to prominence by the proliferation of well-funded right-wing think tanks in Washington and the emergence of more conservative economic theory in several high-profile university economics departments, notably at the University of Chicago (Campbell and Pedersen 2014, chap. 2).

Religious ideology had a similar effect. Historically, white evangelical Christians tended to support the Democratic Party. However, following the tumultuous 1960s and 1970s, which ushered in more tolerant attitudes towards sexual freedom, abortion, unmarried cohabitation, and homosexuality, evangelicals turned towards the Republican Party and became more active in politics. Led during the 1980s by the Moral Majority, this movement pushed conservative social issues on to the political agenda, including in particular the anti-abortion crusade, which further polarized American politics (Waldman 2016, 185–6).

Party Politics

H&L saw a stable two-party system as one important support for American solidarity. But since the early 1970s both political parties began experiencing internal splits and shifting to the right, with the Republicans moving further than the Democrats. The moderate wing of the Republican Party saw an important yet restrained role for government. But they were gradually pushed aside by more conservative people, including Reagan, who famously said that government wasn't the solution to the problem, it was the problem! In fact, by today's standards Reagan was pretty moderate. He cut taxes but then raised them when budget deficits ballooned. He cut welfare spending but did not eliminate programs entirely (Bunch 2009). Similarly, despite George H.W. Bush's campaign promise "Read my lips, no new taxes!" as president, he too raised taxes to control deficits. But the Gingrich Revolution in Congress and then the election of George W. Bush as president in 2000 marked a much sharper rightward shift in the party. It was driven by increasing flows of conservative money into political campaigns and increasingly conservative political rhetoric and policy ideas coming from the Washington think tanks. The rise of talk radio and cable news programs contributed as well, notably Fox News. Defenders of the Second Amendment to the Constitution, which ensures the right of citizens to own guns, jumped on the conservative bandwagon led by the National Rifle Association, another powerful Washington lobby.

On the Democratic side Nixon's resignation from the presidency in the wake of the Watergate scandal alienated many moderate Republicans who switched allegiance temporarily to the Democratic Party. Many of these new Democrats were relatively affluent, middle-class, well-educated professionals, not to mention white, which put them at odds with the more ethnically and racially diverse working-class voters that formed the more liberal New Deal coalition upon which the party's electoral fortunes had rested for decades. As a result, the Democratic Party also began to split and shift to the right (Edsall 1985).

The general rightward shift was exacerbated by America's declining economic hegemony. First was the decreasing political strength of unions, which had traditionally supported the Democratic Party. Union membership declined since the 1950s to only about 11 per cent of all workers today. This was due in part to the shrinking number of manufacturing jobs noted earlier (Fantasia and Voss 2004; Goldfield 1987; Rosenfeld 2014; Western 1997). Second, business interests were shifting to the right as international competition increased and firms had a harder time passing along the costs of tax increases and environmental and other forms of regulatory compliance to customers in the form of higher prices. This too hurt the Democratic Party (Ferguson and Rogers 1986; but see Bai 2007).

Three institutional changes also contributed to the rightward shift of both parties as well as further polarization within them. One was a series of campaign finance reforms, which facilitated the flow of more and more money into elections beyond the control of the parties themselves. Because Republicans tend to have more money than Democrats the advantage went to the Republicans (Center for Responsive Politics 2016; Mayer 2016). Second, when Gingrich became Speaker of the House in 1995 he implemented a harsh whipping system that further diminished moderation in the Republican ranks. Democrats eventually followed suit. Third was gerrymandering, which became so egregious after 2000 that the Supreme Court denounced it but did little to stop it. Because Republicans gained increasing control over state-level politics and the population was shifting towards Republican states, they benefited the most from gerrymandering – often in ways that undermined the voting power of blacks and Hispanics. As a result, there were fewer competitive races for Congress, which allowed the incumbents to embrace more ideologically extreme politics (Waldman 2016, 225–9, 238). The possibilities for gerrymandering (and eviscerating voting rights) would have been diminished if a more centralized form of government was in place. But the United States is a federalist system. Although H&L view federalism as a mechanism reinforcing American solidarity, in this sense it had the opposite effect.

The Financial Crisis, Obama, and Obamacare

Many of the problems noted above came into full light in the wake of the 2008 financial crisis. The crisis first manifested in the subprime mortgage market where many people had been sold dangerously misleading adjustable rate mortgages but who, as it turned out, could not afford them in the long run. Given the wage stagnation and other economic problems facing middle- and working-class families, noted earlier, this was their only hope for achieving the most important piece of the American dream – buying a single-family house. This was especially so for poorer blacks and Hispanics, who were targeted aggressively by various unscrupulous mortgage companies and banks. Unfortunately, their mortgage rates adjusted just as interest rates were rising and housing prices were falling nation wide. Millions lost their homes through foreclosure. Millions more lost vast amounts in their retirement savings and investment accounts. The Great Recession was in full swing. Unemployment skyrocketed to 10 per cent by 2010.

The disaster was particularly hard on people who had been suffering from wage stagnation, rising indebtedness, overwork, and all the rest. Their economic situation deteriorated sharply. They blamed a variety of possible culprits, including the federal government, greedy Wall Street banks, deceitful mortgage lenders, and those "other" people once again. In terms of those other people, much of the blame this time was directed at immigrants from Mexico and Latin America who were said to be flooding across the border taking jobs from American workers. Issues of class and race layered again, but this time in an atmosphere especially electrified thanks to the 9/11 attacks that had put Muslims – a new minority group – in the racist crosshairs of many conservative Americans.

The election of Barak Obama, the first black president, didn't help. This was immediately a thorn in the side of racist America. But things got worse when Obama embraced Bush's $700 billion economic rescue package and effectively nationalized General Motors, AIG, Fannie

Mae, and Freddie Mac, and bailed out some of Wall Street's biggest investment banks. Public concerns over creeping socialism as well as favouritism for Wall Street grew. Things got worse when Obama introduced the Affordable Care Act to reform the health-care system in ways that were again portrayed by conservatives as incipient socialism. During 2009 when Congress was debating the legislation, all hell broke loose as racial animosity and economic angst boiled over. The Tea Party emerged, initially a decentralized grassroots movement but one that was soon backed by well-funded conservative organizations and very wealthy individuals (Skocpol and Williamson 2012). Republicans were seething and took to the streets variously portraying Obama as a socialist, communist, fascist, foreign-born, traitorous, and black terrorist out to destroy America. Racism infused much of this as yet another wedge was driven between the Democrats and Republicans.

The Rise of Donald Trump

Everything discussed so far set the stage for the rise of Donald Trump to the presidency. Trump's campaign resonated with the fears and anxieties of many Americans, which stemmed from the trends described above. His major campaign theme, "Make America Great Again," was in part a promise to revitalize the economy and create more jobs for Americans – a clear reference to the wage stagnation and overwork of recent decades as well as people's concerns for the economic future of themselves and their kids. He also promised to foster an environment where more Americans could become rich and achieve the American Dream. Table 1.1 reports CNN exit polling after the election based on a sample of 24,537 respondents.[3] It shows that although there were not large differences in support for Trump and Clinton in terms of people's incomes, Trump won nearly two-thirds of the vote of people who believed the economy was in poor shape and of people who felt that life for the next generation would be worse than today. Put differently, it was not class per se that mattered but rather the prospects of economic

3 Trump's support as reported in exit polls covered a wide range of people, but those most likely to support him *during the campaign* were people with less than a high school education; reporting ancestry as simply "American"; living in a mobile home; working in "old economy" jobs like agriculture, construction, manufacturing, and trade; having a history of voting for segregationists; being unemployed; being born in the United States; being an evangelical Christian; having a history of voting for liberal Republicans; and being a white Anglo-Saxon Protestant (Irwin and Katz 2016).

Table 1.1 2016 CNN Exit Poll Results

	Support for Clinton (%)	Support for Trump (%)
Income:		
$50,000 or less per year	52	41
$50,000 or more per year	47	49
Condition of national economy:		
Good	77	18
Poor	31	63
Life for the next generation of Americans will be …		
Better than today	59	38
Worse than today	31	63
About the same as today	54	39
Effect of international trade:		
Creates US jobs	59	35
Takes away US jobs	31	65
Does not affect jobs	63	30
Race:		
White	37	58
White men	31	63
White women	43	53
Non-white	74	21
Black	88	8
Latino	65	29
Education:		
College graduate	52	43
Non-college graduate	44	52
Age:		
8–29 years	55	37
30–44 years	50	42

	Support for Clinton (%)	Support for Trump (%)
45–64 years	44	53
65 and older	45	53
Illegal immigrants working in the US should be ...		
Offered legal status	60	34
Deported to home country	14	84
Ideology:		
Liberal	84	10
Moderate	52	41
Conservative	15	81
Financial situation compared to four years ago:		
Better today	72	24
Worse today	19	78
About the same	46	46
Feelings about the federal government:		
Enthusiastic/satisfied	76	20
Dissatisfied/angry	36	58
Opinions of Obama as president:		
Approve	84	10
Disapprove	6	90
View of Obamacare:		
Did not go far enough	78	18
Was about right	82	10
Went too far	13	83

Source: CNN Politics 2016.

stress and downward intergenerational mobility. Similarly, Trump won roughly two-thirds of the votes of people who believed that international trade was taking away American jobs.

Trump's call for building a wall along the Mexican border to keep out job-stealing immigrants built on America's history of racism and resonated to a degree with the distorted understanding of a racial underclass as well as a misinterpretation of the causes of America's recent unemployment crisis and the general economic hardship of the middle and working classes. Job loss stemmed from outsourcing to foreign countries, automation, and the general restructuring of the economy from manufacturing to services, not immigration. His call for restricting Muslims from entering the United States played to racism as well. Not surprisingly, then, exit polling found that he won a majority of the white vote but only about 21 per cent of the non-white vote. Notably, nearly two-thirds of white men voted for him. Relatively less educated people tended to vote for Trump as well. Insofar as Trump's strategy appealed to less-educated white men, it worked like the old Southern Strategy but with a few twists. The concern seemed to be less with African Americans than Hispanics and the appeal was not just to people in the south but nation-wide. Given all this, it is no wonder that he had the support of so many members of the Tea Party and a variety of right-wing extremists, including David Duke, a former Imperial Wizard of the Ku Klux Klan. His racist comments about African Americans certainly contributed to his loss of the African American vote 88 per cent to 8 per cent.

Demographic change contributed to Trump's success. Trump's racist condemnation of Hispanic immigration as a growing threat to Americans undoubtedly explains why he lost the Hispanic vote 65 per cent to 29 per cent. Of course, the relationships between demographic change, race, and economic concerns are intertwined in complex ways, but they surely help account for the fact that 84 per cent of Trump supporters said that illegal immigrants working in the United States should be deported. The age structure of the electorate mattered too. Only a third, 37 per cent, of the millennial generation voted for Trump whereas 53 per cent of Baby Boomers did so, an indication that many people nearing retirement were concerned about their finances.

That ideas and ideology were also important is not surprising. Trump appealed to conservatives with considerable effect, winning 81 per cent of the conservative vote. It is worth mentioning that 35 per cent of those polled said they were conservative while only 26 per cent said they were liberal – a manifestation of the rightward shift in American politics described earlier. Equally telling was Trump's appeal to the white born-again and evangelical Christian electorate, who supported him by the same overwhelming margin.

Trump promised to overcome political gridlock and get government in Washington back on the right track because, as a successful businessman, he said he knew how to "make deals." In a similar vein, by using his own fortune to finance his campaign he claimed that he could not be bought by corporate or other interests – an obvious reference to the fact that the rich managed to corrupt the political system through exorbitant spending on political campaigns and lobbying. These arguments seemed to resonate with voters. The public's dissatisfaction with gridlock in Washington was clear in the voting: 58 per cent of those who felt dissatisfied or angry with the federal government went for Trump while 76 per cent of those who felt enthusiastic or satisfied with it supported Clinton.

Events during Obama's presidency also contributed to Trump's victory. Ninety per cent of those disapproving of Obama's presidency voted for Trump while 84 per cent of those who approved of his presidency voted for Clinton. And 83 per cent of those who believed that Obamacare – the Tea Party's galvanizing issue – had gone too far supported Trump while 78 per cent of those who believed it did not go far enough supported Clinton. Lingering concerns about the financial crisis also came into play: 78 per cent of those worried that the financial situation of the country was worse than it was four years ago voted for Trump.

The point is twofold. First, Trump's victory was the tip of a long-developing iceberg largely hidden even to astute observers like H&L. It benefited from and fed off of the gradual confluence of economic, racial, demographic, ideological, and political changes spanning decades in the United States. Ironically, Trump's ascendance was partly the culmination of forces first set in motion by the Republicans' Southern Strategy as well as their aggressive and heavily financed advocacy of neoliberalism – which contributed so much to the policies of the post-stagflation era, including easing regulatory oversight of banking and financial services and thus contributing to the financial crisis. Some leading Republicans, including both former Bush presidents and Mitt Romney, the Republican Party's previous presidential candidate, were so appalled by his racist, misogynist, and xenophobic remarks during the campaign that they repudiated him, and several big Republican donors, the libertarian and politically active billionaire Koch brothers among them, decided to spend their money on Republicans running for legislative office instead of him. The ranks of the Republican Party were never so divided over a presidential candidate in the last half-century.

Second, and more important for the purposes of H&L's argument, the trends that culminated in Trump's election had been slowly dividing Americans along economic, racial, demographic, ideological, and political lines for decades. Upward mobility seemed to have stalled for many but not for others, as economic inequality increased dramatically during the 2000s and people worried about the fate of the next generation. Inequality was first politicized by the Occupy Wall Street movement in 2009 and then Bernie Sander's bid for the Democratic Party presidential nomination in 2016. The effects of declining US economic hegemony were largely responsible. Furthermore, American society had become racially and ethnically more heterogeneous to a point where whites would soon be a minority of the population. Racial and religious tolerance was declining, especially since the 9/11 attacks, which some viewed as indicative of America's declining military hegemony. Federalism had allowed racial gerrymandering. The political preferences of men and women as well as of different generations drifted farther apart. The ideological distance between median Democratic and Republican voters increased significantly, and splits within the two parties widened too. Since Trump's election, the Republican's retention of both houses of Congress and the likelihood that Trump's nominees would push the Supreme Court sharply to the right suggest that the American system of checks and balances is on shaky ground – the Republicans would control all three branches of government. Of course, the presence of upward mobility, egalitarianism, US hegemony, racial and ethnic homogeneity, federalism, a stable two-party political system, and a system of institutionalized checks and balances were all reasons why H&L believed that America was not breaking apart in the late 1990s. It is not clear that their argument still holds, particularly insofar as these various divisions and conflicts are layered upon one another.

Is America Breaking Apart Now? The New American Politics

At the risk of oversimplification, the fundamental battle lines of postwar US politics pitted the left against the right. The left in varying degrees favoured Keynesian government intervention, including welfare state expansion and higher taxes, while the right favoured the opposite. The left was supported by many African Americans and other minorities while the right's base was predominantly white. So to a considerable extent the politics of race were tied closely to the traditional left-right distinction.

But Trump's victory crystalized a new form of American politics. Now in addition to the traditional left-right dimension we have a pro- and anti-globalization dimension. The second is orthogonal to the first, as Figure 1.1 illustrates. Trump capitalized on an anti-globalization position favouring closed borders and restrictions on trade and immigration. It is worth noting that Bernie Sanders was also anti-globalization insofar as he opposed free trade agreements, which he too believed had cost Americans many jobs. The difference, of course, was that Trump was further to the right while Sanders, a self-proclaimed democratic socialist, was further to the left. And Trump's racism and xenophobia were anathema to Sanders. Hillary Clinton, who ran against

Figure 1.1 The New American Politics

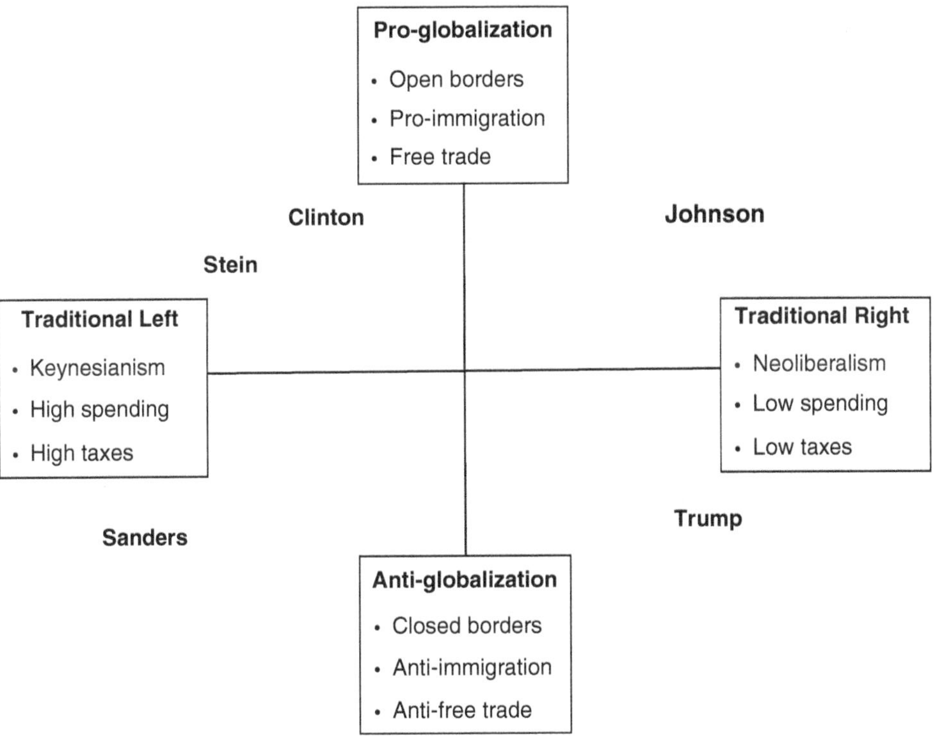

Trump in the general election, was pro-globalization insofar as she was supportive of international trade agreements and less isolationist than Trump in foreign policy matters – she never suggested revisiting the American commitment to NAFTA and NATO, whereas Trump did. She was also more to the left than Trump on many issues. Gary Johnson, the Libertarian Party candidate, was on the pro-globalization right favouring free trade and neoliberalism while Jill Stein, the Green Party candidate, was on the pro-globalization left supporting international cooperation on environmental and climate change issues.

Whereas racism had been largely linked to the traditional left-right dimension in American politics, it has now been detached thanks to the emergence of the pro- and anti-globalization dimension. The anti-immigration view, at least as represented by Trump, focuses on Hispanic and Muslim immigrants. The pro-globalization view is significantly more tolerant, refusing, for instance, to consider mass deportations of undocumented foreigners, which Trump had promised.

Europe has undergone a similar political metamorphosis. France, Denmark, Germany, the Netherlands, Belgium, Poland, and other countries have all recently experienced the emergence of anti-Europeanization/anti-globalization, nationalist, xenophobic, and anti-immigrant political parties and movements. The concern is that Europeanization threatens national sovereignty – the capacity for countries to govern themselves – by shifting control over the cross-border movement of people, goods, services, and capital from national capitals to Brussels (Campbell and Hall 2017, chap. 5). This is the main reason why the British voted in 2016 to leave the European Union in the Brexit referendum. The United States faces nothing like this in terms of having its sovereignty compromised.

Both the Republican and Democratic parties will have to sort out how they handle this new and more complicated form of American politics. The Trump wing of the Republican Party can expect resistance from neoconservatives who oppose anti-global isolationism and favour an expansionist foreign policy. As minority groups continue to constitute an ever larger proportion of the electorate, it will be increasingly risky for the Republicans to continue alienating them if they want to continue winning elections. Perhaps the Tea Party movement will give rise to a real Tea Party – that is, a new third party full of Trump's supporters. Or maybe moderate Republicans will break away and form their own new party. Given Clinton's defeat, the Democrats will have to reconcile demands from the moderate wing of their party with the Sanders wing both in terms of how far left they are willing to go and what sort of position they want to take on globalization issues. Hope for the Democrats may come simply from demographics – the growth of minorities favouring the Democratic Party and from the fact that the very large millennial generation, which so far tends to vote Democrat, will replace the Baby Boom generation, many of whom have grown more conservative in their old age. In any case, it is clear that the rise of Donald Trump, rooted in deep and long-standing societal trends, has ushered in a new era in American politics that will be with us for a while. His campaign capitalized on and may have exacerbated a number of already developing cracks in American social solidarity. Whether America will break apart further is anyone's guess.

REFERENCES

Agiesta, Jennifer, and Sonya Ross. 2012. "AP Poll: Majority Harbor Prejudice against Blacks." https://www.yahoo.com/news/ap-poll-majority-harbor-prejudice-against-blacks-073551680--election.html (accessed May 2018).

Bai, Matt. 2007. *The Argument: Billionaires, Bloggers and the Battle to Remake Democratic Politics*. New York: Penguin.

Bluestone, Barry, and Bennett Harrison. 1988. *The Great U-turn: Corporate Restructuring and the Polarizing of America*. New York: Basic.

Bunch, Will. 2009. *Tear Down This Myth*. New York: Free Press.

Campbell, John L. 2018. *American Discontent: The Rise of Donald Trump and Decline of the Golden Age*. New York: Oxford University Press.

Campbell, John L., and John A. Hall. 2017. *The Paradox of Vulnerability: Small States, Nationalism and the Financial Crisis*. Princeton: Princeton University Press.

Campbell, John L., and Ove K. Pedersen. 2014. *The National Origins of Policy Ideas*. Princeton: Princeton University Press. https://doi.org/10.1515/9781400850365.

Center for Responsive Politics. 2016. *OpenSecrets.org*. https://www.opensecrets.org/members-of-congress/members-list?cong_no=114&cycle=2016 (accessed May 2018).

CNN Politics. 2016. "Exit Polls." https://www.cnn.com/election/2016/results/exit-polls/national/president (accessed May 2018).

College Board. 2015a. *Trends in Student Aid 2015*. Princeton: College Board. https://trends.collegeboard.org/sites/default/files/trends-student-aid-web-final-508-2.pdf (accessed May 2018).

College Board. 2015b. *Trends in College Pricing 2015*. Princeton: College Board. https://trends.collegeboard.org/sites/default/files/trends-college-pricing-web-final-508-2.pdf (accessed May 2018).

Danziger, Sheldon, and Peter Gottschalk. 1997. *America Unequal*. Cambridge, MA: Harvard University Press.

Edsall, Mary, and Thomas Byrne Edsall. 1992. *Chain Reaction: The Impact of Race, Rights, and Taxes on American Politics*. New York: Norton.

Edsall, Thomas Byrne. 1985. *The New Politics of Inequality*. New York: Norton.

Fantasia, Rick, and Kim Voss. 2004. *Hard Work: Remaking the American Labor Movement*. Berkeley: University of California Press.

Ferguson, Thomas, and Joel Rogers. 1986. *Right Turn: The Decline of the Democrats and the Future of American Politics*. New York: Hill and Wang.

Goldfield, Michael. 1987. *The Decline of Organized Labor in the United States*. Chicago: University of Chicago Press.

Hall, John A., and Charles Lindholm. 1999. *Is America Breaking Apart?* Princeton: Princeton University Press.

Irwin, Neil, and Josh Katz. 2016. "The Geography of Trumpism." *The New York Times*, 12 March. https://www.nytimes.com/2016/03/13/upshot/the-geography-of-trumpism.html (accessed May 2018).

Jones, Jeffrey. 2012. "Gender Gap in 2012 Vote is Largest in Gallup's History." http://news.gallup.com/poll/158588/gender-gap-2012-vote-largest-gallup-history.aspx (accessed May 2018).

Judt, Tony. 2010. *Ill Fares the Land*. New York: Penguin.

Kingkade, Tyler. 2012. "State Budget Cuts Drive Up Tuition at Public Universities: New York Federal Reserve Report." *The Huffington Post*, 25 September. https://www.huffingtonpost.com/2012/09/25/state-budget-cuts-drive-tuition-hikes_n_1911044.html (accessed May 2018).

Leicht, Kevin, and Scott Fitzgerald. 2007. *Postindustrial Peasants: The Illusion of Middle-Class Prosperity*. New York: Worth.

Manza, Jeff, and Clem Brooks. 1998. "The Gender Gap in U.S. Presidential Elections: When? Why? Implications?" *American Journal of Sociology* 103 (5): 1235–66. https://doi.org/10.1086/231352.

Martin, Isaac. 2008. *The Permanent Tax Revolt*. Stanford: Stanford University Press.

Mayer, Jane. 2016. *Dark Money: The Hidden History of the Billionaires Behind the Rise of the Radical Right*. New York: Doubleday.

Mishel, Lawrence, Josh Bivens, Elise Gould, and Heidi Shierholz. 2012. *The State of Working America*. Ithaca: Cornell University Press.

OECD. 2011. *Divided We Stand: Why Inequality Keeps Rising*. Paris: OECD.

Pew Research Center. 2014. "Political Polarization in the American Public." http://www.people-press.org/2014/06/12/political-polarization-in-the-american-public/ (accessed April 2016).

– 2015. "Latest Trends in Religious Restrictions and Hostilities." http://www.pewforum.org/files/2015/02/Restrictions2015_fullReport.pdf (accessed December 2016).

Rosenfeld, Jake. 2014. *What Unions No Longer Do?* Cambridge, MA: Harvard University Press. https://doi.org/10.4159/harvard.9780674726215.

Schor, Juliet. 1992. *The Overworked American*. New York: Basic.

Skocpol, Theda. 2000. *The Missing Middle*. New York: Norton.

Skocpol, Theda, and Vanessa Williamson. 2012. *The Tea Party and the Remaking of Republican Conservatism*. New York: Oxford University Press. https://doi.org/10.1093/acprof:osobl/9780199832637.001.0001.

US Department of Justice. 2014. "The Reality of Racial Profiling." The Leadership Conference on Civil and Human Rights. https://www.civilrights.org/publications/reports/racial-profiling2011/the-reality-of-racial.html (accessed May 2018).

Waldman, Michael. 2016. *The Fight to Vote*. New York: Simon and Schuster.

Western, Bruce. 1997. *Between Class and Market: Postwar Unionization in the Capitalist Democracies*. Princeton: Princeton University Press.

Wilson, William Julius. 1980. *The Declining Significance of Race*. Chicago: University of Chicago Press.

– 1990. *The Truly Disadvantaged*. Chicago: University of Chicago Press.

– 1997. *When Work Disappears*. New York: Vintage.

– 2010. *More than Just Race*. New York: Norton.

2 How Homogeneous Need America Be? Nation, Race, and Civility

LILIANA RIGA

What one begs the American people to do, for all our sakes, is simply accept our history.

Baldwin (1965, SM 32)

In two remarkable liberal achievements, America had its first black presidency without political violence. Comparative historical sociology has still to take their fullest measure, but if America's entwined histories of race, nation-building, and violence are any guide, then the sociological brashness of these achievements might yet require a certain reckoning. The challenge is in how to put the question. Hallsian sociology might pose it this way: "What were the underlying social and political conditions that made these liberal – indeed, civil – achievements possible?" A compelling answer lies in John Hall and Charles Lindholm's beautifully elegant 1999 book *Is America Breaking Apart?* Drawing on Smith, Tocqueville, Weber, and Montesquieu, and in response to anxious cultural sociologies of fragmentation, they showed that America's historical institutions and structures, and its homogenizing and widely shared cultural values, have together diffused conflict and accommodated pluralism – albeit on occasion brutally – to enable stability and cohesion. Discordant social noises notwithstanding, America would not likely fall apart; a more diverse America need not be a more fractious one.

The analysis is splendid, forceful, and continually relevant. Nearly twenty years later, the power and suggestiveness of this sociology still speak to why the contentiousness of American social and political life remains nevertheless contained within fairly stable parameters. And it hints at how much (or how little) homogeneity is necessary in the search for political decency and inclusion. Yet the power of Hallsian historical sociology is that occasional reinterpretations are welcome due to an underlying commitment to empiricism, that is, to a commitment to finding more robust and sustainable accounts of the social world. In that spirit, John Campbell, in his contribution to this volume, questions whether significant cracks in America's edifice have started to undermine its very foundations. In this chapter, I in turn question whether Hall's empirical account takes full account of some aspects of American social history. Sitting happily and firmly within the Hallsian framework, I thus insert modest empirical distinctions into the treatments of race and nation in *Is America Breaking Apart*? My aim is to tether its claims to a more elaborate understanding of America's exceptional historical sociology of race. In doing this, I hope to underscore a fundamental Hallsian argument, which is that political civility is a historically rare, desired, delicate, sometimes impermanent, and often violently gotten achievement. But in an equally Hallsian act of anti-romanticism, I think that this also requires a more thorough and more unsettling elucidation of the price exacted in its pursuit.

So I put the question like this: From where have the moral, social, and political costs of America's liberal achievements been extracted, and with what consequences? For everything civility gives, what does it exact in return? My focus is not on retrieving marginalized voices, absences, silences, and invisibilities – although this is always necessary. I am instead interested in how our historical sociology of America's liberal achievements would be adjusted if race were conceptualized as an independent causal variable that *enabled* these achievements, rather than being theorized as *exceptional* to them. If our historical sociology posits race as the central vector of inequality at the core of America's democracy – that is, as a constituent feature of what was a slave society navigating the modern democratic age – then its social inequalities have not only been marked by biologized cultural differences: they've also been shaped and periodically politicized by a form of white *Staatsvolk* nationalism, an effective but uncivil political strategy for nation-building at key historical moments.

Hallsian Sociology and the American Achievement

It has been nearly twenty years since the publication of *Is America Breaking Apart?*, and the challenges to America's reputed civic nationalism are still myriad: growing ethno-racial diversity due to demographic trends, the dislocations of global capitalism and immigration, the rise of a vibrant #BlackLivesMatter movement, an aggrieved sense of "whiteness," widening political polarization, and perennial anxieties of cultural fragmentation and civic decline. As a first approximation, then, we might say that the same challenges of diversity that empowered a black cosmopolitan intellectual to the presidency also then produced a white ethno-nationalist in compensation. This would be in keeping with how liberalism's management of diversity has often been theorized to progress in American political development: formulations include oscillations between white supremacy and egalitarian transformation (King and Smith 2005), racial consciousness and colour blindness (Lieberman 2007), racial nationalism and civic nationalism (Gerstle 2001), conflicting and multiple visions of citizenship and peoplehood (Smith 2003), and an enduring *non*-post-ethnic national identity (King 2005). This approximation would also similarly be in keeping with historical patterns of black American progress, with moments of incremental empowerment and inclusion followed by partial retreats, backlashes, or full reversals.

Hall and Lindholm's *Is America Breaking Apart?*, in contrast, theorized these challenges to American civic and political life and to its cultural homogeneity in a highly original sociology: on the historical record, they argue, American political development has been characterized by distinctive institutions and structures supported by hard-won cultural and value homogeneity, so that its wider cultural frame privileges accommodation over conflict. Powerful homogenizing capacities and accommodative forces in American culture ensure that conflicts and differences stay within limits (Hall 2013, 18; Hall and Lindholm 1999, 147). Stability was facilitated at the end of the eighteenth century, for example, by a background consensus on religion and property rights, allowing for the regulation of conflict and the institutionalization of loyal opposition. The toleration and uniformity of the colonies' communities ensured that religious difference would not layer with other conflicts. But because of uneven economic development and the distinctiveness of the South, this unity was shattered in a second moment – the Civil War – whose brutality nevertheless resulted in a more unified, homogenous nation. Black Americans remained excluded, of course, but did not seek "exit." A third nation-building moment involved the challenge of class in the industrial age of mass immigration at the turn of the nineteenth century, when socialist alternatives were violently defeated by capitalist elites and the courts and, among other things, by fears of (black) labour competition that fuelled working-class racism. And, finally, World War II and the Cold War held mirrors to the central injustice of American life. This allowed the civil rights movement to see some success, which it paid for, in part, by the loosening of the movement's solidarity.

This account is compelling for its consistently unromantic recognition that the jagged road to greater stability and homogeneity comes at a price. Here and elsewhere in his work, Hall never withholds the force of this critique. "There are decidedly vicious elements of American history that are all too easily forgotten," he writes (Hall 2003, 17), counter to "consensus liberalism" theorists, repeatedly insisting that genuine societal alternatives have often been brutally ruled out, particularly in the illiberalisms of America's racial realities. Mindful that "repression and injustice are often involved in the creation of order and the maintenance of stability," he maintains that America is a "society that asserts equality for all, and still is stained by racism"; and indeed even as the de-politicization and fragmentation of the civil rights movement contributed to a certain political stability, it was a deeply morally repulsive route (Hall and Lindholm 1999, 8–9, 10, 66).

But despite the moral ambiguities and social costs involved in the achievements of cohesion and stability, Hall (2013, 92) notes that "the historic uniqueness of the United States perhaps lies in the fact that it was formed through immigration, that it is a polity created from difference." So the "rosier and milder face of American homogeneity can be seen at work in ethnic relations" (Hall 2003, 18), whereby immigrants are fully integrated and ethnic identity has thinning content, being now a choice rather than a destiny. Yet even here there is recognition that melting-pot uniformity creates a social world unfavourable to true diversity (Hall and Lindholm 1999, 145–8). And more than this, "the United States is not a civil society in the fullest sense, though it is indeed a society where – except for the obscene exception of racism – very great personal civility is practiced" (145). So if "there is much to be said for the decencies of a little dullness and the comforts of a measure of conformity," and if American homogenization has been a universal ideal diminishing ethnic particularisms, little of this has been extended to black Americans (147–8).

Thus even America's most remarkable liberal achievements rightly deserve only the two cheers for homogeneity they are given in *Is America Breaking Apart?* But in an analysis drawing on J.S. Mill, Hall

(2013, 92–3, 95–6, 103) argues that background homogeneity and distinctive social practices might nevertheless "allow American nationalism to move beyond its dominant civic core toward elements of genuine civility." Viewed in this way, American political development can be seen as an instantiation of Hall's wider attempts at grappling with a core, defining tension: that between nationalism's pull towards homogeneity and civility's counter-pull towards the liberal accommodation of diversity. This is central not only to his theorizations of nationalisms, but also to those distinguishing civil society from civility, and the possibilities of civil nationalism.

In his 1995 "In Search of Civil Society" and more fully in his 2013 book *The Importance of Being Civil*, Hall articulates a challenging conception of civil society beyond those social spaces and organizations that stand in opposition to the (despotic) state. Locating its historic emergence in the late eighteenth century, Hall (2013, 19) argues that "civil society only 'makes sense' when it contains a heavy dose of civility" – that is, when it moves beyond simple societal self-organization or associational life:

> Civility is based on the recognition of difference and diversity. Caging is dreadful in large part because it presumes that there is one road to truth in all matters ... To say that the recognition of difference is *shared* and the decision to live together with diversity is *mutual* is to note a background consensus, an agreement to differ, that enables civil society to flourish. (22; emphasis in original)

A consensus to agree to live together – without violence and with political decency – but despite *genuine* difference must therefore inhere in any meaningful account of civil society. This social world is attractive and fragile, and its alternatives repulsive (Hall 2013, 1–6, 10). And although it has "weak sociological roots" (Hall 1995, 3–7), civil society's ideological enemies are fierce: despotism and fear, social envy and distrust – made more pernicious by the politics of divide and rule – the insistence on civic virtue, communitarian or moral caging, and, of course, certain nationalisms.

Indeed, Hall (2013, 7) writes, as noted in the introduction to this volume, that in a "fundamental sense nationalism stands opposed to the very base of civility: it seeks unity, in contrast to civility's desire to manage diversity." Nationalism is seen as protean and labile, "characteristically absorbing the flavors of the historical forces with which it interacts" (Hall 2003, 15–16). But he knows that nationalist homogeneity is usually achieved viciously – and this includes civic nationalism, at face value an inclusionary, joinable form. So can we move "beyond narrow national homogeneity to some sort of multicultural civil nationalism" (Hall 1996, 168)? In "How Homogenous Need We Be?" Hall (1996, 163; see 2003, 25) argues that "the deepest bonds are needed if we are to change fundamental values peaceably," so that civility – and liberalism – are easier once homogenization has done its underlying work. Properly understood, then, multiculturalism *is* civil nationalism; it is the recognition of cultural diversity within a "more neutral frame" and with shared commitment to minimal liberal political norms; it is a world of mild relativism, the antithesis of fear-based despotisms. This is as deeply desirable as it is hard to achieve (see Hall 2003, 30; 2013, 26).

In my view, then, Hall's (2013, 26, 83) most subtle and penetrating insight is that while the origins and practices of civility lay in viciousness, civility, properly conceived, is also "a necessary virtue that can help us negotiate a world of pain." But could it be that the depth and consequence of this dynamic for the United States still remains somewhat underappreciated? A careful reckoning of America's history of nation-building assimilation easily matches the cruellest nationalist homogenizing practices of late nineteenth and early twentieth century Germany, Russia, or Hungary – except that the relevant social vector is not ethnicity or religion but rather race. We could do worse than note, in a Gellnerian vein, that American social inequalities have been marked by biologized cultural differences, which have been periodically politicized by an exclusionary ethnic whiteness, in a sort of *Herrenvolk* democracy. To be sure, sociologists of nationalism do not typically discuss American nation-building in this conceptual or linguistic register. But what has it meant for civility and homogeneity that across American history particular racial groups gained political ascendency at the expense of others? Isn't part of American exceptionalism its multiraciality that descends from slavery, even more than its immigrant-based diversity? Isn't *white* ethno-nationalism also a vicious enemy of civility due to its political strategies of uncivilly excluding genuine difference? What would it look like to theorize it as such?

Nation, Race, Slavery

Hall (see 1994, 526–8; 2013, 205–6) sometimes draws attention to Tocqueville's observation that, unlike France, America was "born free."

It was unshackled by the need to transition – or liberalize – from the inequalities of the aristocratic age to the equal social conditions of the coming democratic age. Setting aside the empirical question of its putative early classlessness, this formulation nevertheless obscures a crucial American exceptionalism: it was, in fact, born a slave state in a democratic age – a slave society intrinsically organized around despotically enforced inequality. In a non-trivial sense, America also undertook a unique transition to equal social conditions. Of course the manner and consequences of its liberalization from slavery's despotism – its "decompression," we might say – differed from that of France's *ancien régime*. This is true in the same way that the sociology that descends from slavery differs from that which descends from colonialism, and indeed from European authoritarianisms, including imperial ones; I have in mind Tsarist Russia's emancipation of the serfs followed two decades later by its own Revolutionary Age.

So drawing on a set of Tocquevillian arguments that I learned from Hall, I hope to bring into better view small pieces of the exceptional causal role of race in America's historical liberalization from slavery's inequalities to equal social conditions. The American road passed through civil war, of course, and not revolution. So I offer only two provisional observations to better understand *the political unwinding of the core inequality at the heart of a democratic slave society*. The first involves a nation-building sociology of white ethno-nationalism as a *Staatsvolk* political strategy for managing the historical transition out of slave-based inequality towards more civic (and at moments civil) nationalist settlements. The second hints at how this sociology *un-civilly* underlies persistent social cohesion anxieties – perhaps a neglected source of the cultural fragmentation worries so well theorized in *Is America Breaking Apart?*

Staatsvolk *Liberalization Strategies*

As Hall sometimes does, I, too, begin with Tocqueville. *Democracy in America* opened with Tocqueville's observation that the more he examined American society, the more he "perceived that the equality of conditions is the fundamental fact from which all others seem to be derived, and the central point at which all … observations constantly terminated" (as quoted in Hall 2003, ii). This premise is rather misleading, however, inasmuch as it problematically relegates slavery and black Americans to an exception in an otherwise equal society. And it may be that *Is America Breaking Apart?* does the same, with similar consequences for the ensuing analyses. Interestingly, however, Tocqueville saw something of the inevitable liberalization of a slaving democracy coming, and he hinted at its implications. Noting that the racist prejudices he observed were the exception to an otherwise general enthusiasm for equality, Tocqueville saw what the exit from "Southern despotism" might entail:

> To declare that all the negroes born after a certain period shall be free, is to introduce the principle and the notion of liberty into the heart of slavery … Thenceforward slavery loses, in their eyes, that *kind of moral power which it derived from time and habit; it is reduced to a mere palpable abuse of force* … But if this faint dawn of freedom were to show two millions of men their true position, the oppressors would have reason to tremble. (2003, 403; emphasis added)

In other words, ending slavery would involve not only managing the materialities of social inequality, but also the moral or normative bases for their enforcement: once slavery could no longer be sustained through accepted *mores* or *custom*, the perpetuation of black inequality could only be enforced despotically. And hence begins the challenge of the "decompression." Tocqueville alludes to the sociology of liberalizing a slave society:

> There exists a singular principle of relative justice which is very firmly implanted in the human heart. *Men are much more forcibly struck by those inequalities which exist within the circle of the same class, than with those which may be remarked between different classes.* It is more easy [*sic*] for them to admit slavery, than to allow several millions of citizens to exist under a load of eternal infamy and hereditary wretchedness. (404; emphasis added)

In consequence, "the abolition of slavery in the South will, in the common course of things, increase the repugnance of the white population for the men of color" (355). This begins to theorize the historical predicate of white resentment. Of course civility and barbarism lived side by side under the same political roof, with a certain political decency among whites and cruelty for the rest. Hall and Lindholm (1999, 26–7) recognize this, noting that pluralism might lead to political stability through a process of mutual stalemate, but great tension nevertheless remained in a half-free, half-slave society: "a shared racism underwrote early American unity," they observe in citing Orlando Patterson, and slavery established an equality among whites that reflected the deep connection between freedom and slavery, with the former appreciated in connection to its opposite (18–9).

This is most certainly right, so its consequences might be elaborated even further in the analyses that are then joined. Slavery was viewed as confirmation of the superiority of whites over blacks, Hall and Lindholm (1999, 19) point out, thereby allowing whites to dominate other races. The premise of biological inferiority allowed whites to maintain a belief in human equality in the face of oppression by denying black Americans full human status. As Fields and Fields (2012, 121) rightly note, "those holding liberty to be unalienable, and holding Afro-Americans as slaves, were bound to end by holding race to be self-evident." Hall and Lindholm (1999, 150, 137) similarly observe that this tendency to essentialize difference exists in tension with faith in equality: "to account for real inequality, or even for difference, Americans tend strongly to 'naturalize' distinctions, making biology the source of differences that their ideology cannot otherwise explain."

But perhaps the implied causal – that is, historical – relationship needs deepening, and its consequences examining. As Fields and Fields argue:

> Race as a coherent ideology did not spring into being simultaneously with slavery, but took even more time than slavery did to become systematic. A commonplace that few stop to examine holds that people are readily oppressed when they are already perceived as inferior by nature. The reverse is more to the point. People are more readily perceived as inferior by nature when they are already seen as oppressed. (2012, 121)

In other words, the relevant sociology runs not from inferiority to oppression, but from oppression to inferiority. And indeed we can briefly trace its historicization. The extension of suffrage in the Jacksonian "one man, one vote" era, roughly between the 1820s and the 1840s, gave all non-propertied white males full political inclusion. Hall and Lindholm (1999, 28) point out that this widening of suffrage meant that "politics would be popular and have to pander to electorates." But this "civil" extension radically upended politics in another profound way: America suddenly also became a society in which only black slaves lacked those rights that all others could now and henceforth simply take for granted. Apart from justifying this black exclusion as a matter of self-evident law (albeit one countered by abolitionists), this liberalization newly politicized a racial vector in electoral politics. So the move towards greater civil inclusion had this as its price: America's most significant vector of inequality now required a new set of political strategies to maintain.

One such strategy was the invention of whiteness as ideology, and as strategy for nation-building. The gradual expansion of suffrage in these decades took place against the visible presence of slavery, continually reinforcing the status anxiety of those white publics still to be franchised and who politically understood themselves as "little more than slaves." Political privileges became increasingly more important differentiators, setting in motion white nationalism's developing ideological organization, one finely attuned to the expanding democratic age. In this way, white ideological unity – expressed as a shared interest in maintaining existing forms of inequality – was more than a way of organizing the unequal distribution of power. To say that a shared racism – or white solidarity – underwrote unity is another way of saying that it served as *Staatsvolk* nationalism in the liberalization of a slave society; it provided ideological elite/white cohesion through the nation-building mid-nineteenth century. Whiteness was functional for nation-building, heretofore organizing as a political strategy to manage the transition out of one form of historic inequality towards one of greater equality.

One corollary to this involved the cultural reshaping and revalorization of labour. Jacksonian democracy had also introduced "the dignity of labour" as a civic principle: under conditions of slavery's racially differentiated inequality, of course, white wage-labour had measured its place in the labour hierarchy against slave labour, both in real wages and in the more diffuse "public and psychological" ones. Indeed, instead of deriving American values from the ideals and thought of the founding era, Judith Shklar (1991) famously argued that in America's unique slaveholding democracy the ability to earn from one's labour, combined with equality of political inclusion through the vote, were the two critical indicia of substantive citizenship. Voting and earning embodied a status uniquely juxtaposed against slavery, separating free men from "wage-slavery" and enabling poor white men to distinguish themselves from others similarly positioned by seeing the latter as working less hard. Hence the "work ethic" developed in part as "the ideology of citizens caught between racist slavery and aristocratic pretensions" (Shklar 1991, 64, 91–9). I find this compelling, because it echoes through subsequent decades of policy battles based on racially isolating the deserving from the undeserving in America's labour hierarchy.

Liberalization's Cohesion Anxieties

Therefore one consequence of the political unwinding of the central vector of inequality at the core of America's democratic slave society involved an uncivil white nationalism, effectively a *Staatsvolk* political strategy for managing the gradual liberalization to civic or eventual civil inclusions. A second consequence might then be found in the moral and cultural effects of this unwinding, that is to say, as a source of the disquieting and relentless anxiousness about social fragmentation, one perhaps under-theorized in *Is America Breaking Apart?*

The coexistence of barbarous slavery and despotically enforced inequality in the "land of the free" had created a moral dissonance, a particular American psychology, which we might similarly historicize with the emergence of white solidarity as political strategy. Tocqueville (2003) also hinted at this: "The danger of a conflict between the white and the black inhabitants of the Southern States of the Union – a danger which, however remote it may be, is inevitable – *perpetually haunts the imagination of the Americans*" (407; emphasis added). Could racism and its maintenance have contributed to social anxiety, to a sense of fragmentation, for both victim *and* racist? Might some of the social roots of black exclusion be normatively located in this cohesion anxiety? What does it do to the character of civility to have to continually and studiously keep out of view "the Negroes among us"? How might we think about its moral costs as the slave society navigated a more democratic age? How did the trauma of slavery and its consequences shape its normative management of inequality or hierarchy? Could some of this also contribute to what Hall and Lindholm (1999, 10) analyse as the way in which America is "perennially shaken by self-doubt and moral anguish"?

I cannot answer all these questions, of course, but simply sketch how we might begin within a Hallsian framework. Hall's (see 2013, 23–6; 1995, 7–8) analyses of Montesquieu's *Persian Letters* is hugely compelling, and considering it attunes us to the possibility that, at the very least, one half of America – black *and* white – lived in fear, some trembling as victims of despotism and others trembling from the fragility of their hold on despotic power. What might this look like empirically? One might see it in small things: in the fact that slaves were forbidden to learn how to swim for fear of enabling escape routes; that food was used to control hungry slaves, often generously given in exchange for buying off loyalty, read simply as "non-rebellion" (Johnson 2013, 179, 219). Indeed, the "carceral landscape" of the American South – and by extension the whole of America – suggests that slave owners were trapped in existential fears and anxieties over slave revolts, escapes, bonds between slaves, slaves' own associational lives – not, indeed, unlike Montesquieu's Persian harem, which required simultaneous separateness and total visibility of their subjects (Johnson 2013, especially chaps. 7 and 8). Across the Lower Mississippi Valley, for instance, fear surrounding the fragility of a society organized around extraction and exclusion derived not from enslaving dehumanized people, but from continually needing to de-humanize enslaved people: "slaveholders were fully cognizant of the slave's humanity – indeed, they were completely dependent on it," not least the slaves' ability to withstand pain and physical deprivation, all of which was just one limiting condition to slave-owners' power (Johnson 2013, 207–8, chap. 8). Hall's (1995, 7–8) analysis of Uzbek and the revolt in the harem in *Persian Letters* might be the best place to begin better theorizing the psychological fragility of what was seemingly overwhelming, one-sided despotic power.

More generally, though, and even setting aside the specific and profound traumas of the Civil War, in at least two defining nation-building moments – the mid- and late nineteenth century – maintaining slavery or its consequences caused sociologically diffuse but profound disquiet over social cohesion and fragmentation. With the political extension of slavery to areas gotten from the Mexican-American War, for instance, how could a liberal civil society continue to exist inside a barbarous slave one? While this raging social conflict oddly escaped other American writers of the era,[1] Hermann Melville famously wrestled with it perhaps more earnestly than most, his biography embodying the social forces of the era: his father-in-law judge had decided the case enshrining the 1850 Fugitive Slave Law, very personally forcing Melville to grapple with the relationship between American slavery and the American commitment to freedom, and how the intensity of one solidified that of the other (Rogin 1985, chap. 3, especially 103–9). In a wonderful Tanner Lecture, Toni Morrison (1988, 142) placed Melville's dilemma within the wider phenomenology of the era: a product of his age, Melville "was overwhelmed by the philosophical and metaphysical inconsistencies of an extraordinary and unprecedented idea that had its fullest manifestation in his own time, in his own country, and that idea was the successful assertion of whiteness as ideology." The invention of this ideology itself was the resolution to the tension between liberty

1 As Morrison (1988, 137) noted, at the height of slavery and abolitionism, most American writers chose romance.

and slavery – and this resolution came at the price of how black Americans had sought to resolve it, which was through the contrary assertion of liberty as their natural right (Fields and Fields 2012, 141).

This is not simply to underscore Du Bois's famous argument about the public and psychological wages of whiteness and the scholarship that flows from it (see Feagin 2013; Jung 2015; Roediger 1999). It is rather to note that white ethno-nationalism's work in alleviating the moral disorientations and status jolts of the liberalization of inequalities came at the painful moral cost of sublimating black Americans' claims of liberty, justice, and equality to white cultural claims of liberty, justice, and equality. Sociologists' attention to power can sometimes obscure the ways in which values function to sustain the moral orderings that caste-like hierarchies provide (Haynes and Hickel 2017). So we see early white indentured and coerced labourers' distinctions between deserving and undeserving poor; we see how poor whites learned to hate those next to them, not those above them; and how the public wages of whiteness put a permanent black face to failure – all with the result of creating a more "democratically" robust moral undergirding for sustaining white hierarchies. These, too, were white ethno-nationalism's political strategies for dealing with the anxieties of cultural and social fragmentation.

Blackness, Whiteness, Hierarchy

Of course liberalizing moments of black empowerment historically gave rise to white unity strategies aimed at protecting socio-economic and political statuses at all class levels (Du Bois 1963). Understanding how these political strategies functioned as threats to civility involves a better grasp of how race ideology – or white nationalism – like other historical ideologies, organizes materially, and thus how it can causally operate independently of other sources of social power (on the material organization of ideological power, see Hall 1996, chap. 1; Mann 1986, 10). The political practices involved in slavery, Jim Crow, or indeed mass incarceration might be conceptualized as white divide-and-rule policies, not only sowing deep social distrust and brutally rending the "civility" of civil society, but also organizing and finding expression in very specific material and spatial conditions (on such a view of enslavement, see Johnson 2013). I briefly outline three layered ways in which this ideological organization might perhaps be explored from within a Hallsian framework: (1) through the political invention of segregation as a Tocquevillian practice of divide and rule; (2) through black exclusion from civil society or civic associational life, where American nation-building took place; and (3) through illiberal practices sustaining racial inequalities or hierarchies.

Most immediately, segregation was not simply an organic expression of the operation of a racial caste system. It was a political invention (Hanchett 2000). As a set of political practices, post-slavery spatial segregation had its roots in the battles of the late nineteenth century, initially in the political strategies of white Southern elites before diffusing more widely. White nation-building found expression in new practices of geographical separateness. Assisted by federal funds and local capital, these practices aimed at solidifying vertical cross-class unity. Neighbourhoods in Charlotte, North Carolina, after the Civil War, for instance, were divided neither by class nor race: black and white residents lived in residential and public spaces in "salt and pepper" patterns. Then, in the first Jim Crow separation of public services in 1899, separateness accelerated until 1910 as it formalized first into "checkerboard" and then "sector" patterns (Hanchett 2000). Similar and more well-known white unity politics characterized the Depression Era's exclusionary innovations in housing and neighbourhood redlining, federal mortgage insurance, "contracts for deeds," and those wider postwar (de)segregation struggles underpinned by the privatization of public services and concentrated housing or zoning laws (see Jargowsky 2015; Kruse 2007). Indeed, the Obama administration's 2013 "Affirmatively Furthering Fair Housing" guidelines are only the most recent attempt at fulfilling the unmet antidiscrimination promises of the Fair Housing Act of 1968, to which these earlier segregation practices had given rise.

But because black geographic segregation has been studiously reimagined to solidify white nation-building by promoting white social mobility at the cost of black exclusion, black poverty developed a different ideological character and political infrastructure than white poverty (see Chetty, Hendren, and Katz 2015; Sampson 2012; Sharkey 2009). Both white and black citizens live inside American capitalism, but the spatial organization of poverty is maintained by politically differentiated inclusions and exclusions, not least those directly enforced by the coercive arms of the state – Tocqueville's *ancien régime* style. The public lynching decades of the 1880s and 1890s, of convict lease practices of forced imprisoned black labour until WWII (Blackmon 2008), and even of "racial cleansing" (Phillips 2016) testify to the post-slavery legacy of state-sanctioned violence on black bodies, and to the ways in which America's public spaces were often places of daily humiliations, cruelties, and incivilities. This legacy finds expression in urban policing of black youth in one of the most pernicious and diffuse forms of everyday state violence and humiliation, and the most direct way in which black Americans differentially experience the coercive power of the state (see Epp, Maynard-Moody, and Haider-Markel 2014; Fassin 2013; Muhammad 2011). Anti-black policing and its correlated patterns of incarceration criminalize under the principles of universality and colour blindness, which is arguably one way of making sense of the practices described in the 2015 Ferguson Report, for example, whereby "African Americans experience disparate impact in nearly every aspect of Ferguson's law enforcement system" (US Department of Justice and Civil Rights Division 2015, 62; see also Alexander 2010).[2]

Of course the historic persistence of politically intimate and personalized violence and politically differentiated exclusions render black Americans "conditional citizens"; but they also ensure that race – not ethnicity – becomes a consistent way in which Americans experience "class." Thus the spatialized layering of economic and political exclusions has worked through a second aspect of white nationalism's ideological-material organization: black exclusion from civil society, that is, from the civic and social locations in which nation-building historically took place. America's civil society did not, for most of its history, have voluntary and overlapping associations and memberships where individuals could move freely and without fear, *pace* Hall and Lindholm's (1999, 121–8) description. In addition to the invention of neighbourhood segregation was the purposeful exclusion of black Americans from the expansion of civic associational life during the late nineteenth and early twentieth centuries, a key nation-building moment. America's neighbourhoods were products of federal, state, and municipal policies supported by white urban planners, school boards, local businesses, churches and, most especially, the urban lower-middle classes: police, plumbers, shopkeepers, teachers. These influential white publics, not the state, were the nation-builders of the Americanization moment.

The foundational seedbed era of modern black disadvantage was actually not conceived in the New Deal Era but in Progressive America, where between the 1880s and 1920s a homogenizing white nationalism

2 Despite comprising 67 per cent of Ferguson's population, between 2012 and 2014, black Americans accounted for 85 per cent of traffic stops, 90 per cent of citations, and 93 per cent of arrests (US Department of Justice 2015, 62).

lay the civic and institutional structures for white social mobility.[3] In one of the largest social and political mobilizations in US history, the Americanization's assimilation establishment culturally and civically disciplined the immigrant industrial working class, converting them from "alien non-citizens" into white ethnic citizens. It was civil society nation-building, with all the social coerciveness and exclusionary practices involved in "neighbourliness." The Americanization establishment mobilized more than eighty thousand federal, local, and private agencies in 30 states, twenty-three hundred cities, twelve hundred Chambers of Commerce, more than eight hundred trade organizations, fifty national religious organizations, and thousands of civic associational groupings of all kinds. But civil society's assimilation was exclusively white as it layered "ethnicity" as a substantive social category onto its existing practices of segregation. That is, white nationalism's invention of "ethnicity" was enabled by the uncivil reinscription of a black boundary. As Hall and Lindholm (1999, 129–44) argue, black Americans are "right to believe themselves outsiders in their own country" – indeed, America remains the only Western democracy that actively makes residence requirements for voting more difficult, and it does so for only a studied portion of its citizens. So ethnicity, rather than being a "weak identity marker" with little content and a vague personalized sense of community, as Hall and Lindholm suggest, continues to be a rather strong and visible political marker of whiteness.

These white middle class nation-building processes formed the basis of America's homogeneity, with black exclusion the price exacted in return. As such, the lesson from American history is that civil inclusion might require addressing white unity and its political strategies, not least since white unity has embedded equally in progressive populist social policy (the Progressive Era, the New Deal, the War on Poverty) and in rightist populist policy (Wallace's Southern moment, Reaganism, Trumpism).[4] Hall and Lindholm (1999, 152) argue that antidemocratic capitalist elites are a greater threat than eruptions of populism. But the putative "working class" basis of rightist populist appeals, for instance, rapidly dissolves into a "white working class" if we also permit black

3 This discussion draws elements from work in progress – "The Americanization Moment and Modern American Inequalities."

4 I thank Johannes Langer for discussion on the relationships among populism, race, and nationalism.

(and Latino) Americans to have class interests. White unity, not the ability to address antidemocratic capitalism, is equally the enemy of civil inclusion. Civil society did not create racialized spaces; rather, civil society was itself built on these racializations.

So a third and final aspect of white nationalism's material organization lies in Hall and Lindholm's (1999, 150) conclusion that "the greatest problem of American culture is its inability to conceptualize and deal with inequality," whereby "culture serves as a perfect mask for the structure of interests, permitting considerable harshness and injustice because of its ideology of egalitarian individualism." In racial terms, redistributive policies are difficult because of the devalorization of black Americans through stigmatization and deeply entrenched racism. Indeed, they argue that it is harder to mobilize against economic inequality than it was against Jim Crow, because while segregation was an open breach of American ideals, economic justice does not have a clear target. Therefore poverty should be addressed on a universalist basis or through class mechanisms, perhaps even setting aside differentialist policies: instead of shifting race, shift class, and some of the viciousness of racial inequality will attenuate. Arguably the Affordable Care Act attempted something like this: universalist in application, its significant welfare extensions, particularly through state-level Medicaid expansions, actually had disproportionately beneficial effects for black Americans (Chen et al. 2016). So the wider prescriptive claim is that economic participation and homogeneity will heal racial exclusions: to tackle the inequitable consequences of poverty, Hall and Lindholm (1999, 144) argue, "Americans will accept compensatory policies if they are universal."

But this might also be understood against what I am suggesting has been a historical political liberalization from slavery's inequalities towards full civility, or the political inclusion of genuine difference. This is because the sociology of white nationalism can have its own material and ideological capacities, independent of class. The 2009 subprime mortgage crisis was not universalist in its effects, but it fell inequitably and disproportionately on black Americans for reasons outlined above. Universalist solutions frequently fall aground to the fact that America's historical problems with inequality are often not, fundamentally, universalist. The distributional issues involved in addressing key vectors of inequality do, in fact, have both clear racial beneficiaries and clear racial targets of social distrust.

This claim finds continued, varied, and widespread empirical support: aggregate policy preferences at federal and state levels show that black support for Congressional legislation actually decreases its chances of passage (Stephanopoulos 2015);[5] the first workman's compensation laws were passed in homogeneously white Wisconsin in 1911, but not until 1948 in Mississippi because of white resistance to generosity towards black citizens (Fishback and Kantor 2007); opposition to the Affordable Care Act was driven by belief that undeserving minorities would benefit (Banks 2014; Knoll and Shewmaker 2015); counties with the highest share of slaves in 1860 today oppose affirmative action policies disproportionately more than other parts of the country (Acharya, Blackwell, and Sen 2016); white flight to the suburbs prompted by the northern migration of four million black Americans between the 1940s and the 1970s was motivated by resistance to paying into racially mixed local public services (Boustan 2017); white racism undercut the War on Poverty (Guandango 1996); and black Americans were offered meagre and humiliating social assistance in the Progressive and New Deal eras in racialized distortions that generously assisted white immigrants (Katznelson 2013; Lieberman 2007) – and this at the height of raging anti-immigrant nativism and rightist populism (Fox 2012). Indeed subsequent retrenchment came from those political constituencies where putative beneficiaries were prohibited from voting: cash aid and public employment programs were dismantled in the 1940s because in half of the states, largely black populations (among others) were excluded from political participation and thus unable to express support for redistributive policies (Amenta 1998).

In short, the uncivil exclusion of black citizens made expansions of social welfare for white citizens possible. So in a wider context of racially inflected hierarchies in which status fragility is politicized by divide-and-rule policies, poor and working-class whites have viewed universalist policies not as benefitting them against capitalist elites, but rather as transfers of public monies to non-deserving non-whites. The sociology is such that *both* universalist *and* redistributive policies actually make whites more hostile to government, not less. In terms of inequality, poverty, and the distributional issues these involve – and despite political rhetoric to the contrary – the American struggle has been less about the size of government than about who benefits. This

5 An increase in white support from 0 per cent to 100 per cent increases the likelihood of adoption from 10 per cent to 60 per cent. But as black support rises from 0 per cent to 100 per cent, the odds of enactment actually fall from 40 per cent to 30 per cent (Stephanopoulos 2015, 1583).

strikes me as fundamentally Tocquevillian, and indeed Hallsian, in argument: whites and blacks are locked in the same capitalist system, but they don't *politically* experience it in the same way, as differentiated political privileges, welfare provisions, and the meting out of state violence have disproportionately affected black citizens. This might perhaps be theorized as a state and society in which social inequalities are marked by biologized cultural differences – and politicized as such by white ethno-nationalism.

The Costs of Civility

Inspired by Hall's work on civil society and nationalism, and in particular by his compelling analysis in *Is America Breaking Apart?*, I have only tentatively sketched how race might be better integrated into a historical sociology of civility and nationalism in America's political development. Viewed not as prejudice or attitude, insult, moral character flaw, or identity politics – and so not incidental or exceptional to its sociology – race has been one of the central vectors of American civil and political life (see Jung 2015). The question is how much it has distorted or been exceptional to American civility and liberal nation-building, and how much it has been functional for it. Has the unwillingness to "civilly" address the most fundamental and genuine difference in American society been one price paid for its welfare state, its assimilation of immigrants, its political institutions, and indeed its very civil society and the character of its neighbourhoods and associational life? White ethno-nationalism has perhaps been one of the most consistent ideological threads in American political development, repeatedly inhering to political strategies of left and right in managing the historical liberalization from slavery's inequalities to full civil inclusion. Put another way, America's historic liberalization from slavery's despotically enforced inequalities to its "equal social conditions" – and indeed, in moments, civil inclusions – has come at enormously painful social, moral, and political costs. And this might need greater historical, if not theoretical, reckoning than comparative historical sociologists have so far allowed.

If a key social vector in America's hierarchies is race, then perhaps the election of a black president symbolically but powerfully subverted perceptions of these hierarchies and their status fragilities. We might say that "blackness" in power triggered "white fragility," that it challenged the "racial stamina" of white unity, prompting defensive attempts to re-establish white-dominant racial equilibria (DiAngelo 2011). Extending earlier work on whiteness, there is now a growing sociology grappling with the interiorities of white socioeconomic grievance and cultural anxiety (see Abrajano and Hajnal 2015; Hochschild 2016). Setting the sociological merits of this work to one side, changing demographics and black advancement *have* structurally challenged not only white political power but also the "public and psychological wages" that have variously attached to it or substituted for it (see Kaufmann 2004).

And with this, today, norms of political constraint around race are becoming unbuttoned. Seeing black Americans as racists or as resentful minorities for raising the issue of racism is not new, to be sure. Yet one of the most significant cultural victories of the civil rights moment – a victory somewhat neglected, I think, in Hall and Lindholm's otherwise excellent analysis – was that being a racist became negatively sanctioned in American morality as unacceptably uncivil. But a dangerous sleight of hand also occurred through this cultural approbation: pointing out racism has become as morally repugnant as the possibility of the underlying racism itself. Assisted by scholarly work on "white interiorities" e.g., Hochschild 2016), the bar for defining who is a racist has been raised so high that it can now only be self-ascribed; racism is in your heart, and only if you yourself say so. To the extent that racism is admitted to exist, then, it has often become rather unlocatable. When the accusation of racism becomes a deep personal attack loaded with moral approbation, it is no longer a substantive designation with social consequences, but a moral insult to be avoided. The accusation itself then becomes the moral transgression because it violates precisely "the equalizing etiquette" norms theorized by Hall and Lindholm (1999, 109–20): they understand that, in "cloaking authority relations with the trappings of equality," untidy contestations can offend in part because of the sacralization of the community and its political realm. But when pointing to something as jolting and unsettling as racism becomes more normatively uncivil than the underlying injustice itself, then a profound social cost has likely been extracted from someone somewhere.

One of the most visible of these costs is, of course, the inability to civilly address racialized inequalities. In outlining what they see as Americans' distinct ways of grasping the world, Hall and Lindholm (1999, 83–107) brilliantly argue that Americans' thin, vague, or abstract knowledge of political rights theories serves a key social function: Americans know they have rights, but they're not clear on precisely what they are, so abstract notions of equality, liberty, and justice become malleable in their application and sufficiently vague as to allow them to hold contradictory ideals. "Ideological inconsistency is actually a feature of stability," Hall and Lindholm (1999, 83–7) argue, because disagreements are not over detailed knowledge of principles or of America's mythic collective identity and the bases of its egalitarianism. This may well lend itself to a certain value of homogeneity and stability, but it also comes at the cost of making white America less attuned to black Americans' claims to protections from within the very specificities of these vague inalienable rights.

All of this is just to suggest that a deeper engagement with race might not be empirically isolated from our historical sociology of civil society or nationalism, or indeed from theorizing the conditions of civility and political decency, especially in the context of American nationalism. If ethnic exclusion is sociologically functional for nationalist homogeneity, so too racial exclusion is functional for white ethno-nationalism, and indeed often the bulwarks of civil pluralism have come from racial minorities, not white publics. Without the three-fifths clause, that is, without despotic rule over human property within a democratic state, a government would not have held together; without the invention of white nationalist strategies for keeping white publics together, America could not have built a welfare state. In other words, in key moments, white ideological unity functioned as a kind of nation-building strategy to manage the historic liberalization from a slave-owning democracy to a multiracial one.

If we conceived of these political strategies as nationalizing practices of exclusion, then in any other context we might consider them white ethno-nationalist. Our sociology of nationalism tends to understand its forces in ethnic and religious terms, but less often in racial terms, which are usually reserved for (post) colonial contexts. But could we think of white nationalism as functional for capitalist economic development, and indeed could black Americans not have considered themselves as living under "alien rule" for much of their history? This is not to make a point about the unlikelihood of black "exit" or separatist nationalism, but rather to suggest that white solidarity has been sociologically functional as *Staatsvolk* nationalism. As James Baldwin repeatedly insisted, black exclusion from the American Dream was not an exception to be bracketed, but a necessary condition for it. So, perhaps only one cheer for homogeneity? If America were slightly less homogeneous, that is, if it could properly reconcile its history of genuine difference, it might be more civil.

REFERENCES

Abrajano, Marisa, and Zoltan Hajnal. 2015. *White Backlash: Immigration, Race, and American Politics*. Princeton: Princeton University Press. https://doi.org/10.1515/9781400866489.

Acharya, Avidit, Matthew Blackwell, and Maya Sen. 2016. "The Political Legacy of American Slavery." *Journal of Politics* 78 (3): 621–41. https://doi.org/10.1086/686631.

Alexander, Michelle. 2010. *The New Jim Crow: Mass Incarceration in the Age of Colorblindness*. New York: New Press.

Amenta, Edwin. 1998. *Bold Relief: Institutional Politics and the Origins of Modern American Social Policy*. Princeton: Princeton University Press.

Baldwin, James. 1965. "The American Dream and the American Negro." *New York Times*, 7 March.

Banks, Antoine. 2014. "The Public's Anger: White Racial Attitudes and Opinions toward Health Care Reform." *Political Behavior* 36 (3): 493–514. https://doi.org/10.1007/s11109-013-9251-3.

Blackmon, Douglas. 2008. *Slavery by Another Name: The Re-enslavement of Black Americans from the Civil War to World War II*. New York: Anchor.

Boustan, Leah Platt. 2017. *Competition in the Promised Land: Black Migrants in Northern Cities and Labor Markets*. Princeton: Princeton University Press. https://doi.org/10.1515/9781400882977.

Chen, Jie, Arturo Vargas-Bustamante, Karoline Mortensen, and Alexander N. Ortega. 2016. "Racial and Ethnic Disparities in Health Care Access and Utilization under the Affordable Care Act." *Medical Care* 54 (2): 140–6. https://doi.org/10.1097/MLR.0000000000000467.

Chetty, Raj, Nathaniel Hendren, and Lawrence Katz. 2015. "The Effects of Exposure to Better Neighborhoods on Children: New Evidence from the Moving to Opportunity Experiment." National Bureau of Economic Research working paper 21156. https://doi.org/10.3386/w21156.

DiAngelo, Robin. 2011. "White Fragility." *International Journal of Critical Pedagogy* 3 (3): 54–70.

Du Bois, W.E.B. 1963. *Black Reconstruction in America 1860–1880*. New York: Atheneum.

Epp, Charles, Steven Maynard-Moody, and Donald Haider-Markel. 2014. *Pulled Over: How Police Stops Define Race and Citizenship*. Chicago: University of Chicago Press. https://doi.org/10.7208/chicago/9780226114040.001.0001.

Fassin, Didier. 2013. *Enforcing Order: An Ethnography of Urban Policing*. London: Polity.

Feagin, Joe. 2013. *The White Racial Frame: Centuries of Racial Framing and Counter-Framing*. London: Routledge.

Fields, Karen, and Barbara Fields. 2012. *Racecraft: The Soul of Inequality in American Life*. London: Verso.

Fishback, Price, and Eric Everett Kantor. 2007. *A Prelude to the Welfare State: The Origins of Workers' Compensation*. Chicago: University of Chicago Press.

Fox, Cybelle. 2012. *Three Worlds of Relief: Race, Immigration, and the American Welfare State from the Progressive Era to the New Deal*. Princeton: Princeton University Press.

Gerstle, Gary. 2001. *American Crucible: Race and Nation in the Twentieth Century*. Princeton: Princeton University Press.

Guandango, Jill. 1996. *The Color of Welfare: How Racism Undermined the War on Poverty*. Oxford: Oxford University Press.

Hall, John A. 1994. "After the Fall: An Analysis of Post-Communism." *British Journal of Sociology* 45 (4): 525–42. https://doi.org/10.2307/591881.

– 1995. "In Search of Civil Society." In *Civil Society: Theory, History, Comparison*, edited by John A. Hall, 1–31. London: Polity.

– 1996. "How Homogeneous Need We Be? Reflections on Nationalism and Liberty." *Sociology* 30 (1): 163–71. https://doi.org/10.1177/0038038596030001014.

– 2003. "Conditions for National Homogenizers." In *Nationalism and Its Futures*, edited by Umut Özkirimli, 15–31. London: Palgrave-Macmillan. https://doi.org/10.1057/9780230524187_2.

– 2013. *The Importance of Being Civil: The Struggle for Political Decency*. Princeton: Princeton University Press.

Hall, John. A., and Charles Lindholm. 1999. *Is America Breaking Apart?* Princeton: Princeton University Press.

Hanchett, Thomas. 2000. *Sorting the New South City: Race, Class, and Urban Development in Charlotte, 1875–1975*. Chapel Hill: University of North Carolina Press.

Haynes, Naomi, and Jason Hickel. 2017. "Hierarchy, Value and the Value of Hierarchy." *Social Analysis* 61 (4): 1–20.

Hochschild, Arlie. 2016. *Strangers in Their Own Land: Anger and Mourning on the American Right*. New York: New Press.

Jargowsky, Paul. 2015. "The Architecture of Segregation: Civil Unrest, the Concentration of Poverty, and Public Policy." Issue brief. Century Foundation. https://s3-us-west-2.amazonaws.com/production.tcf.org/app/uploads/2015/08/07182514/Jargowsky_ArchitectureofSegregation-11.pdf (accessed May 2018).

Johnson, Walter. 2013. *River of Dark Dreams: Slavery and Empire in the Cotton Kingdom*. Cambridge, MA: Harvard University Press.

Jung, Moon-Kie. 2015. *Beneath the Surface of White Supremacy: Denaturalizing U.S Racisms Past and Present*. Stanford: Stanford University Press.

Katznelson, Ira. 2013. *Fear Itself: The New Deal and the Origins of Our Time*. New York: W.W. Norton.

Kaufmann, Eric. 2004. *The Rise and Fall of Anglo-America*. Cambridge, MA: Harvard University Press.

King, Desmond. 2005. *The Liberty of Strangers: Making the American Nation*. Oxford: Oxford University Press.

King, Desmond, and Rogers Smith. 2005. "Racial Orders in American Political Development." *American Political Science Review* 99 (1): 75–92. https://doi.org/10.1017/S0003055405051506.

Knoll, Benjamin, and J. Shewmaker. 2015. "'Simply un-American': Nativism and Support for Health Care Reform." *Political Behavior* 37 (1): 87–108. https://doi.org/10.1007/s11109-013-9263-z.

Kruse, Kevin. 2007. *White Flight: Atlanta and the Making of Modern Conservatism*. Princeton: Princeton University Press.

Lieberman, Robert. 2007. *Shaping Race Policy: The United States in Comparative Perspective*. Princeton: Princeton University Press.

Mann, Michael. 1986. *Sources of Social Power*. Vol. 1, *History of Power from the Beginning to AD 1760*. Cambridge: Cambridge University Press.

Morrison, Toni. 1988. "Unspeakable Things Unspoken: The Afro-American Presence in American Literature." In *The Tanner Lectures on Human Values*. Ann Arbor: University of Michigan.

Muhammad, Khalil Gibran. 2011. *The Condemnation of Blackness: Race, Crime, and the Making of Modern Urban America*. Cambridge, MA: Harvard University Press.

Phillips, Patrick. 2016. *Blood at the Root: A Racial Cleansing in America*. New York: W.W. Norton.

Roediger, Philip. 1999. *Wages of Whiteness: Race and the Making of the Working Class*. London: Verso.

Rogin, Michael Paul. 1985. *Subversive Geneology: The Politics and Art of Herman Melville*. Berkeley: University of California Press.

Sampson, R. 2012. *The Great American City: Chicago and the Enduring Neighborhood Effect*. Chicago: University of Chicago Press. https://doi.org/10.7208/chicago/9780226733883.001.0001.

Sharkey, Patrick. 2009. *Neighborhoods and the Black-White Mobility Gap*. Washington, DC: Pew Charitable Trusts.

Shklar, Judith. 1991. *American Citizenship: The Quest for Inclusion*. Cambridge, MA: Harvard University Press.

Smith, Roger. 2003. *Stories of Peoplehood: The Politics and Morals of Political Membership*. Cambridge: Cambridge University Press. https://doi.org/10.1017/CBO9780511490347.

Stephanopoulos, Nicholas. 2015. "Political Powerlessness." *New York University Law Review* 90: 1528–608.

Tocqueville, Alexis de. 2003. *Democracy in America*. Clark: Lawbook Exchange.

United States Department of Justice (Civil Rights Division). 2015. "Investigation of the Ferguson Police Department." https://www.justice.gov/sites/default/files/opa/press-releases/attachments/2015/03/04/ferguson_police_department_report.pdf (accessed December 2017).

3 Roadblocks to Civility: Lessons from Turkish Nationalism

YESIM BAYAR

Understanding the mechanisms of the expansion and maintenance of liberties has been a mainstay of John Hall's intellectual pursuits. This particular direction has been organically linked to his ongoing interest in the sources of civility and political decency in modern societies. Hall has most recently engaged with these issues in *The Importance of Being Civil* (2013), where his call for civility is powerful, unrelenting yet cautious, and coupled with a recognition of its fragility.

The emergence and development of civility in Europe have been nasty and torturous affairs crystallizing as a result, and not despite of, warfare, ethnic cleansing, imperialism, and exclusionary state practices. Writing in the nineteenth century with his gaze on America and France, Tocqueville vehemently advocated that we must never become complacent about our democratic societies and that we must *practise* democracy to keep it alive. In the same spirit, Hall (2013, 82) warns us that civility has "no secure structural base" and thus "when we have it, we should cherish it." He further reminds us that while its maintenance requires continuous care, the enemies of civility are plentiful. One such foe is nationalism, and that is the focus of this paper. More specifically, this discussion asks how and under what conditions nationalism can become a major obstacle to the emergence and development of civility.

Nationalism fundamentally seeks to unify through homogenization. Civility, on the other hand, is, as Hall (2013, 22) puts it, "based on recognition of difference and diversity." It is also about the management of differences. Essentially, civility "allows disagreement to take place without violence and regularizes conflict so that it can be productive" (4). Hence, as noted in the introductory chapter in this volume, a clear opposition is present in Hall's mind between nationalism and civility.

Yet this opposition does not render the study of civility irrelevant to students of nationalism. On the contrary, as Hall reasons, "absolute correspondence between state and nation may not be a universal requirement if arrangements can be made for several nations to live under the same political roof. So questions about civility matter enormously within the theory and practice of nationalism" (7).

Working from these general premises, I have two goals in this paper. The first pertains to my empirical focus. Hall's work on civility and nationalism is primarily grounded in his historical-sociological explorations of the (Western) European landscape. In these works, while Turkey makes occasional appearances, it ultimately remains in the background. By shifting the geographical concentration slightly towards the east, as Berna Turam does in her own chapter, I aim to reflect on the relevance of Hall's arguments to make sense of the Turkish trajectory.

The second goal relates to causes and meanings. For Hall the central endeavour in understanding nations and nationalisms should revolve around structural rather than cultural explanations. Relatedly, he forcefully warns us against giving too much weight to the power of ideas (Hall 1985, 1993, 2006). The critical point here is not to dismiss ideas altogether but to specify when they acquire more significance, why they maintain their hold on society as much as they do, and how their specific content is formed. Hall's (2013, 99) conceptualization of nationalism as a labile force that takes on its character from the social forces with which it interacts is thus situated within this structuralist approach.

The present discussion heeds Hall's warnings against an unqualified emphasis on ideas. Accordingly, it seeks an understanding of the different macro forces that defined the content of Turkish nationalism and that have contributed to its salience. At the same time, however, special attention will be paid to the political elite – how they discussed, formulated, and institutionalized their visions of the Turkish nation – with the aim of underlining how ideas may matter as well as highlighting the contingent character of how nationalist ideas and policies are formulated.

The main arguments outlined here are straightforward. At a general level, the Turkish case presents us with a paradox. When looked at from a long-term perspective, and against modernization theorists' contentions, neither economic development nor the rise in education levels seem to have ameliorated Turkey's record on the protection and expansion of rights and liberties. Significant problems await resolution, especially, but not only, when it comes to the Kurdish population. Reflecting on why these limitations have not been surpassed, this chapter proposes that the salience and force of Turkish nationalism require closer examination as key components of this puzzle.

The discussion is divided into three main sections. The first section is a brief consideration of the Ottoman Empire. The link between empire and nation has often been ignored since the two are considered to be antithetical. Deviating from this perspective, this section briefly outlines those characteristics of imperial rule and exit which were pertinent to the founders of the Turkish Republic. The Ottoman prelude is followed by a more detailed examination of the early Republican period (1920–38). This foundational era is of pivotal significance to students of contemporary Turkish nationalism since the current varieties of nationalism invariably revert to this initial formulation. The character of nationalism that crystallized during this early period was forcefully assimilationist and exclusionary at the same time. The conditions of imperial exit characterized by the trauma of defeat, along with the actions of the military and state elites, were critical for shaping the subsequent understandings of nationhood. The third section narrates these later developments and looks into the power struggles inside the political domain during the post-Kemalist period. This later time demonstrates how nationalist rhetoric can act as a roadblock to political decency.

Imperial Hopes

The Ottomans ruled over a linguistically, ethnically, and religiously diverse population. Effective governance over this diverse landscape necessitated the employment of a variety of administrative tools and strategies. Indeed, a lack of uniformity characterized imperial rule until the nineteenth century. These tools of governance in turn were geared towards managing the existing heterogeneity as opposed to crushing it through homogenization policies. The latter did not make sense to the empire's rulers. Even if one puts aside the amount of material and non-material resources that would have been required for such an endeavour, for the imperial centre differences were not necessarily an obstacle to effective rule. On the contrary, they could be beneficial as a ruling strategy since they could be employed to play disparate groups against each other.

Even though differences were allowed to exist, however, this was not a world defined by political decency in the Hallsian sense. For instance, even though the Ottomans did not use Islam as a weapon and did not demand forced conversion from their non-Muslim subjects, they did not hesitate to use coercion against what they considered to be heretical or deviant forms of Islam (Deringil 2000). Similarly, the oft-celebrated and nostalgically reminisced *millet* system should better be approached with a more sober mind. On the one hand, the system provided non-Muslim religious communities (which belonged to various ethnic and linguistic groupings) with a level of autonomy in their lives. It also provided some level of voice through their intermediaries. On the other hand, it was embedded within an undeniably hierarchical society. Ultimately this system embodied the institutionalization of the inferior status of non-Muslim subjects vis-à-vis their Muslim counterparts. The *millet* system was essentially a response to the heterogeneity of the population (Karpat 2002). However, it was not about the institutionalization of political decency. Neither was it about a nascent pluralism.

In the nineteenth century the imperial centre sought to restructure the state along the lines of its European counterparts. The administrative modernization initiated by the Tanzimat Reforms (1839–76) was geared towards "accommodating the incorporation of the empire into the capitalist logic of expanding Europe" (Keyder 1997, 32). The resolution of economic and military problems was at the top of the agenda. A reconfiguration of state-society relations was also on the horizon. This latter aspect of reforms sought to inspire and heighten the loyalty of imperial subjects. At the same time, however, the empire was vast, the resources to undertake the reforms were slim, and the needs and demands of different regions varied. For example, in contrast to the eastern provinces, increasing levels of commercialization and a general acceleration in economic development had already started to characterize the predominantly non-Muslim Balkan provinces since the eighteenth century. In these areas the rising merchant and manufacturing classes had established close ties with their Western European counterparts. The imperial reforms came too late to these provinces. It was against this background that the protection and encouragement of various European powers in this region gradually made the exit option more attractive. As Keyder (1997, 33) notes, in the cases of Serbia, Greece, and Bulgaria, "nationalism resulted from a mercantile-bourgeois impulse, and was a reaction to the slow pace of economic and political change in the core of the empire."[1] Thus, the more immediate and key issues were not ethnic or religious but primarily revolved around how the economic sphere was structured, and the problems associated with it.

Relatedly, the imperial collapse could not be reduced to nationalist movements. In fact, in different parts of the empire communities were seeking to reform the existing structure rather than to secede from it. For instance, Suny (2015, 65) highlights that "rather than a separate Armenian state, almost all Ottoman Armenians ... hoped for improved existence within the empire." Even by the turn of the century, the opposition of the Armenian *amira* class of wealthy artisans and bankers against the Hamidian regime was not the "nationalist call outside the Ottoman framework until 1915" (Hanioğlu 2008, 83). Similarly, even when the Kurdish organizations, which were founded towards the end of the Ottoman Empire, employed nationalist rhetoric they were not aiming for secession (Klein 2007). Rather, they were seeking to save the empire, and in this sense they could best be described as Ottomanists. Kurdish nationalism would be the product of the nation-building policies of the Republican state.

It was also the case that categories that became relevant to the nationalizing elites of the twentieth century did not resonate with the masses. It was not ethnic designations as much as designations of locality or religion that had some relevance in people's lives. Linguistic distinctions similarly lacked force. Neither of these were attached to notions of sovereignty or national consciousness. When Ottoman intellectuals started to debate issues around Turkish language, for instance, their concerns were social and philological, not nationalist (Kushner 1977). Similarly, when article 18 of the 1876 Constitution stipulated that the representatives in the Parliament must be able to speak Turkish, this was formulated as a pragmatic decision and not as an attempt at homogenization or the awakening of national consciousness (Karal n.d, 317). Language was not coded around identity as it would be under the Turkish Republic; it was first and foremost about facilitating communication.

---

1 Recent scholarship has been revising the content of the unrest in the Balkans. Mazower (2000), for example, suggests that revolts against Ottoman rule were tied to a project of Westernization as opposed to being the "revival of nations." Similarly, Malešević (2012) highlights the complexity of the region's history, and critiques the reducing of these processes to full-blown nationalist movements.

During the late nineteenth century, and as part and parcel of the efforts to reorganize the relationship between imperial subjects and the centre, the notion of Ottomanism was formulated. Ottomanism emphasized the equality of subjects regardless of ethnic, religious, or linguistic differences. Yet, despite the high hopes of the imperial centre and intellectuals, its reception was mixed. Both Muslim and non-Muslim subjects felt disgruntled, perceiving the centre's measures as threats to the existing communal ties, privileges, and power relations. At the Sublime Porte, and inside the Ottoman Parliament, Muslim and non-Muslim representatives seemed to exemplify the Ottomanist idea. However, and notwithstanding the extensive powers inscribed into the Constitution in his favour, Abdulhamid II was not happy about sharing power even symbolically. Indeed, he would use the war with Russia (1877–8) as an excuse to disband the Parliament shortly after it opened its doors in 1876.

Despite this initial setback and continuing tensions and problems, energies were persistently extended towards saving the empire. To this end, different options were debated and assessed. Even as late as the Second Constitutional period (1908–18) Ottomanism, in its varying guises, remained on the table. To this was added the alternative route of Turkism. These two alternatives were accompanied by a third route that privileged the increasingly Muslim character of the empire, and that the renowned intellectual Yusuf Akçura referred to as Islamism. In fact, these different notions of the empire continued to exist side by side until its dissolution. At the turn of the century, lacking a coherent agenda, the Young Turk administration would deploy these alternative visions interchangeably (Hanioğlu 2008).

In brief, then, the eventual strengthening of the nationalist route to the exclusion of others was not in any way predetermined, and came about gradually. At its inception the nationalist formula was conceptualized first and foremost as a way to save the empire. Its full blossoming would only come about as the result of military defeats and the resistance movement that followed World War I.

Early Republican Anxieties

The Turkish Republic was founded in 1923 following a string of defeats in wars (the most important of which were the Balkan Wars of 1912–13 and World War I), the signing of the Treaty of Sevres (1920), which sought to partition the remaining Ottoman lands, and the

National Resistance Movement (1919–23), which opposed the partitioning of the remaining lands by the Allied Powers. Extensive population movements followed. It was these series of events that added up to a trauma of defeat that in turn would greatly impact the formulation of Turkish nationalism during the early years of the Republic (1920–38) when the Republican People's Party ruled the country singlehandedly.

There is great value in trying to differentiate between different types of nationalisms and using them as ideal types. Hall's tripartite classification of nationalisms is useful here. This classification differentiates between ethnic, civic, and civil nationalisms (Hall 2013, 88–90). When applied to the Turkish case, what one unmistakably observes is the resilience and continuity of an ethnic component with some civic elements (with its harsh, assimilationist overtones) thrown into the mix. This particular combination certainly characterized the nation-building project of the Republican elite.

The particular crystallization of Turkish nationalism took shape under significantly different conditions than its European counterparts. In contrast to the Risorgimento nationalism of Italy, for example, Turkish nationalism was part and parcel of a top-down nation-building process. Formulated by intellectuals, military officers, and civil servants of the defunct Ottoman Empire, this particular strand of nationalism was reactionary, harshly assimilationist, and removed from the strands of liberal nationalism that had their roots in Western Europe. Nevertheless, this state-directed nationalism was not grounded in an expansionist rhetoric. Neither was it established on bloodlines. Rather, it combined heavily assimilationist and non-assimilationist/exclusionary rhetoric and policies, which were complemented by an accent on ethnic elements (especially during the 1930s). The specific direction and content of these policies also highlighted how religious and ethnic communities were differentiated under the new regime. Furthermore, the Republican cadres built and legitimized their power around the success they had during the Nationalist Resistance Movement. From their very inception the powers of the state, the military, and the nation were conceptualized as inextricably linked to each other. The state and the military would be the guardians of the nation. They would move the nation forward to take its well-deserved place inside the league of civilized nations. The primary role of the people, on the other hand, would be to work for the nation/state to attain those goals articulated by the political elite.

The Republican cadres were an educated group of Muslim men with secular outlooks on life. The inner core of this elite and some of its important ideologues predominantly came from the borderlands of the Ottoman Empire. They had first-hand experience of the shrinking of the imperial territories and the mass population migrations that had followed. Intellectually, their influences were eclectic, and included positivism, social Darwinism, and Turkism. Mustafa Kemal, the founder of the Republic, took his inspiration from "German vulgar materialism; Thomas Henry Huxley's moral Darwinism; H.G. Wells's cosmological juxtaposition of time, space, and the human in history; Gustave Le Bon's elitism; nationalism; racial anthropology; and early twentieth-century authoritarianism, as well as the ideas of the Enlightenment" (Hanioğlu 2011, 228–9).

For this Republican elite, the trauma of defeat brought in its wake a significant sense of insecurity. Concurrently, the dissolution of the empire entailed a tremendous loss of dignity, which had to be regained. To this end, it was thought imperative to diagnose the reasons behind the Ottoman collapse. The parliamentary discussions of the 1920s and 1930s, regardless of the issues at hand, were inundated by speeches to this effect; and there was agreement on some central points. First, it was "Ottoman cosmopolitanism" that was to blame for the collapse. Turkish nationalism would be based not on continuities but on a strong sense of rupture from the past. Of particular importance here was the *millet* system. The Republican cadres persistently contended that Ottoman tolerance had gone too far, and had only aided the secessionist movements inside the empire and bred treason. In fact, the argument went, those non-Muslims remaining in Turkey were still unabashedly bold despite their hitherto treacherous activities – demanding more rights whereas they should be content with what they had (*TBMM*, 3 January 1923, 166; 4 January 1923, 177–8). Such an attitude, they concurred, could not be tolerated.

Thus, the attack on "Ottoman cosmopolitanism" was primarily an attack on the non-Muslim population in Turkey. The Jews, Greek Orthodox, and Armenian communities were labelled and attacked again and again as traitors, as the unfaithful children of the Ottomans. "They [had] lost the right to live within the bosom of Turks," it was declared (*TBMM*, 4 January 1923, 178). Neither should they have the right to be represented in the Parliament. Despite the significant decrease in the size of the community after the Genocide of 1915, Armenians were forcefully targeted. In 1923, Mustafa Kemal himself pronounced that "in this blessed country Armenians have no rights at all. The country is yours, it belongs to Turks" (*ASD* 1997, 130). Two years later, Niyazi Bey stated that "a government which would allow Greeks and Armenians into this country is a government which would be loathed as a whole" (*TBMMGC*, 18 February 1925, 509). Another MP, Ismail Suphi (Soysallıoğlu) Bey, addressing Parliament prior to the Lausanne Convention where a massive population exchange between Greece and Turkey was to be negotiated, emphasized that "if the Greek Orthodox were to remain in Istanbul it would mean that a ... den of evil would stay" (*TBMMGC*, 25 December 1922, 1155).

This exclusionary rhetoric would soon translate into policies in a wide variety of areas. In 1926, for example, "being Turkish" became a condition to enter civil service. The law, which effectively banned non-Muslims from seeking state employment, would remain in effect until 1965 (Aktar 2000). In 1924, based on stipulations of the Law of Attorneyship, the Istanbul Bar Association started to review its members' files. The files were assessed on subjective criteria such as "good moral character," and out of 960 files that were evaluated a disproportionate number of non-Muslim lawyers lost their permit to work (Levi 1992, 52–4). In the educational sphere, as early as 1923 minority schools were placed under scrutiny, and the language of instruction was regulated to ensure linguistic assimilation. In 1925 the state made it mandatory for teachers working at these schools to have Turkish as their mother tongue. Those teachers who failed the language test lost their jobs. During the same period, unable to pay the high salaries of their Turkish teachers, a number of Jewish schools had to close down (Bali 2001, 190–2). Similarly, the "Citizen, Speak Turkish!" campaign of 1928, which received the direct support of the government, primarily targeted non-Muslim and particularly Jewish citizens. Language became one of the most significant tests of loyalty for non-Muslim citizens. Writing in 1925, the Jewish-Turkish intellectual Avram Galanti (1981, 548) would highlight that "those elements who live in Turkey and whose language is not Turkish ... could be Turks by word, name and officially. However, they cannot be Turks by soul, idea and heart. Because they cannot feel Turkishness."

Calls for assimilation were bold and persistent. Despite their declarations of willingness to follow the Republican dictates, however, non-Muslim citizens would be relegated to the fringes of the nation. The immigration policies that worked against non-Muslim applicants as well as the confiscation of Armenian and Greek Orthodox properties would starkly manifest the rules of belonging to the nation. Ultimately, with these and other sweeping changes, the Republican cadres formulated a matrix of nationhood that was akin to the *millet* system in spirit: religion was still an important gauge determining the rules of belonging. While equality was formally declared, a hierarchy of citizenship based on religious lines was created and practised.

At the same time, the nation under the Republic was presented and envisioned as staunchly secular. This secular outlook was institutionalized through a number of changes that included the closing down of dervish lodges and brotherhoods (1925), the abolition of the caliphate (1924), the closing down of religious schools, and the unification of the education system. In fact, these and similar changes did not add up to a genuinely secular society. Rather, and with the founding of the Directorate of Religious Affairs, the state brought religion under its own control. The Directorate's mission would be to formulate and disseminate the "right" type of Islam that should be followed by citizens in their private sphere. As Webb (2007, 206) succinctly puts it, this type of secularism was not about the "emancipation of the individual but of the state as the vehicle of national destiny." It thus became an organic aspect of the nationalist rhetoric with its emphasis on civic virtue.

Within this formulation of nationhood, the Kurds were initially considered to be the "true owners of the nation" alongside Turks. Yet, although the Kurds had largely supported the National Resistance Movement, the Republican elite feared their secessionist tendencies. In the eyes of the Republican cadres, Kurds occupied an especially tentative position inside the nation after the Sheikh Sait rebellion of 1925, in which a small group of Kurdish nationalists, with the support of the Kurdish *ulama* in the region, were able to galvanize the discontent in the area, which was most directly due to the abolition of the caliphate. But there was also the sense that the Kurds were left behind once the Nationalist Resistance Movement was won. The establishment of autonomy in the primarily Kurdish eastern regions, for instance, turned out to be an empty promise after all. The reluctance of the political elite to listen to the reasons behind Kurdish discontent and their excessively harsh response to the rebellion would be instrumental in triggering a series of similar, smaller-scale rebellions throughout the 1930s. The resistance to a secular, centralized state within these areas, accompanied by the political elite's already existing insecurities over national unity and solidarity, would result in decades of state oppression. The nationalist elite persistently sought to linguistically and culturally assimilate the Kurdish citizenry, sometimes employing extreme measures – including forced resettlements and pogroms.[2] The nationalist cadres would consider Kurds as "potential Turks" but, while not banished to the fringes of the nation like non-Muslim citizens, their loyalty, and the *exclusivity* of that loyalty, would require constant proof.[3]

These assimilationist and coercive policies against the Kurds would be persistent and would extend beyond the Kemalist era. Writing about linguistic assimilation in the eastern regions of the country, Aslan (2015, 62) underlines that "the main reason why the state required complete eradication of minority languages was the constant fear of territorial dissolution, separatism, and disloyalty to the state ... Such mistrust of Kurdish-speakers was a result of a general feeling of insecurity among the state elite who had experienced the gradual dissolution of the Ottoman Empire." Hence, the conditions of imperial exit and its reassessment in the hands of the Republican cadres would shape the initial period of nation-building, and would accordingly imprint Turkish nationalism with its highly assimilationist and dissimilationist/exclusionary character and policies.

For the Republican elite, the unity, security, and vigour of the nation could only be solidly anchored around homogeneity. For this to take root, in turn, discipline was of paramount significance. Recep Peker, an important ideologue of the Kemalist era, exemplified this line of thinking when he wrote:

> We have the mission of establishing a "disciplined" society where [everyone] thinks, writes, says, works, earns, has "freedoms" and at the same time recognizes all limitations which are necessary to protect and keep society alive and ... sincerely follows and believes the decisions/judgments of state authorities and the national chiefs. (1933, 1)

In this disciplined nation citizens were asked to unquestioningly trust in their state even for the exercise of their rights and freedoms. As another important ideologue of the times, Mahmut Esat (Bozkurt) Bey (Bozkurt 1930, 5565–6), poignantly put it: "Those who do not know

2 The most notorious was the Dersim pogrom of 1938 where more than ten thousand Kurds were killed through air strikes and gassing, and close to twelve thousand people were forced to relocate (Aslan 2015, 51).

3 See Yeğen (2007) for a detailed discussion of Kurds under the Republican regime.

how to swim in the seas of freedom will have the state teach them." Nationalist ideology was the foundation of this unified and disciplined society. During debates on some constitutional amendments in 1937, Şemsettin Günaltay asked his fellow parliamentarians: "After these principles of the Turk find their place in the constitution, can opinions be aired against these [principles of nationalism, republicanism, secularism, statism, and reformism]? Can a liberal come forward and defend liberal principles? Can a communist come forward and defend communist principles?" His answer was a decisive "No, they won't. They cannot" (*TBMM* 5 February 1937, 65). In sum, then, the vision of nationhood was based on a zealously formulated idealization of homogeneity in all spheres of life.

Ultimately, the Kemalist project remained top-down, and in important ways it failed to resonate with the masses (Yılmaz 2013). Yet, in fundamental ways this period did draw the contours of the Turkish nation. The axes of the central struggles during the post-Kemalist period would revert to this foundational moment when nationalist ideology was solidified around a trauma of defeat as well as the notion of rupture with the past, and institutionalized around the marriage of a strong state and military as the nation's true guardians.

Post-Kemalist Struggles and Nationalism

The 1950 elections were a turning point in post-Kemalist Turkey. The Democrat Party (DP), whose constituency was primarily rural and commercial, had a resounding victory at the ballot box. Fundamentally, Democrats were populists and supporters of majoritarian democracy. They also were Kemalists. At the same time, however, they sought to imprint their own interpretation of Kemalism through loosening the state's staunchly secularist outlook (Ahmad 2003, 108). It was under their rule, for example, that calls to prayer started to be made in Arabic as opposed to Turkish. Religious orders were tolerated, and religious schools (*Imam Hatip*) were opened.

In general, during the post-Kemalist era, the role of religion in society was debated. Writing about these debates for the period 1944–69, Aytürk (2014, 702) remarks that the "nationalist worldview, which could not penetrate the Turkish periphery in its Kemalist version … started to make significant inroads in its newly fashioned Islamic guise." Differently put, the efforts to establish a particular form of secularism were directly tied to the nationalist rhetoric. As Anderson (2008, 9) puts it, "the ambiguity of Kemalism was to construct an ideological code in two registers. One was secular and appealed to the elite. The other was crypto-religious and accessible to the masses. Common to both was the integrity of the nation as supreme political value." It is of equal significance to note, then, that "Islam delimited the nation … [and] Turkish secularism has always depended on what it repressed" (9).

During the DP's rule, while the pious citizens were feeling the effects of change compared to earlier periods, in other respects the government continued to adhere to the main vision of Kemalism. For instance, the early Republican nationalist reflexes proved to be alive when the government took sides on the Cyprus issue, which was then employed as a tool against non-Muslim citizens. It was under the DP's rule and with its tacit sanctioning that the 6–7 September 1955 pogroms took place. The assaults targeted non-Muslim businesses and citizens in Istanbul, and cost lives and inflicted material damage on businesses and private properties (Güven 2005).[4]

The experiment with multiparty democracy was interrupted by a military coup in 1960. The military had for some time been feeling slighted by the DP. The growing economic problems and the associated public unrest gave them the excuse to seize power.[5] In terms of the ideological landscape the 1960 coup did not signify a radical shift from the Turkish nationalist route that had been formulated in the preceding era. Rather, the military, acting in alliance with the Republican People's Party (RPP), was not only (re)taking control over the state but was once again in a position to reassert the Kemalist ideological makeup and bolster its political power. After all, both actors defined themselves as the guardians of the Turkish nation.

The military coup was justified as a people's movement to safeguard the nation, and it accordingly sought the pacification of Atatürk's enemies (Öztürk 1966, 1.852–5). These enemies included the DP, Islamists, Zionists (or, as was interchangeably used, the Jews), and communists. All of these groups, it was argued, had been "gnawing at our national conscience" and seeking the disintegration of the nation (Öztürk 1966, 2.1005). Turkish nationalism was proposed as the solution to all these threats. The character of Turkish nationalism was further depicted as

---

4 The 6–7 September pogroms were also directly tied to talks over the future of Cyprus and the government's need to rally public support behind it. For a more detailed discussion see Güven (2005).

5 On the discontent among the military preceding the coup, and a concise discussion of this period, see Kandil (2016, 158–68).

unifying, as cultural nationalism (as opposed to nationalisms with racist overtones), against Islamism, developmental and progressive, humane, and anti-imperialist. As in the early Republican period, nationalism was set against Ottomanism. Mehmet Özgüneş's statements were characteristic of the majority opinion inside the Parliament as well as among the top members of the military:

> For this idea [Ottomanism] we had left our Turkishness behind but Arabs did not give up their Arabness. They shot the Turkish army and Turkish soldiers behind their back who had come to their aid in Yemen. We cannot give up nationalism ... Ataturkism means Western-type nationalism ... Our nationalism is cultural nationalism. (Öztürk 1966, 2.1083–4)

Complementing this was the accent placed on the work that lay ahead. The fight against Islamism, communism, and pan-Slavism, for example, could succeed by strengthening the national consciousness and by returning to "Atatürk's principles." According to the RPP cadres, the DP had dangerously strayed from these principles – most importantly from the secularism principle. Consequently, it was argued that "Turkey has been smashed to bits in terms of its ideal" and "the spiritual union, the national unity in Turkey can only be realized by the leadership of Atatürk's nationalism" (Öztürk 1966, 2.982).

Relatedly, the fight against "divisive movements" required special attention. Members of the National Unity Committee, which was composed of military officers, were particularly adamant about addressing this issue. Not surprisingly, non-Muslims remained under the surveillance of the political elite and the military. During debates about whether the nationalism principle should be included in the new constitution, Suphi Gürtoprak insisted that

> the whole issue is about preventing minorities from playing any role in the future. If we do not insert the nationalism principle into this constitution, our government will not be able to do anything when the minorities say to us, "You cannot turn us toward a particular direction. We want our own schools, etc." (Öztürk 1966, 2.1075)

Similarly, fears over territorial integrity, which was a significant theme of the early Republic, continued to delimit the vision of nationhood. For some, two crucial and interrelated problems were the lack of national consciousness and the possible threat of secession. The latter of course was tied to the perceived actions of the Kurdish citizens, who remained a suspect population. In his address to Parliament, General Cemal Gürsel stated:

> Go to a village in Anatolia and ask the citizen "who are you?" They would say "Praise be to God, I am Muslim." He would not say "I am Turkish." There is no such conscience present yet. Let us not lose our Turkishness, our nationalism because of some others' ideas ... You know the struggle we are in with the Kurdish movement. If we say we are getting rid of nationalism, are they going to come back to us? Turkey should be Turkish/ Turk. (Öztürk 1966, 2.1078–9)

The military and the political elite alike recognized the limits of the Kemalist project especially in reaching out to and resonating with the rural communities. Indeed, the DP leadership's efforts aimed to establish rapport with such communities. In the Kurdish areas in particular these attempts were accompanied by an initial relaxation of the hard and oppressive policies of the previous decades (Aslan 2015, 120–1). Yet this instrumental approach did not amount to a genuine transformation in the management of diversity. Instead, and following the constitutional recognition of Kurds in Iraq by the end of the 1950s, the political elite started to worry. The DP returned to the Kemalist rhetoric and action, and without any qualms resorted to oppressive measures (Aslan 2015, 122). As mentioned earlier, the same fears were shared by both the military officers of the 1960 coup and the RPP leaders. The reproduction of the earlier decades' policies was a result of a concern over re-empowering the state (along Kemalist lines) as well as reinstating and bolstering their own power inside it.

In the following decades, socio-economic transformations spearheaded by urbanization and migration to cities sharpened, and increasingly brought into focus the deepening of social inequalities (Watts 2010). These changes in turn shaped the Kurdish demands for economic and cultural rights. The state policy remained actively opposed to such demands, and in fact once again acquired an increasingly oppressive and coercive character.[6] Thus, the military and political actors inside Parliament remained active players in defining the social landscape. Following the 1980 coup, the military's power over the ideological

6 Such state measures would eventually be a factor in pushing Kurdish activism towards violent tactics and the founding of the Kurdistan Workers' Party (PKK) in 1978 (Aslan 2015, 129).

sphere would manifest itself by its endorsement of a "Turkish-Islamic Synthesis." This synthesis was not to be confused with the emergence of civility. On the contrary, it was part and parcel of the military's fight against leftist ideologies and movements.

The post-1980 period was also a period of integration into the global markets as well as Turkey's application for full membership in the European Union. These developments were underlined by the "prevailing feeling [of] 'elevating the country to the level of modern civilization'" as Atatürk had envisioned it (Bora 2011, 59). However, this particular climate was short lived. As Bora further notes, "The Gulf War can be seen as a turning point in the transition from this atmosphere of self-confidence and optimism to one defined by the perception of threat" (59). The transformations in the region, especially inside northern Iraq, fuelled fears regarding the perceived threat to national unity coming from the Kurds. The economic crises of the 1990s further encouraged this erosion of self-confidence and played a part in the intensification of integral nationalism.

The founding fathers of the Republic were nation-builders. They defined their mission primarily along transformative lines as they sought to redefine the cultural, social, and political spheres of the new nation. When it came to power in 2002, the Justice and Development Party (AKP) similarly assigned to themselves a transformative goal. At the same time, however, they refrained from speaking the same language as their pro-Islamist predecessors. Rather, they defined themselves as "conservative democrats" and employed a rhetoric that appealed to a wide cross-section of the population, including middle-class business owners, rural constituencies, the lowers classes in urban areas, intellectuals, and religious and ethnic minorities (Tugal 2007).

As is well documented by now, during the first years of its rule, the AKP initiated much-needed legal changes in order to adhere to the European Union's 1993 Copenhagen criteria. A decade into its rule, it had weakened the military's power inside the political sphere. Although these developments were undertaken with an eye to securing and legitimating the AKP's own political power vis-à-vis its competitors in the political sphere (Keyder 2004), they nevertheless were considered to be changes in the direction of further democratization. It was in the light of these changes and in a post 9/11 world that the AKP was framed as "a beacon of democracy in the Muslim world" by Turkey's Western allies (Keyder 2004, 84). Soon, the AKP's reaction against the staunch secularism of the Kemalist establishment opened a venue for pious Muslims to have their voices heard. Similarly, its critique of coercive policies not only against the pious but also against Kurds raised hopes of significant shifts towards a more inclusive state policy with the possibility of ending the conflict. Indeed, the government did take steps to initiate reforms regarding Kurds' cultural rights, including their linguistic demands. Ultimately, however, all of these steps remained tentative and contentious. As Aslan (2015, 158) concludes, "the AKP government's acknowledgement of Turkey's ethnic diversity and Kurdish cultural demands was laden with significant ambiguities and the actual implementation of the reforms encountered serious setbacks." At the same time, the steps taken were delimited by a nationalist rhetoric that largely reproduced some aspects of its Kemalist counterpart.

In contrast with their Kemalist predecessors, AKP ideologues and politicians emphasized historical continuities as opposed to ruptures in rewriting history. Consequently, they brought into sharp focus what is termed a "neo-Ottomanist" vision (Saraçoğlu and Demirkol 2015). This approach utilized the characterization of Turkey as a bridge between East and West, but did not privilege one over the other. Rather, as the former Prime Minister Davutoğlu suggested:

> The more you draw the bowstring toward Asia, the faster your arrow will travel in the direction of Europe; that is, if you have [strategic] depth in Asia then to that extent you would have regard and acceptance in the eyes of Europe. We should establish self-confidence and societal motivation. (2011, 93)

Establishing societal self-confidence, according to AKP cadres, rests on recognizing "our true heritage" and on raising morally upright and pious generations. While such an emphasis differentiates their vision of the nation from its Kemalist predecessor(s), the AKP has also reproduced the early Republican vocabulary, in its insistence, for instance, on "one language, one flag, one nation." Similarly, there has not been a sustained transformation in resolving the Kurdish conflict.[7]

Today, the AKP employs its version of the nationalist rhetoric in expanding, maintaining, and legitimating its political power. The absolute instrumentalization of Islam in the hands of the AKP should also be understood in this context. For the AKP the "struggle is not against a foreign state [but] against the 'enemy within,' which is thought to have

---

7 Undoubtedly, regional conflicts and shifts as well as the actions of the PKK are also of significance in the intensification of the integral nationalist rhetoric and policies.

alienated the people and the state through Western mimicry" (Aktoprak 2016, 9). Relatedly, "for AKP the ideal civilization is Islam, the state is the Ottomans; among the ethnic identities Turkishness is attributed the role of a big brother within the Muslim brotherhood" (25). In the final analysis, the antithesis of civility – a highly exclusionary rhetoric (and its commensurate policies) that insists on homogeneity and that condemns all groups other than the pious Sunni Muslim and Turkish as suspect populations – continues to define the Turkish landscape.[8]

Conclusion

This discussion is admittedly a brief and partial one, yet the main contours of the Turkish narrative are still useful in suggesting a few general points regarding Hall's works on civility and nationalism. To start off, there is much clarity to be gained from following Hall's (2002, 2013) distinction between the development of states before nations versus nations before states. The former route characterizes the European experience. The latter, as Hall argues, presents challenges that make the marriage between nationalism and liberalism quite difficult if not unlikely. The Turkish trajectory confirms these points. It also manifests, parallel to Hall's main contentions, the weight of the political sphere in shaping the possibilities for and limitations on the development of civility.

More specifically, this examination highlighted the significance of foundational moments in a nation's history. The foundational period discussed here entailed sweeping changes that attempted to punctuate the rupture with the nation's imperial past. Secularism – its specific formulation and institutionalization – was central to these changes. It was the initial formulation of Turkish nationalism coupled with this particular notion of secularism that would become influential in defining the political and ideological struggles in Turkey.

In its early stages, a trauma of defeat characterized the content of Turkish nationalism and its institutionalization. This trauma then shaped the formation of a hierarchy of citizens, which – in a slightly different form – still continues today. The salience of a highly exclusionary

8 Equally limiting nationalist rhetoric (albeit with different emphases) is employed by other actors inside the political sphere. For a discussion of how these competing nationalist rhetorics manifested themselves during the 2011–13 constitutional debates, see Bayar (2017).

and coercively assimilationist nationalist ideology has been reproduced over decades by various actors inside the political sphere with the aim of expanding, reinstating, and legitimizing their power. During the early Republic, the nationalist ideology was understood as a transformative force. In the subsequent periods, this official/state nationalism would be depicted as a stabilizing force. More recently, the AKP's rhetoric has underlined its exclusionary stance towards pious Muslim populations. While some hitherto excluded groups (i.e., Sunni Muslim pious citizens) today have rightly gained their voice, society remains dangerously polarized on multiple axes. Ultimately, the Turkish narrative is about the processes through which the foundationalist nationalist ideology persists – albeit differently interpreted – and continues to be an impediment to constituting political decency.

REFERENCES

Ahmad, Feroz. 2003. *Turkey: Quest for Identity*. Oxford: Oneworld.

Aktar, Ayhan. 2000. *Varlık Vergisi ve Türkleştirme Politikaları*. Istanbul: Iletişim.

Aktoprak, Elçin. 2016. "Postkolonyal Bir 'Dava' Olarak 'Yeni Türkiye'nin Yeni Ulusu." *Ankara Üniversitesi SBF Dergisi* 71 (1): 1–32. https://doi.org/10.1501/SBFder_0000002383.

Anderson, Perry. 2008. "Kemalism." *London Review of Books* 30 (17): 3–12.

ASD (*Atatürk'ün Söylev ve Demeçleri*). 1997. Vol. 2. Ankara: Atatürk Kültür, Dil ve Tarih Yüksek Kurumu.

Aslan, Senem. 2015. *Nation-Building in Turkey and Morocco: Governing Kurdish and Berber Dissent*. Cambridge: Cambridge University Press.

Aytürk, Ilker. 2014. "Nationalism and Islam in Cold War Turkey, 1944–69." *Middle Eastern Studies* 50 (5): 693–719. https://doi.org/10.1080/00263206.2014.911177.

Bali, Rifat. 2001. *Cumhuriyet Yıllarında Türkiye Yahudileri: Bir Türkleştirme Serüveni*. Istanbul: Iletişim.

Bayar, Yeşim. 2017. "Constitutional Debates and Nationalist Visions." *Nationalism & Ethnic Politics* 23 (3): 340–60. https://doi.org/10.1080/13537113.2017.1344792.

Bora, Tanıl. 2011. "Nationalist Discourses in Turkey." In *Symbiotic Antagonisms: Competing Nationalisms in Turkey*, edited by Ayşe Kadıoğlu and Fuat Keyman, 57–81. Salt Lake City: University of Utah Press.

Bozkurt, Mahmut Esat. 1930. "Muasır Demokrasilerin Istırapları." *Ayın Tarihi* 21 (71): 5555–68.

Davutoğlu, Ahmet. 2011. *Teoriden Pratiğe: Türk Dış Politikası Üzerine Konuşmalar*. Istanbul: Küre Yayınları.

Deringil, Selim. 2000. "'There Is No Compulsion in Religion'": On Conversion and Apostasy in the Late Ottoman Empire, 1839–1856." *Comparative Studies in Society and History* 42 (3): 547–75. https://doi.org/10.1017/S0010417500002930.

Galanti, Avram. 1981. "Türkleşmek Yolu." In *Atatürk Devri Fikir Hayatı*, edited by Mehmet Kaplan, Inci Enginün, Necat Birinci, Zeynep Kerman, and Abdullah Uçman, 543–56. Ankara: Kültür Bakanlığı Yayınları.

Güven, Dilek. 2005. *Cumhuriyet Dönemi Azınlık Politikaları ve Stratejileri Bağlamında 6–7 Eylül Olayları*. Istanbul: Iletişim.

Hall, John A. 1985. *Powers and Liberties: The Causes and Consequences of the Rise of the West*. Oxford: Blackwell.

– 1993. "Ideas and the Social Sciences." In *Ideas and Foreign Policy: Beliefs, Institutions and Political Change*, edited by Judith Goldstein and Robert O. Keohane, 31–54. Ithaca: Cornell University Press.

– 2002. "A Disagreement about Difference." In *Making Sense of Collectivity: Ethnicity, Nationalism and Globalization*, edited by Siniša Malešević and Mark Haugaard, 181–94. London: Pluto.

– 2006. "Structural Approaches to Nations and Nationalism." In *The Sage Handbook of Nations and Nationalism*, edited by Gerard Delanty and Krishan Kumar, 33–43. London: Sage. https://doi.org/10.4135/9781848608061.n4.

– 2013. *The Importance of Being Civil: The Struggle for Political Decency*. Princeton: Princeton University Press.

Hanioğlu, Şükrü M. 2008. "The Second Constitutional Period, 1908–1918." In *Turkey in the Modern World*, edited by Reşat Kasaba, 62–111. Cambridge: Cambridge University Press.

– 2011. *Atatürk: An Intellectual Biography*. Princeton: Princeton University Press.

Kandil, Hazem. 2016. *The Power Triangle: Military, Security, and Politics in Regime Change*. Oxford: Oxford University Press. https://doi.org/10.1093/acprof:oso/9780190239206.001.0001.

Karal, Enver Ziya. n.d. "Tanzimattan Sonra Türk Dili Sorunu." In *Tanzimattan Cumhuriyet'e Türkiye Ansiklopedisi*, vol. 2, 314–32. Istanbul: Iletişim.

Karpat, Kemal H. 2002. "Millets and Nationality: The Roots of the Incongruity of Nation and State in the Post-Ottoman Era." In *Studies in Ottoman Social and Political History: Selected Articles and Essays*, edited by Kemal H. Karpat, 611–46. Leiden: Brill.

Keyder, Çağlar. 1997. "The Ottoman Empire." In *After Empire: Multiethnic Societies and Nation-Building*, edited by Karen Barkey and Mark von Hagen, 30–44. Oxford: Westview.

– 2004. "The Bell Jar." *New Left Review* 28: 65–84.

Klein, Janet. 2007. "Kurdish Nationalists and Non-Nationalist Kurdists: Rethinking Minority Nationalism and the Dissolution of the Ottoman Empire, 1908–1909." *Nations and Nationalism* 13 (1): 135–53. https://doi.org/10.1111/j.1469-8129.2007.00281.x.

Kushner, David. 1977. *The Rise of Turkish Nationalism, 1876–1908*. London: Frank Cass.

Levi, Avner. 1992. *Türkiye Cumhuriyetinde Yahudiler*. Istanbul: Iletişim.

Malešević, Siniša. 2012. ""Wars That Make States and Wars That Make Nations: Organized Violence, Nationalism and State Formation in the Balkans." *Archives Européennes de Sociologie* 53 (1): 31–63. https://doi.org/10.1017/S0003975612000021.

Mazower, Mark. 2000. *The Balkans*. London: Weinfeld and Nicolson.

Öztürk, Kazım. 1966. *Türkiye Cumhuriyeti Anayasası, Temel Metinler*. Vols. 1 and 2. Ankara: Türkiye Iş Bankası Kültür Yayınları.

Peker, Recep. 1933. "Disiplinli Hürriyet." *Hakimiyet-i Milliye* 23 (April): 1–3.

Saraçoğlu, Cenk, and O. Demirkol. 2015. "Nationalism and Foreign Policy Discourse in Turkey under the AKP Rule: Geography, History and National Identity." *British Journal of Middle Eastern Studies* 42 (3): 301–19. https://doi.org/10.1080/13530194.2014.947152.

Suny, Ronald Grigor. 2015. *They Can Live in the Desert but Nowhere Else: A History of the Armenian Genocide*. Princeton: Princeton University Press.

TBMM (*Türkiye Büyük Millet Meclisi Zabıt Ceridesi*). 1920–7. Ankara: TBMM.

TBMMGC (*Türkiye Büyük Millet Meclisi Gizli Celse Zabıtları*). 1920–4. Ankara: Türkiye Iş Bankası.

Tugal, Cihan. 2007. "NATO's Islamists: Hegemony and Americanization in Turkey." *New Left Review* 44: 5–34.

Watts, Nicole F. 2010. *Activists in Office: Kurdish Politics and Protest in Turkey*. Seattle: University of Washington Press.

Webb, Edward. 2007. "Civilizing Religion: Jacobin Projects of Secularization in Turkey, France, Tunisia and Syria." Unpublished PhD diss., University of Pennsylvania.

Yeğen, Mesut. 2007. "Turkish Nationalism and the Kurdish Question." *Ethnic and Racial Studies* 30 (1): 119–51. https://doi.org/10.1080/01419870601006603.

Yılmaz, Hale. 2013. *Becoming Turkish: Nationalist Reforms and Cultural Negotiations in Early Republican Turkey, 1923–1945*. Syracuse: Syracuse University Press.

4 Urban Civility Defying Political Authoritarianism? Unpacking Turkey's Reversal of Democracy

BERNA TURAM

Turkey's reversal of democracy has been concurrent with the rise of a new urban civility in large cities. Paradoxically, the increasing repression by the pro-Islamic Justice and Development Party (AKP) since 2007 has coincided with the flourishing of new democratic practices in Istanbul's contested sites. Experiencing the shift in a staunchly secularist downtown neighbourhood of Istanbul from exclusive and homogeneous to an inclusive and mixed place, a young local resident of Tesvikiye, Merve, shared with me these thoughts:

> It is not just the new faces of [Muslim] piety that disturb Tesvikiye's old-timers. My secularist parents and their friends cannot stop complaining about not knowing the people who walk on "their" streets, and who move into their neighbourhood. [In contrast,] my partner and I really enjoy the new anonymity in this place. [Unlike the old-timer residents whose families lived here for generations], people move in and out quite often ... It is much more fun than the sterile streets of Tesvikiye in the past ... Headscarved visitors wander, eat, and shop next to hipsters and LGBTQ, while Jewish locals and Armenian jewellers stay put in their old neighbourhood without discontent.

From its early phases (Hall 1977, 1992), John Hall's sophisticated take on the main ingredients of civility, such as tolerance, mutual respect, consent, and individual freedom, has evolved as he published dozens of books and numerous articles. Hall's theory is especially known for establishing the centrality of civility from the level of the individual (and his or her quality of daily life) to the larger institutional context of politics. The work has bridged several disciplines, including sociology, political science, political philosophy, history, and political economy.

It culminated in his *The Importance of Being Civil* (2013): the book adds probably the final element of the Hallsian idea that civility is the cornerstone of a liberal democracy, as the latter is not attainable without political decency.

Despite the importance of civility, the bulk of political theory fails to capture its significance because of misleading associations. Civility is often overshadowed by its presumed association with the world of emotions and prescribed ideals rather than descriptive reality. More often than not, civility is also wrongly reduced to micro-forces, symbolic interaction, or behavioural aspects of social life, and is thereby disconnected from macro-level power politics. In sharp contrast to these misperceptions, the Hallsian paradigm displays and establishes that civility is an all-encompassing quality of both social and political life, and that it is, thereby, manifested in multiple layers of the interaction between the two. Hence, when the idea of civility is trimmed down to mannerisms framed by class distinction *à la* Elias (2000), it becomes difficult to see its broader implications and cross-class political qualities, particularly those of accommodation and inclusion despite intersectional differences and disagreement. In this regard, as an exception, I find much value in Frank Trentmann's chapter in this volume on civility (its presence or absence) among ethnic Germans as the internal refugee crisis unfolded there in the immediate post–World War II period.

Accordingly, I adopt in this chapter the Hallsian concept of civility by situating it into "urbanity" as a set of socio-economic and political conditions rather than a settlement or a territory (Boudreau 2017; Lefebvre 2003). Hence, by "urban civility," I am not simply referring to a geographically framed cultivation of good or refined manners in the city. Rather, I use the term as the sum of democratic practices of inclusion and accommodation circumstanced by specific contestation of power, and as the formation of respect and trust. In line with the Hallsian vision, the urban civility analysed in this chapter also has a liberating edge. In interaction with urbanites, contested urban space emancipates residents from existing ideological camps, including but not limited to Islamist versus secularist ones. Urban civility opens the way for individual ways of life and collective experiments with forming new bonds and alliances across ancient fault lines.

As we witness the peril of democracies, weak and stable, through a crude decline of civility, the Hallsian wisdom about political decency comes to the forefront of our most immediate concerns and anxieties. Among several cases of reversals of democracies, such as Brazil, India, Poland, and the United States, the case of Turkey in the new millennium provides a distinct laboratory to showcase the ways in which the rise of repressive regimes in today's world comes along with a gradual erosion of civility in social and political life, rather than with a sudden collapse of political institutions and democracy.

Until a couple of years ago, Turkey was considered the "model democracy" of the Muslim world. The Turkish Republic was not only applauded for its competitive multiparty electoral democracy since the 1950s but also for successful modernization and secularization throughout its republican history. Indeed, standing out as the only Muslim-majority nation-state governed by secular rule of law, including the civil code, Turkey with its smooth integration of pious Muslims into the secular polity and the market in the early years of the millennium was no small success. Last but not least, the Turkish Republic was one of the earliest even in Europe to enfranchise women and integrate them into the parliament and workforce, including professions of great power, such as those in the judiciary, medicine, and most academic disciplines (Arat 1989; Tekeli 1994).

While the democratic trajectory of Turkey has never been smooth (for a more historical overview, see Yesim Bayar's chapter in this volume), and was periodically disrupted by military coups up until 1998, the post-2007 period has seen the regime sink into political repression at an unprecedented pace. Soon after the brutal crushing of the democratic Gezi protests in 2013, the most secular democracy of the Middle East became torn by deep political polarization, continuous terrorist attacks by ISIS, violent clashes with Kurdish militia, as well as a failed coup in July 2016 followed by a longer-than-typical state of emergency.

On the one hand, the recent Turkish political trajectory displays how vulnerable civility is when faced with political authoritarianism and its non-liberating political projects. On the other hand, the Turkish case reveals the ways in which civility, embodied in new forms of democratic practices in the city, provides resilient "sanctuaries" against political repression. When everything fell apart, dashing freedoms and rights in social life and institutionally, the last resort of resilience was urban space, particularly metropolitan Istanbul, which persisted in sheltering and cherishing democratic practices. Only when the secularists disagreed about how to accommodate pious Muslim ways of life did urban space previously designated as secular begin to generate inclusionary practices and new alliances across historically formed polarization (Turam 2015).

This chapter, by situating the case of Turkey within the Hallsian framework, attempts to reveal and analyse the value of civility embraced by new forms of democratic urbanism in large cosmopolitan cities, which continue to provide a "breathing space" for freedom- and diversity-seeking democratic urbanites. The ethnographic evidence collected in Istanbul's contested urban space also complicates Hall's theory by juxtaposing these spaces of refuge against the repressive and unjust authoritarian rule, which encroaches on the last remaining islands of freedom in Istanbul. I argue that close proximity to, and constant mobility in, the diverse metropolis endows individuals with a toolbox of urban civility. This toolbox includes a wide range of mundane practices and ways of life that render inclusion and mixing not only possible but also desirable and attainable. This urban experience acquires a primacy in power struggles when the hegemonic government and weak opposition entirely fail in contestation, (dis)agreement, and cooperation.

The speed with which Turkey as a case study sank into authoritarianism poses a series of pressing questions. From a conventional perspective of democratization, one might easily fall into the trap of assuming that the successful integration of moderate pious Muslim actors into the secular state culminated in authoritarianism and the violation of rights and freedoms. In fact, many angry secularist observers from within Turkey and the West were quick to essentialize "Islam" and re-establish the orientalist notion of the incompatibility between Islam and civil society (see, for the existing debate, Gellner 1996, and his critics Eickelman 1998; Turam 2004; and Zubaida 1995). The ethnographic data on democratic urban practices suggest that the reversal of democracy must not be blamed on inclusion of Muslim piety within secular power politics. The decline of democracy has everything to do with political authoritarianism – not Islam as a religion – and the historical roots of lack of trust between opposing political camps.

Bringing the Hallsian "ingredients" of civility to the centre of analysis, this chapter makes two points. First, by exploring the conditions under which new forms of urban civility achieve democratic inclusion of pious Muslims and mixing in the city, it illustrates how Istanbul's contested sites defy the prevailing political indecency at the institutional level. Second, the root cause of the disease of authoritarianism in Turkey and elsewhere, I argue, is the inability of the political elite to achieve these levels of inclusion and cooperation accomplished in contested sites of the city. This failure is due to their incapacity to exercise the main premises of civility in political institutions. Instead, ideological hostility exploited hunger for power and led to bad political rule manifested in irreconcilable divides and deep polarization within the state. In alignment with the Hallsian paradigm, the next section traces the historical roots of how the state and the former elite set the weak trajectory of trust between ideologically antagonistic groups.

The broader aim of this paper is straightforward. Existing mainstream literature that is focused primarily, if not exclusively, on party politics (or the polity) fails to provide an in-depth analysis or satisfactory explanation of the reversal of democracy. That reversal is better explained by a Hallsian theory of civility. The AKP has been in power uninterruptedly since 2002 by using the advantages – and simultaneously undermining the strengths – of the institutional channels of democracy. Concretely speaking, former prime minister and current president Erdogan has so far been brought to power by free and fair elections six times – five times as prime minister and one time as president. The seventh voting was a referendum in April 2017 determining a regime change from a parliamentary to a presidential system. It was nevertheless a referendum, although referendums are the least favoured part of the democratic procedure because they are most prone to the tyranny of the majority.[1] As the voters had the capacity and choice to opt for or against a presidential rule that consolidates all power in the hands of one man, a conventional focus on electoral procedures no longer suffices to either explain or prevent the decay of democracies. Although the documented electoral fraud renders the referendum illegitimate,[2] a considerable mass voted to give up their freedoms and to submit to a new dictatorship. This challenge of mainstream political analysis originates from the failure to capture the primacy of civility in the algebra of best political rule. Accordingly, our understanding of the cases of other reversing or weakening democracies would greatly benefit from

1 I am indebted to Yesim Bayar for rightly making me think about the extent to which a referendum under the circumstances of a state of emergency can be considered a legitimate procedure of democracy.

2 The electoral outcome was fraudulent. The government's winning margin was 1.2 million "yes" votes, but by a conservative estimate more than 2.5 million were not officially stamped. The Election Council changed the rule at the behest of AKP officials to accept and count the unstamped votes after the ballot ended, which was a clear violation of the electoral regulations.

bringing the Hallsian concept of civility to the centre of analysis, practice and, hopefully, political recovery and reform.

Urban Inclusion versus Demise of Political Decency: A Conundrum?

"Inclusion moderates political life," Hall argues (2013, 63), and adds, "political integration is the best route to order because softer political rule de-radicalizes." After decades of marginalization of pious Muslims in staunchly secular socio-political life in Turkey, the AKP came to power by free and fair elections for the first time in 2002 with the promise of respecting the secular rule of law. The new Islamist elite assured people it would not only abide by the rules of democracy, but wished to deepen the practice of democracy itself. During its first term (2002–7), the AKP achieved a series of economic and political reforms and cooperated with the agendas and goals of Turkey's acquisition of membership in the European Union. This was a political achievement of inclusion of pious Muslims, while some of the strongest democracies in Europe are still struggling to integrate Muslim immigrants and their pious ways of life into their socio-political systems. Both the West and the democrats of Turkey applauded Turkey's successful integration as a big step towards democratization.

Clearly, liberal democrats in Turkey supported the politics of the pious Muslims in government not because they were partisans of Islamist ideology or participated in pious ways of life, but simply because they respected and defended religious freedoms as any other kind of liberty. By considering the actions (rather than the Islamic image or ideology) of the AKP during the first term, liberal democrats gave credit to the AKP's assurance of deepening democratic freedoms. But they soon began to feel betrayed as they witnessed the Islamist government violating the freedoms and rights of minorities, journalists, academics, and all dissenting groups. The AKP only cared about the freedoms and rights of pious Muslims, or rather its own conservative constituents, while violating a wide spectrum of liberties that contradicted its own interest, agendas, and preferred ways of life (Öktem, Kadioglu, and Karli 2012; Onis 2013; Turam 2012).

The happy story of political reform became gradually overshadowed by the AKP's second term in 2007–11. The first crack in the somewhat smooth democratization process surfaced with the appointment as president of Abdullah Gul, a pious Muslim, from within the pro-Islamic AKP government. As both the prime minister and president were affiliated with the AKP in power, the democrats were alerted to a possible threat to the system of checks and balances by compromising the separation of powers between the legislative (dominated by the AKP), executive (presidential), and judicial powers of the state. Alarmed by the increasing power of the AKP, the military issued a warning (*muhtira*) on its website threatening the closure of the AKP if it undermined the secularity of the Republic. In a country with a history of periodic military coups, the warning hit the government as more than a mere caution. The government's instinct to fight against the perception of a conspiracy of a military coup has since then never faltered. The warning ushered in a polarization between the so-called secularist camp – the judiciary and the military – and the pro-Islamic camp of the government and the presidency.

The deep divides in the state were immediately reflected in splits in the city. The explicit synchrony between the two was not surprising considering Istanbul's social, geopolitical, and economic importance for political rule in Ankara. By April and May 2007, more than a thousand people had marched in the largest three cities, Istanbul, Ankara, and Izmir, to protest the increasing power of Islamic forces in politics. Referred to as the Republican Marches, these protests yearned for the victory of the former secularist elite and the defeat of Islamism. Hence, they were motivated by an ideologically driven power struggle rather than a desire for a genuine pluralist democracy. Unsurprisingly, the divides in both the state and the city led to further incivility, intolerance, and verbal and even occasional physical offences. The streets of large cities, particularly Istanbul, were gradually turning into a hub of contestation in the post-2007 period. A new concept of neighbourhood pressure (*mahalle baskisi*) was coined by prominent Turkish sociologist Serif Mardin to refer to the societal pressure (and the fear of it) imposed by pious Muslims on liberal secular urbanites (Cakir 2008; Turam 2013)

So, why did the smooth non-violent inclusion of previously excluded Islamists into a secular system lead to polarization and a crisis in the state? Hallsian theory underlines a condition for the affinity between inclusion and good moderate political rule. Hall (2013, 68; see also Hall 1995) states that "the character of social movements result[s] from the nature of the state with which they interacted." But at the same time, as one of the leading theorists on the "entwined nature" of civil society and the state (see also Evans, Rueschemeyer, and Skocpol 1985; Mann 2003), Hall warns us that historical trajectory matters tremendously when it comes to political transformation. More specifically, as a historical comparativist, he emphasizes that the state legacy is the main determinant of the nature of all collective action, including grass-roots movements such as the AKP's base. The state legacy of lack of trust in dissent and of minorities as well as of denial of rights and freedoms to political opposition have framed the parameters of repression and authoritarianism in Turkey's past. Accordingly, it should not be surprising to see that an AKP government based on large mass support inherited weaknesses and vulnerabilities linked to the historical legacy of political authoritarianism in Turkey, which is burdened with distrust and betrayal between politically antagonistic groups. Periodic military coups and their bloody aftermaths also accumulated baggage of the politics of fear for different ideological groups, previously the left and in the late 1990s the Islamists, and more recently, particularly in the aftermath of 2013, the liberals.

The new Islamist elite has historically experienced a denial of recognition, respect, and inclusion on the part of the former secularist elite and state structure. Religious freedom – and freedoms of ethnic and sexual minorities – was historically not a strength of the secular Republic. The state separated religion and politics by placing religion under state control through the establishment of the Directorate of Religious Affairs (Gozaydin 2009). In a 99 per cent Muslim-majority state, the headscarf was officially banned in universities and public offices between 1998 and 2013. The gap between the secularist Westernist elite and pious Muslim masses was not easily bridged until the short window of opportunity in the early years of the new millennium, when the AKP did briefly manage to collaborate with secular democrats. The engagement between pious Muslims and the secular state fell short of being institutionalized into a consolidated democracy, as the AKP as a grass-roots movement shared several characteristics of the secular state.

Historically, mutual trust and the respect necessary to share power have never been *fully* achieved on either side at the level of government and opposition parties (Braithwaite and Levi 2001; Levi 1998). When the secularist Westernized elite of Turkey, following in the footsteps of founder Kemal Ataturk, built the political institutions of the Turkish democracy, they did not expect to share power with pious Muslims in the unforeseeable future. Not only was trust lacking between the urban, secularist Western elite and the rural, pious, less-educated Muslim masses, but also, due to the long history of the state's neglect and estrangement, distrust had become chronic and partly institutionalized. Here, Hall's (1995, 9) observation that "societies with a history of social trust are likely to maintain it through changing social conditions, whilst those without it are unlikely to be able to achieve freedom in modern conditions" applies well. Accordingly, the short period of engagement between the new Islamist elite and the old Republican secularists (2002–7) came to an end when it encountered its first obstacles, whether the military's warning to the AKP, the presidential crisis caused by the AKP, or both at about the same time. Since then, the country has experienced a series of events leading to disarray and a deepening of authoritarian rule unprecedented in recent modern Turkish history.

My ethnographic project on the contested urban space started in the context of chaos and crisis on the streets of Istanbul in 2007. The locus of alert that triggered my fieldwork was certain urban spaces in Istanbul – neighbourhoods, campuses, certain streets and squares that had previously been designated as secular but had recently turned into hubs of intense contestation. What was it that alarmed me, a political ethnographer interested in civil society–state interaction, and pulled me so unavoidably into the study of the urban in 2007?[3] Initially, my attention was caught by the level of divisive exclusionary and offensive modes of behaviour in the streets, which concurred with the explicit compartmentalization occurring within the state itself. Istanbul was in a curious state of agitation, which I had never encountered before in my own neighbourhood and the campuses where I was educated or the streets of Istanbul where I spent most of my life. In the following years of my ethnography, it became clear to me that the remarkable signs of incivility in city life were just the tip of the iceberg informing us of fragmentation within political institutions. The decline of civility in urban life was indicative of deep, albeit unspoken, contempt and hostility in power politics, which did not manifest itself fully until the Gezi protests in 2013 and their aftermath. In 2007, no one could have foreseen that the intense levels of incivility roiling the city, in a clash between a secularist backlash and the Islamist ruling elite, were pregnant with an increasingly authoritarian rule that divides and rules both the state and society.

---

3 From a mainstream political science perspective, there was nothing yet that was significant enough to prompt a whole new major research project. Within the parameters of an electoral competitive democracy, the AKP came to power by elections. Although the Turkish military has had a long history of undertaking military coups, it has not engaged in a full-scale coup since 1980. Turkey was displaying outstanding economic perfor-mance, growth, and low inflation rates.

Relying on his constituency's consistent support in elections, President Erdogan was at the time of writing calling for yet another referendum in April 2017 on a full-spectrum regime change from a parliamentary system to a presidential one, in which power would be totally consolidated into one-man rule. The Islamist followers of Erdogan, distrustful of the Westernist elite and the secular Republic, have submitted to his lead unconditionally as the only way to redemption. By 2017 – that is, in less than ten years – all institutional channels of disagreement, negotiation, and collaboration between Erdogan's rule and the opposition have been forcefully impeded; the freedoms and rights of all opposition, dissent, minorities, and the marginalized have been widely violated; the strongest critics from academia and journalism have been criminalized, detained, and jailed without fair trial; and the rules of democracy have been changed and violated arbitrarily with little or no resistance from other branches of the state, which have been intimidated by the threat of persecution or actual criminalization.

This rapid reversal of democracy must not be attributed either to "Islam" or to the inclusion of pious Muslims within secular power politics. Clearly, the failure of the litmus test of civility in political institutions was not a new addition to either the Turkish political repertoire or historical legacy. But in the aftermath of the 2013 Gezi protests, this failure has been carried to a whole different level by the increasingly aggressive neoliberal, authoritarian, and socio-politically exclusivist policies of the AKP. While the causes are to be found in the historical trajectory of political authoritarianism in Turkey, the distrust of and contempt for civil disobedience and non-violent opposition were given unprecedented impetus by Erdogan's personal ambition for socio-political domination. The fragile institutions of Turkish democracy were in progress, albeit with many challenges, when Erdogan took over, but they have been entirely battered and disabled since his second term of rule, from 2007 to 2011.

What Does the Urban Have to Do with Civility and Democracy?

If both the state and the city synchronize in political chaos and they both divide in deep conflict, what does the urban have to do with civility and democracy? If there is an explicit erosion of civility in urban space, when the state sinks into polarization why do we bother to rethink the linkages between the city and political decency? Richard Senett (1998) associates democratic public spaces with the mingling of identitarian differences. In sharp contrast, another camp in social sciences focuses on the clash of differences in the public sphere as the source of democratization (Davis and de Duren 2011). Alternatively, Habermas coined the term "communicative action" to highlight the ability of the public sphere to generate consensus when people are allowed to freely discuss and disagree.

Despite their interest in the public sphere, most social sciences avoid focusing on the city as an explanatory variable (or locus of analysis) for the premises of good political conduct and rule (see, for exceptions, Davis and de Duren 2011; Sassen 2006; Weber 1958).[4] Nevertheless, my findings invite a distancing from the public sphere as the focus of my analysis, for the monolithic conception of the public sphere was not lending itself easily to exploring urban fragmentation. Istanbul was behaving differently from other predominately secularist cities, such as Eskisehir and Izmir, and religiously conservative cities, such as Konya. Similar differences could be observed between Tel Aviv and Jerusalem or New York and many cities in the southern parts of the United States. Moreover, certain contested parts of Istanbul were also acting differently in terms of inclusion where there was neither contestation nor any desire for inclusion.

Hence, instead of a public sphere – ideally open to and shared by everybody – I found disparate public spaces split by invisible fences of neighbourhoods, squares, streets, and so on. In contrast to the idealized notion of the public sphere as the seed of consent *à la* Habermas (Calhoun 1992), the city was sheltering a lot of frictions, cracks, and competing sites that contested power in a similar fashion to the clash between the ruling elite and its opposition. Hence, my ethnographic findings led me to pay more attention to the city as a unit of analysis with its own identity, fragmented political culture, and clashing ways of life that contested its own democratic agenda. Even the "minimum agreement to disagree" that the Hallsian paradigm values as the basis of civility and democracy was absent from the public sphere in Turkey

4 Here, I refer strictly to political science and political sociology as disciplinary literatures. There is no need to mention that urban sociology, political geography, and interdisciplinary urban studies have treated cities as the hubs of the social, cultural, and political. Nevertheless, the main trends in urban sociology and urban studies have predominantly been to view cities as the locus of neoliberal politics, crime, violence, poverty, or socio-economic inequalities in general. In this work, I bring back a Weberian perspective on the city as a liberating force.

post-2007. In contrast to Habermasian presumption, urbanites did not necessarily end up agreeing on anything just because they could freely debate and disagree. Similarly, at the level of political institutions, despite free and fair elections, the competing political parties could not find any common denominator, such as counterterrorism, on which to achieve intra-elite cooperation. Accordingly, the existence of differences or diversity in the city did not directly translate into spatial exclusion or inclusion. Along these lines, I argue that there is no direct correlation between public debate and political pluralism.

Then why do we still care about the link between the city and democracy? Although I was initially caught up by and studied the disputes over ways of life, my research revealed unexpected new alliances in the most unassuming places. I was surprised to come along new forms of cooperation in the deeply divided neighbourhoods and campuses. New bonds were formed among the least-expected people, basically formerly antagonistic groups that included not only pious Muslims and secularists but also feminists, LGBTQ, Kurdish nationalists, and religious minorities, among others. The democratic practices of inclusivity and new linkages in urban space were significant at a time when the political elite and political parties were entirely incapable of cooperating and moving towards a deeper democracy. The new forms of urban civility that created strong affinities between the city and political decency, which I documented between 2007 and 2013, culminated in the democratic protests of Taksim-Gezi in 2013.

Although trust in political institutions, particularly in the state, has drawn the attention of scholars (Hall 1992; Levi 1998; Tyler and Huo 2002), trust in the city, whether as a sanctuary or a safe place, has not been thoroughly studied in the social sciences. But as the recent mayhem in politics across the globe has shown, and as the term "sanctuary cities" in the United States has exemplified, cities have been not only the major hubs for protest and contestation but also safe places for newcomers, dissidents, and minorities (Tetreault 1993; Turam 2015). Istanbul, with its unique geopolitical position between Europe and Asia Minor, or the so-called West and the rest, deserves some highlighting here as one of the most contested cities in the world. On top of the "civilizational," political, and identitarian contestations, Istanbul is also located at an actual physical fault line, the Bosphorus channel, which separates Christian Europe from the predominantly Muslim Middle East.

Despite the historically rooted distrust between antagonistic political camps – Islamists, secularists, Alevites, Kurdish militia, Turkish nationalists, and others – Istanbul has historically housed a wide range of diverse groups, ways of life, and worldviews from the Ottoman period on. No doubt, it has always been one of the hardest cities to be shared between civilizations, between the Byzantium and Ottoman Empires, and later between secularist Republicans and Islamist migrants from the countryside. Although its history has been an arduous experiment in cohabitation, certain Istanbul neighbourhoods, such as Kuzguncuk and Beyoglu, have not only sheltered but also integrated religious and ethnic minorities since the imperial period (see, in particular, Mills 2007, 2010).

With the massive migration of pious Muslims from rural to urban areas since the 1980s, Istanbul initially became divided into Islamist and secularist zones. The presidential crisis, followed by the Republican Marches, then catalysed its transformation from a segregated city into a contested urban space. At the same time, while Istanbul was probably more difficult than ever to share between old secularist residents and the pious Muslim newcomers in the post-2007 period, the city's most contested sites were also bringing people from antagonistic groups into close proximity. Specifically, the pious Muslim residents of Istanbul were crossing the unspoken borders between Islamist and secularist zones, and entering urban sites – neighbourhoods, campuses, squares, streets, and so on – that had previously been designated as "secular." This urban transformation was facilitated by the replacement of the old secularist economic and political elite by the new Muslim pious elite, who were becoming more educated and adopting new bourgeois lifestyles.

The most visible pious Muslims who crossed the unspoken fences into the secular zones were high-spending veiled women, who could increasingly afford the haute couture boutiques of well-off neighbourhoods. They were noticeable because of their headscarves and because they began shopping in places where they had not customarily been seen before. While the critiques of neoliberalism have a low regard for these newly rich Muslims' consumption patterns, other critical voices warned researchers not to single out Muslim women yet again for a "sin" that the whole world commits. Beyond this defence of the growth of bourgeois tastes and behaviour among devout Muslims, it is also important to acknowledge the importance of crossing divisive boundaries, which facilitated a new phenomenon in the city: mixing. After many years of locals reacting in unwelcoming and verbally offensive ways against the headscarved visitors, high-spending Muslims, including the wife of former president Abdullah Gul, became regular customers at the most expensive stores in downtown Tesvikiye. For many headscarved women Tesvikiye became the place to shop, eat, socialize, and wander around the streets.

It is important to note that fashion-conscious pious women were not the only "trespassers" crossing unspoken boundaries in the city. High-achieving pious Muslim students entered the top-ranking liberal universities of the country by achieving competitive scores in the national placement exams. Similarly, businessmen who established larger, and sometimes international, networks also became integrated into the city and free-market economy, which had previously been claimed and dominated by the country's secular elite. The intersectionality of these transformations across space, class, gender, and religious and political orientation prompted deep discomfort as well as intense contestation, as it confused and puzzled old secular Istanbulites (Turam 2013).

In the midst of street-level confrontation, my first finding was revealing. While I was caught up in, and perplexed by, the intensity of the clash between pious Muslim and secular residents in the city, I was mostly surprised to find deep conflict and antagonism *between secular urbanites* (Turam 2015). Beneath the visible disputes between pious Muslims and secularists over their clashing ways of life lay another level of dispute: secular urbanites struggling with each other over how to accommodate the arrival of pious Muslims in their intimate spaces – neighbourhoods, streets, sidewalks, parks, campuses, shops, and so on. They were afraid of losing their beloved city to the pious newcomers. As the regime associated with political Islam was becoming more and more aggressively repressive, the secular urbanites feared being pressured by the pious urbanites into changing their liberal, secular ways of life.

Multiple issues were arising in contested urban spaces. First, urbanites faced the challenge of maintaining civility in a highly diverse city with residents who have conflicting lifestyles, worldviews, and understandings of urban life. The pious Muslims viewed city life, especially in a highly Westernized, cosmopolitan, and secular liberal urban territory with a vibrant nightlife, as prone to moral decay, sexual emancipation and transgression, uninhibited leisure, clubbing, and use of substances such as alcohol that they despised as sinful. A civil cohabitation in shared urban space was presenting a challenge to both old-timer secularist Istanbulites and the newcomer Muslims. Along with these socio-political discomforts and intimidations was a primarily spatial challenge: as the AKP regime crept towards authoritarian rule, the urbanites developed a strong sense of "territoriality" – feelings of entitlement that came with a strong sense of belonging and clinging to urban sites as outlets of their own autonomy.

Paradoxically, these spatial disputes made inclusion of the pious Muslims into these formerly secular places possible.[5] While the ruling elite in government and in opposition were losing their ability to negotiate and cooperate, and were responsible for increasing political violence in the country, the contested urban space enabled a difficult process of mixing across old lines of antagonisms. It offered not only a litmus test but also an actual laboratory to develop everyday skills of mutual tolerance and respect and democratic practices of accommodation. Hall's (2013, 4) description of the value of civility applies neatly here: "Civility is important because it allows disagreement to take place without violence and regularizes conflict so it can be productive." Simultaneous with ongoing contestation, certain urban sites of Istanbul were opening the way for new bridges between formerly antagonistic groups, thereby channelling old conflicts into new forms of familiarities and interactions.

During 2011–12, most of my discussions with secular Istanbulites revolved around violations of freedom, suspicious arrests, and governmental suppression of the press and media. Turkey has slowly become one of the major violators of freedom, competing with China. At the same time, as the urbanites distanced themselves from the overempowered repressive AKP, they came to appreciate the free zones of Istanbul.

Tesvikiye, for example, one of these contested neighbourhoods, has increasingly become a hotbed of international connections. Ethnic and religious minority groups, particularly the largest Jewish community of Turkey and high-end Armenian jewellers historically based in Tesvikiye, have provided links to other metropolises of the world. One of these Armenian jewellers, Jan, became a good friend of mine during the course of our conversations in his jewellery store. His

---

5 Under the increasing hegemony of the AKP, the most visible "trespassers" were the headscarved pious women. Although the neighborhood was diverse and attracted all sorts of people, other minorities, such as Kurds or LGBTQ, did not have a comparable visible presence sufficient to disrupt political exclusion.

words sum up my analysis of an increasingly mixed and inclusive neighbourhood:

> I used to sell almost exclusively to the residents of Tesvikiye. But, now, I rarely have any idea about which customer is from where. Personal tastes have become more eclectic, and carry fewer class symbols. Initially, I was intimidated by the headscarved consumers, because I thought that they would object to my Armenian origins. But it turns out that they care about my jewellery, my *zannaat* [craft] – and not my religion or ethnicity. I personally don't like the Islamic government, but through my chats with devout Muslims I have learned that some of them don't agree with the AKP's anti-democratic moves either … I am happy to be able to interact with these people, with whom I had no contact up until a decade ago.

What we see in the transition of contested sites of Istanbul is the rise of a new inhabitant. This urban inhabitant is often younger, highly educated, middle class, but most importantly, non-ideological – a rare quality in the context of the highly politicized nature of everyday life and the stormy political history of Turkey. For a long time, most of us have mistaken this non-ideological stand that is predominant among the young as mainly apolitical. But, to the contrary, the new inhabitant of Istanbul is a proactive freedom-seeker; yet she does not seek freedom only for herself or her identity group but for everybody. She resists exclusion, discrimination, and paternalistic, authoritarian interventions proactively by her lifestyle. This new non-ideological characteristic of the urban inhabitant adds one more layer to my intersectional analysis: generation. Unlike their parents, the young Istanbulites, including but not limited to the millennials, have not experienced former military coups and the repressive politics of fear in the aftermath of the coups. As they have never learned to be scared of the state, the law, and the police, they also do not shy away from expressing their interests, need for freedom, and defence of rights.

All of these changes in the city that I observed, documented, and analysed for six years culminated with the Taksim-Gezi protests of 2013, which confirmed all of my findings. Gezi put the final dot to my ethnography. Like the inhabitants of contested neighbourhoods, the young Gezi protestors were freed from ideological cages and thereby liberated from the fear of interacting with the other – a fear inflicted by a political historical baggage that has divided both the city and the state.

The urban space deeply divided by contestation is most capable of generating new democratic bonds and alliances over freedoms and rights. Like most social and political phenomena, this is not unconditional. The key to spatial inclusion as the trigger of democratization in urban space is a safe place. People disagree and dispute freely when they feel safe in a place. They open up, mix, and include when they do not feel under threat. They also experiment with new political practices more freely without the fear of being judged, attacked, or violated. The young protestors of Gezi achieved new alliances with people from previously antagonistic groups, including both LGBTQ and some Islamist groups, in their opposition to the authoritarian rule. Gezi's call for freedom for all was a challenge to identity politics and ideological polarization.

Unfortunately, we have not seen a similar achievement in political society, party politics, or the parliament so far. To the contrary, by reducing parliament to a merely symbolic status, Erdogan managed to concentrate political power in his hands in the three to four years following the Gezi protests. But, fortunately, unlike Gezi Park in Taksim Square, which was brutally evacuated by the police, the contested neighbourhoods and campuses I studied persist as the last resorts of resistance against an increasingly repressive regime. The April 2017 referendum showed that more than 50 per cent of Turkish society opposed Erdogan's rule. This unhappy and repressed opposition finds shelter in contested urban sites of Istanbul and some other secularist cities, such as Izmir and Eskisehir. In these cities, certain campuses and neighbourhoods hang on to their liberating political culture because they are still, first and foremost, safe places. Ironically, this safety is attained by keeping the police physically outside their boundaries, as in the case of some campuses, or keeping them at least at bay, as with Tesvikiye even during the Gezi protests.

Urban space matters. Bringing space to the centre enables us to see the democratization of everyday practices, which are often obscured under an authoritarian government. As the AKP undermined and violated checks and balances with the excuse of the state of emergency, the only medium of resistance left to the opposition was the spatiality of freedom. When the regime cracks down on all parts of civil and political society and criminalizes all dissent – whether from Kurds, Alevites, intellectuals, academics, journalists, women, LGBTQ, or others – the free zones of contestation hold their position in the city, albeit with increasing difficulty. When the regime confiscates the private property of people associated with oppositional groups and dissent, and when it closes down schools, universities, and companies associated with oppositional groups, democratic bonds and alliances continue in the most unexpected places – that is, in the *cracks of the city*.

Conclusion: Spatializing Hallsian Civility?

Any religion in the hands of bad political rule can be twisted to the ends of injustice and political indecency; Islam in its essence is no more conducive to political authoritarianism than any other politics of religion or ethnicity. Viewing the city as the locus of urban civility challenges essentialist arguments about Islam and pious Muslims, and suggests that the Turkish political crisis is caused by the political authoritarianism of the current regime and its historical precedents. In sharp contrast to an increasingly repressive political rule that violates the main tenets of political decency, evidence from Istanbul's contested sites allows for a rethinking of the Turkish case. Here, the Hallsian understanding of civility and how it works proves to be particularly helpful.

The metropolitan city is remarkably vulnerable to conflict and divisions within the state. At the same time, however, contested urban space is highly capable of deflecting conflict away from the state and generating democratic spaces and practices of urban civility. New forms of urban civility in Istanbul are not merely about deliberation and public debate, but are actual experiments with democratic practices of bonding, integrating, and collaborating across ancient fault lines. I argue that these places have an agency, because they generate spatial inclusion and mixing, which facilitates politically decent means of disagreement, contestation, and eventually trust and cooperation.

Conventional political science prioritizes political institutions, particularly the state, party politics, and political society, as the main agents of democratization, while dismissing divided cities as a source of disorder or political instability. Counterintuitively, by relying on the Hallsian concepts of civility, political decency, and primacy of individual freedoms, I argued that divided urban space becomes a source of contestation and force for democratization. Moreover, unlike abrupt urban protests across the globe, everyday contestations in urban space are not destined to be brutally attacked by police or to fade away rapidly under security states. In contrast to tumultuous flashy protests, urban civility sinks in, simmers, and flourishes in city life by gradually melting into mundane everyday life patterns, habits, and routines.

However, spatializing the Hallsian concept of civility is not easy, and the task runs up against several limitations and challenges. On the one hand, the Hallsian perspective welcomes the constructive role of conflict and disagreement as a condition for political decency when it is handled within the framework of civility. Accordingly, I argue that inclusion and democratic pluralism are not the result of the reduction of conflict, but of the ability to form new and shifting alliances out of these conflicts. On the other hand, civility in Hallsian thought concerns *a certain general quality of life* rather than a spatially limited privilege or an advantage confined to a certain realm. Hence, it is reluctant to be reduced to a space, no matter how monolithic and all-encompassing that space may be, as in the case of the public sphere. Hallsian civility is unbound by spatiality and therefore exists only under liberal democratic regimes.

A rethinking of Tocqueville (2003) on the democratizing spirit in everyday life raises further questions about how state and civil society may intertwine. Tocqueville uses the term "the art of association" to highlight the ways in which Americans were able to deepen democracy through their mundane everyday practices. He explains the political skill of association in terms of mores and sensibilities, or as "habits of the heart." However, these democratic habits in America developed under a new democratic regime that did not have much historical baggage of political distrust. What Tocqueville refers to as the "habits of the heart" developed through interactions with democratic institutions. In contrast, in Turkey the gap between the democratizing trends in the city and the authoritarianism of the regime has dramatically increased in the aftermath of the 2013 Gezi protests.[6]

The question becomes, then, whether or not civility ever travels from its historically conventional habitat, the liberal democracies of the West (Hall 2013, 1995). Importantly, while Hall refuses to fall into rigid historical determinism, the arduous struggles of civility to survive in authoritarian regimes speak to the difficulty of its transferability across the globe (Hall 2013, 37). But in this dark age, the vulnerability of civility looks more global than ever, while its primacy and preciousness

6 The 2015 Turkey Progress Report prepared by the European Commission pointed to concerns about freedom of expression. The report also mentioned that Turkey had not yet ratified the 2005 UNESCO Convention on the Protection and Promotion of the Diversity of Cultural Expressions.

become ever clearer. As national territories of consolidated democracies divide and polarize along the axis of political (in)decency, spatiality of civility might be becoming a more serious consideration. The endeavour of spatializing trust, freedom, and civility, while remaining within the Hallsian framework, becomes even more important and timely when we consider Hall's careful distinction between prescriptive and descriptive analysis. Are free and safe places in current world politics becoming a hope or dream for minorities, immigrants, and marginalized groups, and will they persist in the face of rising exclusionist, repressive political rule? These are all very pressing questions that the Hallsian paradigm raises for scholars of political reform and democracy across a long continuum from political sociology, political economy, and political philosophy to political geography.

Despite its timeless primacy for political decency, then, civility remains one of the least understood concepts of political theory. According to the Hallsian paradigm, we do not all need to be similar or on the same page. We do not even have to like each other. If one is lucky enough to be present in one of those precious moments when Hall reveals parts of his inner world, one might hear him say that romance and pain are perhaps often overrated. For a good life and good political rule, all it takes is a basic agreement to respect, include, and accommodate each other despite our differences and disagreements. Perhaps now more than in many other historical periods, this formula sounds like a magic prescription to cure what seems to be a terminal disease in the age of Trump, Putin, and Erdogan.

Hall's stance is thus more than a mere defensive theoretical position or a form of intellectual resistance. There is an admirable genuineness to the Hallsian worldview. An insightful, and witty political sociologist, Hall is the very embodiment of civility in his personal life. He juxtaposes a warm romantic view of the world embedded in cosy communal or civic values against his politics of civility, which may be seen as a colder and more formal political arrangement. First and foremost, it is a commitment to respect the individual and individuation. In this political arrangement, people "show" (though not necessarily "have") respect for each other's freedoms and ways of life (Hall 2013, 6–7). This renders the politics of civility formal rather than merely symbolic or (inter)personal, because it is routinized by democratic practices and institutionalized by the game rules of democracy. Regarding his juxtaposition of civility and romanticism, Hall (2013, 7) reasons that "if this limits [civility's] general emotional appeal, it most certainly increases its merits in my eyes."

REFERENCES

Arat, Yesim. 1989. *The Patriarchal Paradox: Women Politicians in Turkey*. Fairleigh Dickonson.

Boudreau, Julie-Anne. 2017. *Global Urban Politics*. Cambridge: Polity.

Braithwaite, Valerie, and Margaret Levi. 2001. *Trust and Governance*. New York: Russell Sage.

Cakir, Rusen. 2008. *Mahalle Baskisi* [Neighbourhood pressure]. Istanbul: Dogan Yayincilik.

Calhoun, Craig, ed. 1992. *Habermas and the Public Sphere*. Cambridge, MA: Massachusetts Institute of Technology.

Davis, Diane, and Nora Libertun de Duren, eds. 2011. *Cities and Sovereignty: Identity Politics in the Urban Sphere*. Bloomington: Indiana University Press.

Eickelman, Dale. 1998. "From Here to Modernity: Ernest Gellner on Nationalism and Islamic Fundamentalism." In *The State of the Nation: Ernest Gellner and the Theory of Nationalism*, edited by John A. Hall, 268–71. Cambridge: Cambridge University Press.

Elias, Norbert. 2000. *The Civilizing Process*. Oxford: Blackwell.

Evans, Peter B., Dietrich Rueschemeyer, and Theda Skocpol, eds. 1985. *Bringing the State Back in*. Cambridge: Polity/Cambridge University Press. https://doi.org/10.1017/CBO9780511628283.

Gellner, Ernest. 1996. *Conditions of Liberty: Civil Society and Its Rivals*. New York: Penguin.

Gozaydin, Istar. 2009. *Diyanet: Turkiye Cumhuriyetinden Dinin Tanzimi.* [The organization of religion in the Turkish Republic]. Iletisim: Yayinevi.

Hall, John A. 1977. "Sincerity and Politics: The 'Existentialists' vs Goffman and Proust." *Sociological Review* 25 (3): 535–50. https://doi.org/10.1111/j.1467-954X.1977.tb00303.x.

– 1992. "Trust in Tocqueville." *Policy, Organisation and Society* 5 (1): 16–24. https://doi.org/10.1080/10349952.1992.11876775.

– 1995. "Introduction." In *Civil Society: Theory, History, Comparison*, edited by John A. Hall, 1–31. Cambridge: Polity.

– 2013. *The Importance of Being Civil: The Struggle for Political Decency*. Princeton: Princeton University Press.

Lefebvre, Henri. 2003. *The Urban Revolution*. Minneapolis: University of Minnesota Press.

Levi, Margaret. 1998. "A State of Trust." In *Trust and Governance*, edited by Valerie Braithwaite and Margaret Levi, 77–101. New York: Russell Sage.

Mann, Michael. 2003. *Incoherent Empire*. London: Verso.

Mills, Amy. 2007. "Gender and (Mahalle) Neighborhood Space in Istanbul." *Gender, Place and Culture* 14 (3): 335–54. https://doi.org/10.1080/09663690701324995.

– 2010. *Streets of Memory: Landscape, Tolerance and National Identity in Istanbul.* Athens: University of Georgia Press.

Öktem, Kerem, Ayse Kadioglu, and Mehmet Karli, eds. 2012. *Another Empire: A Decade of Turkey's Foreign Policy under the Justice and Development Party.* Istanbul: Bilgil University Press.

Onis, Ziya. 2013. "Sharing Power: Turkey's Democratization Challenge in the Age of the AKP Hegemony." *Insight Turkey* 13 (2): 135–52.

Sassen, Saskia. 2006. *Territory, Authority and Rights: From Medieval to Global Assemblages*. Princeton: Princeton University Press.

Senett, Richard. 1998. *The Spaces of Democracy*. Ann Arbor: University of Michigan Press.

Tekeli, Sirin. 1994. *Women in Modern Turkish Society*. London: Zed.

Tetreault, Mary Ann. 1993. "Civil Society in Kuwait: Protected Spaces and Women's Rights." *Middle East Journal* 47 (2): 275–91.

Tocqueville, Alexis de. 2003. *Democracy in America*. Clark: Lawbook Exchange.

Turam, Berna. 2004. "The Politics of Engagement between Islam and the State: Ambivalences of 'Civil Society.'" *British Journal of Sociology* 55 (2): 259–81. https://doi.org/10.1111/j.1468-4446.2004.00018.x.

– 2012. "Turkey under AKP: Are Civil Liberties Safe?" *Journal of Democracy* 23 (1): 109–18. https://doi.org/10.1353/jod.2012.0007.

– 2013. "Primacy of Space in Politics: Bargaining Rights, Freedom and Power in an Istanbul Neighborhood." *International Journal of Urban and Regional Research* 37 (2): 409–29. https://doi.org/10.1111/1468-2427.12003.

– 2015. *Gaining Freedoms: Claiming Space in Istanbul and Berlin*. Stanford: Stanford University Press.

Tyler, Tom R., and Yuen Huo. 2002. *Trust in the Law: Encouraging Public Cooperation with the Police and Courts*. New York: Russell Sage.

Weber, Max. 1958. *The City*. New York: Free Press.

Zubaida, Sami. 1995. "Is There a Muslim Society? Ernest Gellner's Sociology of Islam." *Economy and Society* 24 (2): 151–88. https://doi.org/10.1080/03085149500000007.

5 Under Stress: Civility, Compassion, and National Solidarity – The Refugee Crisis in Germany after 1945

FRANK TRENTMANN

Civil society and nationalism have been two major themes in historical sociology, and John Hall (1995, 1998) has made seminal contributions to the literature of each. The animating spirit of civil society, Hall (2013) has argued, is civility and the tolerance of different viewpoints that spring from it. Nationalism, by contrast, cherishes homogeneity and sameness. It rests on a belief in the primacy of a nation and seeks to mobilize its members to fulfil its destiny. The two visions have often been treated as belonging to different historical eras. Civil society emerged in the seventeenth and eighteenth centuries as Enlightenment thinkers sought to overcome religious fanaticism and violence (Colas 1998), while nationalism began as an outburst of romantic and ethnic politics in the nineteenth century, helped along by "modern" forms of industry, transport, and mass communication (Hall 1993). Nationalism, in its extreme form, limits the space for difference associated with civil society because it consolidates and elevates one ethnic community above all others. The primacy of one ethnic or language group requires the exclusion of others.

In historical sociology as in international relations, attention has been on the rivalry and tensions arising from competition *between* nations and ethnic groups – as, for instance, in Liliana Riga's or Matthew Lange's chapters in this volume. There is, however, a second stage where civility and nationalism can collide, and that is *within* a national group and *within* a nation-state when people of the *same* ethnic background and citizenship come into conflict with each other. It is important to appreciate the essential tension at the heart of nationalism. The nation is simultaneously an aspirational project and a social reality. Claims to its primacy are in the first instance just that: claims. Ideology, identity formation, and force are needed to make all members of a national community embrace it. National solidarity is fragile and can fragment. A national community may suppress other kinds of social bonds and ideals, such as class, gender, or religion, but it rarely eliminates them (Bjork 2008). We therefore should consider tension and conflict between co-nationals as well as that between different national groups. Civility, in other words, is not only what one national group withholds from another. It is also a trait that can be in greater or shorter supply in relations between co-nationals.

The following pages explore the fate of civility in an extreme case: Germany at the end of the Second World War, a society that had ruthlessly aspired to create a racially pure "national community" or *Volksgemeinschaft* but ended up in total defeat. What does "living with difference" look like when those different beings are co-nationals in need of help? And, in turn, what does their treatment reveal about the presumed strength of national identity and solidarity relative to other social bonds and interests? The internal refugee problem in Germany at the end of the Second World War enables us to explore the tension between compassion and national solidarity at a moment of crisis. Between 1944 and 1946, some twelve million German refugees fled or were expelled from East Prussia, Silesia, the Sudetenland, and other parts of Central and Eastern Europe and took refuge in what remained of Germany, under Allied occupation. These were ethnic Germans, although with their own customs and accents. The local welcome they received from their fellow Germans varied considerably. What were the factors that made for greater or lesser civility in different parts of Germany? What role did religion, work, family, and local identity play in antagonism or assimilation?

The varied experience of these refugees and their interaction with local inhabitants and "host" cultures, I suggest, raise questions about the nature of civility, and its scope and links to social action. Civility, as defined by Hall, refers to a permissive attitude: the willingness to allow for behaviour or opinions different from one's own. It may require a tolerant outlook but, as such, is not especially demanding. We are letting other-minded folk think, speak, and live as they wish, but we do not have to do a lot ourselves. This laissez-faire mentality might be sufficient when individuals and groups with diverse ideas and customs have sufficient means and resources. But such civility would not mean very much if some had no access to food or shelter and are thus incapable of leading the kind of lives they value (and we may wish to respect) (Sen 1999). To be meaningful, civility here requires social action as well as mental disposition. It needs to be viewed in relation to empathy and charity. This chapter, then, seeks to widen and activate the concept of civility beyond the typical confines of the Hallsian paradigm. Methodologically, this means extending it from the history of ideas to social history and interactions in everyday life: doing performs values. Modern societies have shown remarkably different forms and degrees of civility-in-action.

National Solidarity – and Its Limits

The twelve million Germans displaced at the end of the war were part of a longer story of forced population movements stretching back to the First World War and the Nazi-Soviet population transfers between 1939 and 1941, but few of them recognized this. They were not "refugees" (*Flüchtlinge*) like the others, they insisted, but "expellees" (*Vertriebene, Ostvertriebene,* or *Heimatvertriebene*), a term that came to be the authoritative official one in West Germany after 1950; in Soviet-occupied East Germany, by contrast, the official category of *Umsiedler* or resettlers silenced any reference to the forced nature of their migration.[1] In West Germany, the federation of expellees renounced hatred and revenge in their Charta of 1950 but at the same time asserted a divinely ordained universal human right to *Heimat* (homeland). Most had not given up hopes of return, and documenting their violent expulsion was a way of upholding their claim. It was the expulsion itself that dominated letters, newspapers, monuments, and gatherings in the post-war years, with stories that tended to start with the collapse of the Third Reich and advancing Soviet troops and occupation, followed by harrowing accounts of rape, murder, suicide, and suffering during the flight west. From the first multivolume official collection of sources and witness accounts in the 1950s to the controversy about a dedicated museum for the expellees in the 1990s and 2000s, it was the experience of expulsion that was the focus of public and academic attention (Beer 1998; Schieder 1951–61).

1 I use the terms "refugee" and "expellee" interchangeably for the immediate post-war years, as did contemporaries, before the term "*Vertriebene*" gained official acceptance.

But the expellees' arrival in the west is as important a story as their flight from the east. These were not just very large population movements – the *Vertriebene* made up 17 per cent of West Germany in 1950. Most of them arrived in communities with radically different socio-economic structures, cultural traditions, and religious milieus from their own. The local "host" populations and the new arrivals also occupied very different positions in the history of the German nation. According to the 1950 West German census, 4.4 million expellees came from the eastern territories that had been part of Germany in 1937, such as Pommern and East Prussia, the latter of which had been a province of Prussia since 1773 and was part of the German empire at its foundation in 1871. Another 3.6 million, however, were ethnic Germans from places outside Bismarck's empire, including the Sudetenland, Polish Silesia, Hungary, and Romania (Nellner 1959). Geography added a further irony. It just so happened that the largest streams of refugees reached safety in the two regions with a strong sense of their regional and cultural autonomy that had been the most reluctant joiners of Bismarck's unified Germany: Schleswig-Holstein in the north (the final destination for treks across the frozen Baltic) and Bavaria in the south (across the border from Czechoslovakia). In Bavaria in 1950, the *Vertriebene* made up 21 per cent of the population, in Schleswig-Holstein a third; by contrast, they were 10 per cent in Nordrhein-Westfalia and only 5 per cent in the Rhineland-Palatinate. In 1948, a British observer noted that "*Saufliichtling*" (refugee pig) had replaced "*Saupreusse*" (Prussian pig) as an insult in Bavaria (Pohl 2009, 57). In Schleswig-Holstein, refugees were denounced as "Poles" or "Prussians": "into the North Sea with that shit," some said (Kossert 2008).

Core sociological categories collided: class and status, religious identity, community and nation. The local reception of the newcomers varied across time and space, and is best treated as a process, from the moment of arrival through the provision of housing, the search for work, and participation in communal life all the way to assimilation. Empathy and prejudice, assistance and refusal were unevenly distributed across this course, reflecting local cultures and attitudes to outsiders as well as highly uneven material endowments.

The differences began with the initial welcome. The refugee commissioner of the Evangelische Hilfswerk, the main Protestant charity, reported on his trip through the refugee camps in Rhineland in November 1946. In Solingen, forty-two adults and fifty-four children were put up in a cold hall, but at least they had two ovens. The communal meals were "good and free" and they received donated shoes and clothing. There was even a nursery (ADE 1946a). When he visited Schleswig-Holstein and Lower Saxony a few months later, by contrast, he reported how in Campen, for example, most refugees slept in straw heaps on the cement floor of poorly insulated temporary Nissen huts. The light cables had been taken down by the local farmer, who used them to illuminate his farm. Refugees were denied peat for fuel. "The farmer even refuses them drinking water, so that they have to fetch their water from a ditch" (ADE 1946b). As it happened, the farmer was also the elected head (*Kirchenmeister*) of the local congregation (ADE 1947). In Bavaria in March 1946 thousands were arriving every day, and the refugee commissioner despaired about the refusal of many local authorities to get involved in the relief effort (ADE 1946c).

Although there were local exceptions, there was a clear regional divide: a warmer reception in the Rhine and Ruhr and colder treatment in the north and south. Partly, this had to do with overall numbers – sparsely populated Schleswig-Holstein took a good third of all refugees, and many towns and districts almost doubled in size overnight. The Rhineland, by contrast, had only taken in 7 per cent by the end of 1946. On the other hand, the Rhineland and many western and central regions had been heavily bombed, and many towns and cities lay in ruins. It should have been more difficult to welcome refugees there than in rural Schleswig-Holstein and Bavaria, where farms and houses stood essentially intact.

It might be assumed that the lucky ones who still had their home and possessions by the end of the war would have been more ready to help, but the reverse tended to be the case. In the Rhine and Ruhr, many inhabitants had been bombed out themselves and were more understanding of what the *Vertriebene* were going through. Camps were not only for distant strangers but for nearby locals, too. The new arrivals from the east were just the latest wave of migrants. More often than not, property stood in the way of charity, for two principal reasons.

The first was that a lot of the property involved was farmland, and land was scarce. Small farmers were interested in cheap agricultural labourers, not in handing over a few of their acres to now-landless former farmers from the east. Farmers and independent traders were least likely to find their way back into their old job in the new country. The campaign to compensate Germans for at least a part of their war-related losses – which became law in 1952 – only helped to raise suspicion in host communities. Many locals doubted the *Vertriebene* had lost as much as they claimed – for their accounts to be true, some said, the German Reich would have needed to stretch all the way to the Urals. Refugee housing colonies were referred to as "We owned ..." (Lehmann 1991, 39).

A second and related factor was the precarious state of the economy after the war, which put a premium on goods that could be bartered in the black market. Most *Vertriebene* had little to offer except their sweat. Significantly, it was expellees with special skills or higher education, and civil servants in particular, who most easily found their way back into a job. In other words, the low esteem in which refugees were held resulted not only from cultural prejudice: it also reflected the low value of labour in a shadow economy. The currency reform of 1948 and then the economic miracle went some way to rebalance the values of property and labour (Schulze 2001, 45).

Class and property divided locals and the new arrivals, but it was religion that often made the gulf between them unbridgeable. While Germany had been home to both Protestants and Catholics since the Reformation, most small towns and villages were characterized by a single faith. The migrants shook up this ordered landscape, as Protestants arrived in Catholic heartlands and Catholics in Protestant ones. Even Protestants, though, misunderstood each other, especially in northwestern parts of Germany, where Lutheran migrants entered pietist heartlands.

An observer noted the resulting clash of cultures in the village of Gersdorf in Hesse. The established population belonged to the reformed Protestant church inspired by Zwingli and Calvin. Their life and faith followed the principles of simplicity, sobriety, and self-discipline. Pleasure and entertainment were taboo, not to mention fashion and refinement. Middle-aged women wore "grey, brown or black." The local church was plain, their "flats without any luxuries. Meals had to be good and hearty, but they attached no value on its delicate preparation" (Kurz 1950, 34). By contrast, the 128 Sudeten Germans who arrived in 1945–6 were Catholics who enjoyed life, food, and clothes. They chatted, kissed each other's hands, and dressed up for Carnival. In addition, the local core value was self-reliance. People only accepted a gift if they were able to reciprocate immediately, the observer noted; children who accepted food from other families were "reprimanded or even punished" (Kurz 1950, 39). While this culture of self-reliance was not unique to reformed Protestants, it arguably made it harder for the locals in Gersdorf to act charitably.

The refugees from the east were often perplexed by the degree to which local life revolved around religion. As one German from Prague told an investigator in Marburg (Hesse) in 1949, "How backward you all are. Everything here is like the middle ages. You are still fighting the wars of religion" (Volk 1950, 140). Such a sentiment is understandable. The fate of the Sudeten Germans and other national minorities outside the German nation-state had hinged on their nationality (not their religion). For their host communities, by contrast, it was the reverse. Nationalism, then, was more brittle than is sometimes allowed. Even when locals looked at the newcomers through national glasses, racial categories could still exclude them from the national community. In Winsen, south of Hamburg, the local pastor was convinced that the refugee stream was an Allied plot to break German resistance by means of a "*völkische* dissolution [*Auflösung*]" (Schulze 2001, 101). Another pastor in nearby Eversen (Lower Saxony) feared that the "original character of our people [*Volkstum*] would lose its authentic quality [*Echtheit*] if mixed with such strange and alien elements [*land- und artfremdem Character*]" (Schulze 2001, 44).

Germans Helping Germans

Although religion could be a source of division, the German Lutheran and Catholic churches also played a major role in creating solidarity by distributing food, clothes, and shelter after 1945. The churches were critical mediators between host communities and the new arrivals. All these moral efforts did not suddenly arise in a vacuum. The Nazis had operated an extensive system of welfare provision and collection drives, with constant appeals to solidarity and sacrifice. Patriotic collections for the Winter Aid program provided clothes, coal, and even beds (Evans 2005; Stoddard 1940; Tennstedt 1987). Of course, there were fundamental differences before and after 1945. The Nazis strove to strengthen a racial *Volksgemeinschaft* and win a war of conquest, while after 1945 the churches appealed to Christian charity and solidarity in misery. Nonetheless, for givers and recipients alike, post-war charitable campaigns resonated against a background of similar efforts during the war.

The Nazis had mobilized moral resources for helping fellow Germans but, as victories turned to defeat, they also tested and spent a lot of them. In 1943–4, Germans from bombed Hamburg and other cities were taken by train to Lower Saxony and Bavaria, the "air raid shelter of the Third Reich." The Nazis set up soup kitchens and put on entertainment. At the same time, the secret reports of the security service of the SS revealed the real limits of national solidarity. In August 1943, mothers from Hamburg arriving in Bavaria were unable to obtain any diapers, and some were obliged to take the train to Passau to find food. In Styria, evacuees complained that the food was fit only for pigs. In return, rural villagers denounced city dwellers as spoilt and lazy. Three months later, when Munich and Nuremberg were also bombed, the locals blamed their misfortune on godless Hamburgers: "We owe that to you. It happened because you are not going to Church!" (18 November 1943 in Boberach 1984). Rather than breaking down regional loyalties, the Nazis reinforced them, putting on cultural *Heimat* programs for evacuated communities, complete with actors and singers from back home.

These cultural programs outraged locals; they also tended to reinforce regional identities. In Bayreuth, for example, the Reich propaganda office had planned ahead and used actors from Hamburg to make evacuated audiences feel more at home in Bavaria. There were speeches praising "unser Hamburg" (our Hamburg). The actors, the security service wrote, built a "unifying bridge to their homeland." Recognition of their Hanseatic pride, the security service reported, prompted respect from the locals and led to greater tolerance. The bond to a provincial *Heimat* could be stronger than to the German nation, but at the same time was something Germans from different provinces could understand about each other.

In regions where the host population had themselves experienced the trials of migration, such as the Warthegau (where Baltic and Russian Germans were resettled after 1940), help was most forthcoming, all the way to offering the evacuees one's own bed. Elsewhere, appeals to take in bombed-out families fell on deaf ears and sometimes needed to be backed up by threats and police action. Many of those ordered to evacuate thus tried hard to stay in their hometown, within a community they knew. In Witten, in October 1943, two hundred local women demonstrated when the authorities tried to cut their food rations in order to force them to return to their assigned place of evacuation (12 April, 19 August, 11 October 1943 in Boberach 1984).

The Nazi relief system left a challenging legacy for charitable aid after the war. On the one hand, Germans had been trained into habits of giving. On the other, a lot of that giving had been coerced, and after twelve years there was donation fatigue. As elsewhere, the Nazis had centralized the charitable sector. A 1934 law on donations required all drives to have government approval and show they were about public needs. In 1937, the Nazis prohibited house and street collections by Caritas, the main Catholic relief organization. Church collections were now confined to churches and for church purposes. And even these were a thorn in the Nazis' side because every penny and mark that went into a collection bag during a mass held in memory of fallen soldiers was a penny or mark missing from the tin for the regime's Winter Aid program (18 December 1941 in Boberach 1984).

Like the country as a whole, the charity infrastructure was in need of complete reconstruction in 1945. The Red Cross, CARE, and other groups provided an extensive international humanitarian aid program (Reinisch 2013; Steinert 2007), but just as important were efforts organized by the defeated Germans themselves. The Protestant and Catholic churches here took the lead. The Catholic Caritas association, founded in 1897, was well established. Already in spring 1944 Protestant leaders had discussed plans for a charitable body based on "self-help," and the Evangelische Hilfswerk was set up in August 1945. Other bodies had started their life under the Nazis. The Kirchliche Hilfsstelle in Munich originated as an auxiliary of the Reichsverband für das katholische Deutschtum in 1943, designed to look after Catholic clergy in the territories in the east occupied by the Nazis. In 1945–6, it switched to looking after millions of Catholics driven out of the east and being resettled in Bavaria and other parts of western Germany.

Between 1945 and 1948, the Evangelische Hilfswerk raised 200 million Reichsmark in donations. Just as important, it organized collections in kind. In Hessen-Nassau, a region with 1.6 million inhabitants, 800,492 kg of food were donated during the 1948 harvest festival. Even people in Schleswig-Holstein (with a local population of 2.5 million), often criticized for their harsh and un-Christian attitude towards refugees, gave 390,000 kg of potatoes. In the first ten years after the war, donations to the Protestant charity produced a formidable 115 million kg of clothes, medication, and food, worth more than 300 million DM; to give a sense of comparison, all monetary donations from abroad in 1948–9 amounted to 16.8 million DM, with the bulk coming from the Lutheran World Federation (ADE 1949; Zentralbüro des Hilfswerks 1955, 163–72).

The emphasis on charitable "self-help" was significant for moral as well as material reasons. For the church organizations, the donation drives were consciously designed as a way to inculcate charitable habits among the young. "From their earliest years, children are trained to have open eyes and an open heart for the needs of their neighbour" (*Mitteilungen*, March 1953, 7). More broadly, "self-help" provided a language of shared Christian fate and penance that tied the suffering of the refugees to the sympathy of their local hosts and their duty of care.

The millions of expellees were a constant reminder of the lost war and raised sensitive questions about responsibility. To ask who should help the refugees triggered discussion about who was responsible for their plight in the first place. The Nuremberg trial (1945–6) and the troubled and partial process of denazification gave voice to a strong popular reaction against charges of collective guilt. The expulsion of Germans from the east amplified the growing sense among ethnic Germans that they were special victims and pushed Jews, foreign coerced labour, and other Nazi victims down to the bottom of a hierarchy of moral concern and social support. In this view, the mass of innocent German refugees and their suffering far outweighed the few victims of Lidice and other massacres that were sometimes given as a reason for the former's eviction. "How can anyone," one typical article asked, "use the execution of 187 men and deportation of 103 children as a way of justifying the expulsion of 2.5 to 3 million Sudeten Germans? In the Prague concentration camp 'Hagibor' alone more than 800 people died of hunger in the year after the war, mainly elderly and infants." Those responsible for this new suffering were as guilty as the Nazis' hangmen and had no right to accuse "innocent" German people (Bundesarchiv Koblenz 1946a). Leading bishops reinforced this view. "Others should not dishonour the entire German people and let them do further penance," Archbishop Conrad Gröber of Freiburg wrote in his 31 December 1945 pastoral letter, "for ugly things [*Scheusslichkeiten*] which a part of the German people did, misled by criminal dispositions or principles" (Bundesarchiv Koblenz 1945). Here was the increasingly popular refrain that, except for a few Nazi fanatics and perpetrators, most Germans had been powerless, ignorant, and thus innocent all along. References to Germans' innocence and the sense of injustice done to the refugees mutually reinforced each other.

At the same time, exonerating "ordinary" Germans completely carried the risk of eliminating a feeling of remorse, and with it a sense of shared destiny and compassion for the refugees from the east. If the war crimes had been committed by a few Nazis in the east, why suddenly expect Bavarians or other Germans in the west to take responsibility for the fallout?

The churches and their charities, therefore, had to perform a difficult moral balancing act. While catering to their congregations' fixation on their own victimhood, they also called for compassion and care in the name of a shared historical responsibility. In this way, the refugee crisis amplified the tension within the churches about their own role during the Nazi era. In October 1945, the newly founded Evangelical Church of Germany (EKD) made a public confession of guilt in Stuttgart, acknowledging "with great sorrow ... the infinite suffering that through us [*durch uns*] has been brought to many people and countries" and accusing themselves "for not having been more courageous, faithful and loving in offering resistance" (EKD 1945a, 60f.).

The regional churches grudgingly accepted the Stuttgart declaration but resisted calls for an institutional overhaul. Restoration and a concern with ongoing pastoral care trumped denazification and confronting guilt head on. Church elders in Schleswig-Holstein asked the leaders of the EKD why they focused exclusively on German guilt and did not simultaneously speak of the guilt of others. Of course they heard a lot about it, Asmussen responded, "but we would be bad pastors if we talked so much of the guilt of others that the ears of our own people would be blocked for the word of our own guilt" (EKD 1945b, 377).

The literature about post-1945 Germany has mainly focused on the refusal to confront guilt Asmussen warned against. But while personal and collective acts of denial were plentiful, they should not obscure entirely those moments when national guilt was addressed. During the internal refugee crisis, acknowledgment of *some* collective guilt could be turned into a source of Christian solidarity. The refugees, many letters and sermons said, were atoning for the sins of the whole German nation (Bundesarchiv Koblenz 1946b). A Catholic sermon in support of refugee aid in early 1946, distributed by the Munich Kirchliche Hilfsstelle, spelled out the link between the refugees' suffering and collective sin and repentance:

> The refugees were enduring the punishment of God that had descended over us as representatives for the entire nation [*Volk*], and as representatives they have to atone in a special degree. That is why no-one can say "What do I care about these refugees, I want to have my peace, I did not want the war." Their suffering and fate concerns us all. In some way, we all have to atone for sins that have been committed in the name of the German people, and the nature of our atonement is to help those who have

> lost their *Heimat*. We have been spared, not because we have been better, but because He wants to give us an opportunity to become better. (Bundesarchiv Koblenz 1946c)

Calls for individual charity were thus coupled with an appeal to a collective solidarity forged by shared historical responsibility and suffering. All Germans needed to recognize "solidarity in misery" (*Solidarität des Elends*), Eugen Gerstenmaier, the head of the Evangelische Hilfswerk, told an ecumenical meeting on refugees in Stuttgart in June 1947. The "path to freedom," he said, required "the courage to truth [and] will to justice." "We … know that certain parts of the ethnic Germans had been the favoured hunting grounds of the Nazis, especially of the SS; but we also know that many resisted the attempts of seduction and terror." Christianity was a "Praxis," not a theory, and the main task now was to prove itself through its practical deeds in forging solidarity (*Mitteilungen*, August 1947, 72f.). "All of Germany has lost the war," Gerstenmaier stressed. "Not only the Silesians and East Prussians. And, sadly, also not just the NSDAP." "We are those who have been cheated," he added a few months later at a public demonstration, "but towards the rest of the world we cannot act as if we just had been taken in, innocuously. We need to take responsibility for finding ourselves in the situation we are in today." "At the same time, as Christians we are not prepared to justify it … with the formula 'you have done the same or worse'" (*Mitteilungen*, December 1947, 132f.).

The refugee problem was about empathy and a sense of collective responsibility but, at its most fundamental, it was about the prospect of democracy in post-war Germany. Antagonism between locals and newcomers made many refugees long for a return east and created a potential breeding ground for refugee lobbies challenging the post-war settlement. In Memmingen, the Swabian part of Bavaria, the refugee representatives sent the local Christlich-Soziale Union (CSU) an "appeal for humanity" in October 1946, demanding to be treated as brothers and equals. "You cannot honestly expect that we will carry the consequences of Hitler's war all by ourselves while you yourselves are holding onto all your property." The choice was simple: "either reason and humanity will win out and together we will build a new state out of genuine democratic conviction, or intolerance and egoism will triumph and destroy the state" (Bundesarchiv Koblenz 1946d).

The church-led charities saw themselves as vital mediators. Much of the day-to-day work was done by pastors, deacons, welfare workers, and other full-time staff. But a lot also relied on volunteers. In 1954, for example, 168 pastors, welfare workers, and nursery teachers cared for the many thousand new refugees from the GDR. Hard as it was, their task would have been impossible without an additional 226 volunteers, many who served full time (Zentralbüro des Hilfswerks 1955, 171). We read a lot about hard-hearted locals, but who were the people in the vanguard of empathy?

Reports from volunteers in the field give some rare insight into the biography and motivation of these men and women. We can distinguish three groups. The first had established roots in Christian charity and welfare work, stretching back to the years before Hitler. They often came from aristocratic or bourgeois families. A second group was converted by the horrors of war. Some found solace for their own bereavement in helping refugees and disabled veterans, others volunteered to express their gratitude to God for their family's miraculous survival. Finally, there were those who had themselves been refugees or bombed out, such as Annemarie Hörich. Ms Hörich had lost everything in the "Neumark" (East Brandenburg, now Poland) in February 1945. In May 1946 she reached Erbach in Hesse as an "Ostflüchtling" together with her mother and her three-year-old son. She found a room and received clothes from the Evangelische Hilfswerk. Half a year on, she heard that the local pastor was looking for an assistant in a nearby parish. There was nothing more beautiful, she reported to the Hilfswerk, than helping those in need. Refugee aid was often literally "self-help." One of the few positive stories the Protestant refugee commissioner was able to report from north Germany was from Giessen, where the Hilfswerk ran both a transitional camp and the Hotel Lenz. There were plenty of volunteers. The heart and soul was the wife of the local pastor, Mrs Scriba, a mother of ten children who herself had been bombed out.

The place of gender in the charitable relief effort calls for one further note. Caring had long been singled out as a female mission, and it will not come as a surprise that women played a central role in feeding, housing, and assisting the expellees. What also deserves attention is the considerable number of men working alongside them, as volunteers or full-time charity workers, including war veterans and disabled pensioners. The iconography of the donation drives underlines the multiple gendered roles of carers and caring. There was the mother and child, an image reaching back to Käthe Kollwitz's woodcuts and the Pietà. But posters and flyers also appealed to men to lift up their downtrodden brothers instead of walking past. The comradeship of war now fused into a comradeship of compassion. Historians have noted how ideals of masculinity softened in the 1960s, but this was not entirely a sixties phenomenon. The charitable campaign to assist refugees and returning POWs already nurtured the image of male caring and empathy in the post-war crisis (van Rahden 2017).

Legacies

The arrival of millions of ethnic German co-nationals posed a huge cultural and political challenge for the young democratic Federal Republic. It involved a clash of civilizations not so different from those that in recent years have been associated with the arrival of refugees from different races and religions. For Germans in Schleswig or Bavaria, Germans from East Prussia or the Sudetenland were also strangers. In 1949, the British reported that the refugees in eastern Holstein saw in a military conflict between East and West the only way to improve the German situation. In refugee camps, prophetic stories of revenge and a third world war made the rounds. The *Vertriebene* founded their own party, the Bund der Heimatvertriebenen und Entrechteten (BHE), and won 12 per cent of the vote in the Bavarian elections in November 1950, and for the following twelve years served in that state's coalition governments. In 1951, the refugees in Schleswig-Holstein felt so abandoned and frustrated by the slow and piecemeal progress of resettlement to other regions in the west that they threatened to march on Bonn with a quarter million people – since they had managed to walk across the Baltic, they said, such a second trek would be a stroll (Bundesarchiv Koblenz 1952). Working, housing, and living conditions continued to diverge sharply between old and new residents. A large survey in Bavaria found that in 1951 two-thirds of refugee households still lived in a single room. Fully 40 per cent held on to the hope of returning to their *Heimat* (Pfeil 1951, 75).

Integration was an enormous undertaking, but in due course modernized and opened up previously closed communities, especially in Bavaria. The details of this story lie beyond the scope of this chapter. What interests us here is what this process reveals about the core dispositions and actions examined in these pages: recognition, empathy, charity, and learning to live together.

Growing mutual respect and understanding were partly facilitated by public assistance and official recognition. In addition to providing partial compensation for their losses, the state's social housing program doubled the number of flats available to the *Vertriebene* between 1952 and 1955 (Pfeil and Buchholz 1958, 168). Crucially, migrants were redistributed from rural to more urban and industrial regions. As victims of the Red Army, the refugees also gained political status in the course of the Cold War as a reserve army against communism. Both Christian Democrats and Social Democrats courted their vote, eliminating the space for a separate revanchist party. In 1957, the BHE failed to cross the 5 per cent hurdle in the federal elections and was finished as a national political force. Just as important was public support for the migrants' customs and traditions. The state of Bavaria introduced dedicated music, sport, and radio programs and stressed the tribal fraternity (*Stammesverwandschaft*) between Silesians, Bavarians, and Swabians. Saint Hedwig (1174–1243), the patron of Silesia, hailed from a Bavarian aristocratic family, the Bavarian state secretary noted in 1947, and Silesians shared Bavarians' love of music and *Heimat*. By the early 1950s, many small towns had their own *Egerländer "Gmoi"* (community) and the *Egerländer* marched in their costumes at Bavarian song and dance festivals. In exchange, locals started to attend their midsummer celebrations. Radio Bavaria broadcast medleys of old Bavarian songs followed by a Silesian choir that had re-formed in Regensburg. On Tuesday evenings, listeners could tune in and hear about the culture of the *Vertriebenen*. Other programs visited new industries set up by refugees and praised their ambition and hard work (Pohl 2009).

After 1970, when Willy Brandt's Ostpolitik recognized first the Eastern borders and then Poland, effectively extinguishing any hope of return, the *Vertriebenen* organizations popularized an image of themselves as silenced and forgotten victims. In the 1950s, however, the story was one of growing visibility. Towns and state governments stepped forth to adopt provinces in the east, creating concrete, personal links between host communities and the refugees. Bayreuth chose the Sudeten spa town of Franzensbad (Františkovy Lázně in the CSSR). Schleswig-Holstein became the godparent of all of Pommern. Cinemas screened romantic, nostalgic *Heimatfilms* such as *Die Zeit mit Dir* (The Time with You) where a returning POW falls in love with a refugee girl. In 1956, two in three West German newspapers carried special *Vertriebene*-supplements; the expellees themselves maintained an impressive 350 papers with a circulation of over two million (Kurth 1959). Bavaria, in 1953, passed a special *Kulturparagraph* that guaranteed the *Vertriebene* support for their distinctive culture. Communities put up signposts to Danzig and other towns in the east, and erected memorial plaques, boulders, and large crosses of the German East (known as

Ostlandkreuz). Many towns began to include those who had died during the expulsion in their commemorations of the German soldiers who had fallen in the two world wars (Scholz 2015).

Helpful as such public recognition was, integration ultimately hinged on respect and understanding in private life. The two decisive spheres were work and family. Not surprisingly, loss of occupation heightened a sense of dislocation. Better-educated *Vertriebene* managed to resume their professions more quickly and benefitted from greater self-esteem and respect in their new community; 63 per cent of civil servants and 88 per cent of members of the professions reported in 1953 the same or higher position as they had held in 1939 – a remarkably high number compared to the prospects of refugees today. A thirty-four-year old female teacher in Bavaria in 1950 praised the "wonderful camaraderie" she enjoyed with the local teachers: "I have not been made to feel once by any family that I am a so-called refugee, who is looked at as a second-class person" (Pfeil 1951, 96). The loss of one's old occupation, moreover, did not automatically mean social decline. A former salesman was working as a courier for a doctor in 1953 but said he felt subjectively just as well as before the war. What mattered to him was that he earned as much respect from patients now as he had from customers before (Bohnsack 1956, 34).

Work also had a unifying effect, especially in workplaces that depended on cooperation. In a clothing factory in Rotenburg an der Fulda in 1949, the forty-eight-year-old technical director (himself an evacuee from the Rhineland) stressed that they did not know separate groups of locals and refugees: "we are all mixed together … because in our work, each depends on the other and no-one can refuse to chip in … all that interests me is performance [*Leistung*]" (Jäger 1950, 109f.). The economic miracle that followed was important, not only because it generated work and earnings but because it prized such a shared culture of achievement.

The true test of respect and integration happened in the family. Given the prejudice and antagonism that greeted the refugees on their arrival, it is astonishing how quickly they married into their host communities. Already in 1948, half the *Vertriebene* in Bavaria counted locals among their acquaintances. More joined mixed gardening clubs than separate refugee ones. Every second marriage by a *Vertriebene* was a mixed one. By 1952, mixed marriages had risen to 72 per cent in Bavaria as a whole, although there remained regional variations by faith and culture (Pfeil and Buchholz 1958, 166). While impressive, these figures should not be overrated. According to one contemporary investigator, established inhabitants were as likely to marry an expellee as an upper-middle-class person was to wed an unskilled worker. Marriage was often a union between partners who had both suffered losses, although rarely between social equals. In Mardorf, for example, male refugees tended to marry poorer brides who had been orphaned or fallen on hard times. Former merchants and skilled mechanics married the daughters of small farmers or shopkeepers who had died or whose sons were missing in action (Apel 1950, 166).

Putting down new roots rarely meant full assimilation, though. While public support for revanchist groups remained limited, many *Vertriebene* cultivated a strong sense of their lost *Heimat* in private. In 1997, a seventy-three-year old woman who had been raised in East Prussia recalled a family scene from the late 1950s at the outskirts of Hamburg. "I could not have had it any better," she said. She was married to a man from Hamburg, they had a young daughter, and her husband had just built them a house. "We are sitting at the table, and I don't know, but the little one suddenly says, yes, papa, don't you know, once the Russians are gone, then we will go home. My husband almost fell off the chair." She had always told her daughter about "home," but her husband had shown little sympathy. "I never became a *Hamburgerin*," she confessed, "I am still an East Prussian" (FZH 1997). For many, the experience of flight and rape heightened a sense that their *Heimat* had been a place of safety, a "*Geborgenheitsgefühl*." Assimilation was often accomplished only by the second generation, and in many cases it was they who made their parents see the connection between their own loss and the suffering Nazi Germany had wrought on others. Many communities, similarly, opened up only so much of their culture. Years after marrying into the community, one refugee, for instance, was still asked to pay a fee for using the shared village boar to mate with his sows, until he put his foot down and refused (Lehmann 1991, 50).

What were the legacies of the assistance to the *Vertriebene* for moral dispositions and practices such as empathy, care, and compassion? The charitable campaign after 1945 did build up moral capital that was then channelled in new directions. It was a short step from helping refugees from East Prussia to sending parcels across the border to families in East Germany and assisting the new wave of political refugees fleeing the GDR in the 1950s. But moral concern quickly moved further afield, too. Already in November 1953, the Evangelische Hilfswerk drew attention to suffering in Korea and Palestine. In 1957, it stressed in its joint Christmas collection with the Innere Mission that "we ourselves received aid from our brothers across the world in our time of need and hunger. Now it is on us to make a sacrifice for the starving of the world, be it in Palestine, in Syria, in Jordan or Hong Kong. Every day we have reasons to be grateful" (ADE 1957). In 1959 Brot für die Welt (Bread for the World) institutionalized this mission.

During the refugee crisis in 2015, the plight of the Germans expelled from the east was invoked to prompt charity towards a new wave of arrivals from Syria. It would be misleading, though, to think that the flight and reception of those earlier millions from the east automatically predisposed Germans to help strangers in need in general. It was a crooked path. Germans' relations with Greek and Turkish "guest workers" were marked by distance, and in the 1970s, with unemployment rising, by growing antipathy, racism, and discrimination; in 1973 the government imposed a ban on recruiting further guest workers, but family reunions ensured that the number of immigrants continued to rise. Germany took in refugees from Chile in 1973. There were private donations and pledges to serve as godparents, but numbers were tiny; by 1974, the state of Hesse had taken in 165 Chilean refugees. The focus was on humanitarian motives, not on the specific German experience of the *Vertriebene*. And acts of charity coexisted with hate mail targeting the Chileans as dangerous communists. It was the crisis of the boat people in Vietnam, in 1978–9, that triggered a humanitarian response of altogether new proportions where leading journalists and aid workers invoked their own past as refugees; Rupert Neudeck, who launched the "Cap Anamur" – a private aid initiative inspired by French activists – had himself fled Danzig in 1945 as a young child. The culture of compassion proved fragile, however. By the end of 1979, West Germany had taken in thirteen thousand refugees from Indo-China. Less than a year later, most Germans were worrying that "the boat was full" and journalists were warning that the rising number of asylum seekers was creating a dangerous atmosphere of alienation and racism. In 1981, the state governments decided to close their door to any further refugees saved by German ships (Bösch 2017). In 1993, Germany excluded from asylum people reaching the country via her safe neighbours. Eighty-five thousand Roma were deported to Romania that year, notwithstanding persecution there and under the Nazis. The reaction to foreigners has swung between two extremes: private donations, organized charity, and support for asylum has coexisted with right-wing attacks and blaming foreigners for unemployment and a housing crisis (Aziz 1991).

While caring could foster more caring, suffering and receiving aid did not automatically make people more empathic and compassionate towards others in need. This became acutely apparent in the late 1980s when those in need happened to be co-nationals by law: ethnic Germans from the Soviet Union, Poland, and Romania and ethnic Poles who had been German citizens in 1937 (or had ancestors with German citizenship). Between 1988 and 1991, over a million people with German ancestry arrived in the Federal Republic. They did not meet a "welcome culture." "I don't have any sympathy for those people, really," a woman who had fled Lower Silesia after the war said in 1989. "Why do we have to take in so many? ... One should not talk about revenge, but they did not treat us well in those days ... Did we not already leave them all our possessions?" (Lehmann 1991, 178). In her view they were Poles, not fellow German refugees. Others complained that the newcomers were not "real" Germans, because they did not speak German. Faced with a parallel rise in asylum seekers, the government in the early 1990s first introduced restrictions for entry for ethnic Germans, then tightened language requirements, and finally imposed quotas.[2] The fact that many *Verbriebene* from the east had themselves been attacked as "Pollacks" when they reached what remained of Germany at the end of the war did not make them any more understanding towards these new arrivals. As these examples indicate, private morals are connected to public morals: a personal sense of what is right and wrong was coloured by memories of past injustice; collective ideas of the nation, such as the widespread view that German citizenship should be rooted in the German language; and long-standing official proclamations that Germany was not a land of migrants. These were formidable obstacles for empathy and civility, for ethnic Germans from the east as well as for foreigners.

Outlook

The reception and integration of German refugees from the east in post-war Germany is marked by its own historical characteristics, but it can

---

2 In 1993, the Kriegsfolgenbereinigungsgesetz (law dealing with the consequences of the war) limited the number of "Spätaussiedler" to 220,000. In 1999, the quota was lowered to 103,080 (http://www.bpb.de/apuz/156779/spaet-aussiedler-in-deutschland).

also be read to open up questions of wider concern for students of nationalism and civility. This chapter has extended the Hallsian paradigm to consider dynamics located *within* a single ethnic or national group. But the implications of this exercise reach beyond the case of post-war Germany.

The first implication concerns the power of the nation and national identity in the modern world. In much of the literature, nationalism advances with a steadily growing integral force. Often, this integral force is assumed rather than documented. Such an ideal-typical point of view tends to ignore fractures as well as tensions within nations. In times of crisis, such as the Second World War and the post-war years, national bonds could be thinner than presumed. Germans from Danzig or Silesia could not count on fellow feeling and support from people in Schleswig or Bavaria because they were co-nationals. Nationalist and fascist appeals did not automatically translate into collective solidarity. Total war is a great modernizer, but not across the board. While fostering a sense of national endeavour, the Second World War arguably also heightened the attachment to a more bounded, provincial *Heimat*. We know about the significance of "German home towns" from Mack Walker's classic book of that title. National unification, in 1871, and industrial modernity might have changed the role of *Heimat* and homelands, but it did not erase them. The post-war years revealed a tension within nationalism: between loyalty to *Heimat* and loyalty to the larger nation. The regional clash of religious identities weakened the integrative pull of the nation further. After the catastrophic collapse of the Nazis' "*Volksgemeinschaft*," *Heimat* enjoyed a renaissance as a safe zone of identity, celebrated in the mostly nostalgic genre of *Heimat*-movies in the 1950s. The federal state system of the Bonn republic probably reinforced this localism.

The refugee crisis in post-war Germany also raises questions for the popular correlation in the literature on nation-states and social policy between ethnic homogeneity and welfare provision. Such an affinity may well be at play in contemporary Denmark, which is held up as a case in point. But this does not necessarily mean that ethnically homogeneous nations naturally produce more generous welfare services for their citizens. The friction between fellow ethnic Germans after 1945 over basic resources such as housing and water serves as a reminder that there are plenty of identities and interests that can cut across shared ethnic nationality. We need to recall as well just how small and limited state public spending was before the 1960s – 8 per cent of GDP in OECD countries in 1960. For most of the modern period, welfare came in the form of charity and was handed out by voluntary and religious bodies. These were not untouched by nationalism and ethnicity, but they followed their own ideals of solidarity and compassion in addition to that of the nation-state. This level below the nation-state deserves more attention.

A second set of observations concerns the place of morality and civility in accounts of modern society. On the back of the renaissance of civil society in the late 1980s and 1990s, civility has made most of the running and we have learnt a lot about its evolution and the disposition towards living with difference. Such conceptual clarification should not, however, run the risk of empirical isolation. In the eighteenth century, civility was part of a package of moral sensibilities and action that included empathy, the central concern of Adam Smith's *Theory of Moral Sentiment*, as well as compassion and charity. We need to put these moral faculties back into the story. And that means that we need to reconnect mentalities to actions. Civility and solidarity do not go very far if they do not involve caring, giving, and receiving. These have a history. How cultures of compassion and caring (or hatred and revenge) have developed over time in different settings calls for more research. In addition to the ideal of tolerance, we also want to know what civility looked like in practice and see it as moving along a spectrum of different historical outcomes.[3] Its depth and scope vary. As the case of post-war Germany clearly shows, civility was unevenly distributed among regions, groups, and individuals. There can be more or less caring inclusion of some but exclusion of others. Civility is rarely complete.

For civility and empathy to happen, subjects and objects of concern first need to be seen and heard. While compassion and caring are individual experiences and practices, therefore, they also require social imagination and political communication. Morality is political. Accounts of post-war Germany tend to be overshadowed by the question of collective guilt and Germans' denial of it. This is important, but it can easily blind us to the fact that political discourse and mobilization had additional motives. When the German refugees

---

3 One reason for our impoverished understanding of morality in the modern world has been the lop-sided treatment of "moral economy" in social history as a pre-capitalist phenomenon and form of rebellion. For critiques and fresh perspectives, see Fassin (2009) and Trentmann (2007).

portrayed their own victimhood, it was not only to distract from German crimes or their own role in Nazi Germany. It was also aimed at their fellow Germans, to win their empathy and assistance. War and defeat were presented as a shared national destiny calling for shared sacrifice and mutual assistance. We have here an illustration of the politics of recognition that cultivates the terrain of moral attention and care.

REFERENCES

ADE (Archiv für Diakonie und Enwicklung, Berlin). 1946a. ZB 894, Dr. von Freyberg, "Bericht über die VII. Informationsfahrt vom 13–30 November 1946 durch Flüchtlingslager im Rheinland."

– 1946b. ZB 894, Dr. von Freyberg, "Bericht ueber die V. Informationsfahrt durch Fluechtlingslager in Westfalen, Ostfriesland und Oldenburg vom 30. August bis 12. September 1946."

– 1946c. ZB894, "Bericht über eine Informationsfahrt von Vertretern des Evang Hilswerks durch die Flüchtlingslager an der Bayr. Ostgrenze zischem dem 14. und 23. März 1946."

– 1947. ZB 894, von Freyberg, "Bericht über die VIII. Informationsfahrt vom 10.1.1947 bis 19.1.1947 durch Flüchtlingslager in Schleswig-Holstein und Hamburg."

– 1949. Allg. Slg, 503, "Was tun die Deutschen."

– 1957. Allg. Slg 376, Adventsammlung 29 November–12 December 1957.

Apel, Karl. 1950. "Mardorf." In *Die Entstehung eines neuen Volkes aus Binnendeutschen und Ostvertriebenen: Untersuchungen zum Strukturwandel von Land und Leuten unter dem Einfluss des Vertriebenen-Zustromes*, edited by Eugen Lemberg and Lothar Krecker, 152–61. Marburg: N.G. Elwe.

Aziz, N. 1991. "Zur Lage der Nicht-Deutschen in Deutschland." *Aus Politik und Zeitgeschichte* B 9 / 92. 21 February.

Beer, Mathias. 1998. "Im Spannungsfeld von Politik und Zeitgeschichte." *Vierteljahrshefte für Zeitgeschichte* 46: 345–89.

Bjork, James E. 2008. *Neither German nor Pole: Catholicism and National Indifference in a Central European Borderland*. Ann Arbor: University of Michigan Press. https://doi.org/10.3998/mpub.217738.

Boberach, Heinz, ed. 1984. *Meldungen aus dem Reich, 1938–1945: Die geheimen Lageberichte des Sicherheitsdienstes der SS*. Herrsching: Pawlak.

Bohnsack, Else. 1956. *Flüchtlinge und Einheimische in Schleswig-Holstein*. Kiel: Institut fuer Weltwirtschaft.

Bösch, Frank. 2017. "Engagement für Flüchtlinge: Die Aufnahme vietnamesischer "Boat People" in der Bundesrepublik." *Zeithistorische Forschungen* 14: 13–40.

Bundesarchiv (BArch) Koblenz. 1945. Z 18/110: Hirtenschreiben.

– 1946a. Z 18/113: Berichte und Kommentare; anon. c. May 1946: Der Fall Lidice.

– 1946b. Z 18/99. "Heimat der Kirche: Gedanken zur Fastenzeit für unsere Flüchtlinge," edited by Katholische Flüchtlingsdienst (Berlin: n.d. [1946]).

– 1946c. Z 18/101. "Predigt zur Förderung der caritativen Flüchtlingshilfe."

– 1946d. Z 18/96. "Flüchtlingsobleute in Stadt – u. Landkreis Memmingen" to Landesleitung CSU 25 October 1946.

– 1952. B 125/1/fol.1. "Proklamation der Treck-Vereinigung Schleswig-Holstein e.V." February 1952.

Colas, Dominique. 1998. *Civil Society and Fanaticism*. Stanford: Stanford University Press.

EKD. 1945a. *Die Protokolle des Rates der Evangelischen Kirche in Deutschland*, 1, 18–19 October 1945.

– 1945b. *Die Protokolle des Rates der EKD*, Asmussen to Landesbruderrat Schleswig-Holstein, 27 November 1945.

Evans, Richard J. 2005. *The Third Reich in Power, 1933–1939*. New York: Penguin.

Fassin, Didier. 2009. "Les économies morales revisitées." *Annales* 64 (6): 1237–66.

FZH (Forschungsstelle für Zeitgeschichte). 1997. Hamburg, Werkstatt der Erinnerung, WdE 512.

Hall, John A. 1993. "Nationalisms: Classified and Explained." *Daedalus* 122 (3): 1–28.

–, ed. 1995. *Civil Society: Theory, History, Comparison*. Cambridge: Polity.

–, ed. 1998. *The State of the Nation: Ernest Gellner and the Theory of Nationalism*. Cambridge: Cambridge University Press.

– 2013. *The Importance of Being Civil: The Struggle for Political Decency*. Princeton: Princeton University Press.

Jäger, Günter. 1950. "Der Wandel Rotenburgs an der Fulda." In *Die Entstehung eines neuen Volkes aus Binnendeutschen und Ostvertriebenen: Untersuchungen zum Strukturwandel von Land und Leuten unter dem Einfluss des Vertriebenen-Zustromes*, edited by Eugen Lemberg and Lothar Krecker, 83–111. Marburg: N.G. Elwert.

Kossert, Andreas. 2008. *Kalte Heimat: Die Geschichte der deutschen Vertriebenen nach 1945*. Munich: Siedler.

Kurth, Karl O. 1959. "Presse, Film und Rundfunk." In *Die Vertriebenen in Westdeutschland; ihre Eingliederung und ihr Einfluss auf Gesellschaft, Wirtschaft,*

Politik und Geistesleben, edited by Max Boehm, Friedrich Edding, and Eugen Lemberg, 400–421. Kiel: F. Hirt.

Kurz, Karl. 1950. "Der Wandel des Dorfes Gersdorf, Kreis Hersfeld." In *Die Entstehung eines neuen Volkes aus Binnendeutschen und Ostvertriebenen: Untersuchungen zum Strukturwandel von Land und Leuten unter dem Einfluss des Vertriebenen-Zustromes*, edited by Eugen Lemberg and Lothar Krecker, 32–43. Marburg: N.G. Elwert.

Lehmann, Albrecht. 1991. *Im Fremden ungewollt zu Haus: Flüchtlinge und Vertriebene in Westdeutschland, 1945–1990*. Munich: Beck.

Mitteilungen aus dem Hilfswerk. 1947. Newsletter. Evangelisches Verlagswerk, Stuttgart.

– 1953. Newsletter. Evangelisches Verlagswerk, Stuttgart.

Nellner, Werner. 1959. "Grundlagen und Hauptergebnisse der Statistik." In *Die Vertriebenen in Westdeutschland*. Vol. 1, *Ihre Eingliederung und ihr Einfluss auf Gesellschaft, Wirtschaft, Politik und Geistesleben*, edited by Eugen Lemberg and Friedrich Edding, 61–144. Kiel: F. Hirt.

Pfeil, Elizabeth von. 1951. *Fünf Jahre später: die Eingliederung der Heimatvertriebenen in Bayern bis 1950*. Frankfurt am Main: Metzner.

Pfeil, Elizabeth von, and Ernst Wolfgang Buchholz. 1958. *Eingliederungschancen und Eingliederungserfolge*. Bad Godesberg: Bundesforschungsanstalt fuer Landeskunde und Raumordnung.

Pohl, Karin. 2009. *Zwischen Integration und Isolation: zur Kulturellen Dimension der Vertriebenenpolitik in Bayern (1945–1975)*. Munich: Iudicium.

Reinisch, Jessica. 2013. *The Perils of Peace: The Public Health Crisis in Occupied Germany*. Oxford: Oxford University Press. https://doi.org/10.1093/acprof:oso/9780199660797.001.0001.

Schieder, Theodor. 1951–61. *Dokumentation der Vertreibung der Deutschen aus Ost-Mitteleuropa*. Bonn: Bundesministerium für Vertriebene.

Scholz, Stephan. 2015. *Vertriebenendenkmäler: Topographie einer Deutschen Erinnerungslandschaft*. Paderborn: Ferdinand Schöningh.

Schulze, Rainer, ed. 2001. *Zwischen Heimat und Zuhause: Deutsche Flüchtlinge und Vertriebene in (West-) Deutschland 1945–2000*. Osnabrück: Secolo.

Sen, Amartya. 1999. *Development as Freedom*. Oxford: Oxford University Press.

Steinert, Johannes D. 2007. *Nach Holocaust und Zwangsarbeit: Britische humanitäre Hilfe in Deutschland; Die Helfer, die Befreiten und die Deutschen*. Osnabrück: Secolo.

Stoddard, Lothrop. 1940. *Into the Darkness: Nazi Germany Today*. New York: Duell, Sloan & Pearce.

Tennstedt, Florian. 1987. "Wohltat und Interesse. Das Winterhilfswerk des Deutschen Volkes: Die Weimarer Vorgeschichte und ihre Instrumentalisierung durch das NS-Regime." *Geschichte und Gesellschaft (Vandenhoeck & Ruprecht)* 13: 157–80.

Trentmann, Frank. 2007. "Before 'Fair Trade': Empire, Free Trade, and the Moral Economies of Food in the Modern World." *Environment and Planning D: Society & Space* 25 (6): 1079–1102. https://doi.org/10.1068/d448t.

van Rahden, Till. 2017. "Sanfte Vaterschaft und Demokratie in der frühen Bundesrepublik." In *Männer mit "Makel": Männlichkeiten und gesellschaftlicher Wandel in der frühen Bundesrepublik*, edited by Bernhard Gotto and Elke Seefried, 142–56. Berlin: de Gruyter.

Volk, Kurt. 1950. "Allendorf, Kreis Marburg." In *Die Entstehung eines neuen Volkes aus Binnendeutschen und Ostvertriebenen: Untersuchungen zum Strukturwandel von Land und Leuten unter dem Einfluss des Vertriebenen-Zustromes*, edited by Eugene Lemberg and Lothar Krecker, 133–42. Marburg: N. G. Elwert.

Zentralbüro des Hilfswerks, ed. 1955. *Dank und Verpflichtung: 10 Jahre Hilfswerk der Evangelischen Kirchen in Deutschland*. Stuttgart: Evangelisches Verlags-Werk.

PART TWO

International and Comparative Contexts

6 Nationalism and Imperialism as Enemies and Friends: Nation-State Formation and Imperial Projects in the Balkans

SINIŠA MALEŠEVIĆ

Traditional historical accounts tend to view nationalism and imperialism as two mutually exclusive phenomena: whereas imperialism is seen as an ideology centred on extending a polity's power through the use of coercion, violence, and colonization, nationalism is often identified with the popular aspiration to establish a sovereign and independent nation-state. The Hallsian perspective challenges such a simple dichotomy by describing many forms of late imperialisms as being fully compatible with nationalist projects. More specifically, Hall argues that unlike the early capstone empires, which had neither the organizational means nor the interest needed to penetrate the societies under their control, the nineteenth-century modernizing empires managed to increase their power by penetrating their societies and nationalizing their polities. As he puts it, "the power could be increased by nationalizing one's empire, increasing force through coherence" (Hall and Malešević 2013, 17).

This chapter extends Hall's analysis by looking at the other side of this relationship: how nation-states deployed imperial and quasi-imperial designs to boost their nationalist legitimacy at home and power prestige abroad. In this context I explore the historical dynamics of nationalism and imperialism in the nineteenth-century and early twentieth-century Balkans. In particular, I compare and contrast the Serbian and Bulgarian nationalist and quasi-imperial projects. I look at how they both used discourses and legacies of their respective medieval empires of Tsar Dušan (Serbia) and Simeon the Great (Bulgaria). I also explore the contradictions and paradoxes involved in the attempts to reconcile the national and the imperial during the project of nation-state formation – something that other contributors to this volume, such as Luyang Zhou, also consider.

Nation-States and Empires: The Clash of Ideologies?

In the contemporary political discourse, the term "empire" is largely used in a pejorative sense. No rulers, apart from the Japanese emperor, employ this term to describe their polities. Instead this label is mostly deployed to discredit a country's foreign policy. Hence American and Russian use of force abroad is regularly described as imperial in the sense that it infringes upon the Charter of the United Nations, which explicitly states that its members are not allowed to use force "against the territorial integrity or political independence of any state" (article 2). In sharp contrast, a "nation-state" is nearly universally regarded as a legitimate mode of territorial rule. This view is grounded in the idea that such polities represent a political expression of what is regarded to be the dominant and natural form of group identity – nationhood. Although the international community might object to attempts to carve out new nation-states in the territories of existing polities, the ideological motivation behind such an ambition is likely to be regarded as legitimate. In other words, the powerful states might protest or even intervene against nationalist movements, but they would seldom question the central principles underpinning the existence of such movements, as their own states are built on the same ideological tenets.

Obviously this clear-cut distinction between an empire and a nation-state reflects the times we live in, in which the nation-state is not only the dominant form of state organization but also perceived to be the sole legitimate mode of territorial rule (Malešević 2013). In this widely shared understanding, an empire and a nation-state stand for the two mutually exclusive models of polity. While empires are conceived to epitomize the politics of incessant territorial conquest and wars, social hierarchies, exploitation, and inequality, the nation-state model is perceived to stand for political equality, peaceful resolution of conflicts, individual freedoms, and the preservation of national identities (Meyer at al. 1997; Parsons 1977). This traditional view, which sharply separates these two forms of polity, has recently been questioned by several historical sociologists, historians, and political scientists who aim to show how empires and nation-states have more in common than has been recognized. For example, Kumar (2010, 119) argues that "empires and nation-states may in fact best be thought of as alternative political projects, both of which are available for elites to pursue depending on the circumstances of the moment." In a similar way, Münkler (2007) sees these two models of statehood as highly compatible. Exploring their dynamics in the modern era, he maintains that "there remains only a complementary, not an alternative, relation between the two types of border: imperial structures are superimposed on the state order, but they no longer replace it" (6).

In particular, these studies challenge the conventional quasi-evolutionary understanding whereby the nation-state model was destined to replace the imperial orders. Instead they indicate that the imperial structures are much more durable and resistant, leaving open the possibility of their periodic re-emergence in the near future. As Burbank and Cooper (2010) argue and document, neither empires nor nation-states operate as fixed and mutually exclusive entities. Instead, they are characterized by sovereignty that is "shared out, layered, overlapping." They emphasize that nation-states and empires are variable political forms capable of developing "multiple ways in which incorporation and difference were conjugated" (16–17). One strand of new scholarship attempts to show that the imperial model of organization has never been fully displaced by the nation-state, but instead has metamorphosed into novel forms of governance. Thus, some argue that nominal nation-states such as the United States, China, Russia, or even the European Union are in fact empires or hybrid forms such as "nation-empires," "continental empires," or "incoherent empires" (Mann 2003; Münkler 2007; Zielonka 2006). More radical accounts claim that the contemporary world is witnessing a transition from conventional nation-state-centred imperialism towards "empire," which they see as a novel system "configured *ab initio* as a dynamic and flexible systemic structure" enveloping the entire globe (Hardt and Negri 2001, 13).

These emerging critiques of the traditional dichotomous view are quite persuasive and illuminating. However, their focus has largely been on the form of the polity and less on the ideological projects that sustain such political orders. In other words, while they tell us a great deal about the structural or economic organization of the two polity models, they have less to say about the differences and similarities between the ideological doctrines that underpin these projects: imperialism and nationalism.

It is here that the Hallsian perspective provides a clear way forward. While Hall (2017) also shares the view that empires and nation-states have more in common than is usually thought, he also explores the socio-historical sources of this commonality. For Hall not all imperial orders are alike, and the ideological compatibility is only possible in polities that attain a substantial degree of organizational development.

More specifically, he distinguishes between the pre-modern, capstone-type imperial orders and the modernizing empires. The central feature of the capstone empires, such as those of ancient China, Egypt, or the Roman world, is that the rulers controlled vast territories, populations, and resources but had no organizational means to penetrate fully the societies they nominally controlled. By "capstone" Hall means a form of imperial state organization where the "elite sat atop a series of separate 'societies,' which it did not wish to penetrate or mobilize; perhaps the key to its behaviour was its fear that horizontal linkages it could not see would get out of control." Hence such governments were not concerned with "intensifying social relationships" but primarily with "seeking to prevent any linkages which might diminish [their] power" (Hall 1985, 52). Since capstone imperial orders did not possess organizational means to penetrate their social order, they had to rely on the local notables, whom they generally distrusted. In such an environment there was no organizational room to develop society-wide ideological doctrine capable of homogenizing the social order. Although all pre-modern empires were built around specific proto-ideological doctrines such as Confucianism in ancient China or the civilizing ethics of the late Roman Empire, the capstone character of such polities worked against society-wide normative homogenization. In other words, such imperial orders were defined by deep cultural divides, with the small, often court-based elite partaking in "high" literate culture and the illiterate peasantry immersed in local, kinship-based cultural traditions. In this context imperialism was by and large an ideological project of the elite centre, something that for the most part had no resonance with the rest of the society.

In contrast to these capstone systems, the modernizing empires of the eighteenth and nineteenth centuries were significantly better integrated. There is no doubt that these were still highly hierarchical orders characterized by deep social inequalities, narrow levels of political representation, and the general lack of wider social rights. Nevertheless these modernizing empires possessed relatively advanced organizational structures that allowed for greater social penetration. In line with the arguments made by Sombart (1913), Tilly (1992), and Mann (1986), Hall (1988) contends that the intensified interstate warfare in early modern Europe stimulated the development of autonomous and viable state infrastructures. Moreover, Hall (1985, 1988) argues that the sudden and dramatic rise of western European empires in the seventeenth, eighteenth, and nineteenth centuries owes a great deal to the multipolarity of the medieval European order, where no ruler was strong enough to establish a unified European empire. As the political and ideological powers were split between the Catholic Church in Rome on the one hand and the numerous small kingdoms on the other hand, this unusual geopolitical environment ultimately stimulated the rise of autonomous towns, and of banking and trading centres that later proved highly instrumental in the rise of capitalism, state bureaucracy, and civil society. This rather different historical trajectory of Europe as against the rest of the world meant that the European imperial dynamics incorporated many organizational elements that were less present elsewhere. Hence the leading eighteenth- and nineteenth-century empires such as the British, French, or Dutch had no resemblance to the capstone model of imperial order. Instead, the rulers of such empires were eager to utilize technological and organizational advances and develop better communication and transport systems. They were also interested in finding ways to incorporate their populations within the state structure. Although these imperial orders intended to retain the existing hierarchical structures, it soon became apparent that further territorial expansion, including the ongoing acquisition of colonies, entailed the simultaneous extension of some citizenship rights to the non-aristocratic groupings. Hence it is no coincidence that the British, French, and Dutch colonial expansion abroad often went hand in hand with the gradual concession of religious, political, and economic rights to various social strata at home. As these processes unfolded over time, large sectors of the population became better integrated into the imperial project. Thus many members of the middle class and of even lower social strata were employed by the imperial state throughout the globe as administrators, traders, workers, teachers, soldiers, policemen, nurses, and so on. Furthermore, with the expansion of citizenship rights, the growth of literacy rates, and the rise of civil society, imperialism became gradually challenged by other ideological discourses – from liberalism, socialism, and anarchism to nationalism.

The rise of nationalism in particular has generally been regarded as the most serious threat to the imperial projects. For example, Hiers and Wimmer (2013) argue that the proliferation of nationalist movements in the late eighteenth, nineteenth, and early twentieth centuries was the main cause of imperial downfall. Analysing the historical experience of the Ottoman, Habsburg, French, British, Portuguese, and even Soviet imperial projects, they argue that "in all cases of imperial collapse nationalist movements played an important, and sometimes, crucial role" and conclude that "the rise and global proliferation of nationalist movements has been a crucial factor in reshaping the structure of the state system over the past two hundred years" (212–13). Hall is more cautious about this relationship between nationalism and imperialism. While accepting the view that from the nineteenth century onward nationalism becomes a dominant ideological matrix for the legitimization of state rule, he does not see these two ideological doctrines as necessarily being on a collision course. Instead, for him, modernizing empires differ from their capstone predecessors in that they possess organizational means and ideological know-how to accommodate both the imperial creeds and the nationalist practices. Such empires differ from their capstone predecessors in two important ways: (1) while the pre-modern empires did not recognize rivals and proclaimed their ambition to conquer the whole world, the modernizing empires accepted a world of multiple empires; and (2) whereas the capstone orders were culturally heterogeneous and had neither the means nor aspiration to create culturally uniform polities, the nineteenth-century empires engaged gradually in the process of cultural homogenization. As Hall (2013, 227) emphasizes, previously "nationalism and imperialism were separated from each other, making any notion of intimacy between them ridiculous"; modernizing imperial states were different in the sense that they aspired to become nation-states, and in so doing "they attempted to homogenize different peoples into a singular identity." This process in part reflected the dominant ideological shifts in the world but also, for Hall, the fact that the imperial rulers realized they could increase power by nationalizing their empires, "increasing force through coherence" (Hall and Malešević 2013, 17). In this way, the imperial polities could on the one hand stifle the rise of competing nationalist and other social movements and on the other hand could also attain a greater degree of political legitimacy.

However, this attempt to nationalize the empire was neither smooth nor uncontested. Rather, all modernizing empires were stretched between the ambition to preserve their territorial conquests and to increase the cultural homogeneity of their populations. In this context Hall (2013, 229) differentiates between the traditional agrarian empires and the overseas trading polities, arguing that the former were able to nationalize deeper and faster than the latter. Thus, unlike the Ottomans, Romanovs, and Habsburgs, who all expanded as composite imperial orders directly incorporating diverse populations and their territories within the empire itself, the British and French maintained geographical and political distinctions between the inner-core territories and the overseas possessions. This distinct historical legacy was critical for any attempt to model the imperial order. While the French, British, and Dutch polities could embark on the gradual nationalization of their core territories, this process was beset with enormous organizational difficulties and ideological tension in the agrarian composite empires. For example, the Ottoman and Habsburg attempts to nationalize the empire instantly generated a nationalist backlash from movements representing the cultural diversity of the empire. In this situation, nationalization from the centre often tended to create "national movements where none existed before" (Hall 2013, 230), which ultimately weakened the social cohesion of the empire and threatened the very existence of such polities. In contrast, the British or French empires could pursue nationalization at home while still maintaining imperial possessions abroad. Although this situation was also beset with tensions and periodic conflicts (such were the cases of Ireland and Algeria, to name only two), this model lasted until the mid-twentieth century. Hence, for Hall, the modernizing oversees trading empires were quite capable of combining imperialism and nationalism.

The Hallsian perspective offers a nuanced understanding of the multifaceted relationship between the imperial and national. Hall shows convincingly how and why modernizing empires can utilize nationalist ideas and practices. However, I argue that the Hallsian perspective can be extended further to explore the other side of this complex relationship. In other words, my aim here is to show that the imperial states are not the only ones trapped in this ideological ambiguity of the national and the imperial. The elements of this ideological cacophony were just as present in some polities traditionally seen as the epitome of a small nation-state. In this chapter I analyse how the nineteenth- and early twentieth-century Balkan states combined nationalism and imperialism to increase their political legitimacy and international prestige. As this was not a uniform process across the region, I zoom in on the different experiences of Bulgaria and Serbia.

Nationalism and Imperialism in the Balkans

Scholars of nationalism regularly identify the Balkans together with Latin America as the cradle of early nationalist movements (Anderson 2006; Kedourie 1993; Minogue 1996; Mouzelis 2007). For example, Wilson (1970, 28) describes the First Serbian Uprising (1804) as "the first of the great nationalistic movements of the nineteenth century," while Minogue (1996, 120) insists that in the Greek case "nationalism long precedes the coming of industrialism." Similarly, Anderson (2006, 49–55) argues that nationalism originated in the New World as "the Creole pioneers" resisted the European imperial order. However, more recent scholarship is highly sceptical of such assessments (Biondich 2011; Centeno 2002; Malešević 2012a, 2012b; Roudometof 2001). For example, Centeno (2002, 25) argues that the early nineteenth-century Latin American "wars of independence" had little to do with nationalism and much more with imperial decline: "the wars of independence produced fragments of empire, but not new states. There was little economic or political logic to the frontiers as institutionalized in the 1820s … the new countries were essentially mini-empires with all the weaknesses of such political entities." In a similar way, I have tried to show how the early nineteenth-century Balkan uprisings were not driven by coherent nationalist agendas but emerged as an unintended consequence of pronounced social unrest coupled with wider geopolitical changes (Malešević 2012a, 2012b). The central aim of this new scholarship is to show that one should not take pronouncements of nineteenth-century national ideologues and political and cultural elites at face value and simply assume that they reflect popular sentiments. Instead, by looking at the organizational dynamics and the level of society-wide ideological penetration of nationalist ideas and practices, one can demonstrate that this ideology develops quite late in both regions. Most Latin American countries, to use Centeno's (2002) description, remained mini-empires in the sense that only a small number of people, descendants of white settlers residing in large cities, identified with the new states.

Despite their different colonial history, the nineteenth- and early twentieth-century Balkans exhibited a similar pattern of deep divide between the minority – the largely urban population – who were the principal proponents of nationalist ideas and the large, mostly peasant majority generally indifferent towards nationalism. In this context the conventional narratives of popular revolts against the decaying imperial order bear no resemblance to the historical reality. Rather than leading us to see the emergence of independent Serbia, Bulgaria, or Greece as the product of strong nationalist movements rebelling against the Ottomans, the evidence points to the conclusion that such movements were weak and marginal and that nationalism largely developed after independence (Malešević 2012a, 2017; Roudometof 2001). Moreover, in these conventional narratives nationalism and imperialism are ordinarily depicted as mutually exclusive ideological projects.

Hence, the traditional historiography is almost exclusively focused on contrasting Serbian and Bulgarian nationalisms with the Ottoman, and later also Habsburg, imperial creeds. Nevertheless, Hall's (2013) argument about the interdependence of imperialism and nationalism in this period also resonates quite well in the context of small Balkan polities. This is not to say that the imperial and nationalist discourses deployed in nineteenth-century Britain or France are similar in any way to those used in Bulgaria or Serbia. Obviously the imperial powers, as Hall (2013) rightly argues, were eager to nationalize their polities in order to increase force through coherence. In contrast, the new nation-states such as Serbia and Bulgaria were built around the emerging international principles that delegitimized the Ottoman's imperial dominance over their territories. In some respects, while the embrace of nationalism by the great imperial powers was a reluctant strategy for their long-term survival, the reliance on nationalist idioms was the cornerstone of Serbia's and Bulgaria's existence. However, the historical reality has proved to be much messier. Although both Bulgaria's and Serbia's political elites invested enormous economic, political, and ideological resources to build their polities as fully fledged nation-states, they also drew extensively on imperial rhetoric and practice. Hence, rather than incessantly opposing the imperial model of governance, the new states often blended nationalist with imperial discourses and practices. For one thing, both states strongly emphasized their deep historical roots, often invoking imperial legacies to legitimize their new polities. For another, the new Balkan rulers attempted to model their states on the existing European polities, many of which remained deeply imperial in their structure and organization.

Bulgaria

In the Bulgarian case this imperial legacy encompasses the early medieval states that were regularly depicted as the cradle of Bulgarian culture: the First and Second Bulgarian Empires, which are understood to provide the foundation for modern-day Bulgaria. Although the First Bulgarian Empire (seventh to eleventh century) was established by the non-Slavic Bulgar tribes, it gradually incorporated various local groups, eventually becoming a slavicized polity. The nineteenth-century dominant discourses centred on the "unbroken continuity" between the First and Second Empires and contemporary Bulgaria. This rhetoric was focused in particular on the expansion of the state's territory under several notable rulers (including Krum, Boris I, Simeon the Great, and Ivan

Assen II, among others), the Christianization of the population, the development of the first written codes of law, the establishment of the semi-autonomous Bulgarian Eastern Orthodox Church, and adoption of the Cyrillic alphabet (Fine 1991, 94–201). In this narrative the reign of Simeon the Great (893 to 927) was accorded a special place. Many of the nineteenth-century and even some early twentieth-century state formation discourses were framed as attempts to resurrect Simeon's empire in the modern guise. In this period Simeon the Great was celebrated as the ruler who defeated the mighty Byzantine Empire and the always threatening Magyars and Serbs.

Under his rule the Bulgarian state attained the greatest territorial expansion in its history. This period has also been generally regarded as the era of cultural advancement and economic growth. The emphasis was regularly placed on gaining independence for the Bulgarian Orthodox Church and Simeon's support for cultural activities, such as translations of Christian literature in Slavic idioms (with the newly created Cyrillic script as well as the slightly older Glagolic script). Prominent intellectuals, politicians, and military leaders were inspired by the idea of reviving the glories of the medieval empire, employing such slogans as "back to Simeon the Great" (Daskalov 2005, 230). During the early and middle nineteenth century, when Bulgaria was still part of the Ottoman empire, such references to the golden age of Tsar Simeon were for the most part confined to a very small circle of intellectuals, political activists, and other professionals, many of whom were educated abroad. Their intention was to invoke the legacy of the medieval empire in order to justify establishment of an independent state. Initially there was no clear blueprint of what the new polity was to look like, with some advocating a pan-Slavic entity under the protectorate of the Romanovs, others envisaging a quasi-federal Orthodox Christian Balkan empire, and yet others advocating the creation of a sovereign Bulgarian state (Roudometof 2001). Nevertheless, the main focus was on delegitimizing the Ottoman rulers while simultaneously justifying the need for a new Balkan territorial order. In this context the references to the medieval Christian and Slavic empire were used to emphasize the cultural difference vis-à-vis the Ottoman Muslim and non-Slavic empire. Hence, rather than calling upon the principles of "national freedom," as the later-day nationalist historiographies tend to dramatically overplay, the early activists often used the imperial legacy of the past to challenge the imperial rule of the present.

With the establishment of a semi-independent Bulgaria in 1878, the medieval imperial legacy was largely deployed to uphold the nationalist project. Hence the political, military, and cultural elites constructed, institutionalized, and reproduced the narratives of ancient glories in the educational system, mass media, and public sphere in order to mould the majority peasant population into nationally conscious Bulgarians. This process was intensified after Bulgaria gained full independence in 1908 and reached its peak during the Balkan wars of 1912–13. During this period Bulgarian nationalists largely focused on the legacy of the 1878 Treaty of San Stefano. Under this preliminary agreement between the Russian and Ottoman governments, Bulgaria was recognized as an autonomous principality encompassing large territory in the Balkans. However, the 1878 Berlin Treaty quickly revised these territorial gains and made the new Bulgarian polity much smaller.

This decision of the Great Powers infuriated generations of Bulgarian nationalists, who continued to hail the San Stefano agreement as the only fair solution to the Bulgarian national question while perceiving the Berlin Treaty as deeply unjust towards the Bulgarians. As Hranova (2011) and Dimitrova and Kaytchev (1998) demonstrate, the education system was highly instrumental in voicing this deep discontent. The late nineteenth and early twentieth-century school textbooks lament how "unfair" the Berlin Treaty was, like "a knife which cut up the Fatherland into five pieces" (Bobchev 1881, 289 as cited in Dimitrova and Kaytchev 1998, 54). This narrative emphasizes the moral failings of the Great Powers, insisting that their unjust decision partitioned the Bulgarian nation, thus "lacerating living parts off the people's body" (Dimitrova 2003, 58). Leading textbook writers such as Nikola Stanev were adamant that both the Berlin Treaty and the Second Balkan War were unnatural as they did not allow for the proper unification of the entire nation. Instead, the outcome of these events, in his view, was "the figure of Motherland crying for scattered children (Thrace, Macedonia, Dobrudzha)" (Dimitrova 2003, 58). Although most scholars tend to focus on the nationalist content of such narratives, what is equally important is the parallel invocation of the medieval imperial legacies. For example, a number of highly influential novels and popular books published in the late nineteenth and early twentieth centuries draw explicit links between modern Bulgaria within its "natural" San Stefano borders and its medieval counterparts. Hence geography and history textbooks tended to reproduce images of Greater Bulgaria that incorporate the medieval and the San Stefano treaty maps while directly linking the ancient and contemporary rulers (Hranova 2011, 37). One such textbook proclaims King Simeon the Great as motivated by exactly the same ambition that drove contemporary nationalist Bulgarians – to unite the nation "on three seas":

> Now the whole Bulgarian nation, which inhabits almost the whole Balkan Peninsula, was united for the first time in one state, under the rule of one king's will [Simeon I]; now it made up one whole, towards which all our kings aspired and towards which we, too, aspire now. (Ganchev 1888, 24 as cited in Hranova 2011, 37–8)

In a similar way, the novels of the early twentieth century tended to depict medieval rulers as contemporaries motivated by the same goals of national unification. For example, the highly popular writer Fani Popova-Mutafova's 1938 novel *Ivan Assen* was set in the thirteenth century where the main protagonist, emperor Ivan Assen II, is portrayed as a nationally conscious Bulgarian bent on liberating his homeland:

> God Himself had marked the boundaries of this blessed land: the three seas and the wide white river ... from the throne of Holy Sofia, one will would guide the flowering of the great kingdom: the will of the Bulgarian king ... And there was no one other than the Bulgarian king who could unite, rally around his throne, weld into one, the rebellious, eternally warring nations. (Popova-Mutafova 1938, 20–1 as cited in Hranova 2011, 37)

The same idea of "unbroken continuity" with the imperial past was echoed by historians such as Yordan Venedikov, whose 1918 book was based on this very premise: "By a strange coincidence imposed by the inexorable laws of international life, today we are fighting in the same places, against almost the same enemies, and for the same goals for which our ancestors fought under the House of Assen" (Venedikov 1918, 1 as cited in Hranova 2011, 38).

Most of these narratives follow a standard nationalist template where there is no distinction between the medieval imperial polities and the contemporary nation-states. In these popular accounts the emperors, such as Simeon the Great or Ivan Assen II, do not differ much from the modern nationalist figures. Thus, instead of acknowledging sharp feudal hierarchies where such overlords had no interest in peasant masses, the novels and textbooks present them as modern individuals driven by the ideology of nationalism. Nevertheless, while nationalism is the driving force of these historical portrayals, what is also important in these narratives, but rarely acknowledged, is the centrality of imperial legacy. Political sovereignty and territorial unification are not deduced only from the popular will of the Bulgarian populace, but also from the historically rooted claims of previous imperial glory. Hence, when various nationalists invoke the indivisibility of Bulgaria "on three seas" they regularly also invoke the imperial legacy of the "three ancient provinces" – Moesia, Thrace, and Macedonia.

In addition, the persistent references to the medieval empire were used to depict the new independent polity as an equal among the well-established European states. In this context, and especially in the early years, the focus was less on creating a nation-state than on providing a structural framework for the existence of an independent and viable polity. Hence, to achieve international recognition and support from the Great Powers, the semi-independent Bulgaria accepted Alexander of Battenberg as its first legitimate ruler. This practice, quite common in the late nineteenth-century Balkans, of appointing a foreign aristocrat as a head of the new state had very little to do with nationalist ideology and was much closer to the imperial conventions of the *ancien régime*. When Alexander abdicated in 1887, he was replaced by another foreign-born aristocrat, Ferdinand Maximilian Karl Leopold Maria of Saxe-Coburg and Gotha, who remained in power until 1918. The new ruler maintained his Catholic religion, and so the Bulgarian Orthodox Church was deeply opposed to his ascent to the throne. To enhance his claim to the throne, Ferdinand I in 1908 took the title "Tsar of the Bulgarians," which was traditionally associated with Simeon I, by this imitation hoping to appease church leaders.

The persistent references to old imperial legacies were particularly pronounced during the 1912–13 Balkan wars, when Ferdinand often referred to Bulgaria as the seventh Great Power in Europe. During the First Balkan War (1912), when Bulgaria fought the Ottoman Empire, Ferdinand often framed his country's war aims in terms of the re-creation of the new empire ("new Byzantium") and defined the war effort as "a just, great and sacred struggle of the Cross against the Crescent" (Aronson 1986, 86–7). As Crampton (2007, 149) notes, Ferdinand "was to dream in 1912 of a triumphal coronation in Constantinople" where he imagined himself as an heir to Byzantine emperors.

Furthermore, in order to boost its international status, the new state adopted models of political and economic organization from the Western European polities. In this process it often introduced many imperial features into its state structure, from the military to foreign affairs to education and civil service. For example, its 1879 Tarnovo constitution was largely modelled on the 1831 monarchist Belgian constitution. Since Ferdinand tightly controlled the ministries of foreign affairs and war, he was in a position to impose an imperial imprint on the military and foreign affairs offices (Crampton 2007, 149). The imperial imagery was also present in the mass media, which often glorified the new state and its rulers as modern-day Byzantines.

Serbia

Serbia gained independence from Ottoman rule much earlier than Bulgaria, and in this sense is often perceived as the pioneer of early nationalism. For example, the First Serbian Uprising (1804–13) has traditionally been interpreted as one of the earliest cases of a very successful nationalist movement. However, as I have argued elsewhere, this and the subsequent early nineteenth-century Serbian uprisings were mostly social rebellions focused on local concerns that eventually tapped into the broader geopolitical transformations of the region (Malešević 2012a). Hence neither the leaders of these rebellions nor the ordinary population involved were significantly motivated by nationalist ideology. While the majority of the population consisted of illiterate peasants who had no conception of what the nation was, leaders such as Đorđe Petrović (known as Karađorđe) and particularly Miloš Obrenović were largely motivated by personal ambition: a quest for political control and the possibility of expanding their pork trade business with the Austrians (Malešević 2012a, 48; Meriage 1977). Obviously the pronounced religious differences with the Ottoman rulers played an important role in mobilizing the peasantry to resist the local janissaries, but in the early nineteenth century such differences still did not have any nationalist resonance. Even the leaders of these uprisings insisted that they fought renegade ayans and janissaries aiming to "restore the order on behalf of the Sultan" in Istanbul (Roudometof 2001, 231). And when Obrenović became the head of the Principality of Serbia in 1830 he continued to dress as an Ottoman aristocrat (Pavlowitch 1981). Hence it seems that the imperial ethos still dominated early nineteenth-century Serbian politics.

Although nationalist ideas gained influence once Serbia became a fully independent polity in 1867, this did not mean that the imperial rhetoric disappeared. On the contrary, just as in the Bulgarian case, the imperial discourses and practices were deployed extensively to increase domestic and international legitimacy. Like their Bulgarian counterparts, the Serbian rulers invoked the legacies of the medieval Serbian empires. Hence the mass media, educational system, and public sphere all glorified the early polities of Serbs stretching from the ninth-century First Serbian Principality under the Vlastimirović dynasty to the tenth- and eleventh-century grand principality of Raška under the Vukanović dynasty, which was followed by the kingdom of Serbia under the Nemanjić dynasty established in 1217. The Nemanjićs were particularly praised for founding an independent Serbian Orthodox Church in 1219 when King Stefan's brother Rastko (Sava) was ordained as the first archbishop. Most of the focus in the late nineteenth century, however, was firmly directed to the legacies of the Serbian Empire under Tsar Stefan Uroš IV Dušan (1346–55).

This emperor, often called Dušan the Mighty, has been credited with creating a large empire that incorporated much of the present-day Balkan Peninsula. He was generally perceived as one of the most powerful European rulers of his time, capable, like Simeon the Great, of challenging the power and legitimacy of the Byzantine Empire. Dušan was also celebrated for implementing the empire's first constitutional program (i.e., the Dušan code), which consisted of a complex set of laws that regulated most segments of life in the empire. He also supported the Serbian Orthodox Church, which during his rule acquired a Patriarchate, and promoted the cultural and economic development most notable for building many large monasteries (Fine 1991). This image of the powerful and enlightened ruler has been reproduced through the folk poetry that was very popular in Serbia during Ottoman times. However, with the establishment of an independent Serbian state in the mid-nineteenth century, Dušan's empire acquired an exalted place in the public sphere: this period saw a firm focus on celebrating medieval glories and formulating projects that in one way or another were devised as a resurrection of Dušan's empire.

The early plans involved maps of a Greater Serbian state that would encompass all lands where Serbs were assumed to constitute the majority of the population: Franjo Zach's plan from 1843 and the 1844 *Načertanije* of Ilija Garašanin, Serbia's interior minister and later prime minister. Garašanin's plan was particularly influential, as its stated aim was not to "limit Serbia to her present borders, but [to] endeavour to absorb all the Serbian people around her" (Cohen and Riesman 1996, 3). Although this clearly was an idea driven by nationalist aspiration, the reality of mid- and late nineteenth-century Serbia was much more complex, as it blended this nationalism with strong imperial idioms. As in the Bulgarian case, the emphasis was on legitimizing the very existence of an independent state. To this end the medieval imperial legacy was deployed to challenge the Ottoman's, and to some extent later also the Habsburg's, right to rule Serbian lands. Like the Bulgarian new rulers, the Serbian political elite made much of the Christian Orthodox and Slavic roots of their imperial past. Rather than relying solely on revolutionary nationalist rhetoric and practice, which could have been challenged by the still-imperial Great Powers, these rulers were intent on demonstrating unbroken continuity between Dušan's empire and the new state. Both the Serbian and Bulgarian governments were initially keen to downplay nationalist rhetoric and accentuate their imperial heritage.

Although the two states shared much in terms of external legitimacy, there were some noticeable differences in how political legitimacy was attained domestically. For one thing, unlike Bulgaria, which became ruled by a foreign monarch, an independent Serbia was governed by the local rulers. This difference originates in the fact that Serbia's road towards independence started much earlier and was shaped by several successful uprisings, which forced the Ottomans to gradually negotiate more and more autonomy for Serbia's new rulers. Although Karađorđe and Obrenović were initially envisaged as temporary leaders in charge of autonomous, but still Ottoman, provinces, they eventually established themselves as the lawful rulers. For another thing, as Serbia did not have its own aristocrats, most of whom were killed during the Ottoman period, the new rulers created their own royal, and mutually competing, dynasties. Hence the head of the First Serbian uprising, Đorđe Petrović Karađorđe, became "Grand Leader of Serbia" (*Veliki Vožd*), and his descendants embraced the royal titles (princes and kings). Their right to rule was consistently challenged by the progeny of Miloš Obrenović, who led the Second Serbian Uprising and on that basis also became the Grand Leader of Serbia. Obrenović, who was responsible for Karađorđe's death, was later enthroned as the first prince of Serbia. The fact that both of these newly established royal houses stemmed from commoners and thus could have been perceived as deeply illegitimate fostered very different internal dynamics in Serbia as compared to Bulgaria. Whereas in the Bulgarian situation internal legitimacy was tied in part to the legacy of the medieval rulers and in part to "imported" European nobility, in Serbia both dynasties were engaged in fierce conflict and expended enormous effort to delegitimize each other (Malešević 2017). Each was eager to prove its imperial credentials by invoking imagined and fabricated links with the Serbian medieval nobility while simultaneously denouncing its rival claimants. In this way the imperial discourse and corresponding rituals became a cornerstone of the state's legitimation practices.

This is not to say that nationalism was irrelevant as a mode of political communication and rule justification. On the contrary, precisely because Serbia had such weak imperial foundations, nationalism was regularly deployed to sustain the competing claims to rule. Rather than acting as inherent ideological enemies in late nineteenth-century Serbia, then, imperialism and nationalism were often best of friends. The two competing royal houses, to enhance their domestic and international legitimacy, frequently employed both imperial and nationalist rhetorics; both royal houses invested heavily in establishing their aristocratic origins while also utilizing nationalist ideology in an attempt to gain domestic popular support. Both the Karađorđevićs and Obrenovićs courted European royals and had their sons and daughters married to the members of European royal families. Once independence was granted, the focus moved to the Habsburgs, and the two royal houses built alliances with the Austrian rulers. Later they shifted their diplomatic gaze towards other European courts: Russia, France, Germany, and Britain. The royal houses cultivated the support of one or more of the Great Powers. The Karađorđevićs were often supported by Russia and France while the Obrenovićs gained the support of Austria and Germany. The two dynasties also used royal pageantry, including the coat of arms and flag, both of which deliberately incorporated imperial symbols of Tsar Dušan: yellow flags with the red two-headed eagle. Both dynasties were also eager to prove that they possessed genuine aristocratic heritage. For example, the Karađorđevićs traced the origins of their dynasty to the Montenegrin Vasojevići clan, who themselves claimed to be descendants of the Nemanjić dynasty (thus including Dušan the Mighty). These imperial trappings were just as important domestically to show that each dynasty had a legitimate claim to rule while also delegitimizing the competing dynasty.

Nevertheless, to strengthen their mutually exclusive claims the two royal houses also relied on nationalism. As the overwhelming majority of the population was illiterate, however, and tended to identify largely in religious or local, kinship-based, terms, it became important to create institutions that would transform peasants into Serbs and thereby foster a wider support base for the (national) royal family. Hence each royal household, when in power, supported the establishment of educational institutions, mass media, and cultural organizations centred on the glorification of nationhood. From the mid-nineteenth century onwards, the state fostered publication of primary and secondary school textbooks that promoted fiercely nationalist narratives (Jelavich 1989, 47–75; Roudometof 2001, 127). The ministries for culture also sponsored mass media devoted to propagating nationalist and monarchist causes, and in this period the government founded key national institutions such as the National Library (1832), the National Museum (1844), the Serbian National Theatre (1861), and the Serbian Royal Academy of Sciences (1886).

Although Bulgaria and other independent Balkan states went through similar processes of nation-state–building, the Serbian case was different in that nationalism was often deployed as a political strategy to enhance one dynasty's right to rule while simultaneously delegitimizing competitors (Malešević 2017). The history of late nineteenth and early twentieth-century Serbia was characterized by excessive violence between the two royal households, with numerous assassinations, coups, and forced abdications. This conflict at the top spread to the military and political establishments, which gradually became involved in protracted struggles over legitimacy. In this context, nationalism developed as a strategy to attain popular support at home. The decline of the Ottoman Empire provided an opportunity for the rulers to augment their legitimacy through the rise of expansionist nationalism. In this novel historical environment, the traditional imperial claims were supplemented with the new imperial forms of nationalism. In other words, the rulers advocated territorial conquest as means to realize nationalist goals. Hence, the military victories in the Balkan wars acted as quick enhancers of political legitimacy. By dramatically expanding the territory and population of Serbia in 1913, the Karađorđevićs ultimately prevailed over the Obrenovićs. Since the Serbian state doubled in size and acquired over 1.2 million new inhabitants, imperial nationalism was judged to be a viable way forward for the new state.

Nationalizing Empires and Imperializing Nation-States

Both conventional historiography and mainstream historical sociology make much of the distinction between empires and nation-states. In this dominant view empires signify deep social inequalities, territorial conquests, and supremacy of one ethnic group over others. A nation-state, in contrast, is thought to involve a social order defined by political equality, cultural homogeneity, and popular sovereignty. In this understanding, the ideological projects that underpin these two models of polity organization are judged to be mutually exclusive: whereas imperialism denotes an ambition to extend state power through violence and colonization, nationalism is associated with popular self-rule, autonomy, independence, and the preservation of cultural authenticity.

There is no doubt that as ideal-types empires and nation-states represent very different models of polity organization. Nevertheless, as John Hall (1985, 2011, 2013, 2017) rightly emphasizes, no polity is a static entity, but rather is continuously shaped by broader geopolitical changes on the one hand and by the vagaries of domestic politics on the other. In this sense, the nineteenth-century empires, such as those of Britain, France, and Germany, differed profoundly from their ancient, capstone counterparts such as the Roman or Chinese. While the traditional imperial orders could manage cultural differences through excessive violence or plain ignorance, the modernizing empires had no choice but to respond to changing international and domestic conditions. As Hall (2011, 20) makes clear, the combination of the global struggle for territory, resources, and state prestige abroad and rising nationalist movements at home forced the imperial rulers to nationalize their empires. The general hope was that national homogenization would halt domestic centrifugal forces, prevent secessionism, strengthen the empire, and ultimately prolong its life. However, the historical record indicates that once "nationalism and imperialism were joined together in a powerful mixture" (Hall 2011, 20) the path was laid down towards further expansion and violence. For Hall, World War I was the outcome of this deadly cocktail: nationalizing homogenization combined with imperial ambition. What Hall's analysis shows is that in a rapidly nationalizing late nineteenth-century world the imperial rulers could do little else than attempt to nationalize their empires.

This Hallsian argument is potent and persuasive, but it does not fully address the other side of this relationship: how nation-states embraced the imperial rhetoric as they sought to boost their political legitimacy at home and abroad. It is true that the late nineteenth and early twentieth centuries were characterized by blurred boundaries of imperialism and nationalism. However, it was not only a case of nationalizing empires: this process was equally present on the other side of this dichotomy, with some nation-states donning the imperial garb.

The Balkan polities are usually taken to epitomize the small nation-state driven by popular nationalisms. In this understanding, Serbia, Greece, Bulgaria, and other states were seen as the beacons of early nationalism standing against the imperialist ambitions of the Great Powers. One should question such assumptions. Not only was popular nationalism very weak there until well into the twentieth century, but these states also cherished their own imperial projects. Hence, rather than resisting imperialism and pursuing nationalism, the Bulgarian and Serbian new rulers regularly combined the two ideological projects in order to enhance their political legitimacy. While the Great Powers attempted to nationalize their empires in order, as Hall (2013) stresses, to increase force through coherence the Balkan polities were eager to imperialize their nation-states. Despite the different means and strategies deployed, they embraced imperialism for the same reason that compelled the Great Powers to adopt nationalism: to increase their power. Furthermore, the embrace of imperial doctrine was not just confined to proclamations, rituals, rhetoric, and imagery. With the 1912–13 Balkan wars, Serbia and Bulgaria both became involved in the quasi-imperial quest for territory previously controlled by the Ottoman Empire. In this context, the two governments combined imperialism with nationalism to justify their spoils of war. While nationalist arguments were regularly deployed to legitimize inclusion of ethnic brethren living outside the boundaries of the homeland, imperialist doctrine was often invoked to validate the right to expand one's territory.

The experience of these two small Balkan states indicates that conventional historical analyses that differentiate sharply between different forms of polity organization and the corresponding ideological matrices cannot fully account for the complex and often contradictory social reality. The late nineteenth century was a world abounding in what we would perhaps consider strange types of polities: imperializing nation-states and nationalizing empires. Rather than taking for granted that nation-states and empires have nothing in common and that nationalism and imperialism are always enemies, we must understand that the historical reality is full of hybrid ideological and organizational forms. The Hallsian perspective shows how this is possible, and why it matters.

REFERENCES

Anderson, Benedict. 2006. *Imagined Communities*. London: Verso.

Aronson, Theo. 1986. *Crowns in Conflict: The Triumph and The Tragedy of European Monarchy, 1910–1918*. London: J. Murray.

Biondich, Mark. 2011. *The Balkans: Revolution, War and Political Violence since 1878*. Oxford: Oxford University Press. https://doi.org/10.1093/acprof:oso/9780199299058.001.0001.

Bobchev, Stefan. 1881. *Istoriia na balgarskiia narod*. Plovdiv: n.p.

Burbank, Jane, and Frederick Cooper. 2010. *Empires in World History: Power and Politics of Difference*. Princeton: Princeton University Press.

Centeno, Miguel. 2002. *War and Debt: War and the Nation-State in Latin America*. University Park: Penn State University Press.

Cohen, Philip J., and David Riesman. 1996. *Serbia's Secret War: Propaganda and the Deceit of History*. College Station: Texas A&M University Press.

Crampton, R.J. 2007. *Bulgaria*. Oxford: Oxford University Press.

Daskalov, Roumen. 2005. *The Making of a Nation in the Balkans: Historiography of the Bulgarian Revival*. Budapest: Central European University Press.

Dimitrova, Snezhana. 2003. "Traumatizing History: Textbooks in Modern Bulgarian History and Bulgarian National Identity (1917–1996)." *Studies in Ethnicity and Nationalism* 1 (3): 56–72.

Dimitrova, Snezhana, and Naum Kaytchev. 1998. "Bulgarian Nationalism, Articulated by the Textbooks in Modern Bulgarian History, 1878–1996." *Internationale Schulbuchfoschung* 20 (1): 51–70.

Fine, John V.A. 1991. *The Early Medieval Balkans*. Ann Arbor: Michigan University Press. https://doi.org/10.3998/mpub.8108.

Ganchev, Dobri. 1888. *Uchebnik po Balgarskata Istoria za Dolnite Klasove na Gimnaziite i za Triklasnite Obshtinski Uchilishta* [Bulgarian history textbook for junior high school grades and three-grade municipal schools]. Plovdiv: Hristo G. Danov.

Hall, John A. 1985. *Powers and Liberties: The Causes and Consequences of the Rise of the West*. Oxford: Blackwell.

– 1988. "States and Societies: The Miracle in Comparative Perspective." In *Europe and the Rise of Capitalism*, edited by Jean Baechler, John A. Hall, and Michael Mann, 20–38. Oxford: Blackwell.

– 2011. "Nationalism Might Change Its Character, Again." In *Nationalism and Globalisation: Conflicting or Contemporary?*, edited by Daphne Halikiopoulou and Sofia Vasilopoulou, 17–26. New York: Routledge.

– 2013. *The Importance of Being Civil: The Struggle for Political Decency*. Princeton: Princeton University Press.

– 2017. "Taking Megalomanias Seriously: Rough Notes." *Thesis Eleven* 139 (1): 30–45. https://doi.org/10.1177/0725513617700453.

Hall, John A., and Siniša Malešević. 2013. "Introduction: War and Nationalism." In *Nationalism and War*, edited by John A. Hall and Siniša Malešević, 1–28. Cambridge: Cambridge University Press. https://doi.org/10.1017/CBO9781139540964.001.

Hardt, Michael, and Antonio Negri. 2001. *Empire*. Cambridge, MA: Harvard University Press.

Hiers, Wesley, and Andreas Wimmer. 2013. "Is Nationalism the Cause or Consequence of the End of Empire?" In *Nationalism and War*, edited by John A. Hall and Siniša Malešević, 212–54. Cambridge: Cambridge University Press. https://doi.org/10.1017/CBO9781139540964.013.

Hranova, Albena. 2011. "History Education and Civic Education: The Bulgarian Case." *Journal of Social Science Education* 10 (1): 33–43.

Jelavich, Charles. 1989. "The Issue of Serbian Textbooks in the Origins of World War I." *Slavic Review* 48 (2): 214–33. https://doi.org/10.2307/2499114.

Kedourie, Elie. 1993. *Nationalism*. Oxford: Blackwell.

Kumar, K. 2010. "Nation-States as Empires, Empires as Nation-States: Two Principles, One Practice?" *Theory and Society* 39 (2): 119–43. https://doi.org/10.1007/s11186-009-9102-8.

Malešević, Siniša. 2012a. "Wars That Make States and Wars That Make Nations: Organised Violence, Nationalism and State Formation in the Balkans." *Archives Européennes de Sociologie* 53 (1): 31–63. https://doi.org/10.1017/S0003975612000021.

– 2012b. "Did Wars Make Nation-States in the Balkans? Nationalisms, Wars and States in the 19th and Early 20th Century South East Europe." *Journal of Historical Sociology* 25 (3): 299–330. https://doi.org/10.1111/j.1467-6443.2011.01409.x.

– 2013. *Nation-States and Nationalisms: Organisation, Ideology and Solidarity*. Cambridge: Polity.

– 2017. "The Mirage of Balkan Piedmont: State Formation and Serbian Nationalisms in the Nineteenth and Early Twentieth Century." *Nations and Nationalism* 23 (1): 129–50. https://doi.org/10.1111/nana.12267.

Mann, Michael. 1986. *The Sources of Social Power*. Vol. 1, *A History of Power from the Beginning to AD 1760*. Cambridge: Cambridge University Press.

– 2003. *Incoherent Empire*. London: Verso.

Meriage, Lawrence. 1977. "The First Serbian Uprising (1804–1813): National Revival or a Search for Regional Security." *Canadian Review of Studies in Nationalism* 4 (2): 187–205.

Meyer, John W., John Boli, George M. Thomas, and Francisco O. Ramirez. 1997. "World Society and the Nation-State." *American Journal of Sociology* 103 (1): 144–81. https://doi.org/10.1086/231174.

Minogue, Kenneth. 1996. "Ernest Gellner and the Danger of Theorising Nationalism." In *The Social Philosophy of Ernest Gellner*, edited by John A. Hall and Ian Jarvie, 113–28. Amsterdam: Rodopi.

Mouzelis, Nicos. 2007. "Nationalism: Reconstructing Gellner's Theory." In *Ernest Gellner and Contemporary Social Thought*, edited by Siniša Malešević and Mark Haugaard, 125–39. Cambridge: Cambridge University Press.

Münkler, Herfried, H. 2007. *Empires: The Logic of World Domination from Rome to the United States*. Cambridge: Polity.

Parsons, Talcott. 1977. *The Evolution of Societies*. New York: Prentice Hall.

Pavlowitch, Steven. 1981. "Society in Serbia, 1791–1830." In *Balkan Society in the Age of Greek Independence*, edited by Richard Clogg, 137–56. London: Macmillan. https://doi.org/10.1007/978-1-349-06019-1_7.

Popova-Mutafova, Fani. 1938. *Yoan Assen: Istoricheski Roman* [*Yoan Assen*: A historical novel]. Sofia: Drevna Balgaria.

Roudometof, Victor. 2001. *Nationalism, Globalization and Orthodoxy: The Social Origins of Ethnic Conflict in the Balkans*. Westport: Greenwood.

Sombart. Werner. 1913. *Krieg und Kapitalismus*. Munich: Duncker & Humbolt.

Tilly, Charles. 1992. *Coercion, Capital and European States*. Oxford: Blackwell.

Venedikov, Yordan. 1918. *Vek*. Vol. 12, *Voynite za Obedinenieto na Balgarite* [The wars for the unification of the Bulgarians in the twelfth century]. Sofia: Pechatnitsa na S.M. Staikov.

Wilson, Duncan. 1970. *The Life and Times of Vuk Stefanović Karadzić, 1787–1864: Literacy, Literature and National Independence in Serbia*. Oxford: Clarendon.

Zielonka, Jan. 2006. *Europe as Empire: The Nature of the Enlarged European Union*. Oxford: Oxford University Press. https://doi.org/10.1093/0199292213.001.0001.

7 The Despotic and Infrastructural Powers of Democratic, Autocratic, and Authoritarian Regimes

MICHAEL MANN

I have enormous respect for John Hall as a scholar and a writer – and as a perennially helpful critic of my own drafts. I first met him in the early 1980s when we were co-organizers, along with Ernest Gellner, of a seminar series called "Patterns of History" at the LSE. I was mightily impressed by his unfailing knack of homing in on the central underlying idea of each seminar paper we heard, and then critiquing it acutely but sympathetically. He has done the same for me over the years, and he and I have often done research along parallel lines. From that seminar series I wrote the first volume of *The Sources of Social Power* (1986), and he wrote *Powers and Liberties* (1985), his being much shorter, better written, and pithier than mine. More recently, he and I have both emphasized the enduring importance of the nation-state (Hall and Campbell 2015; Mann 1997). He is a fervent liberal democrat, yet is conscious of the tensions and the temptations of democracy, especially where connected to ethnicity or nationalism. I also wrote along these lines in my book *The Dark Side of Democracy* (2005).

We differ in one important respect. He has not hesitated to mix normative with scientific analysis, and I envy him the assurance with which he does this. More specifically, he sees the "civilized acceptance of difference" as essential if liberal democracies are to cope with the fault lines of class, religion, race, and national identity; and he sees the maintenance of privacy and social group autonomy as essential protection against the state (Hall 2013). I am impressed by all this, although as a social democrat I seek more protections against capitalism as well. He believes democracy provides the best possible polity for modern societies. As well as its moral virtues, he stresses its efficiency and its durability, which he says are much greater than in autocratic or authoritarian regimes. I will not discuss here the ethnic problems of democracy, but

I will differ a little in tone by emphasizing other failings of real-world democracy. I will situate this amid a comparative analysis of democracy, autocracy, and authoritarianism, while my theoretical approach is derived from a distinction I made many years ago between despotic and infrastructural power. Some of the conclusions I reach echo the arguments made by John Campbell and Liliana Riga, in their respective contributions to this volume, about the evolution of democratic life in the United States.

Theory: Despotic and Infrastructural Power

In my article "The Autonomous Power of the State" (1984), I distinguished two different kinds of political power: despotic power (DP), which is the range of actions that the state elite is empowered to take without routine consultation with civil society groups; and infrastructural power (IP), the capacity of the state to actually penetrate civil society and so get its actions logistically implemented throughout its territories. Soifer (2012) has said that an infrastructurally powerful state has the ability to painlessly extract fiscal resources, to impose order and the rule of law, and to possess efficient administration of basic services. In his detailed study of Latin American states (Soifer 2015), he measures the infrastructural strength of states in terms of data on education, coercive capacity, and tax extraction. I would add the ability to regulate and redistribute economic resources. Extensively, the state's arm reaches over all of its territories, while intensively the state can deploy enough "weight" to back up its rules (as Soifer [2008] puts it). In this chapter I explore the despotic and infrastructural powers of states in the world today.

IP comprises both *physical* infrastructures like roads or radios or schools, and *social* infrastructures, the human relationships through which the regime persuades others to implement and enforce its laws and dictates throughout the realm. IP comprises all means – physical or social – by which commands are actually implemented. The distinction between despotic and infrastructural power enables us to see more clearly that states can be "strong" in two different ways. Though many historic monarchies and empires were strong in DP, they tended to be weak in IP. Their commands were mainly interpreted and executed by local notables whose powers were substantially autonomous of the ruler. Conversely, modern institutionalized democracies are despotically weak – leaders only rule with the consent of the people. Yet they have far more IP. For example, our salaries are taxed "at source," without any action from us, and most of us cannot evade this, though we may cheat a little and the very rich cheat a lot. However, the democratic state is a two-way street, for it also has less autonomy from its citizens. In earlier times states without their own resources mostly taxed wealth that visibly moved around – much weaker infrastructural power. Modern non-democratic states lie between these two. Although almost all states in the Middle East and North Africa (MENA) do tax their citizens, the ability to collect taxes is quite low. Egyptian and Jordanian tax revenues are less than 15 per cent of national GDP, compared to the OECD countries' average of 35 per cent.

From this distinction I constructed four ideal-typical states. Where both DP and IP were low, I termed the state "feudal" (as in medieval Europe); where IP was weak but DP high, it was "imperial" (like the Chinese Empire); where DP was weak but IP strong, the state was "democratic" (like Britain or the United States today); and where both are high, the state was "bureaucratic" (like the Soviet Union). Two of these labels have seemed inappropriate to me. I revised them first in Mann (2008), but now I make a second revision. The term "imperial," the combination of high DP but low IP, is fine for empires but is not an appropriate term for many contemporary regimes. So I now term this combination "autocratic." The word "autocrat" conveys the sense of a regime with arbitrary powers but not deep implantation in civil society. It rules over but not within society. I do not confine the term to rule by a single person, for autocracies can involve collective rule too, but again there is some separation between this elite and civil society. The term "bureaucratic" was devised to describe modern despotisms like the Soviet Union, but bureaucracy is a characteristic of all modern states, including democratic ones. The Soviet Union was a party-state in which a top-down ruling party embedded in society enforced state commands. "Authoritarian" is my preferred label here, for it is a despotism that through a ruling party has more penetrative and more durable infrastructures, and it has more transformative goals than autocracy, which is often devoted merely to keeping the autocrat or the autocratic elite in power. This yields the two-by-two table presented in Table 7.1.

Real-World States

These are ideal types. Most real-world states do not fit within a single box. The line from democracy to authoritarianism has many gradations. The widely used "Polity Data Set" scores all countries of the

Table 7.1 Two Dimensions of State Power (Revised)

	Infrastructural Power	
Despotic Power	Low	High
Low	Feudal	Democratic
High	Autocratic	Authoritarian

world with populations above 500,000. These scores range from +10 (full democracy) to −10 (full autocracy), with some countries placed at all twenty-one numerical points on the scale (the latest version is Polity IV, 2015, easily accessible on the web). True democracy would combine competitive, representative, and open elections, broad political participation, and effective checks on executive authority, yet all so-called democracies are imperfect in at least one of these respects. The United States scores a full 10 on the Polity scale yet many of its elections are partially bought by big money. All Western democracies are somewhat flawed, while many other self-styled democracies are more deeply flawed, holding phony elections, banning parties and assemblies, and refusing to accept election results. Democracy rules the world of ideals, but not the real world. Autocracies are not perfectly despotic either. There are different degrees and types of autocracy, as Geddes (1999) and Svolik (2012) have demonstrated, while there is often no clear borderline between autocratic and authoritarian regimes. Yet even in these regimes rulers need to adhere to the wishes of some groups in civil society. The infrastructures that link regimes to their people are my subject matter here.

I focus on recent and contemporary states so I will not discuss the feudal category in Table 7.1, except to note that feudal despotism with weak penetration into civil society gave the people as well as the state considerable autonomy from each other, so that most of the people enjoyed freedom of a very different kind from those in modern democracies. They could mostly avoid the state, keeping away from its feeble tentacles. Indeed, in many African countries most people want as little to do with the state as possible – and it is possible. The state cannot exert much infrastructural power, while the people don't want it to. But my analysis will concern the contrast between long-lived democracies with high scores, like the United States and western European states, and countries with low scores, like most states of the Middle East or

Africa or Central Asia. I will also distinguish autocratic from authoritarian states, since they have different social infrastructures.

The division between the modern and the pre-modern is decisive in determining the extent of physical infrastructures. Railroads, automobiles, aircraft, national education systems, radio, television, telephones, computers, and other technological miracles of modernity make for easier communication and control from centre to periphery, and vice versa. All but the weakest autocratic regimes today have more penetrative physical infrastructures than had even major empires of the past. There is also an intermediary category, which we might call "skilled" infrastructures, blending physical tools of communication with specialized social skills, like the practices of vaccination, accountancy, censuses, and statistics. These have also tended to intensify through history, though not so uniformly, since many ancient states had censuses.

In contrast, social infrastructures have not simply intensified through time. Some ancient societies had strong social relationships between the state and the population. Greek city-states are obvious examples, for the polis *was* the citizen body.

So what are the problems of modern democracy? Let me first note that even countries that score 10 on the Polity scale exhibit some imperfections. Though institutionalized democratic states do rule in a broad sense with the consent of the people, this is mediated by four blockages on the free upward flow of infrastructural power. First, and most importantly, infrastructural diffusion is blocked by the greater resources of the powerful, especially by the economically powerful. This is the most important reason why democracy in practice is less virtuous than in principle, and I will discuss it at length below. Second, downward power with despotic overtones is manifest in the emergence of "deep" national security states, which I will again discuss below. Third, political parties channel and often redefine and distort popular sentiments. In most countries the choice of candidates and party lines is made by small groups of people, traditionally in smoke-filled rooms. Primaries add more popular participation, though this is usually confined to party members, who add their own distinctive biases. In India, the parties are engaged in genuine electoral competition, but the party leaders are not elected and indeed they run their parties as autocracies. Fourth, some downward flows come from distinctive inequitable constitutional arrangements. In the United States the Constitution allocates two senators to both Wyoming (585,000 population) and California (30 million), which is indefensible in terms of democratic norms. Moreover, in the 2016 presidential election Hillary Clinton received almost three million more votes than Donald Trump, yet he was elected president because of an electoral college system that privileges rural over urban areas. All four imperfections can block or distort the upward flow of infrastructural power in a democracy, although the first two are more important than the last two.

In contrast, of course, despotic regimes do not want to rule with the consent of the people or even of a broad cross-section of the most powerful groups in civil society. Despots would ideally wish to rule unchallenged, but they cannot in reality rule unassisted. They came to power with the help of allies whose needs cannot be ignored, and nor can they simply ignore popular sentiments. They need downward infrastructures linking them to supporters throughout the realm. They must rule through local elites who, unfortunately for despots, also possess autonomy. The ruler's response is to develop infrastructures that will bind them to him/her. Let us consider these.

Revenue Infrastructures

The need to extract revenue to finance operations is a basic need of all regimes. That is why penetrative infrastructures persuading people to pay up are usually needed. In democracies there is no avoiding this need, and indeed government revenues and expenditures are probably the most persistent and publicized of all political issues. Some social groups have more power than others to determine the type and level of taxation, but all the social infrastructures of democracy – the parties, the parliaments, the media – are dominated by debate about taxes. Democracy is at its most developed level in this arena.

However, regimes can in principle bypass or at least mollify this if they have an independent revenue-gathering capacity of their own that does not need the consent of the people. Some taxes require a lesser degree of consent, like bond issues, import and export taxes, and sales taxes. Soifer (2012) argues that the greater the proportion of direct to indirect and resource taxes, the greater the (two-way) infrastructural power. Better still for despotism are resources supposedly "belonging" to the regime, as with profit-making nationalized corporations or the royalties extracted automatically from economic enterprises. The oil and natural gas industries in producer countries are the major modern examples. Since the revenue belongs to the regime either in profit or in royalties, there is less need to tax the people. Similar possibilities have long existed. Monarchs had revenue-yielding estates of their own, and were often held to own all underground mineral rights. Even today any minerals found underneath my English house would belong to the Duchy of Cornwall, that is, to Prince Charles, as his lawyers recently informed me – a reminder doubtlessly occasioned by the arrival of new fracking technologies. But in countries like Norway or the United States democracy is so entrenched that the possession of oil or gas reserves and fracking activities are subject to open political debate – and their governments depend mostly on income and sales taxes, anyway.

Blanton and Fargher (2008) found that most of the early states of history with their own revenue sources were autocratic, while those needing to extract taxes were forced to cede some political rights to the community and to establish some form of representative institutions. "No taxation without representation" turns out to be an ancient mantra, traceable all the way back to early Sumerian states of the third millennium BCE.

Today those autocratic and authoritarian regimes with large revenues of their own can shower the people with subsidies on essential commodities, job expansion in the public sector, and more spending on education, health, and housing. All this can happen without yielding representative institutions. The major spur to democratization in the West was taxation. Since major oil and gas revenues bypass this, a powerful historical stimulus to democratization is absent. This is especially so of the small Gulf States and Saudi Arabia, where oil and gas profits or royalties form most of GDP. Authoritarian communist regimes also have had considerable freedom from taxpayers, for the regime effectively owned all the major industries and collective farms, took their revenue, and then distributed wages and benefits out of this sum. In these cases the regime can avoid developing infrastructures of active support within the people. Under Marshall's (1963) typology of citizenship rights, as he wrote in the section "Citizenship and Social Class," they grant social rights while withholding civil and political rights, hopefully heading off insurrection at the pass. Obviously the provision of social benefits generates infrastructures of their own, but these are more top-down than bottom-up control by the people. Yet the recent recession has caused a general belt-tightening of social citizenship, making many non-democratic rulers uneasy.

Repression

Repression is a second way of bypassing the need for extensive infrastructures in civil society. Autocratic and authoritarian regimes deploy considerable repression to protect themselves both from popular revolt and from defections by their allies. Democracies have tended to use it only in emergencies, although states of emergency are becoming more common with the emergence of the "deep" national security state, where government can act secretively, without routine consultation, to tap our phones, hack our emails, conduct arbitrary arrests, and even torture in the name of "the war against terror." As in previous wars, we have little recourse and our right to individual and group privacy is reduced. Most Western states are currently becoming less democratic as surveillance infrastructures intensify.

Such democratic repression is much feebler than the terror wielded by some autocratic and authoritarian states. Nonetheless, repression is costly, and no regime has the ability to wield it continuously. Instead it is deployed erratically in episodes of exemplary repression. It can keep the ruler in power, which is perhaps all that many autocrats aspire to, but it can rarely encourage positive commitment from the people. Repression tends to stifle social and economic development – and this ultimately weakens the despot. But "ultimately" is a long time and repression may be effective in the short- and medium-term. It has the great virtue for the regime of lessening the need for other social infrastructures. The active cooperation of the masses is not required.

Nonetheless, repression requires its own infrastructures binding those entrusted with repression to the political rulers. Repression may take two main forms. The first is judicial. Democratic regimes rely heavily on this. Opposition demonstrations will be tolerated within established legal limits but, if these are breached, opponents will face a peaceful yet implacable judicial process. A despotic regime is fortunate indeed if it can deal with opposition through judicial enforcement of its arbitrarily declared laws. In practice it must resort to military power, by either the armed forces or paramilitary security police. Democratic regimes rarely deploy the army at home and they rarely have large paramilitary forces. In stably institutionalized democracies the military is also subordinated to the civil authority, while elections guarantee unchallenged change from one government to another. The rules of the game are respected and transitions are peaceful. Institutionalized democracies produce more order than do autocratic regimes, which is the opposite of what autocrats claim. New democracies are more problematic. Before democratic institutions are firmly in place, escalating factional violence and military coups are possible.

Reliance on military force requires harmonious relations with a loyal officer corps. Armies and paramilitaries have more effective Weberian-type bureaucracies and command structures than do the civil authorities in autocratic regimes. They can act as a cohesive force to repress opposition – or to challenge the ruler. Thus autocrats shower favours on generals, often donating to them formerly nationalized companies or licences to monopolize trade. Egypt, Syria, Indonesia, Ethiopia, and Rwanda have all sought to buy off the military in this way. They also humour them with the latest toys – aircraft, missiles, tanks, and the like.

Yet army training inculcates a caste-like *esprit de corps* that gives soldiers a sense of their own collective interests, which may be distinct from those of the ruler – hence many military coups. In Uganda President Milton Obote had to rely more and more on his army, showering it with favours, depending more on generals he felt he could trust. General Idi Amin became his mainstay, but in 1971 Amin led a coup and established one of the most vicious of modern dictatorships. Roman emperors had coped with such threats by forming Praetorian Guards to protect themselves from both the people and the military. Today some autocrats have "palace guards" or security police paramilitaries as a Praetorian Guard against the army. But there are many cases of failure. In 2001 President Laurent Kabila of the Congo was killed by his own palace guard. The Shah of Iran's refusal to allow a unified High Command unintentionally weakened his army's ability to take collective action against the enormous popular demonstrations of 1979. He relied on the security police, the SAVAK, but it lacked the numbers and equipment to cope with really massive demonstrations. In Egypt Mubarak had also built up his security police, privileging its commanders over army generals in his distribution of the spoils of office. But the police could not handle millions of demonstrators in Cairo in 2011. In both cases an alienated military stood aside and the regime fell, major failures of repressive infrastructures (Kandil 2016).

Hence a second strategy is to factionalize the army, privileging supposedly loyal generals and units with the spoils of office while frequently rotating other generals or giving them air force or naval postings – things that lessen their ability to mount coups. This produces many loyal higher-level officers who would have much to lose if the regime fell, but it also produces alienated officers susceptible to the promises of rival politicians. These strategies carry the disadvantage of weakening either the loyalty or the unity of the repressive infrastructures (Kandil 2016). In contrast, democratic rulers are more successful in keeping civilian control over the armed forces (so are most authoritarians, which I discuss later). They sleep easier at night in this respect, though authoritarians may stay awake at night worrying about single-party factionalism, and democrats about the next election.

Civil Administration: Bureaucracy and Patrimonialism

Public civilian employees are entrusted with implementing state directives. Though all state administrations have defects, and bureaucracies never reach the level of efficiency lauded by Max Weber, bureaucracies in institutionalized democracies generally implement directives more fully than those in autocratic administrations. They may drag their heels or advise their political masters that a proposed policy is impracticable, or fight over departmental responsibilities, or they may leak, but they rarely block directives. Personal loyalty is not required, since obedience is structured into the bureaucratic hierarchy. Bureaucracy is a good thing in democracies because it ensures a smoother flow of infrastructural power, both upward and downward.

Most autocratic administrations have proportionally more public employees than do democracies, but that is attributable to a desire to boost employment to reduce discontent rather than to increase administrative efficiency. In fact it usually reduces efficiency, since finding work for them bloats both tasks and costs. Nor is there a simple hierarchical chain of command in autocrats' ministries, as there broadly is in both democracies and authoritarian states. Autocratic administrations are more personalized and politicized. Staffing is not by meritocracy but by elite desires to favour clients, friends, and relations. Loyalty is as much personal as structural. We call this patrimonialism. Networks of patron-client relations intervene between ruler and ruled, reducing the direct two-way communication of controls and resources, for at each layer of administration the patrons possess some autonomy from the state. Patrimonialism exists to one degree or another in virtually all regimes, but is more crucial to autocracies.

Many regimes seek to bolster patron-client loyalty by recruiting patrons from their own kin, ethnicity, tribe, region, or religion, like Tikritis in Saddam's Iraq, Alawites in Syria, the Al Saud tribe in Saudi Arabia, the Al Khalifa family in Bahrein, Sinhalese in Sri Lanka, Tigray in Ethiopia, or the successive Hutu and Tutsi regimes of Rwanda. Through kinship, common origin, and ethnic-religious ties, the rulers hope to create loyal patron-client infrastructures spreading across the realm. They offer to them a spoils system, redistributing public resources towards friends and away from enemies. The spoils grew from the 1980s as neoliberal policies privatized state enterprises and rulers gave them to friends and kin, including military and security police chiefs.

Yet patrimonial "in-groups" foster "out-groups" discontent at being excluded from a share of the spoils, and potentially capable of their own national or regional organization, especially if they share a common religious, ethnic, or other identity. The clash of regime and out-groups may result in further ethnic or religious polarization, as those who had worn their ethnic or religious identity lightly are forced into a more sectarian identity. This is the path towards civil war and ethnic cleansing, as in Syria today. Where political parties are allowed, the autocratic regime will seek to divide and rule among them too, as in Jordan and Morocco, where opposition parties are allowed but deterred from joining together to form a coalition. Another quasi-democratic version of this is the ethnocratic polity, where a majority ethnic or religious group has the force of numbers to guarantee victory in free elections. Then it can use laws to discriminate against the minority, as in Israel, Sri Lanka, or until recently Rwanda and Northern Ireland.

The breadth of the in-group coalition is crucial. If the spoils are distributed only within a narrow circle of regime family and friends, their loyalty may be assured but many elites may feel excluded and alienated and become restive, denouncing cronyism, nepotism, and corruption. Patron-client networks can be supportive provided spoils are distributed quite broadly. But it needs skill to maintain a balancing act between the core elites who can be truly relied on for loyalty and those more independent elites who, if disaffected, might desert the regime. This balancing act is not easy to accomplish, for it requires intelligent flexibility, which is difficult to maintain over a long period of time. The most vulnerable regimes (apart from those discredited in war) are personalist, exclusionary, and internally factionalized autocracies (Mann 2012, chap. 9). Support bases may be limited to a set of elite groups and military officers whose loyalty seems assured. These may then be reduced down to a circle of friends and kin whose loyalty seems certain. But this involves the exclusion of many elites from a share in the spoils of office, which may result in their supporting oppositional movements. Elite support for the regime matters more than that of the people as a whole. If the regime stays cohesive, broad based among elites, and in control of repressive force, it will outlast popular storms because of popular fear of the military and of disorder.

Civil Administration: Corruption

Corruption does not usually increase despotic power but it does restrain the smooth flow of infrastructural power, both upward and downward. In autocratic regimes the salaries of officials are rarely separated from the fruits of office. As was the norm in most historical states, officials can appropriate resources flowing through their departments, a process resulting in officials' palaces and foreign bank accounts. This looting of the state results less from morally corrupt individuals than from the entire patron-client reward system of autocracy, whereby each level of administration has sufficient autonomy to appropriate the fruits of office. In autocracies and quasi-democracies in which elections are held, corruption may be denounced and become a major issue in elections and in demonstrations, but it rarely ends. The rulers themselves are often the greatest looters. All this greatly limits the flow of infrastructural power through the various levels of administration.

Corruption is widespread in all regimes, however. In authoritarian single-party regimes elites may collectively set up their own networks of special party stores, schools, dachas, and the like, perverting the egalitarian ideals of the party. Looting of state resources was more openly tolerated in fascist than communist regimes, since the fascist ethos was the survival of, and the spoils to, the fittest. Yet in the collapse of Soviet communism and in China's transition to market capitalism looting occurred on a truly massive scale, as party officials sought to appropriate state resources as their own private property, or to collaborate with entrepreneurs to establish politically protected enterprises. Regional and local party fiefdoms appeared, enjoying considerable autonomy.

Democratic regimes are also corroded by corruption, but of lesser quantity and different quality. Looting is rarely on the same scale as in autocracies. Most democratic scandals involve rather trivial benefits – gifts, free holidays, preferment for a friend or relative, and the like. If revealed by insider leaks to journalists, they are taken up by opposition politicians and become scandal, forcing personal resignation or electoral defeat. Francois Fillon is a contemporary example, a scandal of just under one million US dollars paid to his family, plus suits and watches given to him totalling about twenty-five thousand US dollars, destroying what had seemed an assured route to the French presidency. In democracies few politicians or bureaucrats gain great personal wealth from the fruits of office except after they leave, when they can sell their supposed expertise and influence and become rich – as Henry Kissinger, Bill Clinton, and Tony Blair have conspicuously done.

Recently established democracies are vulnerable to larger corruption. Two scandals have broken out in Brazil in the new century. The Mensalao scheme involved public funds illegally paid to Congress deputies in exchange for backing the Workers' Party government in crucial votes. When the Supreme Court finished its trials in 2012, twenty-five politicians, bankers, and business executives had been convicted, including high-ranking officials of the Workers' Party. Second, in Operation Car Wash Brazil's biggest construction firms overcharged state oil company Petrobras for building contracts. In exchange Petrobras executives and politicians were personally given back part of the overpayment. Prosecutors alleged that these kickbacks helped finance Workers' Party campaigns, and also helped ex-president Lula build his retirement villa. Currently four presidents of Brazil and six current standing ministers are under investigation. The scale of Brazilian corruption will be stupendous if these allegations are proved. Perhaps massive corruption lies unexposed in other democracies too.

But "democratic corruption" has two distinctive qualities. First, the gifts accepted are more likely to go into party funds or personal re-election finances rather than simply into coat pockets. In the 2012 US election it cost about $1 billion to become president, $10 million to become a senator, and $1 million to become a member of the House. In 2016 Hillary Clinton raised the amazing sum of $1.4 billion, with Wall Street being the main source. This was not charity on the part of donors, but self-interest – the possibility of influencing the next president. Donald Trump's war chest was "only" just under $1 billion. In France, where parties which achieve at least 5 per cent of the vote get certain campaign expenses paid by the state, a current scandal concerns the Front National, which has been overcharging the state and appropriating the surplus. In Brazil the bulk of the appropriated funds went to re-election campaigns, although some Brazilian politicians were also seeking personal wealth, like the construction and Petrobras executives.

The second quality of democratic corruption is the nature of the barter, with funds directly or indirectly given to politicians or officials by corporations in return for friendlier policies, like exemptions from government taxes or regulations or permissions for mergers and takeovers, all of which would bring them very big profits. In Korea unparalleled economic growth has been attributed by most scholars to the intimate relations existing between a state with an efficient Weberian-style bureaucracy and the chaebol, the country's giant corporate conglomerates (see, e.g., Amsden 1989; Weiss 1998). Yet at least six of the bosses of the top ten chaebol, which together generate revenue equal to over 80 per cent of GDP, have been convicted of corruption. They were then pardoned by the president of the day – too big to jail! In 2017 a Samsung scandal unfolded over illegal payments totalling thirty-six million dollars given to a confidante of the president in return for approval of a Samsung merger. This has resulted in the dismissal of President Park Geun-hye and the indictment of Samsung's de facto boss, Lee Jae-yong. Lee is following family tradition. His father, the previous Samsung boss, was twice convicted of bribery and tax evasion but was pardoned by the then president (Mozur and Sang-Hun 2017; Sang-Hun 2017).

Nor are longer-lived democracies immune from corporate influence and corruption. Obviously corporations have always enjoyed predominant influence over governments in capitalist countries, and nowhere more so than in the United States. But in recent years the United States has seen this influence intensified by the legalization of corrupt practices, now called "lobbying" (for overall accounts, see de Figueiredo and Richter 2014; Drutman 2015; Kuhner 2014). Lobbying gets results. In one study (Witko 2011), for each additional $201,220 paid as campaign contributions, a corporation could on average expect to receive an additional 107 contracts worth roughly $5.3 million in additional revenues. Take the example of American corporate tax. The nominal rate of corporation tax is currently about 40 per cent if we add average state and local taxes to the 35 per cent nominal federal tax. Donald Trump made much of this in his election campaign, arguing that it was exceedingly high. Yet so many exemptions have been granted by governments to individual corporations or entire industries that the average actually paid by all corporations is only about 15 per cent. Here lobbying results in massive savings by corporations and industry associations and substantial campaign funds given by corporations to politicians. This is perfectly legal.

Over three billion dollars have been spent on Washington lobbying in each year between 2008 and 2016! In 1998 the total had been only $1.45 billion, and in 1975 it had been under $100 million. On the demand side, figures on individual races reveal the same phenomenal growth. In 1976, the average cost of running for a House seat was $86,000; by 2006 it had reached $1.3 million. The range of donors has also narrowed. Before the 1970s voluntary associations, labour unions, and diverse political pressure groups had spent more than business did. Now ninety-five of the one hundred biggest lobby spenders are representing business interests. At all levels of government – federal, state, and local – lobbyists often write the politicians' bills for them. A "revolving door" has also opened: by 2007 two hundred former members of the House and Senate were registered lobbyists. This had been rare before the 1970s, when it had been considered a somewhat tainted practice.

Lobbying has an innocent side. It can be just a means of informing government of how an existing or proposed piece of legislation might affect an industry or corporation. But where accompanied by campaign contributions, it becomes an exchange of bigger profits for corporations and other special-interest groups for payments to politicians. It is carefully made into an indirect exchange, and the biggest expansion has been of specialist lobbying firms mediating the links between politicians and corporations. Moreover, lobbyists focus on the building up of friendly relations with politicians and their staffers so that mutual sympathies and friendships will only indirectly lead to mutual gifting. Bribery becomes indirect, blurred, and difficult to prove. But it is impossible to believe that the major corporations of America, whose very being is calculation of profit, would engage in all this expenditure unless it was profitable. And on the other hand it is hard to believe that politicians, dominated as they are by the desire for re-election, would not be prepared to give favours to business if it resulted in sizeable campaign contributions. In their eyes, the end justifies the means – the end being their own re-election, which reaffirms true political values, and the means are only little tinkerings with legislation. But as Cicero lamented as the Roman Republic decayed, "One realizes finally that everything is for sale."

The country that invented the word "lobbying" is not immune either (Cave and Rowell 2014). The word originally referred to encounters in the lobby of the Houses of Parliament, at Westminster. Lobbying in the United Kingdom (no longer confined to that place) has grown considerably since the mid-1990s, and in 2007 was worth $2.3 billion (£1.9 billion) and employed fourteen thousand people. Three-quarters of it is estimated to be by business. The revolving door is as important as it is in the United States, and the lobbyists also write much of the legislation. Yet British lobbying is more discrete, and campaign contributions are fairly well regulated so that scandals tend to be small and rare. In 1994 the Cash for Questions affair broke, as a simple market exchange. Two Conservative MPs were accused by the *Guardian* newspaper of accepting bribes to ask questions on behalf of an Egyptian businessman. Their libel case against the newspaper collapsed amid mounting evidence of their guilt. One resigned his seat in Parliament, the other lost his seat to an anti-corruption candidate. But these are minor cases.

There is much lobbying also at the European Union, and many similarities between the European and American systems, but there is one important difference. Brussels officials are not usually elected so do not need campaign funds, unlike their American counterparts. A comparative study of lobbying success in the two systems (Mahoney 2008) produced significant differences in results. In the United States, 89 per cent of corporations and 53 per cent of trade associations succeed, while only 40 per cent of citizen groups and 37 per cent of foundations succeed. In the EU the success rates are also quite high – 57 per cent for trade associations and 61 per cent for lobbying firms – but citizen groups and foundations win equally (56 per cent and 67 per cent, respectively). Policymakers in the EU do not need industry's euros, so there is not the same unique subservience to their interests.

The causes of increased lobbying come from both sides of the exchange. Business lobbying increased in two phases. The first came as reaction against Keynesian political economy of the 1960s, which favoured legislation to regulate private enterprise and protect workers and consumers. In 1972, faced with growing compliance costs, slowing economic growth, and rising wages, leading American CEOs formed an organization to increase their political influence on the Hill. Their lobbyists succeeded in stifling a threatening Labor Reform Act, in securing extensive deregulation, and in reducing business taxes. This became part of the neoliberalism of the 1980s (as it did in Britain). In the second phase business focused on selective regulation protecting each industry or corporation from the chill wind of the market through tax exemptions, subsidies, and other privileges. The lobbyists originally seeking more business freedom from the state turned to seeking advantages within it.

On their side the politicians became more capitalistic. Since the mid-1980s election spending in the United States has increased more than fivefold as costly media advertising campaigns intensified, aided by the liberalization of regulations governing campaign finances. This culminated in the determination by the Supreme Court in the "Citizens United" case in 2010 that the Constitution protected the rights of corporations just as it did individual rights, and so corporate groups were entitled to make campaign contributions unrestricted by government regulation, just as individuals are. Though the principle also applies to other collectivities, like labour unions and voluntary associations, the big money resides with business. This amounts to a capitalist takeover of democracy, the blocking of upward flows of infrastructural power, and the distortion of downward flows by capitalist institutions. But it also transforms market capitalism into crony capitalism, giving politically connected corporations unfair advantages over corporations merely operating in the market (Kuhner 2014, 249–50). It does not increase the despotic powers of the state but of corporations, which are of course internally authoritarian. In the United States the distortions currently prevent necessary regulation of the financial services industry, which a decade ago greatly damaged the world economy, and the necessary regulation of climate change, which is a threat to human life on earth. Capitalism unleashed equals democratic corruption. No wonder populist backlash to such corrupt politics, however confused, is increasing.

Democracy depends on the separation of powers. This is generally assumed to mean separation between the legislative, executive, and judicial branches of government. Equally important, however, is the separation between the different sources of social power. This mutual conspiracy of corruption between politicians and capitalists is in effect a merger of political and economic power, rather than a mutual checking of each other's power. Moreover, the commercialization of politicians indicates that crony capitalism is dominant in this merger. Like John Hall, I believe that market competition in the economy helps preserve democracy, but corporations buying up government is a wholly undesirable dimension of capitalism. But attacking this has been less central for liberal democrats than for social democrats, who are readier to use government to curb the excesses of capitalism and restore equality between the power sources.

Political Party Infrastructures and Authoritarian Regimes

In stably institutionalized democracies political parties link national politicians with national party members, local cells, local government councillors, and sympathizers. These parties' infrastructures penetrate broad swathes of the country, generating commitment among activists and sympathizers. They are the life-blood of democracy and, as we have just seen, of its corrupt perversions. The most effective and long-lived modern despotic regimes have also based their rule on a party system, but on a single party whose members penetrate civil society as agents of regime control, and to a lesser extent pass popular sentiments and grievances upwards through the party hierarchy. Single-party rule is the best survival strategy for a despotic regime, since it offers infrastructural protections both against resistance from below and to a lesser extent from factional disputes among allies (Svolik 2012).

The classic examples have been ruling communist and fascist parties. Fascist regimes did not last long, since their own militarism destroyed them. But communist parties have been longer lived. Their infrastructures comprised 83 million members in China in 2015 (8 per cent of total population), 19 million in the Soviet Union in 1986 (10 per cent of total population), 1.5 million in Vietnam in 1976 (4 per cent of total population), and 800,000 in Cuba in 2011 (8 per cent of total population). In such highly ideological parties many members were initially zealots, although careerism later became more important, since promotion to higher positions has depended on party membership and surface zeal. Both increased obedience to one's superiors. Since other political parties were eliminated early, there were no organized out-group challengers, and hostility to the regime could only surface at the local level. Any sign of broader organized infrastructures was immediately repressed (Lee 2007). No single-party regime has been overthrown from below.

Repression is normally the job of party security police rather than the army. Indeed, they could be used to effect purges of the military. Communist and fascist parties were able to subordinate the military to civilian control (though this was not so of the hybrid fascist/military regime of inter-war Japan) just as have democracies. However, these regimes were muddied by the existence of two distinct hierarchies of administration, one of the party, the other of the civilian ministries, though the party infrastructures tended to dominate.

Single-party regimes tend to generate single despots, like Stalin, Mao, Castro, and the Kim dynasty, while factional disputes among party elites are endemic. At first these regimes, unlike democracies, lacked institutions for settling factionalism, for preventing the rise of a dictator, or for determining leadership succession. Some communist regimes after Stalin and Mao began to remedy these weaknesses by institutionalizing collective decision-making and introducing mandatory retirement age and term limits (Svolik 2012, chap. 4). This is not the party democracy of communist theory, since lower echelons have had little influence on party decisions. But informal constitutionalism among party elites has so far worked well for over thirty years in China and Vietnam, giving a stability of rule and succession rivalling all but the oldest democracies. In the post-Stalin Soviet Union the Presidium also developed rules concerning membership, protocols, decision-making, and succession procedures. These worked for twenty-five years.

John Hall argues that democracies remain more effective than authoritarian regimes. He contrasts the cases of Britain and Nazi Germany during World War II. As he says, the Nazis in Germany could not put nearly as many women in the labour force as democratic Britain could. Nor could they get workers to put in as much overtime. Britain with more (democratic) infrastructures could penetrate the workforce to get more out of them than could authoritarian Germany. Yet in the same war the massive mobilization of the Soviet population, including women, achieved by Stalin's communist party might seem to negate this argument. Moreover, the Soviet Union had the highest economic growth rate of the inter-war period, while after 1950 China led the way in growth, in reducing mortality rates, and in stabilizing population size. China is still seen as a possible model of development by many poorer countries. It is now developing more comprehensive and longer-range environmental policies than democracies, which are dominated by the short-term electoral cycle (Mathews 2014). Single-party regimes are despotic and often extremely cruel, but in some ways they are more infrastructurally effective than democracies – though this depends on the survival of the regime.

Nonetheless, it is doubtful they can outlive institutionalized democracies. Party factionalism in the post-war context of a stagnant economy and declining ideological commitment to communism led to conflict that brought down the Soviet Union. China and Vietnam remain communist survivors, maintaining authoritarian party rule even while now bringing capitalists inside party institutions. It is an open question whether Cuba will develop similar institutions after the Castros have departed, while North Korea is still stuck in a dynastic dictatorship. But we ask the survival question of communism, not of Western democracy.

Some other autocrats have also attempted single-party rule. For seventy-one years the Mexican PRI maintained single-party rule, developing constitutional rules governing party elites. Presidents could rule only for six years and a successor was chosen through power-sharing among party elites. Japan's LDP held power for fifty years. MENA examples have been the Baathist parties, the Tunisian RCD, and the Islamic Republic of Iran (which could also use the infrastructures of mosques, madrassas, and revolutionary guards). In Malaysia the UNMO has ruled for over sixty years, ever since the first post-independence election in 1959. Through time it became dominated by the "iron fist" of Mahathir Mohammad, sole ruler until 2003, when he hand-picked his successor. According to Slater (2003), Mahathir subordinated and used the infrastructures of a hierarchical party, always winning flawed elections and thus wielding both despotic and infrastructural power. Various African countries have also had enduring one-party rule, although their regimes have been much less effective, since they had feeble infrastructures.

Svolik (2012, 110–17, 193–5) measures regime stability and survival by the duration of uninterrupted succession in office of leaders. He finds that single-party regimes last between two and three times as long as either regimes without parties or autocratic regimes that permit multiple parties. However, they are closely followed by multi-party regimes in which the regime party has over 75 per cent of the seats. Duration then reduces as the percentage of government party seats reduces. Thus government parties consistently increase survivability. Geddes (1999) argued that this was because they could allow greater participation and popular influence on policy while retaining regime dominance. Svolik (2012) adds that these parties satisfy careerist aspirations within the party structure – just as I noted for communist parties. So why are single parties not more common? First, they are not easy to create. The strong ones are not simply created by fiat from the top, for they initially embody a transformative ideology welling up from a popular movement. Second, regimes based on traditional upper classes, especially landowners, prefer patron-client controls to the riskier strategy of a mass mobilizing party.

Ideological Infrastructures

An ideology shared by rulers and ruled or an ability to silence subversive ideologies help maintain routine obedience to regime directives. Long-lived democracies do not need to flourish much ideology beyond conventional homilies of the people and nation, for they can achieve considerable "facticity," caging the population within routine practices and "rules of the game" that do embody belief in democracy but that more importantly make alternatives almost unthinkable. This facticity is the core of their legitimacy, not adherence to a formal ideology. This is much less the case in newly established democracies, which are more vulnerable since the rules of the game may not be universally accepted and memories of alternative politics remain thinkable.

The greater the consensus or the greater the absence of alternatives, the less the need for repression. Autocratic regimes, unlike authoritarian regimes, generally lack much ideological ballast, especially in their early years. But both routinely fall back on repression, although they can add control of most traditional communications media. Networks of churches and schools, mosques and madrassas have also mostly reinforced conservative autocratic regimes. If the citizens lack access to alternative views or have no knowledge of how many others might hold those views, they are unlikely to challenge the regime.

After the fall or domestication of communism and fascism, the most recent important political ideology has been radical Islam, whose infrastructure of mosques, madrassas, and internet (and prison classes abroad) carry messages threatening established regimes or legitimizing their own. Transnational internet media also threaten state monopolies of ideological infrastructures. The internet, social media, cell phones, and Al-Jazeera helped mobilize large crowds during the Arab Spring, although they were not the primary mobilization infrastructures. But most regimes of all types have sought to use such media to spy on those they suspect of opposition. Authoritarians and autocrats also try to censor the transnational media, with China in the lead, while IS has led in internet communication of subversive messages. This new terrain of ideological struggle is also expanding as a site for interstate conflict, with Russian-American rivalry in the vanguard.

All regimes claim the rather pragmatic ideology of being able to bring economic benefits to the country, but economic growth is fickle. A regime that presides over economic recession will feel vulnerable. Much more effective is the claim made by autocratic and authoritarian regimes that they provide order so that attempts to overthrow them would lead to disorder. They envelop themselves in an ideology of order, hierarchy, and discipline, which is internalized by many. In institutionalized democracies order is taken for granted and the political regime can be changed with little risk of disorder. But overthrowing an autocrat may be risky, possibly opening the way to violence and chaos. Military coups are one way to reduce this risk, for after brief skirmishes they can usually impose order, while formerly close allies already entrenched within the state can usually overthrow an autocrat without disaster. But popular insurrections are more problematic. In the aftermath of the uprisings called the "Arab Spring" several countries were plunged into disaster. Most Libyans, Iraqis, and Yemenis probably presently yearn for another effective dictator, while Egypt actually has one. Only the Tunisian rebels largely achieved their goals, though their hold remains a little tenuous. Many Chinese and Russian people today admire the few brave dissidents in their country. But they do not join them, not only through fear of repression, but also because they fear disorder would ensue if the Chinese Communist Party or the Putin regime fell.

Conclusion

I have tried to specify the relationships between despotic and infrastructural power in three types of political regimes – democratic, autocratic, and authoritarian. Autocratic states are more despotic and less durable, with less infrastructural power than democracies, as expected. This is because they have to rule through patron-client networks that enjoy some autonomy from the state. Autocrats can devise methods of binding them to the state, but these result in tensions between included and excluded elites, and it is not easy in the long run to maintain a balance between them. That is the main reason why autocracies are generally shorter lived than democracies.

Yet authoritarian states basing their power on a single party have as much infrastructural power, can be as effective, and are almost as durable as democracies. This has been obvious in the case of communist regimes, but it is also true of some other autocratic regimes generally lacking much ideology and which have managed to practise single-party rule. If democracy was the greatest power invention of the eighteenth and nineteenth centuries, the single party is the twentieth-century equivalent. Many have argued that the greater the infrastructural power, the less the despotism. "As infrastructural power grows, in other words, despotic power declines," says Ron (2003, 19). This is not true of authoritarian regimes.

In general I have upheld my original view that democracies are low on despotic power and high on infrastructural power, though this is truer of longer-lived democracies than newer democracies. However, I have noted worrying contemporary trends. On the one hand, the rise of the "deep" security state amid a "war against terror" has increased state despotic tendencies almost everywhere, including in long-lived democracies. There is no sign at present that this might be declining. Governments are still discovering new surveillance techniques made available by micro-electronic technologies. These are also potentially useful in policing the increasing numbers of people made redundant, poor, and restive by current trends in the global capitalist economy. It is doubtful if this genie can be put back in the bottle. On the other hand, capitalist corruption is weakening democracies' infrastructural power, since the flows between people and state are being increasingly blocked by the buying of politicians and officials by capitalist corporations – which are themselves internally authoritarian. Add on to this that we are in a period in which autocratic and authoritarian models of social development seem capable of rivalling democratic models across parts of the world, and that the main traditional opponents of rampant capitalism, socialist movements, are declining almost everywhere, and the result is that I am not over-sanguine about the global future of democracy. John Hall has identified "civility" as the cultural bedrock of democracy. He identifies two of its principal enemies as unrestrained capitalism and war – as I have done here. But I wonder if he finds me now to be too pessimistic about the future of democracy.

REFERENCES

Amsden, Alice. 1989. *Asia's Next Giant: South Korea and Late Industrialization*. New York: Oxford. University Press.

Blanton, Richard, and Lane Fargher. 2008. *Collective Action in the Formation of Pre-modern States*. New York: Springer. https://doi.org/10.1007/978-0-387-73877-2.

Cave, Tamsin, and Andy Rowell. 2014. *A Quiet Word: Lobbying, Crony Capitalism and Broken Politics in Britain*. London: Bodley Head.

de Figueiredo, John M., and Brian Kelleher Richter. 2014. "Advancing the Empirical Research on Lobbying." *Annual Review of Political Science* 17 (1): 163–85. https://doi.org/10.1146/annurev-polisci-100711-135308.

Drutman, Lee. 2015. *The Business of America Is Lobbying*. New York: Oxford University Press. https://doi.org/10.1093/acprof:oso/9780190215514.001.0001.

Geddes, Barbara. 1999. "What Do We Know about Democratization after Twenty Years?" *Annual Review of Political Science* 2 (1): 115–44. https://doi.org/10.1146/annurev.polisci.2.1.115.

Hall, John A. 1985. *Powers and Liberties: The Causes and Consequences of the Rise of the West*. Berkeley: University of California Press.

– 2013. *The Importance of Being Civil: The Struggle for Political Decency*. Princeton: Princeton University Press.

Hall, John A., and John Campbell. 2015. *The World of States*. London: Bloomsbury.

Kandil, Hazem. 2016. *The Power Triangle: Military, Security, and Politics in Regime Change*. Oxford: Oxford University Press. https://doi.org/10.1093/acprof:oso/9780190239206.001.0001.

Kuhner, Timothy. 2014. *Capitalism v. Democracy: Money in Politics and the Free Market Constitution*. Stanford: Stanford University Press.

Lee, Ching Kwan. 2007. *Against the Law: Labor Protest in China's Rustbelt and Sunbelt*. Berkeley: University of California Press.

Mahoney, Christine. 2008. *Brussels versus the Beltway: Advocacy in the United States and the European Union*. Washington, DC: Georgetown University Press.

Mann, Michael. 1984 "The Autonomous Power of the State: Its Origins, Mechanisms and Results." *Archives Européennes de Sociologie*, 25. Reprinted in Michael Mann, ed., *States, War and Capitalism*. Oxford: Basil Blackwell, 1988. https://doi.org/10.1017/S0003975600004239.

– 1986. *The Sources of Social Power*. Vol. 1, *A History of Power from the Beginning to AD 1760*. Cambridge: Cambridge University Press.

– 1997. "Has Globalization Ended the Rise and Rise of the Nation-State?" *Review of International Political Economy* 4 (3): 472–96. https://doi.org/10.1080/096922997347715.

– 2005. *The Dark Side of Democracy: Explaining Ethnic Cleansing*. Cambridge: Cambridge University Press.

– 2008. "Infrastructural Power Revisited." *Journal of Comparative International Development* 43 (3–4): 355–65.

– 2012. *The Sources of Social Power*. Vol. 3, *Global Empires and Revolution, 1890–1945*. Cambridge: Cambridge University Press.

Marshall, T.H. 1963. *Sociology at the Crossroads and Other Essays*. London: Heinemann.

Mathews, John. 2014. *Greening of Capitalism: How Asia Is Driving the Next Great Transformation*. Stanford: Stanford University Press. https://doi.org/10.11126/stanford/9780804791502.001.0001.

Mozur, Pau, and Choe Sang-Hun. 2017. "Samsung Heir's Arrest in South Korea Intensifies Calls for Cleanup." *New York Times*, 17 February.

Ron, James. 2003. *Frontiers and Ghettos: State Violence in Serbia and Israel*. Berkeley: University of California Press.

Sang-Hun, Choe. 2017. "South Korea Removes President Park Geun-hye." *New York Times*, 9 March.

Slater, Dan. 2003. "Iron Cage in an Iron Fist: Authoritarian Institutions and Personalization of Power in Malaysia." *Comparative Politics* 36 (1): 81–101. https://doi.org/10.2307/4150161.

Soifer, Hillel. 2008. "State Infrastructural Power: Approaches to Conceptualization and Measurement." *Journal of Comparative International Development* 43 (3–4): 231–51. https://doi.org/10.1007/s12116-008-9028-6.

– 2012. "Measuring State Capacity in Contemporary Latin America." *Revista de Ciencia Política* 32 (3): 585–98.

– 2015. *State Building in Latin America*. Cambridge: Cambridge University Press.

Svolik, Milan. 2012. *The Politics of Authoritarian Rule*. New York: Cambridge University Press. https://doi.org/10.1017/CBO9781139176040.

Weiss, Linda. 1998. *The Myth of the Powerless State*. Ithaca: Cornell University Press.

Witko, Christopher. 2011. "Campaign Contributions, Access, and Government Contracting." *Journal of Public Administration: Research and Theory* 21 (4): 761–78. https://doi.org/10.1093/jopart/mur005.

8 Resistance and Nationalist Violence: A Hallsian Approach to Nation-Building in a Colonial Context

MATTHEW LANGE

John A. Hall's enormously impressive *œuvre* is multifaceted and extensive, and both traits make it difficult to generalize about a "Hallsian" approach. Yet two characteristics are present throughout the majority of his work and are hallmarks of Hallsian sociology. One key element is the subject matter. Hall's work focuses primarily on states and nations, and a central concern is the interrelationship between the two, with states shaping nations and nations affecting the characteristics and policies of states. He notes, in turn, that nation-states have been the dominant actors in the world over the past two hundred years but recognizes that there is nothing natural or ideal about them, as nation-states are usually very difficult to build, something that several chapters in this volume illustrate. During the last few decades, states, nations, and nation-states have been brought back into sociological analysis, and Hall played an important role in this process (see Campbell and Hall 2015; Hall 1986, 1994, 1998; Hall and Malešević 2013; Paul, Ikenberry, and Hall 2003).

The second defining characteristic of the Hallsian approach is the productive marriage between sociology and history. The focus is on big and classical sociological questions, and the analysis is informed by diverse social theorists, especially Ernest Gellner, Adam Smith, and Max Weber. At the same time, a rigorous employment of history both informs sociological understandings and serves as direct evidence for the arguments being advanced.[1] The Hallsian combination of sociology and history has contributed to the resurgence of comparative-historical

1 See Hall and Bryant (2005) for Hall's assessment of historical methods in sociology.

sociology, a development in which Michael Mann, also a contributor to this volume, has played a major role as well. The approach offers, in addition, a template for replication: it urges us to look beyond historical particularities for more general understandings, while the importance it gives to historical knowledge highlights the many blind spots and limitations of grandiose social theory (see Hall 1985, 1995, 1996). One important limitation of social theory recognized by Hall is its bias towards "Western" industrialized societies – a problem that the Hallsian approach seeks to address in part by turning to the history of other parts of the world.

In this chapter, I apply a Hallsian approach to the study of overseas colonialism. In line with the subject matter of Hallsian sociology, I consider the impact of states on nation-building and nationalist violence in former colonies. Analytically, I combine the particulars of history and the generality of social theory. Most importantly, I follow Hall's lead by using historical understandings to revise theories of social change in Western Europe so they can be applied to other social environments. In so doing, I follow the comparative-historical orientations of many of the chapters in this volume – such as those by Joseph Bryant, Luyang Zhou, and Yanfei Sun and Dingxin Zhao.

States and Nationalist Violence in Former Colonies

Modernization theory claims that modern social transformations – including the rise of powerful states and organized mass religions – facilitate nation-building through their positive effects on social homogeneity. This theory is now almost universally dismissed for its claims that all countries modernize in the same way, but a number of influential scholars accept that states and religions shape social homogeneity in influential ways and explore how state and religious differences explain variation in nation-building. For example, Wimmer (2016) notes that a history of centralized statehood promotes social homogeneity, as older states are generally more effective and promote shared language among core populations for long periods of time. Gellner (1983) arrives at a similar conclusion but takes a different theoretical route: he links historical states to high culture and views the latter as an influential determinant of nation-building. Linked to Gellnerian high cultures, historical states commonly support particular religions and thereby contribute to more religiously homogenous populations, and mass, organized religion is an important building block of nations (Hroch 1985; Loizides 2009; Marx 2003; Mosse

1975; Smith 1993). Although not taking a modernization perspective, ethnosymbolists make complementary claims about states and religions. Anthony Smith (1986), for instance, notes that histories of statehood and organized, mass religion can facilitate nation-building by providing a variety of myths and symbols that nation-builders can manipulate to predispose people to perceive, believe in, and value nations.

While states and religion can facilitate successful nation-building in these ways, such effects depend on whether state and religious actors use their influence to forge unified nations and whether minorities are willing to assimilate. A Hallsian approach, in turn, directs attention to the influence of social and historical environments and forces researchers to question whether context promotes variation in nation-building. Within Western Europe, for example, states and other influential actors commonly worked hand in hand to build nations, and resistance to nation-building policies was relatively limited. Most importantly, Western European states usually collaborated with and co-opted religions in ways that not only limited opposition to nation-building but also allowed states to exploit religious resources to build nations. One important contextual factor explaining these characteristics was widespread international warfare, which not only kick-started nation-building efforts relatively early but also created foreign enemies that could unify new nations (Mann 1986; Tilly 1985). And in combination with the Reformation, this international competition helped to fuse religion and state, with the Treaty of Westphalia reinforcing the sovereign's right to enforce official state religions. Finally, European nation-building was – historically speaking – very early and occurred just as new technological developments were making possible the rise of "imagined communities" (Anderson 1983). Due to timing, both national alternatives and opposition to nation-building were relatively weak.

In colonial environments, things are very different, and these differences might make a history of statehood and large, organized religions more of an impediment to nation-building than a building block of nationalism. Whereas non-colonial states facing international threats commonly have an incentive to build unified nations, overseas colonial states ruled over peoples who were usually perceived as innately alien and incapable of assimilating into the imperial *Staatsvolk*. Most colonial officials therefore made no effort to build nations among the colonized and fixated on colonial control. And because pre-colonial states and mass religions commonly mobilized anti-colonial resistance, colonial officials might have been most likely to implement policies impeding nation-building in environments with these elements.

Colonialism, Resistance, and Nation-Building

Colonial powers combine four main strategies to deal with anti-colonial resistance: indirect rule, direct rule, coercion, and division. Through indirect rule, colonial powers attempt to undercut resistance by delegating considerable autonomy and authority to local elites. In allowing indigenous elites to maintain some degree of power and authority, colonial authorities hope these elites and their subjects will be more likely to accept colonial domination. Direct rule, by contrast, sees indigenous elites and their institutions as a source of anti-colonial resistance and attempts to contain that resistance by eliminating their autonomy. Although direct and indirect rule are opposing strategies, they can be combined to form hybrid forms of rule that attempt to exploit the benefits of each (Lange 2009). Moreover, colonial powers commonly use each as distinct forms of rule in the same colony, with some regions and peoples ruled more directly and others ruled more indirectly.

Whether using direct rule, indirect rule, or some combination of the two, colonial powers also commonly employ coercive and divisive strategies of control. Because colonial officials lack legitimate authority, coercion is inevitably employed to maintain colonial rule. This strategy restrains anti-colonial resistance by severely punishing those who resist colonialism, through prison, physical violence, and murder. Divisive strategies attempt to limit anti-colonial resistance by increasing competition and conflict between different segments of the population, a technique that is commonly referred to as "divide and rule" (Abernethy 2000; Lange 2015, 2017; Mamdani 2012). According to Abernethy (2000), overseas colonial powers combine three divisive sub-strategies to shore up control: isolating communities from one another, increasing competition between communities, and creating communal hierarchies. While most theorists focus on the overt aspects of divide and rule, others note it also had more hidden components. The legibility of populations facilitated colonial control, and colonial officials recognized and institutionalized a variety of ethnic, religious, and racial categories in an effort to better control the population (Cohn 1987; Wyrtzen 2015). These categories contribute to divisions on their own and reinforce divisive strategies.

Whereas direct rule, indirect rule, and coercion can have mixed effects on nation-building among the colonized, divisive strategies of control strongly and consistently obstruct nation-building by dividing peoples into distinct categories and institutionalizing competition. Colonialism is therefore most likely to impede nation-building when divisive strategies are components of control efforts. Colonial decisions to employ divisive strategies depend on a variety of things, but one influential factor is the level of anti-colonial resistance, something that is linked to the presence of pre-colonial states and religions. People living in regions with powerful pre-colonial states are usually able to resist colonial conquest, and colonial powers, if successful, commonly have great difficulty breaking this resistance after conquest. Such resistance is usually promoted by the presence of large populations possessing a variety of mobilizational resources and is usually greatest when pre-colonial states support an organized religion, as the latter provides a variety of mobilizational resources – organizational, communicational, and ideological – that prove difficult for colonial powers to contain. Colonialism was therefore most dependent on elaborate and intensive strategies of control in such environments, something that pushed colonial officials to attempt to rule through division.

Divisive strategies of colonial control, in turn, have the greatest benefits for colonizers in regions with powerful pre-colonial states and religions, and the fewest drawbacks. Indirect rule poses considerable risks in places with powerful pre-colonial states and religions because the main institutions of colonial resistance stay intact and remain powerful. Pre-colonial states also hinder the effectiveness of direct rule and coercion as strategies of colonial control. Given the size and organization of the populations in places with pre-colonial states, heavy reliance on either of these strategies is necessarily costly and logistically difficult. Moreover, both direct rule and coercion – especially in combination – commonly increase powerful and widespread grievances that contribute to an anti-colonial backlash, and pre-colonial institutions provide powerful mobilizational resources for such a backlash. Divisive strategies, on the other hand, are usually easy to implement in places with pre-colonial states. Although they took different forms, pre-colonial states were empires with core peoples linked to the state and peripheral peoples who – to different extents – were usually excluded and discriminated against by the pre-colonial state and its core peoples. Colonial states can easily exploit these divisions – heightening divisions, competition, and antipathy between majorities and minorities – to gain support from minorities, making nation-building a very difficult task. Thus, given a powerful base of anti-colonial resistance as well as cleavages that colonial officials can exploit in implementing divide and rule, the impact of pre-colonial states and religions on nation-building might be very different in colonial contexts than in Western Europe.

Missionaries and Nationalist Divisions in a Colonial Context

A growing literature finds that missionaries contributed to many of the outcomes commonly attributed to colonialism (Cogneau and Moradi 2014; Lankina and Getachew 2012; Woodberry 2008, 2012), but few works consider how missionaries affected nation-building and violence (although see Trejo 2009). Because missionaries did not seek political control, they did not employ strategies of domination. Instead, they fixated on conversion, but this goal also had the potential to promote the intensification of ethnic divisions and nationalist contestation, especially when missionaries faced stiff resistance. And, paralleling the discussion of states and colonialism, this resistance was likely greatest in regions with mass, organized religions.

Missionaries commonly affected the contours and salience of ethnicity and, in so doing, contributed to powerful and politicized nationalist divisions. Most notably, many missionaries standardized languages and created systems of writing for previously unwritten languages. In addition, they were commonly the main providers of education and printed an enormous body of work for local consumption (Woodberry 2012), and both of these factors shaped the contours and salience of ethnicity by popularizing various ideas of it (Anderson 1983).

Second, missionaries commonly organized their followers and helped them to pursue communal interests at the regional and national levels, and these activities had the potential to politicize ethnicity, promote ethnic competition, and intensify nationalist contestation. Sometimes missionaries actively organized their followers to pursue communal interests. This was most common when they worked with marginalized minorities and faced opposition from majorities. More commonly, however, missionaries contributed to nationalist divisions and contestation more indirectly by heightening ethnic identities and providing education, organizations, and other resources that facilitate ethnic-based political mobilization.

Third and finally, missionaries contributed to transformations in ethnic hierarchies, something that also shaped the salience of ethnicity and intensified communal competition. Most importantly, missionaries were the main source of education throughout much of the world, and education was an important means of mobility and communal status. And because many communities facing downward mobility saw missionaries as undesirable and therefore avoided them, they perceived the greater mobility of peoples who worked with missionaries as unjust, thereby heightening ethnic divisions and competition. This was especially the case when upwardly mobile communities were minorities who had previously been marginalized by the majority.

Missionary effects on nationalist divisions and competition undoubtedly varied greatly, and resistance to missionary proselytization likely exacerbated their divisive effects. Missionaries were most likely to contribute to nationalist divisions and competition when facing strong resistance, something that was especially likely in regions with large, organized religions. Because missionaries had greater difficulty attracting people who practised Buddhism, Hinduism, and Islam, they commonly worked more closely with religious minorities, which strengthened ethnic divisions, increased the mobility of minorities, and intensified majority resentment against minorities. Moreover, the threat posed by missionaries commonly sparked revival movements in places with well-organized religions, increasing the risk that indigenous elites would adopt and support religious-based nationalisms that excluded and targeted religious minorities.

Comparative-Historical Analysis: Burma and Thailand

In addition to using history to inform classical sociological theory, a Hallsian approach uses historical evidence to support theoretical claims. In this section, I provide a comparative-historical analysis of Burma and Thailand. Specifically, I delve into their different histories of colonialism and missionary influence to explore how context shapes the impact of states and religions on nation-building.

Burma

Also known as Myanmar, Burma is the location of the world's longest-running civil war, which began in 1948, has killed over one hundred thousand people, and pits a state that is dominated by ethnic Burmans – known as Bamars – against an organized opposition comprised of ethnic Karens. Rohingya, Chin, Kachin, Mon, and Shan minorities have also fought the government, making Burma one of the most war-torn countries on the face of the planet since its independence in 1948. In nearly all of these conflicts, minorities have sought greater autonomy, whereas the state and its supporters have fought to protect the Bamar nation.

Burma was a powerful kingdom at the turn of the nineteenth century and controlled lands that roughly coincide with its present borders. Similar to composite states in early modern Europe, a core region controlled peripheral polities by granting them considerable autonomy. The state elite and their core population were ethnic Bamars, who spoke the same language and practised Buddhism, the state-sponsored religion. Evidence suggests that many minority peoples assimilated into Bamar culture in pre-colonial times by learning Burmese and converting to Buddhism. Today, two-thirds of Burmans speak Burmese as their first language, and 80 per cent of Burmans practise Buddhism.

British colonial conquest was a violent and piecemeal affair, occurring through three different wars of conquest in 1826, 1852, and 1885. In all three wars, the British faced strong military resistance but outmatched their Burmese counterparts. Conquest and control are different things, however, and British officials faced considerable opposition throughout the colonial period. Although many minorities initially opposed British rule, they were quickly pacified and soon cooperated with the British. Many Bamars, by contrast, intensely opposed British rule and maintained this opposition throughout the colonial period. For example, after the final conquest of Burma in 1885, the British faced a violent rebellion over the next three years and required over forty thousand Indian troops to keep the region under some semblance of control (Callahan 2003, 25). Other Bamar-led revolts followed, causing Burma to earn the reputation of being among the most lawless of all British colonies.

Given this staunch opposition, it is not surprising that the telltale signs of divisive strategies of control were present in colonial Burma. Most notably, Furnivall (1958, 22) astutely notes that the British ruled minorities and the majority differently and provided minorities with privileged access to positions within the colonial state, both of which promoted extreme national disunity. The case thus highlights how a powerful pre-colonial state contributed to anti-colonial resistance and thereby a particularly divisive form of colonial rule.

The British ruled over the core areas of the former Burmese kingdom through direct rule, destroying the monarchy, eliminating Bamar self-rule, and imposing a system of rule that gave the British greater control over Bamar affairs. This intense form of rule was costly and had become increasingly uncommon among new British colonies, with indirect rule becoming the dominant form of rule by the second half of the nineteenth century. The use of direct rule in Burma was influenced by British fears of Bamar resistance, as direct rule was viewed as a means of removing the most powerful basis of anti-colonial opposition. Moreover, the first regions conquered by the British quickly became major producers of rice and attracted large numbers of Indian settlers, and both of these developments also promoted direct rule. Alternatively, the British implemented indirect rule among the larger minority communities in the north and east for a variety of reasons: it was less costly, these parts of Burma offered limited economic benefits, and the minorities living in these regions became relatively supportive of British rule (Callahan 2003; Selth 1986; Smith 1994). Indirect rule made possible considerable political autonomy and allowed minority communities to maintain a customary system of law. Furthermore, the British restricted access to the indirectly ruled regions, thereby creating rigid boundaries between Bamars and the minority peoples they used to rule (Gravers 2002).

A second way in which the British differentially treated Bamars and minorities was through military and police recruitment. During the first phase of colonialism, the British used Indian soldiers in their efforts to maintain some semblance of control and put down resistance. Shortly thereafter, they began to employ a growing number of indigenous Burmans to fill these positions, although for most of the colonial period they excluded Bamars from the security forces out of fear that they could not be trusted. The privileged Burmans were drawn from three minorities: Karens, Kachins, and Chins, which together comprised 81 per cent of indigenous members of the military in 1931 but accounted for only 15 per cent of the population (Callahan 2003, 35; Selth 1986, 489). During the Second World War, Japan conquered colonial Burma with the help of Bamar nationalists. The British, in turn, enlisted minorities to help combat the Japanese and their Bamar collaborators, thereby pitting minorities against Bamars in violent military battles.

The combination of ruling the majority directly and minorities indirectly and of privileging minorities in the colonial military and administration contributed to powerful ethnic divisions and competition. The use of indirect rule over minorities heightened ethnic divisions and competition by pitting minorities and Bamars against one another. Bamar nationalists wanted a unified nation-state dominated by Bamars, something they believed was present in pre-colonial times but that the British had unfairly destroyed. Minorities, on the other hand, wanted to maintain their autonomy, especially in the face of what they saw as chauvinistic Bamar nationalism. An additional factor was that Mons and Karens were two ethnic minorities whose populations lived primarily in the directly ruled region. Seeing the autonomy of other minorities and being excluded from the Bamar nation, leaders from both of these communities began to demand their own ethnic states similar to those of other minorities.

Importantly, the privileged position of minorities within the colonial security apparatus also contributed to this violence. Many Bamars greatly resented both the British for destroying the pre-colonial political system and the minorities for their collaboration with the British. And because the minorities had formerly been subordinate subjects of the Bamars, the privileged position of the minorities was all the more glaring. This situation contributed to the rise of virulent Bamar nationalism that sought to reinstate Bamar control of the state. The minorities, because of their privileged position within the police and military forces, were well placed to oppose aggressive Bamar nationalism and fight for self-rule. Thus, minority self-rule and autonomy movements faced off against Bamar nationalists, and the outcome was severe nationalist violence between Bamars and a half dozen minority communities.

While the interaction between colonialism and a history of statehood intensified ethnic divisions and competition in ways that prevented nation-building, the case of Burma also offers evidence that missionaries hindered nation-building when they worked in regions with a history of state-sponsored, organized religion. Most importantly, missionaries worked closely with minorities because Bamars vehemently opposed missionaries, and missionary influence among minorities strengthened and politicized ethnicity in ways that increased nationalist contestation. Missionaries thus put Buddhists on the defensive and contributed to religious-based resentment that helped to solidify religion as a central pillar of the Bamar nation, making Christians – as well as Muslim Rohingyas – favoured targets of Bamar nationalists.

Baptist missionaries arrived in Burma shortly before the beginning of British colonial rule but had little influence because the pre-colonial state prevented them from leaving the capital city, forbade proselytization, and declared that any Buddhist who converted would be executed. Once British rule began, however, missionaries gained access to all peoples living in British-controlled territory. Yet they faced considerable resistance from Buddhists. Buddhism, as noted above, was a central institution among Bamars with a sound organizational base, being state sponsored prior to colonialism. Buddhist officials and their followers resented and mobilized against Christian missionary influence, something they associated with colonialism and cultural imperialism. As a result, missionaries eventually worked much more closely with non-Buddhist minorities who had historically been marginalized and exploited by Bamars.

Through their work, missionaries played a particularly important role in heightening ethnic awareness among minorities. The Karens offer one telling example. Missionaries coined the term "Karen" during the colonial period to refer to diverse peoples who lived in the peripheral mountains and forests and spoke a variety of languages and dialects (Jørgensen 1997, vi). Despite the extreme weakness of a precolonial Karen consciousness, the missionaries wore ethnic lenses and believed that the Karens were a distinct "race" and "nation" even when the Karens did not do so themselves. At the same time, the missionaries saw the Karen "nation" as primitive and needing assistance to gain the attributes of an "advanced" and "modern" nation. As one prominent missionary remarked in the late nineteenth century, "From a loose aggregation of clans we shall weld them into a nation yet" (Smeaton 1920, 19). Another missionary noted the success of their nation-building endeavours: "These scattered tribes were becoming a united people. Instead of each clan acting for itself, they proposed to unite; and this was undoubtedly the legitimate result of the new life from the Deliverer. Satan divides and destroys. Jesus unites and saves" (Bunker 1902, 237).

The activities of several missionaries suggest that many worked hard to strengthen a Karen consciousness. Only a few years after the establishment of the Karen missions, American Baptists made the first Karen flag and gave it to the Karens to represent their community (Mason 1862, 267). They also encouraged Karens to organize a national association promoting Karen unity and looking out for the well-being of the community. In many other ways, however, the impact that missionaries had on the development of a Karen national consciousness was more indirect and unintentional. Language offers one notable example.

Shortly after they began working with Karens, Baptist missionaries standardized three Karen languages, made them written languages, and thereby helped to build a common linguistic base on which to build an imagined community. As one British official remarked, "No people can long survive the extinction of their language ... The missionaries, headed by the great Judson, have rescued the Karen language from oblivion and given it a certain permanency by reducing it to writing in the Burmese character" (Smeaton 1920, 219–20). The main reason that the missionaries made this effort was a desire to make the gospel much more accessible to the Karens and thereby facilitate conversion. To allow Karens to read the scripture, in turn, American Baptist missionaries also invested enormous effort in educating Karens by establishing schools wherever the missionaries worked. This education was in one of the three Karen languages used by missionaries, meaning that Karens learned standard dialects shared by many others and made investments in these languages.

Karens flocked to these missionary schools, and went from being illiterate to being among the most educated communities in colonial Burma. Mass literacy, in turn, gave Karens access to literary depictions of the Karen community, something that Benedict Anderson (1983) describes as playing a fundamental role in building a strong and widespread ethnic consciousness. Indeed, the Baptist Missionary Press was established shortly after the beginning of the mission and was prolific, printing tens of millions of pages of material in the Karen languages. These writings depicted Karens as a coherent community with ancient roots instead of as the diverse collection of people that they were. For example, the missionaries established a vernacular newspaper in 1842, which reviewed the current events affecting Karens and continually depicted Karens as a primordial community. One article from 1855 presents a myth that exemplifies Anderson's claims about imagined communities and seems to present the core elements of his theory. It describes how the losing of books (the loss of literacy) caused the demise of the Karen "nation" and prophesizes that the return of books will once again unite the Karen nation (Mason 1860, 75–6). By the early twentieth century, articles in the newspaper did more than describe the Karen nation as real: they actively sought to increase a sense of Karen consciousness. An article from 1916 offers one instance. Entitled "The Karen Language and Karen Loyalty," it describes how language is the basis of Karen identity and demands respect for it as well as for all Karens (American Baptist Historical Society 2015).

As the previous examples highlight, missionaries and the missionary press played an important role in popularizing ethnic myths that supported a Karen consciousness. American missionaries were extremely interested in Karen customs and culture, as knowledge of both proved vital to evangelical success. Dr Francis Mason, who helped translate the Bible into Karen, also collected and published Karen myths and traditions. On this, he writes: "The Karens had no books, but I found they had an abundance of traditions, and I went to work collecting all I could find of every description. I pretty well exhausted the Tavoy Karens from one end of the province to the other, for whenever I found a man who knew something that others did not, I had it written down on the spot" (Mason 1870, 276–7). Among the many myths of Karen origins that Mason gathered, he interpreted and popularized one particular version that describes Karens as originating from the Gobi Desert and migrating to Burma thousands of years ago, and this myth became an important part of the Karen myth-symbol complex. By giving the myth a scientific character and describing the origins of the Karen community in concrete terms, this myth strengthened an ethnic consciousness (Rajah 2002).

In addition to the ideal bases of community, missionaries also shaped the more physical foundations on which a Karen consciousness could flourish by promoting interactions among Karens from all over colonial Burma. One way this occurred was through schools, especially secondary schools that brought together Karens from different regions. Churches also emerged as a central social institution that allowed Karens to interact with one another. As one colonial official described it, "The local church takes the place of the clan-unit, or village. These churches are federally united into associations or missions, which look up to the missionary as their leader. These associations take the place of the confederacies of clans" (Smeaton 1920, 196). Missionaries and their converts organized regular meetings bringing pastors and other Christians together to talk about local and regional affairs, and annual meetings for all Karen Christians brought the leaders of the Karen community together to discuss church governance for the entire community. Such meetings played an important role in making the imagined Karen community seem real, especially since the little contact between Karen clans that existed prior to the arrival of the missionaries was often conflictual. One British official noted the unifying effects of the meetings: "Opportunities are thus given for the Karens to have friendly and social gatherings, which serve to cement a better understanding among the different tribes, who for many years were jealous and suspicious of each other" (McMahon 1876, 255).

Importantly, missionary influence varied greatly among Karens, and anthropologists find that only a minority of contemporary Karens possesses a strong, overarching Karen consciousness (Buadaeng 2007; Jørgensen 1997). If missionaries were the main cause of ethnic consciousness, one would therefore expect that the strongest Karen nationalists were most influenced by the missions, and this is exactly what the evidence suggests. Of the three different Karen languages that missionaries standardized and put into writing – Sgaw, P'wo, and Pau – missionaries had much more influence on the Sgaw. And although Christian Sgaw Karens are a tiny minority of all Karens (approximately 15 per cent), they have almost without exception been the leaders of the Karen nationalist movement, whereas many non-Christian and non-Sgaw-speaking Karens oppose the nationalist movement (Gravers 2002; Harriden 2002; Stern 1968).

In addition to promoting salient ethnic divisions in Burma, missionaries also contributed to nationalist contestation and violence through their impact on Karen nationalism and ethnic hierarchies. Regarding the former, Baptist missionaries promoted Karen self-rule from the time they began working with them. The cost of sending missionaries overseas and high death rates were two influential factors pushing missionaries to embed their movement in the Karen community. Moreover, the American Baptist mission in Burma had an ideology extolling the virtues of self-support and communal autonomy (American Baptist Foreign Mission Society 1927; Carpenter 1883). As one missionary wrote in a letter: "After we have given to the country or people an educated ministry, teachers, the Bible, and a literature, the rest must be self-sustaining. Karens must sustain Karens, is a sentiment I have re-iterated to our native preachers here. Churches must sustain themselves, must begin, must learn, and believe and feel that that is the law of Christ's kingdom" (Carpenter 1883, 159). This promotion of communal autonomy and self-support helped strengthen nationalist desires for self-rule. Along these lines, one internal document of the American Baptist mission noted, "With the development of this policy there has also developed a healthy spirit of independence and power of initiative among the people" (American Baptist Foreign Mission Society 1923, 8).

More than simply pushing Karens to run communal affairs, missionaries also helped organize them to pursue communal interests politically, something that ultimately provoked great anger and resentment among Bamar nationalists. The marginalized position of Karens, widespread Bamar discrimination against Karens, and missionary disdain for "heathen" Bamars all contributed to missionary efforts to organize Karens politically in an effort to protect them. In addition to other more local organizations, in 1881 missionaries helped to establish the Karen National Association, which had the stated purpose of promoting Karen unity and fostering the well-being of the

Karen community. By the 1920s, the association had become increasingly active in colonial politics and began to fight for greater Karen autonomy, infuriating Bamar nationalists by demanding that colonial Burma remain part of colonial India. Eventually, the Karen National Association changed its name to the Karen National Union, which mobilized the Karen separatist movement and continues to fight a civil war against the Burmese state.

While Karen demands for a separate independent homeland fuelled the nationalist civil war after colonial independence, those demands only emerged after discrimination and violence showed that Karens would be forcibly excluded from the Bamar nation. And missionaries also contributed to such exclusion by mobilizing Karens to pursue ethnic interests. In addition, they also readjusted ethnic hierarchies in ways that benefited Karens at the expense of Bamars. Baptist missionaries founded hundreds of schools and helped converts run them. By 1913, the Baptists had established an entire system of education, including nine high schools, three teachers' colleges, two theological seminaries, two bible schools for women, thirty-two boarding schools, and 686 day schools (American Baptist Foreign Mission Society 1913, 9). Although some Bamars and non-Karen minorities attended missionary schools, Karens constituted the great majority of the student body even though they comprised only a fraction of the total population. Relatively high levels of education, in turn, allowed Karens to climb the social ladder and receive many of the best jobs in administration, the military, and the private sector. Many Bamars resented the growing social power of Karens, a resentment intensified by the means through which Karens became upwardly mobile: Bamar nationalists saw Christian Karens as collaborating with colonial officials and missionaries in ways that destroyed Bamar self-rule and culture. As Gravers (2002, 240) notes, "To the Burmans, the Christian Karen supported the foreign demolition of the kingdom and the humiliation of Buddhism," and this motivated violence against Karens.

Thailand

Thailand and Burma share a border that is over two thousand kilometres long and have a long history of conflict and competition. Both have core populations linked to a historical state that practises Buddhism. They also have several ethnic minorities and nearly identical ethno-linguistic fractionalization scores (0.38 for Burma and 0.36 for

Thailand), suggesting similar levels of ethnic diversity. Thailand differs from Burma, however, in that it avoided colonial conquest and rule and has had only one nationalist conflict over the past seventy years, which has been much less violent than conflicts in Burma.

In the absence of colonial rule, indigenous state officials did not attempt to implement any sort of divide-and-rule strategy like in Burma. Instead, under pressure from British and French colonialists in Burma, Malaya, and Indochina, Thai officials copied Western Europe and pursued policies of national unification through the assimilation of minorities into the core nation (Terwiel 2005; Wyatt 2003), beginning with state reforms promoting direct rule throughout the territory in the 1880s. Like in pre-colonial Burma, regions with ethnic minorities in the north and the south had previously paid tribute to the Thai monarchy and retained considerable autonomy, but the reforms reduced local autonomy and created the infrastructural basis for the nation-state. As part of their nation-building efforts, the Thai state expanded its provision of education, made education mandatory in 1921, and taught exclusively in Thai. The state also sponsored Buddhism as the official national religion. While all of these policies sought to build a unified Thai nation, the state began to pursue nation-building policy much more aggressively after conservative nationalists led a successful coup in 1932.

The Thai state's nation-building efforts proved unsuccessful among many Muslim Malays living in southern Thailand and contributed to a backlash, and this conflict remains an important source of nationalist contestation and violence in contemporary Thailand. Because Thai Malays had a history of autonomy, practised an organized religion other than the state-sponsored one, and spoke a different language, they resented Thai centralization and nationalization efforts. Moreover, two of Thailand's southern provinces were transferred to British-controlled Malaysia in 1909, and this contributed to demands for the transfer of the remaining Malay regions as well. As a result of this resistance, officials chose to limit the political reforms in the region until 1932, at which time the abrupt and uncompromising imposition of nationalist policy by the military leadership sparked a Malay backlash. The case of Thai Malays shows that nation-building in non-colonial environments is hardly a given, as a history of autonomy and cultural differences that conflict with nationalization efforts promotes resistance to hardline nation-building. Moreover, the case suggests that nation-building is especially divisive when neighbouring states encourage minorities to resist.

Nationalist assimilation was much more successful among Lao-speaking peoples in northern Thailand. In fact, these efforts were so successful that Lao-speaking Thais presently are not categorized as minorities. In Thailand, the Lao minority is much larger than the Malay population, and one-third of all Thais continue to speak Lao. Prior to the Thai state's nation-building reforms, the Lao lived in six northern principalities, all of which had autonomy from Bangkok but paid tribute to the Thai monarchy. Before this, the regions were ruled by a powerful kingdom – Lan Na – that rivalled the Thai kingdom in power until the Burmese conquered both regions, with Lan Na subsequently joining forces with the Thais to overthrow the Burmese in the late eighteenth century, and thereafter becoming a tributary state of Thailand (Wyatt 2003). In Burma, the minorities who lived in similar tributary states ultimately fought Bamar nationalists to maintain autonomy, but similar violence did not erupt among the Lao in Thailand, who have accepted and been accepted into the Thai nation. The absence of colonialism has much to do with this difference, as government policy reduced Lao autonomy in 1870 and actively assimilated Lao into the Thai nation. This is in stark contrast to Burma, where the British increased minority autonomy and institutionalized national difference. And because Lao and Thai are similar languages, because nearly all Lao practise Buddhism, and because Lao nationalism was not encouraged by external forces, the Lao did not actively oppose nationalist assimilation policy in the way that many Thai Malays did.

Relative to minorities in Burma, the Lao-speaking Thais were also much less influenced by missionaries, as the first missionaries only arrived in 1867 and had limited impact given the concentration of missionaries around Bangkok and the missionary focus on converting Thais and Chinese. The Thai royal family maintained cordial relations with many missionaries and – unlike in pre-colonial Burma – did not outlaw the conversion of Thais, which pushed missionaries to continue trying to convert Thais even when such efforts proved unsuccessful. One consequence of this is that there were few and belated efforts to work among the Lao and other minorities in the hinterlands. In contrast with their work with Karens in Burma, the missionaries working among the Lao offered little education and printed much less material, largely due to their very limited success proselytizing among the Lao and the presence and popularity of Buddhist monastery schools throughout the region. Even when the Lao did attend missionary schools, the schools used the Thai language more than Lao: they taught exclusively in Thai for two decades, then began teaching in both languages for three decades, and subsequently returned to teaching exclusively in Thai (Buadaeng 2007; McGilvary 1912). Though missionaries recognized that using the Lao language would facilitate their missionary work, they wavered in their use of Lao for a variety of reasons: they had already invested in the Thai language, Thai and Lao are mutually intelligible, Lao used a totally different script than Thai, no printed material was readily available in Lao, and missionaries believed that Lao was a dying language that would inevitably give way to Thai (McGilvary 1912, 222–5). The fact that Thailand was not a colony also promoted the use of Thai. Most importantly, Lao students wanted to learn Thai because it was the main language of the government, business, and higher education; and the Thai government as part of their nationalization efforts pressured missionaries to use Thai. By contrast, minorities in Burma clamoured to learn English because it was the language of politics and the economy, and the British did not support the Burmese language among minorities.

It is notable that Karens are the largest officially recognized minority in northern Thailand, and that this group – in sharp contrast to Karens in Burma – has more fully assimilated into the core national community. Although Thai Karens continue to face considerable discrimination from the Thai government (including forced relocation), few have developed a strong Karen consciousness in opposition to Thai nationalism. Instead, anthropologists find that they usually possess dual identities that are equal parts Thai and Karen (Buadaeng 2007). The lack of colonial rule contributed to this outcome, as it prevented divisive policies and made possible relatively early efforts to nationalize Karens in Thailand. Differences in missionary influence also played an important role.

Presbyterian missionaries interacted with Thai Karens beginning in the middle to late nineteenth century, but proved very unsuccessful, a failure the missionaries attributed to not knowing the language (McGilvary 1912, 143). Yet when two Karen missionaries from Burma began working with Thai Karens in their vernacular, they proved equally unsuccessful. Highlighting this limited success, only one missionary text was published in a Karen language, and missionaries did not offer any vernacular education to Karens (McFarland 1928, 33–4). One major reason for this limited influence is that the Thai state – while permitting missionary activities – restrained their presence among minority peoples. And when they did allow missionaries to interact with minorities, they commonly undermined their work. Before the Karen missionaries from Burma arrived, for example, the king's brother informed Thai Karens that they would be punished if they converted, causing the Karens to give the two Burmese Karen missionaries a very cold reception (McGilvary 1912, 144).

By the time missionaries gained greater influence among Thai Karens in the 1950s, the Thai state had established a strong presence in regions where Karens resided. This began in the 1870s with major centralizing political reforms implemented by King Chulalongkorn and eventually included the establishment of public schools. The curricula in the government schools ignored the existence of Karens and other minorities and imparted the Thai nationalist position, and by this time missionary schools were forced to follow the curricula of Thai schools (McFarland 1928, 36). In fact, because Karens had access to government schools, missionaries simply offered financial support and student housing to Karen students who attended those schools (Buadaeng 2007). Thus, whereas missionary schools and presses helped heighten a Karen consciousness in Burma, this did not happen on the Thai side of the border, and political and educational institutions actually taught Karens that they were part of a great Thai nation. This comparison of Karens in Thailand and Burma suggests that the influence of missionaries on nationalist divisions and violence depended on colonialism.

Concluding Thoughts

The hallmark of Hallsian sociology is the marriage between sociology and history in the analysis of states and nations. History helps to correct shortcomings in social theory by highlighting blind spots and biases resulting from broad generalizations, but social theory forces historical analysis to explore patterns instead of particularities. The inclusion of history is particularly relevant when analysing societies outside Western Europe and North America, as leading theorists developed their ideas to explain social change in core regions of the world.

In this chapter, I mimic a Hallsian approach to analyse the impact of historical statehood and organized, mass religion on nation-building and nationalist violence outside the European core. Whereas analyses of Western Europe claim that states and religion proved very valuable for building nations, such claims depend on a particular social context characterized by intense international conflict, close ties between state and religion, and relatively early nation-building. In a colonial context, on the other hand, pre-colonial statehood is a powerful basis of anti-colonial opposition, which contributes to colonial policies that intensify ethnic divisions and competition in ways that hinder nation-building and promote violence. The presence of organized, mass religions contributed to this anti-colonialism and also promoted resistance to missionaries. The latter, in turn, pushed missionaries to focus on minorities, something that also contributed to ethnic divisions and competition.

The comparative-historical analysis of Burma and Thailand highlights how colonial context mediates the impact of states and religion. In Burma, pre-colonial states and organized, mass religion interacted with colonialism and missionary influence to exacerbate ethnic divisions, competition, and antipathy. The British implemented a divisive control strategy to deal with strong anti-colonial resistance. In so doing, they separated minorities from the majority, gave preferential treatment to the former, and ruled them through different forms of colonialism. Missionaries, in turn, focused their work on minorities because of stiff resistance from the Buddhist majority. Through this influence, missionaries helped to mobilize minorities politically, strengthen ethnic divisions, and readjust ethnic hierarchies. Thailand, on the other hand, was never colonized. As a result, statehood and a mass, organized religion did not have the same divisive effects: officials never implemented divisive policies, and missionary influence was more limited and affected by the Thai state's nationalist policies.

REFERENCES

Abernethy, David. 2000. *The Dynamics of Global Dominance: European Overseas Empires 1415–1980*. New Haven: Yale University Press.

American Baptist Foreign Mission Society. 1913. "The Judson Centennial." Collection 4424, Folder 701-2-6. Division of Rare and Manuscript Collections, Cornell University Library.

– 1923. "Sgaw Karen Mission." Collection 4424, Folder 705-2-3. Division of Rare and Manuscript Collections, Cornell University Library.

– 1927. "Report of Devolution Committee of the Burma Mission." Folder 702-4-9. Division of Rare and Manuscript Collections, Cornell University Library.

– 2015. "Karen Language and Loyalty." http://judson200.org/index.php/burma-language-exhibit/57-morning-star-articles/195-karen-language-and-loyalty (accessed 15 September 2015).

Anderson, Benedict. 1983. *Imagined Communities: Reflections on the Origin and Spread of Nationalism*. London: Verso.

Buadaeng, Kwanchewan. 2007. "Ethnic Identities of the Karen Peoples in Burma and Thailand." In *Identity Matters: Ethnic and Sectarian Conflict*, edited by James Peacock, Patricia Thorton, and Patrick Inman, 73–97. New York: Berghahn.

Bunker, Alonzo. 1902. *Soo Thah: A Tale of the Making of the Karen Nation*. London: Oliphant, Anderson, & Ferrier.

Callahan, Mary. 2003. *Making Enemies: War and State Building in Burma*. Ithaca: Cornell University Press.

Campbell, John L., and John A. Hall. 2015. *The World of States*. New York: Bloomsbury.

Carpenter, C.H. 1883. *Self-Support, Illustrated in the History of the Bassein Karen Mission*. Boston: Franklin Press.

Cogneau, Dennis, and Alexander Moradi. 2014. "Borders That Divide: Education and Religion in Ghana and Togo since Colonial Times." *Journal of Economic History* 74 (3): 694–729. https://doi.org/10.1017/S0022050714000576.

Cohn, Bernard. 1987. *An Anthropologist Among the Historians*. Delhi: Oxford University Press.

Furnivall, J.S. 1958. *The Governance of Modern Burma*. New York: Institute of Pacific Relations.

Gellner, Ernest. 1983. *Nations and Nationalism*. Oxford: Blackwell.

Gravers, Mikael. 2002. "Conversion and Identity: Religion and the Formation of the Karen Ethnic Identity in Burma." In *Exploring Ethnic Diversity in Burma*, edited by Mikael Gravers, 227–58. Copenhagen: NIAS Press.

Hall, John A. 1985. *Powers and Liberties: The Causes and Consequences of the Rise of the West*. Oxford: Basil Blackwell.

–, ed. 1986. *States in History*. New York: Basil Blackwell.

– 1994. *Coercion and Consent: Studies on the Modern State*. Cambridge: Polity.

–, ed. 1995. *Civil Society: Theory, History, Comparison*. Cambridge: Polity.

– 1996. *International Orders*. Cambridge: Polity.

–, ed. 1998. *The State of the Nation: Ernest Gellner and the Theory of Nationalism*. New York: Cambridge University Press.

Hall, John A., and Joseph Bryant, eds. 2005. *Historical Methods in the Social Sciences*. London: Sage. https://doi.org/10.4135/9781446261934.

Hall, John A., and Siniša Malešević, eds. 2013. *Nationalism and War*. New York: Cambridge University Press. https://doi.org/10.1017/CBO9781139540964.

Harriden, Jessica. 2002. "'Making a Name for Themselves': Karen Identity and the Politicization of Ethnicity in Burma." *Journal of Burma Studies* 7 (1): 84–144. https://doi.org/10.1353/jbs.2002.0003.

Hroch, Miroslav. 1985. *Social Preconditions of National Revival in Europe: A Comparative Analysis of the Social Composition of Patriotic Groups among the Smaller European Nations*. New York: Cambridge University Press.

Jørgensen, Anders Baltzer. 1997. Foreword to *The Karen People of Burma: A Study of Anthropology and Ethnology*, by H.I. Marshall, v–xi. Bangkok: White Lotus.

Lange, Matthew. 2009. *Lineages of Despotism and Development: British Colonialism and State Power*. Chicago: University of Chicago Press. https://doi.org/10.7208/chicago/9780226470702.001.0001.

– 2015. "State Formation and Transformation in Africa and Asia: The Third Phase of State Expansion." In *Oxford Handbook of Transformations of the State*, edited by Stephan Leibfried, Evelyne Huber, Matthew Lange, Jonah D. Levy, Frank Nullmeier et al., 116–30. New York: Oxford University Press.

– 2017. *Killing Others: A Natural History of Ethnic Violence*. Ithaca: Cornell University Press.

Lankina, Tomila, and Lullit Getachew. 2012. "Mission or Empire, World or Sword? The Human Capital Legacy in Postcolonial Democratic Development." *American Journal of Political Science* 56 (2): 465–83. https://doi.org/10.1111/j.1540-5907.2011.00550.x.

Loizides, Neophytos G. 2009. "Religious Nationalism and Adaptation in Southeast Europe." *Nationalities Papers* 37 (2): 203–27. https://doi.org/10.1080/00905990902745742.

Mamdani, Mahmood. 2012. *Define and Rule: Native as Political Identity*. Cambridge, MA: Harvard University Press. https://doi.org/10.4159/harvard.9780674067356.

Mann, Michael. 1986. *The Sources of Social Power*. Vol. 2, *The Rise of Classes and Nation-States, 1760–1914*. New York: Cambridge University Press.

Marx, Anthony. 2003. *Faith in Nation: Exclusionary Origins of Nationalism*. New York: Oxford University Press.

Mason, Ellen Huntly Bullard. 1862. *Civilizing Mountain Men: or, Sketches of Mission Work among the Karens*. London: James Nisbet & Co.

Mason, Francis. 1860. *Burmah, Its People and Natural Productions*. London: Trubner and Company.

– 1870. *The Story of a Working Man's Life: With Sketches of Travel in Europe, Asia, Africa, and America, as Related by Himself*. New York: Oakley, Mason.

McFarland, George Bradley. 1928. *Historical Sketch of Protestant Missions in Siam, 1828–1910*. Bangkok: Bangkok Times.

McGilvary, Daniel. 1912. *A Half Century among the Siamese and the Lao: An Autobiography*. New York: Fleming H. Revell.

McMahon, A.R. 1876. *The Karens of the Golden Chersonese*. London: Harrison and Sons Printers.

Mosse, George. 1975. *The Nationalization of the Masses: Political Symbolism and Mass Movements in Germany from the Napoleonic Wars through the Third Reich*. New York: Howard Fertig.

Paul, T.V., John Ikenberry, and John A. Hall, eds. 2003. *The Nation-State in Question*. Princeton: Princeton University Press.

Rajah, Ananda. 2002. "A 'Nation of Intent' in Burma: Karen Ethno-Nationalism, Nationalism and Narrations of Nation." *Pacific Review* 15 (4): 517–37. https://doi.org/10.1080/09512740210000294l3.

Selth, Andrew. 1986. "Race and Resistance in Burma, 1942–1945." *Modern Asian Studies* 20 (3): 483–500. https://doi.org/10.1017/S0026749X00007836.

Smeaton, Donald MacKenzie. 1920. *The Loyal Karens of Burma*. London: Kegan Paul, Trench, Trubner.

Smith, Anthony D. 1986. *The Ethnic Origin of Nations*. Oxford: Basil Blackwell.

– 1993. *National Identity*. Reno: University of Nevada Press.

Smith, Martin. 1994. *Ethnic Groups in Burma: Development, Democracy and Human Rights*. London: Anti-Slavery Society.

Stern, Theodore. 1968. "*Ariya* and the Golden Book: A Millenarian Buddhist Sect among the Karen." *Journal of Asian Studies* 27 (2): 297–328. https://doi.org/10.2307/2051753.

Terwiel, B.J. 2005. *Thailand's Political History: From the Fall of Ayutthaya to Recent Times*. Bangkok: River.

Tilly, Charles. 1985. "War Making and State Making as Organized Crime." In *Bringing the State Back*, edited by Peter Evans, Dietrich Rueschemeyer, and Theda Skocpol, 169–91. New York: Cambridge University Press. https://doi.org/10.1017/CBO9780511628283.008.

Trejo, Guillermo. 2009. "Religious Competition and Ethnic Mobilization in Latin America: Why the Catholic Church Promotes Indigenous Movements in Mexico." *American Political Science Review* 103 (3): 323–42. https://doi.org/10.1017/S0003055409990025.

Wimmer, Andreas. 2016. "Is Diversity Detrimental? Ethnic Fractionalization, Public Goods Provision, and the Historical Legacies of Stateness." *Comparative Political Studies* 49 (11): 1407–45. https://doi.org/10.1177/0010414015592645.

Woodberry, Robert D. 2008. "Pentecostalism and Economic Development." In *Markets, Morals, and Religion*, edited by Jonathan Imber, 157–78. New Brunswick: Transaction.

– 2012. "The Missionary Roots of Liberal Democracy." *American Political Science Review* 106 (2): 244–74. https://doi.org/10.1017/S0003055412000093.

Wyatt, David K. 2003. *Thailand: A Short History*. New Haven: Yale University Press.

Wyrtzen, Jonathan. 2015. *Making Morocco: Colonial Intervention and the Politics of Identity*. Ithaca: Cornell University Press. https://doi.org/10.7591/cornell/9781501700231.001.0001.

9 Two Communist Revolutions: A Hallsian Comparison of China and Russia

LUYANG ZHOU

Karl Marx made three predictions of how communist revolution would occur. It would carry a universalistic internationalist ideology, viewing all forms of nationalism as antithetical to transnational proletarian solidarity. It would take place in the most advanced industrialized society and thus be conducted by the urban working class. And because the transition to communism was the consequence of the structural implosion of the capitalist system, the military would play only a minor role in the power takeover – communism would not be made but would instead come on its own.

Marx's vision has been proven as well as refuted by the two major communist revolutions – the Russian Revolution of 1917 and the Chinese Revolution of 1949. Both deviated considerably from Marx's predictions, but the extent to which they did so varied. The Bolsheviks stayed much closer to orthodox Marxism. They declared an anti-nationalist ideology, seized power through an urban coup, and ended the civil war within three years of intense struggle after a two-decade-long engagement in non-military conspiratorial activities. In contrast, the path taken by the Chinese Communist Party (CCP) looked like a heresy. The CCP overtly framed itself as nationalist patriots in pursuit of China's unification and full sovereignty. Apart from the short opening period that took place in cities, the twenty-eight-year-long revolution was conducted almost entirely in the countryside, taking the form of a protracted militaristic peasant war against both the Nationalist Party of China (KMT) and the Japanese.

These disparities have largely been neglected by researchers. Most comparative scholars of the two revolutions underscore the structural commonalities that led both to success (Moore 1966; Skocpol 1979; Wolf

1969), although recently a few have noted their differences (Anderson 2010; Mann 2012, 174–90, 398–414). The "fourth generation" of revolutionary theory (see Goldstone 2001) offers insights into leadership, ideology, organization, and process, but has not yet been extended to a comparative analysis of these two major revolutions. In area studies, an emerging literature is tracing China's economic success and political stability since 1978 back to the CCP's special revolutionary history (Heilmann and Perry 2011; Perry 2007; Saxonberg 2013); yet such work lacks a comparative perspective, and is accordingly rather limited in terms of social-scientific theoretical implications.

In this chapter, I provide a comparative historical explanation of why the Bolshevik and CCP revolutions were so different by leveraging the Hallsian perspective. The focus is on three analytical dimensions: the pace of nationalization (Hall 1993, 2017), the spread of civility and thus political decency (Hall 1987a, 2013), and the extent of military warfare both inter-state and within-state (Hall 1986, 1987b). With regard to the first dimension, although both polities had been undergoing the transition from empires to nation-states, Tsarist Russia encountered greater difficulties than the early Republic of China. This disparity geared the communist elites of the two polities to embrace Marxism in contrasting ways: whereas the Bolsheviks used class to negate and obscure nation, proclaiming their goal to be the establishment of a non-national universal state, the CCP invoked class to cultivate a stronger Chinese nationalism. The analysis here echoes aspects of the arguments made in Siniša Malešević's and Yesim Bayar's chapters in this volume – in so far as attention is paid to the numerous ways nationalism is in important cases "made" in subtle and at times unexpected fashions by elite actors.

With regard to the second dimension, both Russia and China belonged to the East, where civility in the Hallsian sense had not taken root, but the Tsarist state, due to its closer cultural proximity to the West and higher levels of modernity, possessed a bit more of what we may call political decency than was the case with the KMT regime. Preferring to use non-lethal punishment in repressing revolution, the Tsarist state preserved the urban orientation of the Bolshevik movement, while the KMT's brutal massacre physically removed the urbanist CCP members, producing the unintended consequence of making room for ruralists to take over.

As to the third dimension, despite its similar experience of geopolitical decline, Russia retained the status of a military power and kept its army stable until the final days of the Romanov dynasty. The mutual hostility between the old military and the Bolsheviks fuelled the latter's anti-Bonapartist psychology. In contrast, in the prolonged course of fatal defeats, incomplete reforms, and warlordism, China's military power had spread throughout society and strongly influenced the radical elites, who then forged a militant-minded communist section.

This chapter considers each of these explanatory analytical dimensions in turn. I conclude with a reflection on the long-term trajectories of each polity and address the big question of whether the CCP will become the next Soviet Communist Party.

Pace of Nationalization

Marx identifies communist ideology as a psychology antithetical to matured capitalism. However, this was more applicable to communists in the West than to the Bolsheviks and CCP, who made successful revolutions in societies where capitalism was relatively underdeveloped. This raises the question of how the makers of the two revolutions came to be interested in Marxism and how their comprehension of this ideology differed from that of their Western counterparts.

This question has so far been addressed by invoking the non-capitalist elements peculiar to Russia and China: the populist convention among the intelligentsia, the huge agrarian populace imbued with the entrenched tradition of mass rebellion, the arbitrary state repression soliciting unified class consciousness, and the isomorphic effect impelling radicals to mimic the despotic state (Bonnell 1983; McDaniel 1991; Perry 2002; Ulam 1977; Xu 2013). While all these factors had existed in Russia and China for a long time, at least since as the spread of Marxism within the two societies in the nineteenth century, the Hallsian perspective suggests a concurrent trend that can explain the timing of the revolutions: the transition from empires to nation-states (Hall 2013, chap. 10).

For those who made the Bolshevik and CCP revolutions, communism was the response to the question of nationalization. The Bolsheviks, primarily ethnic non-Russians themselves (Riga 2012), wanted to retain the multinational state and considered nationalism as dangerous. They thus invoked communism as an instrument to prevent and curb nationalization. For the CCP, in contrast, communism boosted the process of nationalization. Being ethnic Hans, the CCP had no doubt that in the long term China could become a nation-state. What concerned its leaders was how to cultivate the nascent modern Chinese nationalism so as to swiftly achieve China's unification and full sovereignty.

The leading Bolshevik revolutionaries held a pessimistic view of nationalization, for several reasons. The first was geopolitical calculation, which was popular among the Transcaucasian, Polish, and Lithuanian Bolsheviks, who came from the small peripheral nations that had suffered Russia's oppression for centuries. Because the Russification of these regions was unsuccessful, non-Russians often managed to retain clear separate identities and remained motivated to seek equal status with the Russians. However, the failures of the uprisings in the previous centuries had taught these Bolsheviks, as well as their nationalist counterparts, a lesson: whatever ideological frames the imperial centre undertook, the small nations all the same lacked the military capacity to achieve successful separation. To say the least, even if separation could have succeeded, it would have put these nations in even greater danger. The Orthodox Georgians and Armenians might have been slaughtered by the adjacent Ottomans, and the Poles could have easily been occupied by Germany.

The second line of thinking was particular to the non-Russian Bolsheviks that had been assimilated, including the Ukrainians, Latvians, and Jews. Growing up in the regions where Russification had been more successful, these individuals were educated in Russian and immersed in Russian language and culture, and they largely lost their native national identities. They loathed Tsarism but considered secession from Russia unnecessary. They thus viewed communism as a promising system for maintaining a cohesive state.

The third line of thought came from the Russian Bolsheviks, who took it for granted that the non-Russian periphery must be retained as the geopolitical screen and fence while the dominance of the Russian should be preserved to maintain the common market. To these people Tsarist universalism had become as futureless as its cornerstones – monarchism and Orthodoxy – were becoming obsolete. Communism was viewed as an enlightened framework that could retain Russian domination while making it seem less hierarchical and oppressive.

Unlike the Bolsheviks, the CCP believed that the future socialist China must be a nation-state. Like the Russian Bolsheviks, Chinese communists considered the non-Han peripheries as inseparable parts of China, but did not envisage a centralized multinational movement that synchronically unfolded among all ethnic groups (Liu 2004). Two factors might account for this outlook. First, the revolution started in the post-imperial period, when the non-Han peripheries had de facto separated from China proper. The CCP, trapped in the repression and civil war in China proper, had no practical need to take the minority issue seriously. Second, the CCP, not being in power, was far less pressured to present a formal program detailing how it planned to recover the periphery. In this regard, it faced a simpler situation than the in-power KMT, which had proposed some controversial approaches, such as armed conquests and forced assimilation.

To the CCP, China's nationalization could not happen because the idea of nationalism had difficulties penetrating society and could therefore not function as a vibrant mobilizational force. The national idea stumbled before local identities, floated above the illiterate masses, and lacked the intellectual finesse to shape national pride. The CCP members taking part in the 1911 Revolution saw that nationalist slogans did not suffice to incorporate the local armed forces into a unified political camp. Such fragmentation took root in the context of China's geographical vastness and enormous cultural diversity, and became aggressive as universal Confucianism discredited the military and financial powers began decentralizing. Seeing that ferocious factionalism had caused the end of campaigns, the corruption of the armed forces, and the distortions of formal rules, the CCP felt it necessary to invoke some additional ideologies to dilute the notion of locality. Class, for its emphasis on universalism, appeared ideal in this regard.

The CCP members who engaged in grassroots contentions pointed to a second dilemma. From the chaos of the 1910s many patriots had drawn the lesson that, to gain stronger leverage to counterweigh imperialist powers and their agents, the labourer masses must be introduced to the nationalist movement. To the CCP this prescription was naive. Their own experience showed something different: the nationalist slogan could not penetrate the illiterate populace, who totally lacked any notion of nationhood. They thus looked for an ideology that could make the masses fight for nationalism without exactly understanding what it was. Communism appealed to them because it addressed individuals' most concrete interests, such as food, security, and housing.

The CCP adopted communism also to motivate its members. They were embarrassed by the paradox that they were patriots but had minimal cultural materials for developing national pride. Most of them were educated in the post-Confucian period, an iconoclastic time when successive defeats had led the entirety of Chinese history to be refuted as a mistake. The CCP turned to communism because they were attracted by its orientation towards the future – every nation, regardless of its past, could if engineered correctly reach the communist heaven. This ahistorical perspective would allow the CCP to avoid the Kemalist dilemma: making up an enlightened nationhood that was alien to the populace.

There was no determinism, however. In the Russian case, neither non-national universalism nor the invitation to communism was inevitable. Alternative proposals to a Soviet state existed. Among the Ukrainians, Latvians, and Jews were growing non-Russian nationalist movements, while the rightist chauvinists sought to Russify the empire into a Russian nation-state. The liberals (Kadet), on the other hand, proposed a multinational federation that embraced liberal universalism. Choice was contingent upon individual backgrounds. Nationalists came from upper-class families, possessed more cultural capital, and were relatively old, which imparted to them more access and attachment to national culture, while non-class liberals primarily consisted of gentry, who could not accept the route of class warfare against the upper classes. In comparison, the Bolsheviks were of humble social origins, poorly educated, and young. They were thus excluded from the processes of nationalization while also feeling alienated from the ideologies of class collaboration.

Likewise, in China the question of nationalization triggered different responses among the KMT. According to them, a "national universe" could be created either by liberal civic education or fascist rectification, while national indifference among the populace could be eliminated eventually through the development of mass education. As for the issue of shaping national pride, the KMT opted for an enlightened traditional Chinese culture, which they thought could teach the populace authority and solidarity without using alien Western norms. The KMT's reluctance for radicalization stemmed from its relatively upper-class origins, extensive experience abroad, decent education, and strong attachment to the imperial culture, which armed their brains with more ideological alternatives. By the same token, lacking knowledge of any powerful alternatives, CCP members were easily swayed by Soviet propaganda.

The Bolsheviks and CCPs were not "internationalists" as were communists in capitalist Western societies, in that neither Russia nor China had yet achieved the status of full-fledged nation-states, a prerequisite for thinking in "international" or "transnational" ways. While on the eve of the Great War the European communists strove hard to contain the surging nationalism at home, the Bolsheviks and CCPs were faced with the embarrassing dilemma that they did not see strong nationalism at all, even though the CCP wanted it.

Civility and the Extent of Political Decency

Mocking the peasantry as "a sack of potatoes," Karl Marx never thought this class would be able to make any contribution to a successful communist revolution. This prophecy deeply influenced the Bolsheviks, keeping them from exploiting the rebellious potential within Russia's vast agrarian populace, although the repression of 1905 and the ensuing "Dark Period" had proven that urban conspiratorial activities could achieve little. In contrast, Marx's warning had a far weaker impact on the Chinese communists – after a short-lived attempt at replicating the Bolshevik takeover, the CCP members who had survived the massacre of 1927 moved their focus to the countryside. Following several unsuccessful attempts at retaking the cities, they abandoned the illusion of seizing power overnight by an urban uprising, and instead lapsed into a protracted rural guerrilla war.

There are some accounts of this bifurcation, most of which highlight two variations, which made rural mobilization easier in China than in Russia and hence encouraged the CCP to adopt a less orthodox strategy. First, the Tsarist state remained intact and stable, and had sufficient capacity to put down any uprisings from the bottom. By contrast, the KMT state was fragmented and short of reach, especially in the rural regions. Second, Russia's plane and steppe provided little room for the partisans to hide, whereas China's mountainous topography could shelter the militarily inferior partisans. However, both accounts underestimate the ability of individuals to exert agency and thus fall short of explaining how other historical alternatives were excluded. The Bolsheviks might have engaged in rural agitations as the Socialist Revolutionary Party (SR) did; by the same token, the CCP could have maintained its presence in cities, which was the case with the Chinese Trotskyists after 1928. Had these two alternatives become realities, the two communisms would have had different appearances.

The Hallsian perspective can explain why these alternatives did not materialize by drawing our attention to the style of state repression in Russia and China (Hall 1987a, 114–20). The Tsarist state, despite its despotism, exclusiveness, and brutality, was a "benign autocracy," in the sense that it possessed limited, but nonetheless real, political decency. This was first and foremost manifested in the fact that the regime preferred to use non-lethal punishments when repressing revolutionary movements. Such decency derived from two sources. On the one hand, the Romanov dynasty viewed itself as a European monarchy, which for centuries had driven it to present a civilized image vis-à-vis its Western allies – Russia's use of the death sentence was much less frequent than in France and America (Daly 2000). On the other hand, far from being a modern totalitarian ruler, the Imperial Palace was constrained when attempting to exert arbitrary power. It faced overt or covert resistance from the nobles, the liberal-minded intellectuals, and the professional judicial corps. This check was technical – not comparable to that of the church and liberal towns of medieval Europe – but was sufficient to slow, moderate, or even rescind brutal orders from the Tsar or secret police (Walkin 1962, 32–59).

It was this bounded political decency that allowed the urban-minded Bolsheviks to survive, and to remain a group that would never switch to a rural revolution. They primarily included urban workers and students who lacked the skills for agricultural labour. Influenced by orthodox Marxist ideology, they harboured a strong hatred of the peasant mentality and rural environment: in exile they refused to study local languages and marry local women, fearing that their European and proletarian minds would hence be polluted; they actively plotted escape, and once opportunities opened up they returned to the cities. After the frustration of 1905, while the SR continued its agitation in the rural regions, reasoning that state extermination here had greater difficulty in persisting (Gusev 1975, 53–63), the Bolsheviks judged that their penetration of the working class should be further intensified. The ensuing decade's conspiratorial activities would pursue this goal: the Bolsheviks set up *Pravda*, developed evening schools, established cells in trade unions, and even used double agents who received salaries from the police (Cliff 2010, 241).

The only remaining way to halt Bolshevik activity was to have the stubborn leadership physically removed. However, the Tsarist state would not permit mass killing. Among the 102 Bolshevik central leaders from 1903 to the downfall of Tsarism, only eight died before 1917, either from executions or diseases. The majority suffered repression in the form of intense arrests and exile – on average everyone had been arrested 5.4 times, while certain prominent leaders were imprisoned more than fifteen times. Imprisonment was never lifelong and was often short or shortened. When the Bolsheviks returned to freedom, they continued to dominate the party debates – the ideology of heroism they inherited from the nineteenth-century populist-terrorists idealized the experience of imprisonment. The stronger penal record one had, the higher prestige one could achieve in the party's power hierarchy.

The Tsarist state also showed political decency in that its revolutionary movement was an early comer to modern party politics, which reflected Russia's close cultural proximity to the West. This trend became institutionalized after the 1905 Revolution when the Tsarist state inaugurated the Duma, which somewhat legalized party competition, albeit in a nominal and intermittent manner. This imitation of the Western parliamentary system did not extinguish revolutionary movements as the Tsar expected but, rather, further solidified their ideologies. Provided with a legal platform, the socialist parties, wanting to be easily recognized, deliberately differentiated their own programs from that of their rivals, especially ones trumpeting similar ideologies.[1] For this reason, the Bolsheviks had to keep their distance from the SR's program. Both conducted revolutionary activities, but maintained the tacit demarcation between urban and rural regions.

The CCP's switch to rural agitation is often taken for granted, given China's overwhelmingly agrarian populace and the KMT's bloody repression in cities. Yet far from all CCP members consented to this change. Many stubbornly resisted the transfer, either by staying in cities or by impatiently trying to return. Others simply quit the CCP and became the Chinese Trotskyists. The latter continued conspiratorial activities in cities – in a fruitless manner similar to that of the post-1905 Bolsheviks – in the hope that an impending invasion by Japan would bring down the KMT regime and create an opening for revolution, as occurred with Tsarism during the Great War (Chen 2015, 998; Wang 2015, 1016–17). Such reluctance was not surprising, given that the composition of the CCP leadership before 1928 was very close to that of the pre-1917 Bolsheviks. Most of the leading CCP members were industrial workers, urban intellectuals, or students trained in the Soviet Union. Misled by the mythicized Bolshevik history, they were obsessed with the idea of making a revolution through a decisive urban-led uprising. There were some less orthodox participants in peasant agitations, often with rural origins, but their enterprise was viewed as auxiliary, supplementary to the total attack in cities.

Had the KMT state not resorted to mass killing of the hardline urbanists, the CCP would have likely still ruralized, but the process would

1 I thank Sidney Tarrow for this comment.

have been slower and have confronted more intensive contestation from inside. The KMT regime did not allow for political decency. During its brief cooperation with Soviet Russia from 1922 to 1927, it had learned the Leninist model and transitioned into a semi-fascist system seeking to annihilate competing sources of societal power in order to achieve absolute centralization. This engineering project had, in the legal system, caused the reversal of the emerging trend of judicial professionalization (Li 2012). On the one hand, the court was subordinated to the KMT's arbitrary control, with numerous non-professional party cadres installed from outside. On the other hand, many harsh sentences were processed without the participation of judicial institutions.

Under the KMT's punishment system, the CCP urbanist leadership suffered immense losses. Of the seventy-six central committee members before 1928, as many as 40 per cent were executed; these people would not return to the party as the released Bolshevik leaders did. Unrestrained by any societal powers or judicial procedures, the KMT regime simply killed whomever they arrested. Most executions were conducted at military commands or army prisons in secrecy, following brutal torture, which often led to the arrestees' deaths. To prevent armed rescue by CCP partisans, executions were processed as quickly as possible, typically within two weeks, and sometimes on the very day of or day after the arrest. Such frightening repression deterred resistance – among the survivors, 17 per cent defected while another 18 per cent escaped to the Soviet Union, where the CCP held a secure overseas base. This led to the loss of control over strategic reshaping – communication between Shanghai and Moscow was almost cut off at the beginning of the 1930s, to the extent that CCP members at home could only use envoys to maintain contact with their Soviet superiors (Brandt 1958, 145–6). Hampered by the enormous distance, the Comintern could only issue orders to the CCP based on outdated messages that had been produced months before.

This massive removal of the urbanist-minded CCP leadership created a huge power vacuum at the top echelon of the party hierarchy, allowing the erstwhile marginal CCP members who had engaged in peasant mobilization to take over. Here China's lack of political tolerance again facilitated the revolution's ruralization. As party politics was still in its nascent stage, the KMT and CCP were essentially the only two modern political parties. Thus, the CCP's turn to the countryside was not intended to confront a substantial agrarian alternative that propagated a similar program, like the Russian SR. The KMT itself was replacing "party rule" with "military rule" in the 1930s (Wang 2003, 167–79), illegalizing party politics. Without the need to distinguish itself from an adversary in the countryside, the CCP had a much weaker motivation to stick with its urban ideological orientation, except for tactical reasons such as collecting intelligence and demonstrating compliance with the Comintern. Rather, it quickly embraced the model of China's ancient peasant war.

The Warfare Experiences of the Old Regimes

Marxism maintained that warfare within the capitalist international system could lead to defeats and state breakdown, which would allow communist revolutions to succeed, but objected to the use of the military in an immature capitalist system in order to foment those revolutions (Berger 1977). Both the Bolsheviks and CCP deviated from this canon in that they each dismantled the old social systems through brutal civil wars. However, their ways of waging civil war differed. The Bolsheviks primarily played the role of non-military monitors (commissars), with their duties confined to ensuring the old army would fight faithfully, while CCP members were actively involved with the army, acting both as commanders and monitors. As the Hallsian perspective generally concerns power relations during warfare, and in particular the organizational base of ideology (Hall 1986, 1987b), a Hallsian question can be raised: why did ideological power possess more weight in the CCP civil war than in the Bolshevik one?

This difference seems too easy to explain: the Bolsheviks picked up a defunct state machinery, whereas the CCP fought against an incumbent one and thus needed to create its own armed forces from scratch. Yet closer examination shows that the account must extend to the two groups' mentalities, which had been generated long before the civil wars started. Harbouring an anti-Bonapartist psychology, the Bolsheviks loathed standing armies. Their stubborn insistence on replacing the regular army with militia persisted through the fall of Tsarism in 1917 and the civil war, and was manifested in the well-known provocation of the "Military Opposition," wherein the party elders objected to using the old military experts. Lacking military backgrounds and passion for the military, then, they were left with the passive role of monitor. The CCP, by contrast, was imbued with a martial spirit, viewing massive warfare as the cornerstone of China's struggle for unification and liberation. Many CCP members came from the old army, often from its high ranks, while others learned military skills outside of the army, in a generally militarizing society. Their backgrounds allowed them to play a substantial military role in the civil war.

The root of this disparity lies in the military powers of the two old systems, and in particular whether the old regime could monopolize the military culture. If yes, the military would be counted as part of the reactionary old regime, which led to the revolutionaries' anti-Bonapartist mentality. Such congruence was true of Russia. Despite its setbacks in Crimea and Manchuria, and chronic geopolitical decline, the Tsarist Empire remained a military power until its very final days. Without burning defensive crises, the military issue was never central to Russian society's agenda. Neither the socialists nor the liberals needed to embrace a patriotic discourse to legitimize themselves.

The generally stable state of security also allowed the officer corps to maintain organizational unity and promote gradual reforms, from which could develop an apolitical professional culture. From 1878 onwards officers were encouraged to cultivate political indifference so that they could fully focus on military affairs and be immune to revolutionary propaganda (Kenez 1973, 135–6; Mayzel 1975, 315–16; Steinberg 2010, 73). Professionalism had deepened to the extent that on the eve of the Bolshevik takeover the military was almost ignorant of popular ideologies and simply hated all thoughts that carried dissident tones (Kozlov and Nazemtseva 2015). In the wake of the 1905 Revolution the officer corps and military students proved a solid pillar of Tsarism (Denikin 1991, 109–10); this led the movement to fail. During both of the wars with Japan and Germany, officers blamed revolutionary agitation for Russia's setbacks while eagerly creating revolution-free units in their own troops (Timirev 1998, 76–8).

Given the "reactionary" character of the Tsarist military culture, the Bolsheviks loathed the army and extended their hatred to the idea of making revolution through war. They evaded conscription, defected from service, protested the schedule and discipline in barracks, and celebrated every defeat the imperial army suffered. Meanwhile, being mostly of humble social origin and non-Russian ethnicity (especially Jewish), they were increasingly blocked from entering the armed forces. As the reform of professionalization unfolded, a middle-school diploma became a prerequisite for admission to military academies, which transformed officer membership into a privilege for individuals from economically modest families (Persson 2010, 28–43). The humiliating Russo-Japanese War galvanized a wave of Russian chauvinism, wherein Jews became the scapegoats and were deprived of the right to enter military academies in some jurisdictions (Lohr 2003, 17–23). Moreover, "monarchist patriotism" modelled on Japanese Bushido intensified the pre-existing Orthodox theological teachings (Wright 2005), which further alienated the atheist-minded radicals.

China was in a different situation. On the one hand, successive defeats and intense warlordism had promoted the proliferation of a martial spirit and a general militarist-patriotic culture. On the other hand, the old regime, due to its fragmentation and low level of professionalization, failed to monopolize such a militarist outlook, but allowed it to be shared by the revolutionaries. The geopolitical crises of the mid-nineteenth century had altered the imperial literati's traditional anti-military mentality, propelling intellectuals to embrace the martial spirit (Sutton 1980, 20–1). The politicization of the military was inaugurated in the 1850s and became full blown during the warlordism of the 1910s–20s, in the course of which the military came to view intervention in civilian politics as their obligation (Chen 2008, 23–4). Among the masses, militarization spread as a response to the imperial downfall – to deal with the proliferation of banditry, mafia, and looting soldiers – and local self-defence groups mushroomed. It was within these groups that many future CCP generals experienced their initial confrontation with the military and violence (Rowe 2007).

A military patriotic discourse was thus generated, and every social group had to engage in it. The CCP denounced the old army as corrupt and reactionary and trumpeted the need to create a progressive and patriotic military culture. This was not just a proposal. Both the 1911 Revolution and the North Expedition of 1926, as well as the Taiping Rebellion (1851–64) and the Boxer Rebellion (1900–1) to a lesser extent, had embodied such progressive militarism. Many CCP members took part in the North Expedition, acquiring the training that would enable them to become commanders and commissars in the civil war. The communists also gained war skills from the warlords, as positions within the old officer corps were continually becoming available. The warlords, quickly becoming mercenaries in the post-imperial anarchy, recruited officers in an extremely flexible way, which allowed future CCP members of humble social origin and without education to occupy even high-ranking posts.

In the civil war of the 1930s, the CCP largely combined the military with politics. There was a high degree of interchangeability between commanders and commissars, given that both groups mastered military skills well. The content of the "political work" was far more than non-military supervision over the professional military as in the Bolshevik case: the commissars oversaw the teaching of complicated skills, such as air defence, chemical defence, night fighting, and even hygiene, because without these skills soldiers were likely to panic. The commissars were also supposed to be technically sophisticated enough to perform as model fighters, as the old military discipline had become dysfunctional and had to be replaced by the models of ideologically committed individuals.

Conclusion

The Hallsian perspective has helped us compare the Russian and Chinese communist revolutions. We can now reflect on the consequences of those revolutions in light of what we learned about their causes and specific trajectories. Consider first China's hitherto impressive economic success and political stability. By leveraging a nationalist-communist framework, the CCP has had more flexibility in adjusting its economic system. When the appeal of communism faded, the CCP could emphasize the nationalist part of its ideology. The same option was unavailable to the Soviets, because advocating nationalism would delegitimize Soviet internationalism and cause the non-national state to dissolve, as occurred under Gorbachev's reign. From this we might be able to formulate a general thesis: communism needs nationalism to survive. In the global 1989 most "national communisms" survived while every non-national communism died. Nationalism, thanks to its lack of concreteness, has allowed for more flexibility and room for adjustment.

The repression patterns of the old regimes forged the models of intra-party purges. Given that the reconstruction had been completed by the KMT's massacre, the CCP's later internal purges were not very bloody, which allowed the generation of the revolution-makers to live into the 1980s. Harbouring a strong attachment to the communist regime (Zhao 1994; 2001, 214–16), they carved out the path of marketization without resorting to political liberalization. In contrast, due to the Tsar's practice of non-lethal repression, the Bolsheviks delayed the dirty work of purging until the late 1930s, to be perpetrated by the communist regime itself. Stalin's Great Terror forged a huge break, with the October men wiped out and replaced by a new generation of nomenklatura consisting of technocrats and apparatchiks. These people were at first timid in pushing reforms and then indecisive in defending the party – an approach that explains in part the Soviet Union's change from stagnancy in the 1970s to collapse in the 1980s.

The party-army relationship determined whether the communist regimes could withstand the most intense social unrest released by reforms. Throughout the Mao era the CCP army continued its revolutionary tradition of politicization, which shaped the strong conviction among the officers that the party had created the army and thus the army must defend the party at any expense. This norm was so entrenched that during the Tiananmen protests army non-compliance with the directives of the CCP was quickly overcome (Shambaugh 1991, 552–3). In contrast, the Russian army saw itself as a bystander during the fall of the Soviet Union. The officers were open to the Yeltsin regime, just like many of their Tsarist predecessors had been open to the Bolshevik in 1918. The commissar corps were not against the regime change at all, but rather were calmly switching to a new institution known as "the Officer Assembly," where they were supposed to propagate patriotism, marketization, Eastern Orthodoxy, and anything else the new regime ordered them to preach.[2] It is thus not surprising that the August Coup attempted by a few generals ran into resistance from the entire armed forces.

The Hallsian perspective can also offer insights into the burning question of whether the CCP's legacies of revolution, which had hitherto supported the resilience of the party, could turn shaky or weaken in the future. As Hall (1992, 351–3) suggests, nationalism is easier to manipulate but it can also lead to war. This seems a plausible outcome for China, as its economic strength is drawing close to that of the United States whilst its political regime remains semi-totalitarian and often needs to evoke popular support to consolidate its legitimacy. The Hallsian perspective also stresses that the lack of political decency can turn grievance into violence (see Lange 2013), leaving a society bereft of civility and difficult to democratize (Hall 1994). We should keep a close eye, therefore, on the CCP's current return to Maoist tactics. In parallel, Hall (1987a, 202–3) argues that scientific education, by negating the idea that societies necessarily evolve in one direction, undermines the ideological basis of despotism. As it turns out, this is what is occurring in the CCP army at the moment, where a corps of commander-technocrats is taking shape, while commissars are increasingly assuming the roles

2 *Krasnaia Zvezda* (Red Star), 10 January 1992.

of professional psychologists, social workers, and priests of general nationalism. China's future, in sum, remains quite open.

REFERENCES

Anderson, Perry. 2010. "Two Revolutions." *New Left Review* 61: 59–96.

Berger, Martin. 1977. *Engels, Armies, and Revolution: The Revolutionary Tactics of Classical Marxism*. Hamden: Archon.

Bonnell, Victoria. 1983. *Roots of Rebellion: Workers' Politics and Organizations in St. Petersburg and Moscow, 1900–1914*. Berkeley: University of California Press.

Brandt, Conrad. 1958. *Stalin's Failure in China, 1924–1927*. Cambridge, MA: Harvard University Press.

Chen, Bilian. 2015. "The Real Lesson of China on Guerrilla Warfare: Reply to a Letter from a Chinese Trotskyist." In *Prophets Unarmed: Chinese Trotskyists in Revolution, War, Jail, and the Return from Limbo*, edited by Gregor Benton, 985–1000. Leiden: Brill.

Chen, Zhirang. 2008. *Junshen zhengquan: Jindai zhongguo de junfa shiqi* [Warlord-gentry regimes: Warlordism in modern China]. Guilin: Guangxi shifan daxue chubanshe.

Cliff, Tony. 2010. *Lenin: Building the Party, 1893–1914*. London: Bookmarks.

Daly, Jonathan. 2000. "Criminal Punishment and Europeanization in Late Imperial Russia." *Jahrbücher für Geschichte Osteuropas* 48 (3): 341–62.

Denikin, Anton. 1991. *Put' russkogo ofitsera* [The road of a Russian officer]. Moscow: Sovremennik.

Goldstone, Jack. 2001. "Toward a Fourth Generation of Revolutionary Theory." *Annual Review of Political Science* 4 (1): 139–87. https://doi.org/10.1146/annurev.polisci.4.1.139.

Gusev, Kirill Vladimirovich. 1975. *Partiia eserov: Ot melkoburzhuaznogo revoliutsionarizma k kontrrevoliutsii: Ocherk* [Socialist Revolutionary Party: From petty-bourgeois revolutionaries to counterrevolutionaries: A brief history). Moscow: Mysl'.

Hall, John A. 1986. *Powers and Liberties: The Causes and Consequences of the Rise of the West*. Berkeley: University of California Press.

– 1987a. *Liberalism: Politics, Ideology, and the Market*. London: Paladin Grafton.

– 1987b. "War and the Rise of the West." In *The Sociology of War and Peace*, edited by Colin Creighton and Martin Shaw, 37–53. Basingstoke: Macmillan.

– 1992. "Peace, Peace at Last?" In *Transition to Modernity: Essays on Power, Wealth and Belief*, edited by John A. Hall and Ian C. Jarvie, 343–67. Cambridge: Cambridge University Press. https://doi.org/10.1017/CBO9780511628092.017.

– 1993. "Nationalisms: Classified and Explained." *Daedalus* 122 (3): 1–28.

– 1994. "After the Fall: An Analysis of Post-Communism." *British Journal of Sociology* 45 (4): 525–42. https://doi.org/10.2307/591881.

– 2013. *The Importance of Being Civil: The Struggle for Political Decency*. Princeton: Princeton University Press.

– 2017. "Taking Megalomanias Seriously: Rough Notes." *Thesis Eleven* 139 (1): 30–45. https://doi.org/10.1177/0725513617700453.

Heilmann, Sebastian, and Elizabeth Perry, ed. 2011. *Mao's Invisible Hand: The Political Foundations of Adaptive Governance in China*. Cambridge, MA: Harvard University Asia Center.

Kenez, Peter. 1973. "A Profile of the Prerevolutionary Officer Corps." *California Slavic Studies* 7: 128–45.

Kozlov, Denis I., and Elena H. Nazemtseva. 2015. ""Russkii front pervoi voiny v germanskoi istoriografii, 1920–1940" [The Russian Front during the First World War in German historiography]. *Voenno-Istoricheskii Zhurnal* 2: 38–42.

Lange, Matthew. 2013. "When Does Nationalism Turn Violent?" In *Nationalism and War*, edited by John A. Hall and Siniša Malešević, 124–44. Cambridge: Cambridge University Press. https://doi.org/10.1017/CBO9781139540964.008.

Li, Zaiquan. 2012. *Fazhi yu dangzhi: Guomindang zhengquan de sifa danghua* [Rule of law or rule of party: The partization of the KMT judicial system). Beijing: Shehui kexue wenxian chubanshe.

Liu, Xiaoyuan. 2004. *Frontier Passages: Ethnopolitics and the Rise of Chinese Communism, 1921–1945*. Washington, DC: Woodrow Wilson Center Press.

Lohr, Eric. 2003. *Nationalizing the Russian Empire: The Campaign against Enemy Aliens during World War I*. Cambridge, MA: Harvard University Press.

Mann, Michael. 2012. *The Sources of Social Power*. Vol. 3, *Global Empires and Revolution, 1890–1945*. Cambridge: Cambridge University Press.

Mayzel, Matitiahu. 1975. "The Formation of the Russian General Staff, 1880–1917: A Social Study." *Cahiers du Monde Russe et Sovietique* 16 (3): 297–321. https://doi.org/10.3406/cmr.1975.1241.

McDaniel, Tim. 1991. *Autocracy, Modernization, and Revolution in Russia and Iran*. Princeton: Princeton University Press.

Moore, Barrington. 1966. *Social Origins of Dictatorship and Democracy: Lord and Peasant in the Making of the Modern World*. Boston: Beacon.

Perry, Elizabeth J. 2002. *Challenging the Mandate of Heaven: Social Protest and State Power in China*. Armonk: M.E. Sharpe.

– 2007. "Studying Chinese Politics: Farewell to Revolution?" *China Journal* 57: 1–22. https://doi.org/10.1086/tcj.57.20066239.

Persson, Gudrun. 2010. *Learning from Foreign Wars: Russian Military Thinking 1859–73*. Solihull: Helion and Company.

Riga, Liliana. 2012. *The Bolsheviks and the Russian Empire*. Cambridge: Cambridge University Press. https://doi.org/10.1017/CBO9781139013628.

Rowe, William T. 2007. *Crimson Rain: Seven Centuries of Violence in a Chinese County*. Stanford: Stanford University Press.

Saxonberg, Steven. 2013. *Transitions and Non-transitions from Communism: Regime Survival in China, Cuba, North Korea and Vietnam*. Cambridge: Cambridge University Press. https://doi.org/10.1017/CBO9781139152396.

Shambaugh, David. 1991. "The Soldier and the State in China: The Political Work System in the People's Liberation Army." *China Quarterly* 127: 527–68. https://doi.org/10.1017/S0305741000031052.

Skocpol, Theda. 1979. *States and Social Revolutions: A Comparative Analysis of France, Russia and China*. Cambridge: Cambridge University Press. https://doi.org/10.1017/CBO9780511815805.

Steinberg, John W. 2010. *All the Tsar's Men: Russia's General Staff and the Fate of the Empire, 1898–1914*. Baltimore: Johns Hopkins University Press.

Sutton, Donald. 1980. *Provincial Militarism and the Chinese Republic*. Ann Arbor: University of Michigan Press.

Timirev, Sergei N. 1998. *Vospominaniia morskogo ofitsera* [Memories of a navy officer]. Saint Petersburg: Galeia Print.

Ulam, Adam B. 1977. *In the Name of the People: Prophets and Conspirators in Prerevolutionary Russia*. New York: Viking.

Walkin, Jacob. 1962. *The Rise of Democracy in Pre-revolutionary Russia: Political and Social Institutions under the Last Three Czars*. New York: Praeger.

Wang, F. 2015. "On the Causes of the CCP's Victory and the Failure of the Chinese Trotskyists in the Third Chinese Revolution: A Reply to Peng Shuzhi." In *Prophets Unarmed: Chinese Trotskyists in Revolution, War, Jail, and the Return from Limbo*, edited by Gregor Benton, 1001–24. Leiden: Brill.

Wang, Qisheng. 2003. *Dangyuan, dangquan yu dangzheng: 1924–1929 nian guomingdang de zuzhi xingtai* [party members, party powers and party strife: The organizational state of KMT 1924–1949). Shanghai: Shanghai shudian chubanshe.

Wolf, Eric R. 1969. *Peasant Wars of the Twentieth Century*. New York: Harper & Row.

Wright, Donald. 2005. "'That Vital Spark': Japanese Patriotism, the Russian Officer Corps and the Lessons of the Russo-Japanese War." In *The Russo-Japanese War in Global Perspective: World War Zero*, edited by John W. Steinberg, 591–608. Leiden: Brill.

Xu, Xiaohong. 2013. "Belonging before Believing: Group Ethos and Bloc Recruitment in the Making of Chinese Communism." *American Sociological Review* 78 (5): 773–96. https://doi.org/10.1177/0003122413500784.

Zhao, Dingxin. 1994. "The Defensive Regime and Modernization." *Journal of Contemporary China* 3 (7): 28–46. https://doi.org/10.1080/10670569408724206.

– 2001. *The Power of Tiananmen: State-Society Relations and the 1989 Student Movement*. Chicago: University of Chicago Press.

10 Religious Toleration in Pre-modern Empires

YANFEI SUN AND DINGXIN ZHAO

One of John Hall's many contributions to sociology is his analysis of the relationships between religion and politics and their economic consequences. In his classic *Powers and Liberties*, for instance, Hall (1985) argued that religion, upon entering into politics, shapes the nature of the state and of state-society relations, and that the very competitive church-state relations in Christian Europe gave rise to a highly unstable yet dynamic civilization crucial to the rise of industrial capitalism and nation-states in the West. Following in John Hall's footsteps, in this chapter we analyse another aspect of the religion-state relationship to examine how pre-modern empires' religious policies,[1] indicated by the level of their religious toleration, were shaped by the nature of the religion/belief system that those empires adopted.

Scholars, in part dismayed by the enormous incivility and violence accompanying the modern nation-building process (Bayar in this volume; Hall 2013; Kuru 2009; Üngör 2011; Wimmer 2002), have written more appreciatively of the extensive religious, ethnic, linguistic, and cultural diversity of pre-modern empires (Bang and Kolodziejczyk 2012; Barkey 2008, 2014; Burbank and Cooper 2010; Lavan, Payne, and Weisweiler 2016). While these studies are highly informative, they tend to overlook that pre-modern empires also exhibited vast differences in dealing with religions in their territories: some allowed all kinds of religions to exist and flourish, while others persecuted heretics

1 A pre-modern empire usually controlled multiple urban centres and extensive hinterlands through conquest (sometimes through marriage and inheritance). It also had a very limited infrastructural capacity, and thus had to control the local communities and frontier regions by indirect rule.

and non-believers and carried out forced conversions (but see Barkey 2014). This chapter seeks to map the pattern of variations in these empires' policies towards different religions, including most major pre-modern empires in its analysis, and offers a tentative explanation for the variations.

We proceed as follows. First, we place the pre-modern empires in different tiers according to our measurement of religious toleration. We then briefly discuss the difficult choices faced by a pre-modern empire with limited infrastructural capacity. Finally, we present a theory and a narrative explicating why some pre-modern empires were more tolerant of different persuasions than others. Our central point is that the religious policy of a pre-modern empire was shaped primarily by the nature of the religion/belief system that the empire adopted as the state ideology.

Mapping Religious Tolerance

This chapter only selects from the pool of empires that existed during and after the Axial Age (from the eighth to the third centuries BCE), when rulers had to deal with a wide spectrum of belief systems. We exclude those empires where the Enlightenment ideas of religious liberty had begun to take root. In other words, early modern Western empires, such as the British Empire, the French Empire, the Russian Empire, and the Dutch Empire are not considered here. We also focus on empires that exhibited significant durability, for an obvious reason: only when an empire has lasted a certain amount of time can a pattern of religious policies be observed.

Based on the above criteria, we selected the following pre-modern empires for our analysis: the Achaemenid Empire (550–330 BCE), the Parthia Empire (247 BCE–224 CE), the Sasanian Empire (224–651), the Roman Empire (c. 5 BCE–476 CE), the Byzantine Empire (c. 330–1453), the Carolingian Dynasty (750–887), the Holy Roman Empire (962–1806), the Mongol Empire before its division into four khanates (1206–59) and its continuation in China (Yuan Dynasty, 1271–1368), the Ming (1368–1644) and Qing (1644–1912) empires,[2] and finally various Islamic empires, including the Rashidun Caliphate (632–61), the

2 Even though the pre-modern Chinese Confucian empires display a distinctive pattern when their religious policies are compared with other empires, for the sake of narrative succinctness we selected only the Ming and the Qing empires for our analysis.

Umayyad Caliphate (661–750), the Abbasid Caliphate (750–1258), the Caliphate of Córdoba (929–1031), the Ilkhanate (1256–1335/1353) after its conversion to Islam in 1295, the Golden Horde after its Islamicization in 1313, the Ottoman Empire (c. 1299–1922) before the Tanzimat Reform (1839–76), and the Mughal Empire (1526–40, 1555–1857).[3]

In this chapter, the concept of religious toleration is used to describe the extent to which a pre-modern empire tolerated religions other than those it promoted. The levels of religious toleration are measured according to the following four criteria: (1) the kinds of religions that were permitted or not permitted by the state; (2) the extent of discrimination towards religions permitted by the state; (3) the level of suppression of religions not permitted by the state; and (4) whether a state carried out forced conversions. To be clear, our use of the concept of "religious toleration" has nothing to do with the modern idea bearing the same name,[4] even though a pre-modern empire's more lenient religious policy can also easily be labelled as such from today's point of view. The four criteria permit us to group the pre-modern empires into five levels or tiers of religious toleration, in descending order.

Our first tier, the group of empires with the highest level of religious toleration, includes the Achaemenid Empire during Cyrus's reign, the Parthian Empire, and the Mongol Empire (including the Yuan Dynasty in China). These empires tolerated and patronized a wide variety of religions, had no record of systematic discrimination against any religion, and made no attempts to impose their own religion or gods on conquered peoples.

Cyrus, the first emperor of the Achaemenid Empire (550–330 BCE), is renowned for his liberal religious policy. The inscription on the Cyrus Cylinder, discovered in the ruins of Babylon in 1879, tells us that, after conquering Babylon in 539 BCE, Cyrus showed great respect towards the Babylonian gods. He not only allowed the people he conquered to continue their religious practices, but also actively assisted deported peoples to return to their lands of origin and reconstruct their places of

3 The religious policy of the Safavid Empire does not closely conform to the general pattern of Islamic empires and needs a separate treatment. However, we omit the case due to space constraints.

4 Today's concept of religious toleration is based on the Enlightenment ideas of liberty of consciousness and individual freedom. These ideas are alien to pre-modern empires, whose practices of religious toleration were motivated by other reasons.

worship. Most famously, Cyrus allowed the Jews to return to Jerusalem after decades of captivity in Babylon (Mallowan 1985). Darius continued this practice.[5]

Later rulers of the Achaemenid Empire developed an increasingly stronger bond with Zoroastrianism, an ancient monotheist religion, even though the extent of their patronage of the religion remained unclear. Xerxes, in one of his inscriptions, recorded that he destroyed a "place of *daivas*,"[6] and had established in its place the worship of Ahura Mazda, the supreme God in Zoroastrianism (Rose 2014, 51). This could be an indicator of the ruler's diminishing religious toleration due to his Zoroastrian worship. But the information is too scanty to permit us to draw any clear conclusion.

Under the Parthian Empire, cults dedicated to Greek and Iranian deities were widespread, and syncretic gods that blended deities of different religious traditions were popular. The Parthian Empire adopted a liberal attitude towards a wide variety of religious systems and beliefs. Jews, early Christians, and Buddhists flourished in the territories of the empire (Neusner 1983; Rose 2014, 77–8; Venetis and Mozdoor 2017). Although Zoroastrianism no longer enjoyed the privileged status it had been accorded under later Achaemenid rulers, the Parthia court patronized Zoroastrian priests and sponsored the compilation of sacred Zoroastrian texts (Bivar 1983).

The Mongols were known as the most ruthless and brutal warlords of all time, but their empire was also exemplary among pre-modern empires for its openness towards almost all kinds of persuasions. Shamanism was the religion that the Mongols traditionally practised. Soon after Genghis Khan (c. 1162–1227) began his extraordinarily successful conquest campaigns, he established *yasa*, the Mongols' code of law, and in it enshrined a policy of religious toleration (Aigle 2014, 152; Lane 2006, 207). The Mongol rulers treated all religions and their leaders

---

5 As impressive as Cyrus's and Darius's generosity towards conquered subjects was, their religious policies were still in line with the practices of ancient Near East empires rooted in polytheistic religions (including the Assyrian and Neo-Babylonian empires). Local gods were mostly respected. The conquered people were allowed to continue their religious practices. Deportation of the conquered and desecration and destruction of their temples occasionally happened, but these were motivated by political not religious reasons (van der Spek 2014).

6 *Daivas* were old Indo-Iranian gods, whom Zoroastrianism denounced as false gods or demons.

with respect, and exempted religious personnel from taxation and from public service (Burbank and Cooper 2010, 108). They even organized debates among different religious leaders at the court and other venues. Mosques, churches, lamaseries, and temples were built freely, some of them receiving imperial patronage. All kinds of religions, including Buddhism, Christianity of several varieties, Islam, and Manichaeism enjoyed the freedom to proselytize under the Mongol Empire (Lane 2006).

In terms of religious policies, the Roman Empire before its Christianization was strikingly similar to the Ming and the Qing empires in China. Based on the extent of their religious tolerance, they both sit in the second tier. These empires accepted a plurality of religions, engaged in no systematic discrimination against different kinds of persuasions, and made no attempt to impose a religion on people against their will. However, unlike the empires in the first tier, these empires displayed clear limits on their religious toleration: the Roman Empire showed intolerance towards Christianity and what were deemed immoral cults, while the Ming and Qing empires were harsh on sectarian religions and "licentious cults."

The Romans were polytheists. They believed that Rome's welfare depended on the protection of gods and that impiety would incur divine dissension and punishment. The empire made it a civic duty for Romans to participate in pagan festivals. Later, emperors themselves were elevated to divine status, becoming part of Rome's state religion and increasingly posing homage to them as a test of loyalty to the empire. Before its Christianization, the Roman Empire treated the religions of conquered peoples with openness. Indeed, in their early expansions, the Romans adopted deities and religious practices first from the Etruscans and later from the Greeks (Momigliano and Price 2005, 7911). Greek gods were Romanized and became the mainstay of the Roman pantheon. As the empire expanded to the east, deities of eastern origin also entered the Roman pantheon. Cults worshipping Isis, of Egyptian origin, and Mithras, of Persian origin, for instance, were widespread across the empire (Momigliano and Price 2005, 7919; Witt 1997). Even though the Jews' monotheistic practices were in conflict with the empire's state religion, the empire honoured Jewish monotheism as an ancient tradition and exempted Jews from participating in pagan festivals and emperor worship. The empire's religious toleration did have its limits, however. The Romans repressed religious practices when they created disturbances to the public order and violated the Roman sense of morality. For instance, the empire eliminated the Druids in Gaul and in Britain because of their practice of human sacrifice, and prohibited the cult of Dionysus in Italy for its alleged debauchery (Momigliano and Price 2005, 7921).

The rise of Christianity put the Romans' open religious policy to the test. Christians refused to participate in both the pagan festivals and the imperial cult (de Ste Croix 2006). But they could not claim, like the Jews, that their monotheism was rooted in an ancient tradition. Moreover, unlike Judaism, Christianity had a very strong drive towards proselytism. Its diffusion among different social classes had the potential to subvert the existing social structure; its ability to spread among heterogeneous social groups to produce trans-local networks and communities posed a political challenge for the empire (Mann 1986, 321–5). The Romans' persecution of Christians was well known. What is less well known is that such persecutions were mostly carried out by the local authorities on a sporadic, ad hoc basis, often under the pressure of the "public opinion" of local communities. When the official policy remained ambiguous, many provincial governors followed Pliny's formula (de Ste Croix 1963). They would avoid actively seeking out Christians, and would give the accused a chance to prove his or her innocence by making a sacrifice to the Roman gods and swearing by the genius (i.e., supernatural spirit) of the emperor. Only those who refused to prove their "innocence" faced persecution. The first empire-wide persecution took place in 249, but this short-lived policy was followed by a long period of relative tolerance. During the Great Persecution of 303–12 (303–5 in the western part of the Roman Empire), the emperors issued edicts, ordering Christian churches and texts to be destroyed, banning meetings for Christian worship, and depriving recalcitrant Christians of their legal rights. Later imperial edicts further ordered the arrest of Christian clergy and required all inhabitants of the empire to sacrifice to the Roman gods (Frend 2005). But again the persecution did not last long.

For both the Ming and Qing empires, Confucianism was the state ideology. The imperial court and the bureaucrats at different administrative levels also practised the state cult, as scholars would call it (Feuchtwang 1977). The state cult involved emperors making sacrifices to their own ancestors and to emperors of the preceding dynasties, and emperors and their officials making sacrifices to the deities who were thought to protect the welfare of the empire and the people, or to "great men" such as Confucius (Feuchtwang 1977; Thompson 1996). Both the Ming and Qing empires tolerated and gave patronage to religions such as Buddhism, Daoism, and Islam. While Muslims were more concentrated in certain regions, Buddhist and Daoist temples were widespread across China. Some of them received imperial patronage. The empires were also open-minded about deities of popular cults, including some of these deities in the registers of sacrifice and requiring local officials to offer regular sacrifice to them (Thompson 1996, 78–9). Even Catholicism had a real chance to establish itself as a major religion in China. The Jesuits found ways to serve in the court and gain the trust of emperors. They won privileges for Catholic missionaries to build churches and proselytize. This lasted for almost 150 years, until the Catholic Church's condemnation of Chinese rites – including ancestral rituals – angered Emperor Kangxi (1654–1722), who ordered a ban on Catholicism (Mungello 1994). In contrast with this general policy of toleration, the Ming and Qing empires were heavy-handed in dealing with sectarian religions. These religious movements, often centred on charismatic leaders, propagating messianic messages, and organized into a closely bonded community, were feared to have a high potential for mobilization and rebellion. The empires were also hostile towards cultic practices that were perceived to breach Confucian moral codes, labelling cults worshipping "amoral" or "immoral" deities (such as deities protecting gambling and illicit love affairs) as "licentious cults" (*yingci*) and subjecting them to suppression (Poon 2011, 33; Wang 2017, 179–80). However, campaigns to eradicate licentious cults were mostly initiated by some zealous Confucian scholar-officials, and thus remained local, sporadic, and ineffective (Dean 1998, 48; Wang 2017, 180).

The Sasanian Empire sits on the third tier of the ladder of religious tolerance. The Sasanian Empire was born out of rebellion against the Parthians. Its rulers tried to legitimize their authority by proclaiming themselves to be the direct inheritors of the glory of the Achaemenid kings and defenders of the Zoroastrian faith. After the empire's establishment, it installed one religion, Zoroastrianism, as the state religion, and promoted Zoroastrian orthodoxy across its land, persecuting heresies, notably Manichaeism and Mazdakism (Widengren 1983; Yarshater 1983b), and harshly punishing apostates (Gnoli 2005). But outside its core areas it allowed most other religions to exist, and rarely carried out forced conversion. At times, it would persecute other religions when it felt threatened by their proselytizing. However, except in a very unusual (and short-lived) instance, the Sasanian Empire did not attempt to convert peoples of other religions.[7] Jews, Christians, and Buddhists all developed their own communities in the empire. A very large Jewish community flourished under Sasanian rule, with thriving centres in multiple cities, and with its own semiautonomous leadership (Neusner 1983). Even though they suffered bouts of persecution, Christians were generally tolerated (Asmussen 1983; Williams 1996).[8] In the eastern part of the empire, notably in Bamiyan, Buddhism had its followers (Emmerick 1983; Higuchi and Barnes 1995).

Though there was considerable variation, Islamic empires followed a general pattern. They installed one religion, Islam, as the state religion and persecuted heresies and apostasy. They allowed other monotheistic religions to exist, albeit with some restrictions and discrimination. On the other hand, they treated polytheists harshly and converted them by force. According to our criteria, Islamic empires (with the exception of the Safavid Empire) stand on the fourth rung of the ladder of religious tolerance.

In an Islamic empire, a person's religious belief had serious consequences for his or her social standing, for Muslims enjoyed privileges. Islamic empires granted the other monotheist religious communities, particularly the Jews and the Christians, *dhimmi* (protected person) status and allowed them to continue their religious practices. *Dhimmis*, however, were subjected to forms of discrimination. They had to pay a special tax (*jizya*) and did not enjoy certain political rights reserved for Muslims (even though they were otherwise equal under the laws of property, contract, and obligation). Moreover, *dhimmis* faced restrictions in practising their religion. They were forbidden to build new churches and to proselytize, and the ringing of church bells was also forbidden because it was said to disturb Muslims. It is worth noting that although the Islamic empires did not convert *dhimmis* by force, the structure of

---

7 This very unusual instance happened when Yazdegird II (439–57) sought to impose Zoroastrianism on Armenians, who practised Zoroastrianism before their conversion to Christianity in the fourth century. The Sasanians carried out forced conversions because they regarded the Armenians as apostates of Zoroastrianism (Rose 2014, 108). The forced conversions were soon halted, however, in the face of Armenian resistance.

8 Some of the persecutions were motivated by political rather than religious reasons. The Sasanian Empire was at war with the Roman Empire. When Shapur II learned that the Roman emperor Constantine had received baptism, he ordered the persecution of Christians living in his territory (Rose 2014, 104).

the Muslim society produced strong incentives for conversion: to convert would elevate their social position and widen their opportunities.

Islamic empires were much more hostile towards religions that were not monotheistic, seeing polytheists or pagans as idolaters. Zoroastrians were granted the status of *dhimmi* under Caliph Umar (Gordon 2005, 28). But their status was not secured, as their practice of fire worship was often seen as idolatrous (Choksy 1997), and under the Abbasid rule they were reduced to *kafirs* (non-believers) and regarded as impure (Berkey 2003, 100; Stepaniants 2002, 166). Buddhists too were seen as "idol worshippers." These religions were subject to harsh treatment: their sites were desecrated, destroyed, or turned into mosques; their followers often were forced to choose conversion or death (Berkey 2003).

The Christian empires examined in this chapter, including the Roman Empire after 380, the Carolingian Dynasty, the Holy Roman Empire, and the Byzantine Empire, sit in the lowest, or fifth, tier in religious tolerance according to our criteria. These empires were similar in the sense that they all installed Christianity as the state religion and they all persecuted heresies and apostates. They also forced pagans to convert to the state religion. They allowed Judaism to exist, but under a much higher level of restrictions and discrimination than in Islamic empires.

The Christianization of the Roman Empire was synchronous with the formation of Christian orthodoxy. After Constantine convened the first council at Nicaea in 325, persecution of heresy adopted a more concrete and legal form. The Edict of Thessalonica in 380 established Nicene Christianity as the state religion of the Roman Empire. Any deviation from the orthodoxy thus became a crime against the state. In the Byzantine Empire, persecution of heretics was commonplace. As the imperial right to regulate the church was generally accepted by the ecclesiastical authority, Byzantine emperors frequently allied with like-minded clergy members to excommunicate, imprison, and exile heretics (Hussey 2010, 305). In the Holy Roman Empire, it was the Catholic Church that interrogated and condemned heretics. The secular rulers collaborated when recalcitrant heretics were handed over to the secular authorities for burning (Deane 2011, 95, 114).

Persecution of pagans started under Constantine, who ordered the pillaging and destruction of some pagan temples (MacMullen 1984). Anti-pagan policies continued in the Byzantine Empire. Pagan festivals and sacrifices were banned; pagan temples were destroyed or repurposed as Christian churches; pagan practices were proscribed even within private homes; and pagans were forced to convert to Christianity. In Western Europe after the fall of Rome in 476, forced conversions of pagans were carried out by Christianized kings of Germanic origin. The most notorious example was set by Charlemagne (742–814). During his wars against the pagan Saxons, Charlemagne ordered the Saxons to be baptized. When the Saxons resisted, he massacred forty-five hundred of them in Verden in 782 (Fried 2016, 125). He further issued a legal code that sentenced to death Saxons who rejected baptism. The first of the Crusades was initiated by Pope Urban II in 1095, but it was enthusiastically supported by the secular rulers. Wherever the Crusaders went, they forced non-Christians to convert and massacred those who resisted (Riley-Smith 2005); during the Crusades Jews faced more discrimination and were even massacred (Chazan 1987; Riley-Smith 2003). Jews were more leniently treated by the Byzantine Empire, but even there they suffered more than they did under the Sasanians and the Arabs. It is no wonder that, when the Byzantines were at war with the Sasanians in 602–28 and then the Arabs in 634, the Jews welcomed the invaders, even sided with them, and revolted against the Byzantines (Luttwak 2009, 211; Neusner 1970, 122–3).

The Pragmatic Default and the Ideological Constraint

As Hall (2012, 307) puts it in a memorable passage, pre-modern empires were "puny leviathans." They were leviathans because they occupied a vast expanse of land populated by people of diverse ethnicities, languages, religions, and cultures. They were puny because of their weak infrastructural capacity – they had neither an effective bureaucracy nor modern means of transportation and communication to allow them to penetrate deep into society (Crone 1989, 38–41; Mann 1986, 142–3). As Crone (1989, 47) aptly points out, a pre-modern empire should be "understood in a minimalist rather than a maximalist vein: the state did a little and the subjects did the rest." In other words, the power of a pre-modern empire could never reach the local and frontier societies without compliance from the local elites. Therefore, if rulers of pre-modern empires were pragmatically minded, then accepting local diversity, including religious diversity, would come as a sensible choice (Hall 2012, 307–8). Such a religious policy not only invited cooperation of the local elites and lowered resistance in the newly occupied territory, but also created competing ideologies ideal for divide and rule.

Yet this policy of religious tolerance had one serious drawback: it prevented the development of an empire-wide elite culture and reinforced the centrifugal tendency of the regional elites. Rulers of pre-modern empires thus had an incentive to adopt and promote one religion/belief system as the state ideology. The installed ideology, however, could strongly constrain the religious policies of the state, preventing it from adopting more pragmatic stances towards religious minorities when needed. Given these countervailing factors, it is important to examine the nature of the state religion/belief system and analyse how it shaped the empire's religious policy.

The Nature of the State Ideology and Its Impact on Religious Toleration

In order to understand the nature of a state religion/belief system and its impact on a state religious policy, we need to devise a classification system. Past scholars tend to see religions in the light of the monotheism/polytheism dichotomy and to argue that monotheism fosters intolerance. This argument first appeared in the ground-breaking works of David Hume (1957) and Edward Gibbon (1837), but still resonates in the works of contemporary historians of ancient Rome such as de Ste Croix (2006), MacMullen (1981), and Bowersock (1996).

Gibbon (1837), describing the kind of polytheism practised by the ancient Romans, wrote:

> The superstition of the people was not embittered by any mixture of theological rancor; nor was it confined by the chains of any speculative system. The devout polytheist, though fondly attached to his national rites, admitted with implicit faith the different religions of the earth. Fear, gratitude, and curiosity, a dream or an omen, a singular disorder, or a distant journey, perpetually disposed him to multiply the articles of his belief, and to enlarge the list of his protectors. (vol. 1, chap. 2, 11)

This description captures the logic of polytheistic religions. Polytheists believed that there were many gods and many ways to worship them. Seeing all as more or less valid, they had no qualms about adding new gods and practices to existing ones. For polytheists, the boundary between different religions was fluid, porous, or even nonexistent. By contrast, strict monotheists held that there was only one true God, and that all other gods or beliefs were false. Insistence on hard boundaries between one's own and other religions and intolerance of alternative forms of worship are thus a natural outgrowth of monotheism.

As illuminating as it may be, this monotheism/polytheism dichotomy is an inadequate frame for understanding the nature of a religion and its impact on a state's religious policy. Some belief systems, such as Confucianism and Buddhism, cannot be properly categorized as either polytheistic or monotheistic. More importantly, when Hume and Gibbon and later scholars of Roman history argue that monotheism leads to religious intolerance, what they have in mind is Christianity and Christian empires. But if we broaden the scope of our investigation to include empires that adopted other monotheistic religions, such as Zoroastrianism and Islam, we will notice, as we did above, that these empires treated non-state religions differently. The variation in religious policies among empires with a monotheistic religion as the state religion/belief system calls for a better taxonomy. Our strategy is to disaggregate the one-dimensional monotheism/polytheism dichotomy into two dimensions (see Table 10.1), that is, "zero-sum" versus "non-zero-sum" and "evangelical" versus "non-evangelical" (Sun 2017).

In the table, "zero-sum" denotes a situation in which followers of one religion/belief system see their own convictions as the only source of truth and make a clear demarcation between truth and falsehood, while "non-zero-sum" denotes a situation in which followers do not make such a clear demarcation and are ready to tolerate or even accept persuasions of different origins. "Evangelical" signifies a high level of zeal in imposing one's own religious beliefs on others by persuasion and even coercion, while "non-evangelical" signifies the lack of such zeal and practices.

Table 10.1 provides examples of religions/belief systems falling in each of the four categories. It should be kept in mind that we analyse the nature of religions only in pre-modern empires, because both the beliefs and practices of the religions we examine have experienced great changes in the modern age. Admittedly, even in pre-modern times the degree of zero-sum mentality and the strength of evangelical passion of a religion also varied, sometimes significantly, across different historical periods and different societies. Nevertheless, if we adopt a *longue durée* perspective, and for the purpose of cross-religion comparison, the basic tone of a religion/belief system in terms of its degree of zero-sum mentality and strength of evangelical passion can still be easily discerned.

Table 10.1 Nature of the Religion/Belief System and Proclivity of an Empire's Religious Policy

	Non-zero-sum	Zero-sum
Non-evangelical	Examples: Polytheistic religions, Confucianism	Example: Zoroastrianism
	Proclivity: tolerate all kinds of religions on the condition that they do not breach the mores of the society	Proclivity: suppress heresy and apostasy in their own communities, but rarely impose forced conversion on peoples of different ethnic/religious tradition
Evangelical	Example: Buddhism	Examples: Christianity, Islam
	Proclivity: have considerable toleration for different religions, seek to incorporate deities of other religions into the lower strata of its pantheon	Proclivity: suppress heresy and apostasy, have little toleration for other religions, possibly seek forced conversion

Table 10.1 also summarizes the religious policy that a pre-modern empire with a certain state religion/belief system was most likely to adopt. In what follows, we will discuss the nature of the religions/belief systems listed in the table, as well as how a pre-modern empire's religious policy was shaped by the religion/belief system that empire embraced.

Polytheistic religions and Confucianism fall into the category of non-zero-sum and non-evangelical belief systems. Since the nature of polytheistic religions has already been discussed, we will focus on Confucianism here. Among the state ideologies of pre-modern empires, Confucianism is unique. In pre-modern China, it was the functional equivalent of a state religion in many respects, but it was not a typical religion. Like other state religions of pre-modern empires, it functioned as a major source of political legitimation of empires, guided state policies, provided a moral compass for individuals, and structured social relations. Confucianism also incorporated religious elements, including but not limited to a supernatural concept of heaven, divination, yin-yang cosmology, and ancestor worship (Zhao 2015, 343–4). However, Confucianism's chief concern was with this world, not salvation in the other world. Regardless of whether we see Confucianism as a religion or as a philosophy, it was neither zero-sum nor evangelical. It did not claim to be the only source of truth, nor was it interested in converting others. When people of other faiths, Chinese Jews included, decided to embrace Confucianism, it was usually a voluntary decision. Moreover, since Confucianism did not supply enough "interventionist practices" in the form of prayers, sacrifice, and formulas and chants for the purpose of averting misfortune, overcoming crisis, and attaining salvation (Riesebrodt 2010, 86, 148), it left plenty of space for other religions to fill. Given the nature of Confucianism, then, the Ming and Qing empires had a high level of religious toleration.

In the category of evangelical but not zero-sum religions, we find Buddhism. Buddhism was evangelical, encouraging people to "take refuge" in the three jewels of Buddhism, namely the Buddha, Dharma, and the Sangha (i.e., the monastic community). Yet it was not a zero-sum religion. Buddhism saw itself alone as provider of the right path to enlightenment or nirvana, making it superior to other religions – but it did not condemn other religions as false. The Buddhist cosmology identified six realms of existence, namely gods, demi-gods, humans, animals, hungry ghosts, and hells. According to Buddhism, other religions could not help followers to achieve nirvana, which transcended the six realms, but they could lead their practitioners to accumulate good karma, which in turn would lead to rebirth in the three good realms of gods, demi-gods, and humans. In this chapter we have said little about Buddhist empires due to the scanty information we have been able to collect at this stage of research, but we can postulate: Buddhism's evangelicalism would lead empires that espoused it to actively extend its influence, yet Buddhism's non-zero-sum nature did not give much theological ground for empires to adopt a harsh religious policy or execute forced conversion.

Zoroastrianism can be regarded as an archetype of a zero-sum but non-evangelical religion. Born in the context of Indo-Iranian common beliefs, Zoroastrianism represented one of humankind's earliest attempts to move away from polytheism towards monotheistic salvation. The teachings of Zoroaster exalted a single god, Ahura Mazda, as the supreme being. It also divided the Indo-Iranian pantheon by relegating some devas (i.e., deities) present in folk beliefs to demons and other malicious creatures, and contrasting them with divine beings (Yarshater 1983a). This kind of binary opposition was intrinsic to Zoroastrianism, which saw the world as the stage of the cosmic battle between Spenta Mainyu (the good spirit) and Angra Mainyu (the evil spirit). Human beings were given the choice to follow the good spirit to attain salvation.

Zoroastrianism was zero-sum because it saw itself as the only "good religion" and the only path to truth. Hence, the urge to uphold orthodoxy and root out heresy was very strong in Zoroastrianism. On the other hand, it was not evangelical. It did not generally accept converts; one had to be born into the religion (Stepaniants 2002, 165).

The zero-sum nature of the religion compelled the Sasanian Empire, which installed Zoroastrianism as the state religion, to punish apostasy and heresy, and sometimes wreak havoc on other religions. It was also the reason that the Sasanian Empire became suppressive when Zoroastrianism faced threats from proselytizing religions and sects, including "Christianity to the west, Buddhism to the east and Manichaeism from within" (Rose 2014, xxii). This made it significantly more hostile towards religious diversities than the Roman Empire before Christianization as well as the Ming and Qing empires of China. However, it generally did not seek to impose Zoroastrianism on peoples of other faiths, which gave the land of Zoroastrianism a significant religious diversity. This is why the Sasanian Empire belongs to the third tier on our scale of religious toleration, above the Islamic and Christian empires.

In the category of zero-sum evangelical religions, Christianity and Islam are by far the most important. They both claimed to be the only and ultimate truth and condemned other religions as false. Their vision of the afterlife was equally zero-sum, holding that one's fate was either eternal salvation or eternal condemnation. Since correct belief was the only way to salvation, heresy was not to be tolerated because it would lead people astray from the truth and path to salvation. Neither was apostasy to be stomached, because it was a rebellion against truth. Both religions aimed for universal salvation, making proselytization to the people of other religions/belief systems an obligation. Empires that made either Christianity or Islam their state religion were thus inclined to criminalize heresy and apostasy, and to use the powers of the state, including hard coercion, to impose the "true religion" on other peoples. This explains why empires that took Christianity and Islam as the state religion fall into the bottom two tiers in our measurement of religious toleration.

Islam and Christianity differed in one major regard. While both religions saw themselves as the custodian of God's final revelation, Christianity saw anything subsequent as false and noxious (Lewis 1994, 175–6). Christianity only tolerated Judaism because it saw the Jews as a living testimony to the authenticity of scriptural events (Lipton 1999, 56; Rist 2016, 73–4). At the same time, it maintained that the Jews should be left "scattered in exile from their land and oppressed into servitude" as punishment for their sin of rejecting Jesus (Cohen 1999, 35). Islam, as a latecomer in the lineage of monotheist religions in the Near East, believed that God had previously revealed Himself to the earlier prophets of the Jews and Christians, and that Muhammad was the last in the series of prophets God sent to mankind. For Islam, monotheists such as Jews and Christians were "People of the Book" (*Ahl al-Kitāb*) who should be respected, even though their revelation was incomplete, damaged, and superseded (Lewis 1994, 176). This feature of Islam made it significantly less zero-sum than Christianity, and made the religious policies of pre-modern Islamic empires (mostly clustered in the fourth tier of our religious toleration measurement) overall more lenient than those of the Christian empires (clustered in the fifth tier).

Conclusion and Discussion

Inspired by Hall's work on empires and civility, in this chapter we put forth a five-tier categorization of religious tolerance in pre-modern empires and proposed a theory to explain the observable differences. We disaggregated the monotheism/polytheism dichotomy, used by historians to contrast the Roman Empire's openness to different kinds of religions before its Christianization and its religious intolerance thereafter, to develop a new scheme to analyse the state religion/belief system along two dimensions: zero-sum versus non-zero-sum and evangelical versus non-evangelical. Pre-modern empires whose state religion/belief system was non-zero-sum and non-evangelical tended to adopt the most lenient religious policies, while those whose state religion/belief system was zero-sum and evangelical tended to adopt the most illiberal religious policies. Pre-modern empires whose state religion/belief system was either zero-sum and non-evangelical or non-zero-sum and evangelical tended to adopt religious policies with levels of religious tolerance in between. This explains why most religiously tolerant empires (in the first and second tiers) were either rooted in polytheist traditions or adopted Confucianism as the state ideology. It also explains why empires that adopted Buddhism (non-zero-sum and evangelical) or Zoroastrianism (close to zero-sum and non-evangelical) as a state religion allowed more religious diversity in their territories than Islamic and Christian empires. Finally, while both Christianity and Islam are zero-sum and evangelical religions, Islamic empires showed a higher toleration of other monotheistic religions in their territories than did Christian empires because Islam's concept of "People of the Book" made it significantly less zero-sum than Christianity.

Other factors such as state capacity, state autonomy from religion, and geopolitical situation could certainly also influence the degree of religious toleration of pre-modern empires. But, in comparison with the nature of the state religion/belief system, these are secondary factors. Due to space constraints, we will provide just one example here. The Achaemenid Empire, the Parthian Empire, the Mongol Empire, the Roman Empire before Christianization, and the Ming and Qing empires were all rooted in the non-zero-sum non-evangelical religious/ideological tradition. However, the Roman Empire and the Ming and Qing empires were placed in the second tier in our measurement of religious toleration, whereas the other three empires all sat in the first tier. The reason is the Roman Empire and the Ming and Qing empires had a much higher state capacity (by pre-modern standards) and were more likely to take a managerial attitude towards different kinds of religious activities. But the religious policies of the Romans as well as the Ming and Qing were still much more lenient than the rest of the empires, particularly the Christian and Islamic ones, which shows that state capacity was less important than the nature of state religion/belief system in shaping a state's religious policy.

As this chapter shows, zero-sum evangelical religions, once installed as state ideology, were the source of religious intolerance within pre-modern empires. Christian empires' religious policies tended to be even more intolerant than those of Islamic empires because Christianity was more zero-sum. Intolerance brewed conflicts; forced conversion, inquisitions, religious persecution, and religious wars were all too common in pre-modern Europe. It was amid such perennial conflicts that two polarized sets of modern ideologies were born. One saw compromise and tolerance as the only path to the peaceful coexistence of different communities, which led to the emergence of ideas such as religious liberty and institutions that support them. The other inherited the zero-sum tradition or the zero-sum evangelical tradition of Christianity, which led to the rise of ideologies such as nationalism, communism, and liberal fundamentalism.[9] It seems that the ideas of civility and its nemeses are both children of the Christian tradition.

9 We use "liberal fundamentalism" to denote an ideology that gives Western powers the right to stage wars and other activities to instigate regime changes in non-Western countries. It is one of the most important sources of human rights disasters in recent decades.

REFERENCES

Aigle, Denise. 2014. *The Mongol Empire between Myth and Reality: Studies in Anthropological History*. Leiden: Brill.

Asmussen, J.P. 1983. "Christians in Iran." In *The Cambridge History of Iran*. Vol. 3, *The Seleucid, Parthian and Sasanid Periods*, edited by Ehsan Yarshater, 924–48. Cambridge: Cambridge University Press. https://doi.org/10.1017/CHOL9780521246934.010.

Bang, Peter Fibiger, and Dariusz Kolodziejczyk, eds. 2012. *Universal Empire: A Comparative Approach to Imperial Culture and Representation in Eurasian History*. Cambridge: Cambridge University Press. https://doi.org/10.1017/CBO9781139136952.

Barkey, Karen. 2008. *Empire of Difference: The Ottomans in Comparative Perspective*. Cambridge: Cambridge University Press. https://doi.org/10.1017/CBO9780511790645.

– 2014. "A Comparative Sociology of Toleration within Empire." In *Boundaries of Toleration*, edited by Charles Taylor and Alfred Stepan, 203–32. New York: Columbia University Press.

Berkey, Jonathan Porter. 2003. *The Formation of Islam: Religion and Society in the Near East, 600–1800*. Cambridge: Cambridge University Press.

Bivar, A.D.H. 1983. "The Political History of Iran under the Arsacids." In *The Cambridge History of Iran*. Vol. 3, *The Seleucid, Parthian and Sasanid Periods*, edited by Ehsan Yarshater, 21–99. Cambridge: Cambridge University Press. https://doi.org/10.1017/CHOL9780521200929.004.

Bowersock, Glen Warren. 1996. *Hellenism in Late Antiquity*. Ann Arbor: University of Michigan Press.

Burbank, Jane, and Frederick Cooper. 2010. *Empires in World History: Power and the Politics of Difference*. Princeton: Princeton University Press.

Chazan, Robert. 1987. *European Jewry and the First Crusade*. Berkeley: University of California Press.

Choksy, Jamsheed Kairshasp. 1997. *Conflict and Cooperation: Zoroastrian Subalterns and Muslim Elites in Medieval Iranian Society*. New York: Columbia University Press.

Cohen, Jeremy. 1999. *Living Letters of the Law: Ideas of the Jew in Medieval Christianity*. Berkeley: University of California Press.

Crone, Patricia. 1989. *Pre-Industrial Societies: New Perspectives on the Past*. Hoboken: Wiley-Blackwell.

Dean, Kenneth. 1998. *Lord of the Three in One: The Spread of a Cult in Southeast China*. Princeton: Princeton University Press.

Deane, Jennifer Kolpacoff. 2011. *A History of Medieval Heresy and Inquisition*. Lanham: Rowman & Littlefield.

de Ste Croix, Geoffrey E. M. 1963. "Why Were the Early Christians Persecuted?" *Past & Present* 26 (1): 6–38. https://doi.org/10.1093/past/26.1.6.
– 2006. *Christian Persecution, Martyrdom, and Orthodoxy*. Edited by Michael Whitby and Joseph Streete. Oxford: Oxford University Press.
Emmerick, R.E. 1983. "Buddhism among Iranian Peoples." In *The Cambridge History of Iran*. Vol. 3, *The Seleucid, Parthian and Sasanid Periods*, edited by Ehsan Yarshater, 949–64. Cambridge: Cambridge University Press. https://doi.org/10.1017/CHOL9780521246934.011.
Feuchtwang, Stephan. 1977. "School-Temple and City God." In *The City in Late Imperial China*, edited by George William Skinner, 581–608. Stanford: Stanford University Press.
Frend, W.H.C. 2005. "Persecution: Christian Experience." In *Encyclopedia of Religion*, edited by Lindsay Jones, 7057–62. Detroit: Macmillan Reference USA.
Fried, Johannes. 2016. *Charlemagne*. Trans. Peter Lewis. Cambridge, MA: Harvard University Press. https://doi.org/10.4159/9780674973398.
Gibbon, Edward. 1837. *The History of the Decline and Fall of the Roman Empire*. Vol. 1. London: Frederick Westley and A.H. Davis.
Gnoli, Gherardo. 2005. "Iranian Religion." In *Encyclopedia of Religion*, edited by Lindsay Jones, 4535–8. Detroit: Macmillan Reference USA.
Gordon, Matthew. 2005. *The Rise of Islam*. Westport: Greenwood.
Hall, John A. 1985. *Powers and Liberties: The Causes and Consequences of the Rise of the West*. Oxford: Basil Blackwell.
– 2012. "Imperial Universalism – Further Thoughts." In *Universal Empire: A Comparative Approach to Imperial Culture and Representation in Eurasian History*, edited by Peter Fibiger Bang and Dariusz Kolodziejczyk, 304–9. Cambridge: Cambridge University Press. https://doi.org/10.1017/CBO9781139136952.016.
– 2013. *The Importance of Being Civil: The Struggle for Political Decency*. Princeton: Princeton University Press.
Higuchi, Takayasu, and Gina Barnes. 1995. "Bamiyan: Buddhist Cave Temples in Afghanistan." *World Archaeology* 27 (2): 282–302. https://doi.org/10.1080/00438243.1995.9980308.
Hume, David. 1957. *The Natural History of Religion*. Edited by H.E. Root. Stanford: Stanford University Press.
Hussey, J.M. 2010. *The Orthodox Church in the Byzantine Empire*. Oxford: Oxford University Press.
Kuru, Ahmet T. 2009. *Secularism and State Policies toward Religion: The United States, France, and Turkey*. Cambridge: Cambridge University Press. https://doi.org/10.1017/CBO9780511815096.

Lane, George. 2006. *Daily Life in the Mongol Empire*. Westport: Greenwood.
Lavan, Myles, Richard E. Payne, and John Weisweiler. 2016. *Cosmopolitanism and Empire: Universal Rulers, Local Elites, and Cultural Integration in the Ancient Near East and Mediterranean*. Oxford: Oxford University Press. https://doi.org/10.1093/acprof:oso/9780190465667.001.0001.
Lewis, Bernard. 1994. *Islam and the West*. Oxford: Oxford University Press.
Lipton, Sara. 1999. *Images of Intolerance: The Representation of Jews and Judaism in the Bible Moralisée*. Berkeley: University of California Press.
Luttwak, Edward N. 2009. *The Grand Strategy of the Byzantine Empire*. Cambridge, MA: Harvard University Press.
MacMullen, Ramsay. 1981. *Paganism in the Roman Empire*. New Haven: Yale University Press.
– 1984. *Christianizing the Roman Empire: (A.D. 100–400)*. New Haven: Yale University Press.
Mallowan, Max. 1985. "Cyrus the Great (558–529 B.C.)." In *The Cambridge History of Iran*. Vol. 2, *The Median and Achaemenian Periods*, edited by I. Gershevitch, 392–419. Cambridge: Cambridge University Press. https://doi.org/10.1017/CHOL9780521200912.008.
Mann, Michael. 1986. *A History of Power from the Beginning to AD 1760*, vol. 1: *The Sources of Social Power*. Cambridge: Cambridge University Press.
Momigliano, Arnaldo, and Simon Price. 2005. "Roman Religion: The Imperial Period." In *Encyclopedia of Religion*, edited by Lindsay Jones, 7911–25. Detroit: Macmillan Reference USA.
Mungello, David E., ed. 1994. *The Chinese Rites Controversy: Its History and Meaning*. St Augustin: Steyler.
Neusner, Jacob. 1970. *A History of the Jews in Babylonia v. Later Sasanian Times*. Leiden: Brill.
– 1983. "Jews in Iran." In *The Cambridge History of Iran*. Vol. 3, *The Seleucid, Parthian and Sasanid Periods*, edited by Ehsan Yarshater, 909–23. Cambridge: Cambridge University Press. https://doi.org/10.1017/CHOL9780521246934.009.
Poon, Shuk-wah. 2011. *Negotiating Religion in Modern China: State and Common People in Guangzhou, 1900–1937*. Hong Kong: Chinese University Press.
Riesebrodt, Martin. 2010. *The Promise of Salvation: A Theory of Religion*. Chicago: University of Chicago Press. https://doi.org/10.7208/chicago/9780226713946.001.0001.
Riley-Smith, Jonathan. 2003. *The First Crusade and Idea of Crusading*. London: A&C Black.
– 2005. *The Crusades: A History*. London: A&C Black.

Rist, Rebecca. 2016. *Popes and Jews, 1095–1291*. Oxford: Oxford University Press. https://doi.org/10.1093/acprof:oso/9780198717980.001.0001.

Rose, Jenny. 2014. *Zoroastrianism: An Introduction*. New York: I.B. Tauris.

Stepaniants, Marietta. 2002. "The Encounter of Zoroastrianism with Islam." *Philosophy East & West* 52 (2): 159–72. https://doi.org/10.1353/pew.2002.0030.

Sun, Yanfei. 2017. "The Rise of Protestantism in Post-Mao China: State and Religion in Historical Perspective." *American Journal of Sociology* 122 (6): 1664–725. https://doi.org/10.1086/691718.

Thompson, Laurence G. 1996. *Chinese Religion: An Introduction*. Belmont: Wadsworth.

Üngör, Uğur Ümit. 2011. *The Making of Modern Turkey: Nation and State in Eastern Anatolia, 1913–1950*. Oxford: Oxford University Press. https://doi.org/10.1093/acprof:oso/9780199603602.001.0001.

van der Spek, R.J. 2014. "Cyrus the Great, Exiles, and Foreign Gods: A Comparison of Assyrian and Persian Policies on Subject Nations." In *Extraction & Control: Studies in Honor of Matthew W. Stolper*, edited by M. Kozuh, W. Henkelman, C. Jones, and C. Woods, 233–64. Chicago: Oriental Institute, University of Chicago.

Venetis, Evangelos, and M. Alinia Mozdoor. 2017. "The Establishment and Development of Christianity in the Parthian Empire." http://www.iranchamber.com/religions/articles/christianity_development_parthia.php (accessed June 2017).

Wang, Mingming. 2017. *Empire and Local Worlds: A Chinese Model for Long-Term Historical Anthropology*. Abingdon: Routledge.

Widengren, G. 1983. "Manichaeism and Its Iranian Background." In *The Cambridge History of Iran*. Vol. 3, *The Seleucid, Parthian and Sasanid Periods*, edited by Ehsan Yarshater, 965–90. Cambridge: Cambridge University Press. https://doi.org/10.1017/CHOL9780521246934.012.

Williams, A.V. 1996. "Zoroastrians and Christians in Sasanian Iran." *Bulletin of the John Bylands University Library of Manchester* 78 (3): 37–54. https://doi.org/10.7227/BJRL.78.3.4.

Wimmer, Andreas. 2002. *Nationalist Exclusion and Ethnic Conflict: Shadows of Modernity*. Cambridge: Cambridge University Press.

Witt, R.E. 1997. *Isis in the Ancient World*. Baltimore: Johns Hopkins University Press.

Yarshater, Ehsan. 1983a. "Iranian Common Beliefs and World-View." In *The Cambridge History of Iran*, vol. 3, edited by Ehsan Yarshater, 341–58. Cambridge: Cambridge University Press. https://doi.org/10.1017/CHOL9780521200929.013.

– 1983b. "Mazdakism." In *The Cambridge History of Iran*. Vol. 3, *The Seleucid, Parthian and Sasanid Periods*, edited by Ehsan Yarshater, 991–1024. Cambridge: Cambridge University Press.

Zhao, Dingxin. 2015. *The Confucian-Legalist State: A New Theory of Chinese History*. Oxford: Oxford University Press. https://doi.org/10.1093/acprof:oso/9780199351732.001.0001.

11 Ashoka and Constantine: On Mega-Actors and the Politics of Empires and Religions

JOSEPH M. BRYANT

At critical phases in their early development, both Buddhism and Christianity received the unexpected and substantial patronage of imperial rulers, whose ideological advocacy and material benefactions dramatically advanced their socio-historical trajectories. The parallels between King Ashoka of the Maurya dynasty (r. 269–232 BCE) and the Roman emperor Constantine (r. 306–37 CE) have oft been noted, though rarely with sustained consideration of the strikingly different historical legacies their actions initiated. Ashoka's efforts in support of Buddhism were crucial in raising it to social prominence and facilitating its geo-cultural diffusion across South and East Asia. The distinctive concordance of state and religion he fashioned, however, was neither institutionally reinforced nor sustained by his dynastic successors. Buddhism would not only not become a "state religion" in the land of its origins, it would steadily yield ground to a resurgent and reformed Brahmanical Hinduism in the aftermath of the Mauryan empire's demise (c. 185 BCE). Constantine's embrace of Christianity, in contrast, established both the ideological and the organizational basis for an enduring State-Church alliance and the imminent consolidation of a Christian empire and civilization. How are these divergent outcomes to be explained?

The tradition of inquiry that has investigated the interdependencies of religions and polities most extensively – across epochs and cultures – is that famously inaugurated by Max Weber and further developed by eminent global historians and comparativists, John Hall prominently among them.[1] Yanfei Sun and Dingxin Zhao's chapter in this volume

1 Three immensely influential contributions derive from a legendary "Patterns of History" seminar collaboratively taught at the London School of Economics: Hall (1985), Mann (1986), and Gellner (1988).

contributes to that tradition. The legitimizing function of religions, domestication of the masses, religiously determined systems of life-regulation, salvation religions and "tensions" with the world: the deploy of these and related analytical categories has yielded richly textured insights into the constitution and transformation of societies and civilizations, and therewith an enhanced capacity to comprehend the longer-term trajectories of the diverse histories that comprise the global human drama.

For a significant number of those histories, a royal conversion/patronage event features prominently as a turning point moment, ushering in major cultural changes and reconfigurations in the relations of power and authority. Celebrated instances include the Shah of the Achaemenid empire, Darius the Great (c. 550–486 BCE), on behalf of Zoroastrianism; the Sinhalese monarch Devanampiya Tissa (r. 247–207 BCE), who sponsors Buddhism on the island of Sri Lanka; Tiridates III of Armenia (r. 287–330 CE), whose conversion to Christianity led to its establishment as the official religion of the kingdom; Ezana of Aksum (fl. 340), a ruler of the Aksumite empire who converts to Christianity and founds the Ethiopian Church; Clovis, pagan chieftain of the Franks (r. 481–511), whose Christmas day baptism by the Bishop of Reims hastened the conversion of Frankish tribes to Catholicism; Tang dynasty empress Wu Zetian (r. 684–705), who offsets Confucian hostility to her rule through support of Mahayana Buddhism, in the form of prolific textual production, the commissioning of temples, monasteries, and monumental cave sculptures, and claims that the empress herself is the prophesied incarnation of the bodhisattva Maitreya; Vladimir, Grand Prince of Kievan Rus' (r. 980–1015), who converts to Greek Orthodoxy in 987 and promptly orders mass baptisms across his realm, compliance expedited through violent campaigns against paganism and lavish patronage for the *pravoslavie* or "true glory" of Orthodox Christianity; three of the four regional Khanates of the Mongol empire, which will be guided into the *Dar al-Islam* through conversion of several members of the Ghinggisid royal lineage, beginning with Berke, ruler of the Golden Horde (r. 1257–66), followed by the conversions of Mubarak Shah of the Chagatai Khanate (r. 1252–60) and Ghazan, ruler of the Ilkhanate (r. 1295–1304); and, in what might prove to be the last round of royal conversions of global historical significance, that band of German princes who – along with Henry VIII of England (r. 1509–47) – provided protection for the nascent Protestant movement and went on to support the establishment of Reform churches throughout their territories: men such as Frederick III,

Elector of Saxony (r. 1486–1525), his son Johann the Steadfast (r. 1525–32) and grandson Johann Frederick I (r. 1532–47), Philip I, Landgrave of Hesse (r. 1519–67), and Ernest the Confessor, Duke of Brunswick-Lüneburg (r. 1520–46).

Important particularities adhere to each of these examples, but they also collectively disclose that the decisive sociological consequences of royal conversion episodes are typically twofold. They function as powerful catalysts for *altering the directionality of sociocultural change*, and they often *accelerate the temporal pace of ongoing historical processes*. Explanation of these commonly paired effects is straightforward. A sovereign ruler either claims or is vested with command over the resources of the state, and can thereby deploy the available instrumentalities of power in pursuit of royal projects and dynastic ambitions. As a particularly potent type of "mega" actor – a sociological category encompassing individuals who wield greatly amplified powers owing to their occupancy of leadership positions within large institutions, organizations, or social movements – a king, khan, or emperor stands at the authoritative summit of an entire social system, and can thus issue directives of prevailing force and efficacy.[2] The paramount concerns of royal leadership routinely centre on regime stabilization and maintenance of the status quo by upholding traditional norms and retaining the loyalties and services of allied elites. Occasions do arise, however, when rulers resort to unconventional measures or more radical policies, whether in response to challenges from below, the onset of social crises, or sundry life-changing experiences – growing megalomania included – that inspire a personal sense of "mission" or purpose hitherto lacking in a sovereign's vocabulary of motives.

The transformative actions of Ashoka and Constantine were alike rooted in their conversion experiences, which in turn provided the motivations and rationales for extensive royal benefactions on behalf of their adopted religions. Examination of the similarities and differences between these two momentous cases of "mega-actor" intervention should permit specification of those causal relations that led to their notably dissimilar outcomes: a limited phase of imperial sponsorship for Buddhism within India; an institutionally entrenched and lasting concordance of Church and State within the Roman empire. To facilitate this explanatory task, an analytic matrix of five key considerations will be used to organize and process the pertinent data:

2 For insightful discussion of the concept, see Mouzelis (1991).

1. **Social Contexts and Trend Lines**. Even allowing for quirks of character and biography, royal conversion and patronage decisions are fundamentally political acts, and as such reflective of the social worlds and temporal currents out of which they emerge and to which they respond. The meaning and purpose of such decisions can thus be determined only through examination of the social structure of the society or empire in question – its institutions, world views, ideologies – and the organization of its population in terms of occupation, class, status, gender, and ethnicity. Establishing the temporal horizon of a conversion decision is an equally pressing requirement. Are contemporaries living in an epoch of stability and prosperity, or one of upheaval, decline, and deepening crises? Are the social trends underway compatible with, or potentially subversive of, existing hierarchies and traditions?

2. **Structure of the Religious Field**. The social significance of any royal conversion will depend on the type of religion converted to and its relation to the traditions being relegated, abandoned, or renounced. The spectrum of religious options must accordingly be inventoried, and their interrelations identified – whether competitive or cooperative, exclusionary or inclusive, hierarchical or non-hierarchical (Bourdieu 1971). As a religious field is modified by changes both internal and external, opportunities and pressures for adjustments in royal affiliation and patronage are likely to increase. To the extent that a favoured cult or religion accommodates ancestral practices and beliefs, the likelihood of ensuing social discontent and intergroup conflict will be reduced. Altogether different are the hazards involved in extending imperial support to a religious movement that not only proclaims an exclusive monopoly on sacred truths and divine access but is militantly hostile to all other forms of religious expression. The most consequential difference between Ashoka's advocacy of Buddhism and Constantine's patronage of Christianity will be shown to reside precisely here, in the radically contrasting configurations of the religious fields they responded to.

3. **Ruler Interests**. Since the historic arrival of organized states in the early Bronze Age, pharaohs, emperors, and kings have assiduously laid claim to celestial favour in one form or another, ranging from avowals of descent from the gods to proclamations of divine appointment as mediators of the sacred. Set against this

longstanding pattern of politicized religiosity, it is not surprising that historians have frequently attributed royal conversions to "will-to-power" objectives rather than spiritual fervency, to *raisons d'état* rather than *raisons de l'âme*. Attentiveness to the full range of identifiable or likely motivations is, however, the sounder methodological course, given that practical interests and principled ideals are commonly reinforcing and thus difficult to disentangle for causal assessment. Actions having the appearance of political expediency, for example, might represent tactical or strategic choices in the service of ideals that require temporary concealment prior to public pronouncement. In all cases of royal conversion it will be necessary to identify shifts in the constellation of social forces that variously facilitate and constrain a sovereign's freedom of action with regard to matters sacred and divine.

4. **Opportunity Frames**. Even for mega-actors in command of immense resources and powers, the channelling of will and purpose into effective programs of action requires realistic assessments of the factors that might impede or expedite implementation. As those conditions wax and wane, multiply and diminish, in accordance with ongoing socio-historical processes, the question of "timing" – that is, the seizing of opportune or propitious moments – assumes crucial analytical importance. The "opportunity frame" concept offers a way of balancing and distinguishing between (a) levels of commitment to a project and (b) the strategic and tactical assessments that determine when a course of action should be initiated. Implementation delays, or recourse to ambiguous proclamations and compromise efforts, need not imply weak or wavering commitments, but simply an informed awareness that present circumstances are unconducive for the desired intervention. Royal aspirations to modify or transform religious conventions appear to be particularly prone to temporal lags between the conversion and reform phases, given the strong and impassioned resistance likely to greet any political attempt to depart from or undermine established sacral traditions and affiliations.

5. **Modes of Patronage and Institutionalization**. Once a viable opportunity for imperial support presents itself, decisions must be made regarding (a) the kinds of benefactions and favours to be extended, (b) the sequence and pacing of their delivery,

and (c) the scale of those endowments and the sources of their funding. Depending on the degree of rivalry and antagonism within a religious field, patronage transactions might also receive coercive reinforcement in the form of discriminatory practices or outright persecution of competitor traditions. Decisions carrying greatest weight for longer-term prospects will be those concerning the arrangements through which imperial largesse flows to the newly favoured religion. The pivotal contrast here is between institutionalized modes of patronage and looser, ad hoc procedures that remain reliant upon discretionary disbursements. Over the course of his lengthy tenure as absolute ruler of the Mauryan empire, Ashoka made no effort, either legally or administratively, to secure for Buddhism the advantages he had so lavishly and publicly bestowed; the conventions of royal patronage remained dependent upon the whims of sovereign prerogative. Conversely, the Roman state under Constantine and his successors pursued a path of complementary institutionalization, that is, a process of ever-deepening State-Church coordination that culminated in the legislative establishment of Christianity as the official religion of the empire.

A fully comparative historical sociology of royal conversions still awaits development. The analytical matrix proposed here offers only a limited and provisional reconnaissance, its thematic foci formulated less for purposes of generalizing across cases than for tracking and explicating the social structural and cultural developments involved in two of the most celebrated and consequential royal conversions in world history.

Against the conventions of chronology, our analysis will commence with Constantine and Christianity rather than the historically prior case of Ashoka and Buddhism. There are two main justifications. First, the textual and archaeological evidence available for the reconstruction of both Roman imperial and Christian history is far more abundant and reliably datable than what has survived from the period of the Mauryas and early Buddhism. The fact that Buddhist oral traditions were committed to writing many centuries after the movement's historic emergence poses a number of challenging problems, not least with regard to identifying changes over time. The second rationale invokes methodological expediency, on the assumption that explicating events that did occur should prove less challenging than accounting for the non-appearance of similar phenomena in analogous cases. The traversal of a historical trajectory that connects beginnings with developments and outcomes should, moreover, furnish a few suggestive clues regarding the alternate routes or "detours" that led to different historical destinations elsewhere.

Constantine the Great: Roman Emperor and Servant of the Most High God and His Son Jesus the Christ

Under the soldier-emperor Diocletian (r. 284–305), the mode of governance in the Roman empire was radically transformed through the creation of an imperial college comprised of four ruling emperors. The two senior members in this "Tetrarchy" carried the title of Augustus, with one emperor responsible for the expansive empire's eastern half, the other holding sway in the west. The two junior members, known as Caesars, were likewise assigned to eastern or western zones of operation, where they would assist and implement the policies of their respective senior colleagues. By strategically localizing imperial authority across a quadrant of regions – each with its own court, bureaucracy, and legionary armies – Diocletian was seeking not only greater administrative control and military effectiveness, but also a stabilization mechanism for transferring sovereignty. That objective would be attained through an orderly cycle of timed retirements for the outgoing senior emperors and the concurrent succession of their junior colleagues, who would in turn induct an incoming brace of new Caesars. While successful in shoring up frontier defences and boosting tactical responsiveness, the regional placement of the tetrarchs and their armies obviously courted the risk of setting off yet another round of internecine strife between ambitious military commanders – a scourge that had erupted repeatedly in prior decades. Diocletian's grand political experiment was thus ultimately dependent upon continued solidarity within the imperial college, which could be sustained only on the basis of shared interests among the individual tetrarchs. Despite recourse to political intermarriages and symbolic adoptions within the ruling families, a major breach was not long in coming.

On 24 February 303 an imperial edict was promulgated throughout the Roman empire, effectively mandating the termination of Christianity: members of the illegal *superstitio* are prohibited from assembling for worship; buildings, sacred writings, and related cult paraphernalia are to be confiscated or destroyed; Christians of high status refusing to renounce membership shall be stripped of rank and juridical privileges; Christian freedmen found within the imperial civil service must be enslaved anew. A second edict months later orders the arrest and imprisonment of all clergy unwilling to honour the traditional gods. So began the "Great Persecution" that would rage on and off with varying degrees of intensity and violence over the next decade (de Ste Croix, 2006). From the outset, however, prosecutorial enforcement was not uniform across the empire. Most notably, the Caesar of the west, Constantius Chlorus, limited the repression in Gaul, Hispania, and Britannia to the confiscation and demolition of churches. The legal directive to imprison, torture, and execute the non-compliant was disregarded, whether from humane tolerance or, as Christians would later claim, possible sympathies for the persecuted cult. His benign conduct will prove influential, for Constantius's eldest son is Constantine, a seasoned soldier who had served with distinction under the tetrarchs Diocletian and Galerius. Upon the death of his father at York, 25 July 306, Constantine lays claim to the rank of Augustus, an action duly ratified by the customary approbation of the assembled troops. All pretence of compliance with the edicts of persecution is ended, as the new emperor promptly lifts the ban on Christian religious practices and orders the return of confiscated properties (Barnes 1981). With these actions Constantine has effectively forced his entry into the college of emperors; but this was a tetrarchy still at war with the religion he would presently join and support. To understand how that historically portentous conjuncture came about, we must retrace the interrelational dynamic of the two main trajectories involved.

The Rise of Christianity and the Deepening Crisis of Empire

The public crucifixion of Jesus of Nazareth (c. 33 CE), executed as a blasphemer against the Jewish god and an enemy of the Roman state, cast a menacing shadow of suspicion over the social movement inspired by his actions. Reasons for the alarm are easily located, for Christianity owes its genesis to that explosive mixture of the religious and the political that informs the Messianic promise, of a heaven-sent Saviour who will miraculously deliver "captive" Israel from foreign domination and usher in God's kingdom on earth. Christianity's commitment to that eschatological program is directly coded into its originating discourse of self-presentation: the accredited redemptive agent, Jesus Christ, is literally "Jesus the Messiah" (the Greek term *christos* translating the

Hebrew *mashiach*); and those believing in Jesus the Christ thus become, by nominative extension, Christians, *hoi Christianoi*, that is, "Messianists" or "followers of the Messiah."

That inherited political-cosmological schema suffices to explain why the Jesus movement failed to gain significant traction within Judaism after the crucifixion – a degrading, humiliating defeat that, by traditional expectations, necessarily exposed the falsity of Jesus's Messianic pretentions. Hence the great urgency of Christian midrashic deliberations to rework the Messianic mythos so as to feature and legitimize a "crucified Messiah," a notion that drew heavily on resonant prophetic verses concerning God's "suffering servant" in Isaiah 53, which presents a mysterious figure who will be "pierced through for our transgressions ... and bear the sins of many." From this and similarly adaptable passages in the Hebrew scriptures, Christian exegetes and teachers will elevate Jesus to the role of a universal Saviour, whose redemptive mission is extended to encompass all of humanity: eternal life is promised to those who uphold His commands, eternal damnation for those failing to do so. With Christ's crucifixion rationalized as a universal atoning sacrifice, and His resurrection signifying humanity's ultimate triumph over death, a politically charged sacred narrative has been profoundly (re)scripted, its new logic providing the sustaining impetus for the emergence of a conversionist-salvation cult espousing global ambitions to "baptize all the nations."

In the ensuing decades the Jesus movement would develop into a new form of social organization that featured the multiplication of local congregations across the Roman empire – as "seeded" by missionary evangelization and migration – while also affirming participatory union in the mystical Church of Christ. The main processes of institutionalization are fundamentally driven by the need to channel or "routinize" the Redeemer's salvific charisma for perpetual access and sustaining power. The words and deeds of Jesus and his disciples are passed on in oral traditions that provide storylines and episodes for much of the copious, multilingual textual production that soon follows. Core cultic practices, such as the sacraments of baptism and the Eucharist, re-enact key moments in the earthly ministry of Jesus and thus enable participants to partake of the sanctifying blessings He awards to His faithful. In the initiation rite of baptism, devotees undergo a "washing of regeneration" that cleanses the soul from all sin and effects a transformative rebirth through the miraculous infusion of God's Holy Spirit. Through its indwelling presence the Christian is able to "walk in the newness of life" in joyful anticipation of the imminent Second Coming of the Lord, who will return in glory "to judge the living and the dead." In the liturgy of the Eucharist, congregants commemorate the Last Supper and enter into physical-pneumatic "holy communion" with their Saviour, by consuming the consecrated bread and wine that has been miraculously transmuted into the "body and blood" of Christ. The developing hierocratic order of the Church likewise derives its authority from the founding era, most decisively in the doctrine of "apostolic succession," which holds that the varied potencies and functions Jesus bestowed upon his disciples – such as the power to baptize, "bind and loose" sins, and cast out demons – have been passed on to the continuing line of congregational "overseers" known as bishops. With administrative and pastoral assistance provided by presbyters, deacons, lectors, and other ministerial offices, each *ekklesia* or church will function as a self-governing micro-polity, in service not to Rome but to God's sovereignty.

The new religion would spread rapidly across the empire over its first two centuries, but congregations were typically small and membership growth remained modest and uneven. By the year 200, demographic estimates place the Christian share of the total population of some sixty million at well under 1 per cent, in the range of two hundred thousand members. Internal difficulties along with external pressures combined to significantly deter conversions.[3]

Membership obligations and norms were dauntingly formidable, and rested upon an expectation of exclusive devotional commitment to the new faith. Prior attachments to the "sinful" world outside were to be broken, necessitating difficult kinship breaches as well as "antisocial" disengagements from all activities entangled in idolatrous practices: civic affairs, sacred festivals, and popular entertainments most notably. Believers were also expected to remain "sealed in purity" in the aftermath of their baptismal cleansing; any fall into unrighteous conduct risked forfeiture of eternal life and consignment to hell on the pending Day of Judgment. The strains of maintaining those saintly standards begin to manifest early in the second century, when Christian writings make repeated reference to the *dipsychoi* or "divided souls" who have lost trust in the heavenly promises and are backsliding into worldly temptations. A measure of stabilizing relief would be secured

3 For demographic estimates, see MacMullen (1984), Lane Fox (1987), Stark (1996), and Hopkins (1999).

through penitential reforms extending selective pardon to post-baptismal sins – including a new sacrament of penance that granted a single-use "backup" remission of sins for the wayward – but ethical standards remained high and "mortal sins" like fornication, adultery, and idolatry were still considered unpardonable within the Church.

Core elements of the Christian belief system likewise carried their own barriers to credence and acceptability. Particularly problematic was the dire forecast of imminent world-destruction, construed as a fiery cataclysm that will attend Christ's Second Coming and the settling of accounts in the Last Judgment. A central event in this end-time scenario is the predicted physical resurrection of the dead, a macabre notion widely greeted with bewilderment and repugnance in cultures long accustomed to associating corpses with pollution and reserving prospects of immortality for the soul or mind rather than the body. Far more scandalous and offensive, however, was Christian denunciation of the empire's traditional religions, which were deemed to be not only false, but utterly demonic. Condemnation was total: sacrificial offerings provide sustenance for Satan's malignant forces; temples and statues serve as their favoured haunts; ancient fables and mythologies furnish examples for vice and blind humanity to the truth of the One God. Such unmitigated rhetorical aggression against all aspects of polytheistic culture and society necessarily carried subversive political implications, given that Roman imperial discourse had long insisted that Rome's *imperium* had from its very beginnings been divinely sponsored, in recognition that the Romans exceeded all nations in scrupulous observance of the rites of *religio* and in pious *reverentia* to the gods everywhere.

The first harbinger of inexorable antagonism between the nascent Messianic cult and the Roman state is Nero's infamous decision to scapegoat Christians for the great fire that broke out in Rome in 64 CE. As the historian Tacitus narrates, Nero astutely sought to shift culpability from himself by rounding up and cruelly executing fanatical members of a secretive, noxious *superstitio* widely reviled for "criminal depravities" and "hatred for humankind" (*Annals*, 15.44). Christian tradition would memorialize nine additional persecutions, each purportedly filled with heroic martyrdoms and each theologically rationalized as a testing of faith and punishment for sins. All but the last three, however, were small-scale affairs, either local or regional, and typically occasioned by disturbances or popular protests from below rather than imperial initiative. Given that membership in the illicit cult was a crime punishable by torture, exile, confiscation of property, and even execution, a more immediate and continuous hazard for Christians was the menace of private informants, who regularly filed denunciations with local officials or extorted bribes by threatening to do so. To allay these fears and the reality of punitive repression, martyrdom would be elevated to a normative ideal of unsurpassable glory, repeatedly celebrated in sermons, commemorative texts, and devotional rituals that honoured those who offered up their bodies in defiant affirmation of Christ. This semantic transvaluation – apparent defeat is a higher triumph, horrific death in this world ensures eternal life in that to come – proved so inspirationally effective that Church leaders were presently confronted with the problem of "voluntary" martyrdoms, zealous believers either deliberately provoking arrest or spontaneously demanding inclusion alongside brethren undergoing trial or torture. The incentives for martyrdom were considerable, and included a complete remission of all sins (as a "baptism of blood") along with immediate entry into heaven.

The first two empire-wide persecutions were launched by the emperors Decius and Valerian, in 249 and 257 CE, respectively. The timing marks the violent intersection of two opposing trajectories: for Rome's empire, an ever-deepening, many-sided crisis brought on by institutional malfunctioning and slackening material production; for the Christian Church, an accelerating trend in membership growth and upgrades in organizational capabilities.

Rome's mounting adversity and disarray over the course of the turbulent third century would manifest most alarmingly in the state's growing incapacity to safeguard over-extended borders and maintain stable governance. Frontiers north and south would be breached repeatedly by tribal nomads and barbarian federations bent on plunder, extortionate subsidies, and lands for settlement. In the east a resurgent Persian power – led by warrior kings of the Sasanian dynasty – periodically overran and devastated Roman cities and territories across Mesopotamia and Syria. Collapsing discipline within the legions sparked a chain of regional mutinies and rebellions, as ambitious commanders marched against reigning emperors and rival usurpers in a series of debilitating civil wars, coups, and assassinations. Escalating military demands placed immense strains on the state's fiscal resources, against which the favoured ploy of coinage debasement contributed to pricing chaos and inflationary pressures. The ravages of war and burdens of taxation combined to weaken the agricultural supports of the entire social system, resulting in abandoned fields, food shortages, and contractive dislocations throughout the economy. Social brigandage, long an outlet for oppressed peasants, runaway slaves, and army deserters, rose to new levels of disruption, spurred on by the deteriorating material conditions that attended the state's political instability and defensive vulnerabilities. To anxious contemporaries, an unprecedented succession of natural disasters appeared to forewarn a grander cosmic rupture, as did the outbreak of a virulent plague in 249, spreading mass death and terror across the empire as it flared repeatedly for well over a decade.

For the self-described "sojourners" who were "in this world but not of it," and who prayed daily for the Second Coming of their Saviour and the advent of God's celestial kingdom, the empire's spiralling descent into turmoil and chaos could only strengthen conviction in the eschatological hopes that sustained their faith. Plague, famine, drought, war, rapine, and pillage: all these coinciding miseries and misfortunes signified nothing less than pending fulfilment of the prophesied "end of days." In times of prosperity, apocalyptic assurances of the world's imminent passing rarely attain acceptance beyond the marginal ranks of the alienated and downtrodden; the onset of social crises and rising insecurity invariably widens the appeal. Rome's faltering dominion would thus significantly alter the dynamics of conversion, by eroding confidence in traditional beliefs and weakening attachments to established conventions and norms. Those changing circumstances are conspicuously registered in the first substantial surge in Christian membership, which by the mid-third century is estimated to have crossed the threshold of one million devotees, a fivefold increase over the five preceding decades of calamity and chaos. Though still negligible in absolute numbers – no more than 2 per cent of the total population – proselytizing successes were now regularly including converts from wealthier and educated strata, whose material and cultural resources contributed greatly to enhanced organizational performance. Christianity's appeal was further strengthened by the fact that it provided a sheltering haven in troubled times, protectively insulated and sustained by charitable welfare arrangements as well as intensified bonds of in-group solidarity (Bryant 2010).

The state-initiated persecutions must accordingly be viewed as defensive reactions, their primary objective being to regain divine favour through the suppression of a subversive cult whose deranged followers utter blasphemies against the tutelary deities and perversely refuse their customary worship. Little wonder, then, that Christian sacrilegious deviance was widely identified as the principal cause of the natural disasters and military reversals wreaking havoc across the Roman world.

The emperor Decius's response to the crisis called for a universal supplication of the gods: all inhabitants of the empire (Jews exempted) were ordered to offer sacrifices to the ancestral deities at their local shrines and temples. Monitoring commissions were established to superintend proceedings, and every citizen was required to submit for notarization an affidavit that not only testified to compliance, but also featured a signed declaration of having "always and continuously" offered sacrifices in the past. The Decian edict thus carried a double hazard for Christians, whose prospects for salvation remained contingent upon strict avoidance of all idolatrous practices and steadfast confessional loyalty to Christ. Coerced by the menacing requirement of notarized certification, great numbers of Christians across the empire lapsed into idolatry and apostasy, either by sacrificing to the demons outright or by furtively procuring certificates through bribery and forgery. Defiant and zealous devotees endured imprisonment and torture, many to the point of martyrdom; countless others fled underground. Policing efforts, enforced vigorously at the outset, slackened as military emergencies intervened, with Decius himself slain on a Balkan battlefield against invading Goths (summer 251). Persecution would be renewed six years later under Valerian, who targeted the cult's organizational basis. All forms of Christian assembly would be prohibited, clerics refusing to sacrifice to the gods executed, and high-status individuals stripped of rank and property, and beheaded upon refusal to renounce membership. There is scant mention of apostasies, and martyrdoms accumulated rapidly. Yet another Roman military disaster, however, would bring relief to the Christians. During an attempt to drive back invading Persian forces in the east, Valerian's legions will be routed (summer 260), the emperor himself carted off into bondage. His beleaguered son Gallienus, beset by mutinies and barbarian invasions, quickly terminates a persecution that had encountered surprisingly defiant resistance.

Christian narratives will duly celebrate these consecutive triumphs over Satan's earthly minions, relishing the fate of the persecutors and glorying in the "copious martyrdoms" that testified to the truth of God's promises for his elect. But it was adaptive resilience and the coordinated, organizational efficiency of the Church that ultimately mattered. The most consequential policy adjustment was the fraught decision to readmit the multitudes of believers who had lapsed during the Decian persecution, which was accomplished by extending priestly powers of absolution to cover the hitherto unpardonable mortal sins of apostasy and idolatry. Schism erupted, as traditionalist elements broke away to form their own Church of the Pure; but in developing a more tolerant pastoral position on matters of sin and forgiveness, the pragmatic leaders of the Catholic mainstream had hit upon an arrangement that augured well for future growth potential. In the peaceful lull leading up to the Great Persecution, Christian numbers are estimated to have risen to five or six million members, approximately 10 per cent of the population.

In This Sign, Conquer! Constantine's Conversion and the Making of a Christian Empire

The third-longest reigning emperor in Roman history, Constantine would hold imperial power for more than three decades (306–37). But it was only after he destroyed the tetrarchic system by force of arms in 324 that he exercised sovereign authority over the entire, reunited empire. That political history – the passage from shared rulership to autocracy – provides the key to understanding the emperor's developing relations with Christianity, as it directly charts the escalating enlargement of Constantine's "freedom of action."

After rescinding Diocletian's edicts of persecution upon entry into the imperial college, Constantine proceeded to shore up his position through diplomatic manoeuvring and intensive campaigning against barbarian tribes along the Rhine. An increasingly fractious tetrarchy, riven by competing ambitions, continued its inexorable slide towards civil war. Seizing the initiative, Constantine's Gallic legions crossed the Alps in the spring of 312 with the dual objective of deposing Maxentius, the reigning western Caesar, and of bringing the more populous and economically advanced provinces of Italy and North Africa under Constantine's dominion. That campaign culminates triumphantly in the Battle of Milvian Bridge, outside the walls of Rome, where Constantine's forces delivered slaughter to Maxentius's routed troops. Victory and territorial expansion brought substantial geopolitical advantages in manpower and material resources. What lifts this episode into an altogether different level of historical significance, however, is Constantine's conversion to Christianity.

We have two versions, written by Christians who had personal contacts with the emperor: the rhetorician Lactantius, who also tutored

Constantine's eldest son; and the emperor's biographer, the bishop-historian Eusebius. Lactantius reports that Constantine experienced a dream on the eve of the deciding battle, instructing him to mark the shields of his troops with a Christogram involving Chi-Rho, the first two letters of "Christ" in Greek (☧). Eusebius's fuller account is presented as the emperor's own testimony, conveyed to the bishop many years afterward. Central here is the appearance of a "cross of light" above the sun, bearing the inscription IN HOC SIGNO VINCES, "In this sign, conquer!" The night following, Christ appears to Constantine in a dream and orders him to place the cruciform sign of the Chi-Rho on his military standards (Barnes 1981). Concerns over discrepancies and implausibilities in these accounts need not detain us, for, as sociological studies of conversion have consistently documented, post-conversion narratives tend to compress time horizons and dramatize selected turning-point moments, while also slighting the prior socialization that "primes" the pre-convert's receptiveness to certain messages and signs. The prevailing scholarly view, that Constantine's "cross of light" was a solar halo phenomenon, is eminently credible. But in a world where natural wonders, epiphanies of gods, and dream visitations were recognized and respected channels of divine communication, the historically important fact is that – whatever Constantine dreamed or witnessed – he either readily accepted or anticipated the interpretations provided by the Christian clerics in his entourage.

Constantine remained in Rome for several months, carrying out tasks essential to asserting control over the newly incorporated territories. Nor were the interests of his new religion neglected. A massive building program was initiated, something that would ring the imperial city with six martyr churches located just outside the walls, and two monumental basilicas, the Lateran and Santa Croce, within them. The emperor's treasury financed the immense construction costs, and each church was supplied with large quantities of gold, silver, and bronze liturgical implements and lavished with the finest decorations of precious stones and metals – life-size silver statues of Christ and the Apostles included. Substantial land grants were also assigned to provide steady income for continuing maintenance. Constantine's reconfiguration of the ancient capital's urban landscape – a religious revolution inscribed in brick and concrete – carried the unmistakable provocation that grand commemorative edifices were being erected to honour individuals who had been executed as blasphemers of the gods and traitors to the state (Lenski 2016).

Constantine's early benefactions extended well beyond Rome. Four additional churches were endowed elsewhere in Italy, and the emperor also provided unstinting support for churches in North Africa. In a letter to Anulinus, proconsular governor of Africa, Constantine orders the immediate restoration of confiscated Church properties. Shortly thereafter, the governor is notified of a new policy exempting Christian clerics from serving on civic boards requiring personal liturgical expenditures. His accompanying justification is revelatory, for not only does the emperor assign paramount responsibility for reverencing "the Most Holy Celestial Power" to Christianity, he also asserts that the fortunes of the state and all humanity are dependent upon whether that religion is despised or respected – a declaration all the more striking in that Anulinus had only recently proven himself a diligent enforcer of the edicts of persecution! In another remarkable letter, sent to Caecilianus, the metropolitan bishop of Carthage, the emperor announces pending delivery of three thousand bags of coined money, to be used in defraying operating expenses for "the ministers of the most holy Catholic religion." More astonishing still, Constantine informs the bishop that whenever additional sums are needed, the fiscal procurator has standing orders to comply upon request. The imperial treasury is henceforth an open coffer for bishops of the Catholic Church.[4]

Having liberated Christians in the western half of the empire, Constantine set about advancing their cause in the east. Prior to his invasion of Italy, an alliance had been formed with Licinius, Augustus of the Danubian provinces, who was himself under threat by Maximinus, the eastern Caesar and fierce persecutor of Christians. During their meeting in Milan (February 313), Constantine persuades Licinius to extend freedom of worship to Christians and restore their properties. In a pre-emptive move, Maximinus's forces cross into Thrace and capture several garrisoned cities before Licinius's counter-attacks rout the invaders, thereby ending the eastern civil war.

Notwithstanding Licinius's marriage to Constantine's sister, relations between the two remaining Augusti remained antagonistic, with ongoing disputes over lines of succession. The first military confrontation occurred when Constantine led troops across the border and inflicted

4 All quotations from Constantine's letters are drawn from these sources: Eusebius, *Ecclesiastical History*, X.5–6; *Life of Constantine*, II.24–70; and Optatus, *Against the Donatists*, appendices 3, 5, 9.

two crushing defeats on his brother-in-law's armies, forcing a treaty that ceded the central Balkans to the western Augustus (March 317). A coerced peace meant preparation for war, and with legitimate concerns about the loyalty of his Christian subjects, Licinius reverted to persecutorial measures: the army high command and civil service were purged of those unwilling to offer sacrifice; bishops were forbidden to travel or hold synods; several clerics were executed for treason; churches were closed or destroyed. It was at this low point, Eusebius informs us, that God intervened to "defend His own" through the agency of "His servant Constantine" (*Life of Constantine* 2.2). In the summer of 324, Constantine launched a combined land and sea operation against Licinius, which culminated in total triumph and reunification of the empire under a single sovereign.

The theologically idealized depiction of Constantine as a Christian crusader – canonically established in the writings of Lactantius and Eusebius – has been greeted with varying degrees of scepticism from the time of Gibbon and Burckhardt to the present.[5] The main line of counter-argument proposes that Constantine's journey to faith was more tentative and politically motivated than Christian tradition allows. The retention of pagan deities on the coinage years after his purported visionary conversion is taken for divided loyalties, though the disappearance of such symbolism following imperial reunification in 324 suggests, more plausibly, a sensible aversion to alienating the non-Christian majority before full sovereignty had been won. Constantine's theological discourse has also raised questions about belief and conviction, given his frequent invocation of abstract phrases suggestive of deistic or henotheistic inclinations: "Divine Providence," "the Greatest God," "Supreme Divinity," and similar formulations. Yet here again, given that Constantine erected no temples to this "Most High God," but did initiate the construction of basilicas, baptisteries, and martyr churches dedicated to the Christian divinity, it is far more likely that the emperor's deistic language represents an accommodative rhetorical

5 Gibbon (1776, XX.III), quoting from an "anonymous" poet (mischievously knowing it to be Voltaire), wrote that Constantine "used the altars of the church as a convenient footstool to the throne of the empire." Burckhardt (1949, ix), harsher still, described "a genius driven without surcease by ambition and lust for power ... the murderous egoist who possessed the great merit of having conceived of Christianity as a world power."

strategy to reassure the many rather than appease the few. There is, moreover, abundant evidence in the corpus of imperial letters to document Constantine's zealous commitment to Christianity.

As early as 314, following a failed attempt at resolving a schismatic rupture in the African Church, Constantine writes an encyclical to the Catholic bishops ("my dearest brothers"), which provides a surprisingly full testament to his beliefs. Christ, *Christus Salvator*, is featured prominently, with pointed mention of His great mercy, His triumphant providence, His teachings and judgment. Even the Devil makes an appearance, his inveterate malignancy faulted for having turned the minds of the schismatics "away from the most noble light of the Catholic Law." More remarkably, Constantine also offers a "confessional" disclosure, openly admitting to a life "far from justice" prior to conversion. Yet, despite his meriting punishment for his misdeeds, the merciful and benevolent God has chosen him as "His Servant." Constantine will expand on this "celestial commission" in a letter to the Vicarius of Africa (315), declaring that his foremost obligation is to dispel errors and impieties, so that "all men might show forth true religion ... and render to Almighty God the worship that is fitting."

A series of legislative enactments would give practical realization to the emperor's declared Christian commitments. The facial branding of criminals is forbidden, as the face is made in the image of God (315). Jews found guilty of stoning Jewish converts to Christianity shall be burned alive (315). Manumission of slaves within the Church is granted legal status (316). Litigants may bypass civic courts and seek adjudication from bishops, whose rulings are binding (318). Marriage laws imposing civic penalties on celibacy and childlessness are repealed, in deference to Christian ideals of sexual abstinence and virginity (320). Clerics and their families are exempted from taxation and compulsory public services, in recognition of their charitable support of the indigent (320). Testamentary law is radically modified by legalizing deathbed bequests of property to the Church, overriding traditional rights of family members (321). Sunday is declared an obligatory day of prayer and rest (321).

After Constantine secures absolute authority over the entire empire in 324, his sponsorship of Christianity abruptly assumes a more militant and hostile stance against traditional polytheism. In a letter sent throughout the newly won eastern provinces, he orders relief measures for the victims of persecution and also provides a remarkable "mission statement" recounting his election by God to serve as the "instrument of His will." The Divine purpose? Nothing less than that "the human race" should be brought to "pious observance of God's holy laws." In a second letter Constantine ventures open contempt for ancestral cultic practices, deriding those who obstinately "delight in error" after the "true doctrine" of Christianity has been revealed. He speaks ominously of the "power of darkness," of "sanctuaries of falsehood," but disavows outright coercion against pagans and calls on his fellow Christians to pray for their conversion. Despite the irenic appeal, the disestablishment of polytheism was already underway.

Eusebius reports on a flurry of laws and actions that followed imperial unification, targeting what the bishop calls the "insanity of polytheism" (*Life of Constantine* 2.45). The emperor orders immediate cessation of the customary practice whereby state officials opened public proceedings with incense offerings to the gods. The dedication of new cult-statues is banned; officials are forbidden to participate in idol worship; divination and the consultation of oracles are prohibited. Constantine is also said to have issued an interdict on blood sacrifices, though the strident renewal of this law in 341 by his sons indicates enforcement proved elusive. Intent on degrading the infrastructure of paganism, Constantine directs his agents to undertake systematic spoliation of the sacred treasures housed in the temples and shrines of the eastern provinces: bronze doors and gilded roofing tiles are hauled away; gold and silver statues converted into melted bullion; admired sculptures and other ornaments confiscated. State terror is also selectively applied, as several major temple complexes are ransacked and destroyed at the emperor's behest, the populace "fearful of harm" should they resist. Much of this plunder would be funnelled into financing the second great wave of Constantine's monumental building projects, with numerous basilicas and martyr churches erected across the eastern provinces (in Jerusalem most notably). Adding substantially to these expenses was the construction of Constantinople, the new and decidedly Christian imperial capital strategically located at the empire's east-west juncture along the Bosporus.

Though he once informed an assembly of bishops that he had been divinely appointed to serve as "the bishop of those outside the Church," Constantine's interventions in ecclesiastical affairs were not only historically momentous but pattern-setting for the emperors who followed. His principal concern throughout was to promote unity within the Church, and this necessarily entailed punitive sanctions against dissenters whenever mediation failed. Episcopal synods were the main sites for forging consensus, and Constantine early on usurped the right to summon, organize, and superintend these conclaves, hitherto the exclusive prerogatives of bishops. At the Council of Nicaea in 325, the emperor not only sat regally among the three hundred bishops attending, he participated decisively to press the agenda of his clerical advisors, even to the point of proposing the *homoousios* or "same substance" formula to characterize the theologically disputed relation between Christ the Son and God the Father. Those unwilling to subscribe to the Nicene Creed, or who subsequently revoked their constrained consent, were variously deposed or exiled by imperial command. A series of laws against sundry "heretical" and "schismatic" groups soon followed. The clerics of "superstition and falsehood" are denied the privileges granted to Catholics. As "haters and enemies of truth," their right to assemble, whether in public or private, is disallowed. Their "pestilential" houses of worship shall be seized and delivered over to the true Church. The writings of Arius, chief opponent of Nicene Christology, are to be delivered up and consigned to the flames; those found in possession of his blasphemous compositions shall be executed. Foreshadowing an imminent and lengthy future, the dogmas and anathemas of the claimants of "orthodoxy" thus secured enforcement through the coercive powers of the state.

By the time Constantine was laid to rest inside his rotunda mausoleum to await the promised Resurrection – sins recently cleansed through timely baptism, marble sarcophagus flanked by cenotaphs of Christ's Twelve Apostles – the emperor had set his new religion on a trajectory of growth and empowerment that would inexorably transform the Roman world into a Christian empire. Under his sons and their successors, patronage for the Church would deepen, persecutions against pagans intensify. Though Christians did not achieve demographic majority until sometime in the fifth century, the effective disestablishment of traditional polytheism can be dated to the reign of Theodosius I (r. 379–95). After declaring in 380 that "all the peoples" of the empire should adhere to the Trinitarian creed of the Catholic Church, and issuing several discriminatory decrees against heretical sects, Theodosius turned to the challenge of a still vigorous polytheism. Civil strife seemed ever more likely as militant bishops and gangs of monks, emboldened by prohibitions of sacrifice and divination, had already begun razing temples and smashing idols, often with tacit imperial connivance. Theodosius chose to escalate by issuing decrees that would culminate in a comprehensive ban on all forms of traditional religiosity. In early 391, all inhabitants are forbidden to "pollute themselves" by slaughtering animals in sacrifice, debarred from visiting shrines and temples, and commanded to abandon idolatry. In late 392, a lengthier ruling strikes directly at domestic cult practices, banning offerings of incense, wine, candles, and garlands to the household and familial deities. Blood sacrifice and divination are now classified as capital crimes of "high treason." To promote compliance, all officials are placed on notice that failure to detect and punish these crimes will result in substantial fines. In 399, the sons of Theodosius issue the following ruling: "Let all temples in the countryside be demolished ... With their overthrow and removal, all material basis for superstition will be destroyed" (*The Theodosian Code*, XVI.10.16).

A "revolution from above," initiated by Constantine and forcibly imposed, had resulted in a world keyed to radically different political and cultural arrangements.

Ashoka Maurya: From Warrior King to the King of Dhamma

The brilliant polymath-historian D.D. Kosambi identified chronological uncertainties as the greatest challenge in the reconstruction of ancient Indian history. As he pointedly noted, in comparison to the dynastic annals of imperial China or the abundance of contemporary texts and historiographies for Greece and Rome, India has "virtually no historical records worth the name ... with very little documentation above the level of myth and legend" (1965, 9). The paucity of chronological "anchor points" renders socio-historical synchronizations and sequencing exceedingly difficult, as does the lagging arrival of written texts following centuries of oral transmission. With datable, events-based narratives beyond reach, Kosambi advocated a "combined methods" approach that would go beyond the conventional privileging of literary works by incorporating research findings from archaeology, geography, ethnology, and comparative sociology. While problems of chronology remain, the turn towards social history inspired by Kosambi's work has resulted in a much clearer picture of the main phases of social development in early Indian history, especially as regards the interplay of cultural, economic, political, and military factors (see Allchin 1995; Thapar 2004).

Buddhism and the Rise of Empire

According to widely accepted tradition, the founder of Buddhism, Siddhartha Gautama, attained nirvana and passed beyond this world in his eightieth year, after having taught and gathered disciples over the forty-five years since his enlightenment as the Buddha. The actual dates for his life, however, are uncertain and contested. Until recently, 566–486 BCE was the favoured chronology. But through textual reassessments and inferences from archaeology, a much later dating has gained currency, with estimates ranging between 479–399 BCE and 448–368 BCE (Bechert 1995). By down-dating the historical Buddha a century or more, these new chronologies call into question a number of the social correlations proposed in earlier scholarship. The relevant implications of this disagreement will be considered below, but let us first review those aspects of the history that still command specialist assent.

Buddhism originated as one among a large number of ascetical/spiritual movements that began emerging during the Late Vedic period (c. 800–400 BCE), a time of unprecedented metaphysical speculation and religious ferment. Despite the proliferation of discourses and practices – a spectrum encompassing hedonic advocacy and self-mortification, atheistic materialism and pantheistic mysticism, mastery of body through yoga and control of mind through meditation – all these diverse currents represented creative and critical engagements with the polytheistic Vedic legacy, as conveyed in the sacred Sanskrit verses and enacted in sacrifices and rituals conducted by the priestly Brahmins. Intensive debate among sages and sects was facilitated by a shared conceptual universe, informed by world-constituting categories such as *atman* (self/soul), *samsara* (birth-rebirth cycle), *karma* (actions-effects), *moksha* (liberation/salvation), and *dharma/dhamma* (law/order/duty).

After years meditating and fasting in the company of yogis and gurus, the Buddha came forth as a sage by proclaiming a "Middle Way" between the extremes of hyper-asceticism and sensual indulgence. His new *dhamma* is announced in the Four Noble Truths: (1) life entails *dukkha*, physical and mental suffering; (2) the cause of suffering is *tanha*, our desires and attachments; (3) the cessation of desire brings release from suffering; (4) the elimination of desire is achievable via the Eightfold Path: right views, thoughts, speech, conduct, livelihood, effort, mindfulness, contemplation. Through these dispositions and practices – diligently pursued over one lifetime or several – liberation from the eternal "wheel of rebirth" is obtained and one "crosses over" to nirvana, the bliss transcendent.

As the number of disciples increased, the movement developed into a communal association known as the *bhikkhu-sangha*, or "community of mendicants," an itinerant troupe of salvation-seekers whose ranks included converts from all castes, along with a parallel and much smaller order of nuns. Initiates were pledged to celibacy and penury, their acceptance symbolized by new names and shaved heads. Growing fame attracted patronage from kings and wealthy donors in the form of parks, buildings, and monetary support, which facilitated the gradual transition to settled monasticism. A vast corpus of ethical injunctions and regulations was formulated to maintain discipline within the Sangha, punctuated by a fortnightly ritualized confession of faults before the gathered assembly (Gombrich 1988).

As a mendicant order, monks were dependent upon charitable donations for their basic necessities: a filled begging bowl for the one daily meal, clothing supplies, occasional medicines. Buddhism thus functioned organizationally in a "symbiotic" rather than "congregational" mode, for the lay followers, the *upasakas* (attendants), participated largely on the level of providing material support to the monastics, who in turn offered *dhamma* instruction and prayer blessings. Most importantly, the notion of *dana* or "giving" was elevated to primacy in the *karma* doctrine, as it was said to provide a "peerless field of merit" for those bestowing gifts on the Sangha. Promised rewards included worldly boons and successively higher rebirths, leading eventually to one of the temporal heavens; those refusing faced the prospect of worldly misfortunes and downward rebirths. In addition to *dana*, the Buddhist laity ensured karmic progression through *samsara* by adhering to the Five Precepts: prohibitions against killing sentient life, theft, sexual misconduct, dishonesty, and use of intoxicants.

The Buddha's "middle way" would ultimately prove to be the most successful of the heterodox challenges to the Vedic tradition; but other renunciatory sects – the hyper-ascetic Jains and the fatalistic-determinist Ajivikas most notably – provided stiff competition, not only over metaphysical claims and techniques of mind-body discipline, but also for disciples and donations. Hence the polemical echoes preserved in Buddhist scriptures, depicting the Buddha in serene debate with rival sages over the cogency of their respective positions.[6]

Another form of competition was presented by the custodians of Vedic oral traditions and rituals: the priestly Brahmins, whose authority derived from lineage rather than corporate organization, and who wielded influence wherever caste arrangements had been imposed

6 For an illuminating account of the "struggle for attention space" in ancient India, see Collins (1998).

through conquests or imported by aggrandizing local elites. The Buddha propounded three main objections against Brahmins, two principled, one characterological. The custom of animal sacrifice, often large scale, was symbolically central to the Vedic worldview and served as its foundational ritual expression. The Buddha opposed this practice, both for its gory violation of the *ahimsa* or "non-violence" precept and the negative karma thereby generated. Brahmanical sponsorship of caste was also challenged, largely through its subordination to ethical criteria, as most strikingly conveyed by the Buddha's declaration that anyone – whether Brahmin, Kshatriya, Vaishya, or Shudra – can attain heaven by observing the Five Precepts, or, conversely, fall into low rebirths or hells from immorality. Caste status, in other words, discloses a karmic past; it does not determine the karmic present or future. More polemically, the Buddha insists repeatedly that the "true Brahmin" is one who lives ethically, spiritually, ascetically, unlike the many "Brahmins by birth" who act unjustly and pursue wealth and sensual pleasures. The Sangha itself is institutionally anti-caste, through its universal admission (barring slaves and the disabled) and disregard for all caste regulations governing interpersonal relations. In striking confirmation of the remarkable "field-openness" of ancient Indian religiosity and the wide appeal of the Buddha's *dhamma*, textual and inscriptional evidence indicates that Brahmins not only constituted the largest convert constituency within the Sangha but that they were also strongly represented among the *upasaka* laity.[7]

The setting and stimulus for this Late Vedic efflorescence in metaphysical speculation and new life-patterns was macrostructural transformation: technological, economic, demographic, military, and political.

Following the demise of the city-based Indus Valley civilization and the arrival of migrating/conquering tribes of Aryan pastoralists (c. 1400), northern India entered into a historically obscure post-urban phase of intercultural syncretization, during which indigenous populations – the "dark-skinned" Dasa of the *Vedas* – were variously subordinated to successive waves of warrior-nomads. Political and military

7 For estimates of caste distributions within the Sangha and *upasaka* ranks, based on tabulations of socially identifiable individuals named in the early Buddhist writings and later donative inscriptions, see Chakravarti (1996, 124–31) and Bailey and Mabbett (2003, 117).

power was organized along clan and tribal lineages, with leadership provided by *rajans* (chieftains/kings); successful plundering led on to territorial encroachments. Economic life revolved around livestock rearing and village-based agriculture, supplemented by essential craft services and products; barter served as the mode of exchange.

A decisive catalyst for development took the form of improved smelting techniques and increasing utilization of iron tools (c. 900). Iron axes, sickles, bladed hoes, and ploughshares not only enhanced labour productivity, but greatly increased cultivation surface through forest clearance. The spread of quick-growing rice varieties and more intensive use of irrigated paddies permitted multiple cropping and higher yields. Rising food security spurred population growth; agricultural surpluses sustained craft and occupational diversification as well as merchant trade. These interdependent processes would coalesce in what is known as India's "Second Urbanization," that is, the marked revival of towns and cities that begins to manifest across the northern plains and river valleys in the eighth century and accelerates thereafter. Archaeological excavations disclose not only an increase in settlements over time, but their growing size and population density (Allchin 1995). Literary sources confirm this picture, providing names and descriptions for scores of urban settlements, ranging from bustling market towns along the rivers and roadways on up to a dozen or so *mahanagara* or "great cities" that functioned as centres of commerce and administration. Political transformations were underway as well, as fixed-settlement and growing reliance on agriculture led to the emergence of territorial polities known as *janapadas* (tribal footholds), each named for their respective Aryan lineages that lorded over toiling subjugated populations (Shudras).

Surplus-capture by leading families progressively undermined tribal bonds and strengthened caste arrangements, giving rise to Kshatriyan clan oligarchies in some territories and monarchical states in the more economically advanced Ganges basin. By mid-seventh century, territorial consolidations through incessant warfare had resulted in the formation of sixteen *mahajanapadas* or "Great Realms," the majority of which were now under hereditary kingships in command of standing armies and administrative bureaucracies. Another century or so of warfare effectively eliminated or subordinated the remaining clan oligarchies, leaving four major northern kingdoms to contend for supremacy. Magadha, the eventual victor, was a populous and prosperous state located in the middle Gangetic plain, richly endowed with fertile soils, abundant forest, rich iron deposits, and navigable rivers. Over the next two centuries, four successive Magadhan dynasties would pursue the project of imperial expansion, vanquishing rivals by force of arms and incorporating their territories within an increasingly sophisticated fiscal-administrative apparatus. At the height of its power, India's first empire would encompass some five million square kilometres of the subcontinent's landmass and rule over an ethnically and linguistically diverse population of up to fifty million inhabitants (Thapar 1997, 2004).

Conquest by Dhamma: Ashoka's Religious Politics

It was under the fourth dynasty, the Mauryas (322–185 BCE), that the empire attained maximal territorial extent, spreading beyond the Indus into eastern Afghanistan and down through central and much of southern India. The last major conquest was carried out by its third ruler, Ashoka, whose renown would derive less from his military exploits than from an altogether different form of "conquest."

In 257, twelve years after coronation, the emperor introduced a new method of communication for his vast dominion: royal directives were to be inscribed on massive stones and erected pillars at prominent locations across the empire, to which designated officials would periodically summon the inhabitants for public readings and instruction. Despite the unforgiving hostility of India's climate to the preservation of ancient texts and monuments, over thirty such decrees have survived, in multiple copies with slight regional variations.[8] The most important of these proclamations carried an astounding confession:

> When he had been consecrated eight years [261/60], the Beloved of the Gods, king Piyadassi [Ashoka], conquered Kalinga. A hundred and fifty thousand people were deported, a hundred thousand were killed and many times that number perished. Afterwards, the Beloved of the Gods earnestly practised *Dhamma*, desired *Dhamma*, and taught *Dhamma*. On conquering Kalinga the Beloved of the Gods felt remorse, for when a

8 The extant texts are categorized as Rock Edicts (RE I–XIV), Minor Rock Edicts (MRE I–IV), and Pillar Edicts (PE I–VII); there are in addition several unnumbered local inscriptions. Translations are derived from Thapar (1997). More commonly utilized for communication purposes were perishable materials like wooden boards, palm leaf, and textile banners.

> country is conquered the slaughter, death, and deportation of its peoples is extremely grievous ... and this weighs heavily on his mind ... Beloved of the Gods now considers victory by *Dhamma* to be the foremost victory ... This *Dhamma* inscription has been engraved so that any sons or great grandsons I may have should not think of gaining new conquests ... They should only consider conquest by *Dhamma* to be a true conquest ... for this is of value in both this world and the next. (RE XIII)

With this splendorous edict, the traditional *dharma* of kings – to wage glorious war, reap plunder and territory – is not only derogated and subordinated to the principle of *ahimsa*. Ashoka goes so far as to enjoin the disavowal of militarism upon his descendants! Wide-eyed innocence cannot have been involved, for long before the Kalinga war Ashoka had suppressed rebellions while serving as his father's viceroy. More telling still, his usurpation of the crown entailed the murderous removal of his brothers, the heir designate included (Lahiri 2015). The sheer horrors of violence and warfare were thus nothing new to the emperor, whose embrace of radical pacifism must accordingly be traced to changes within. Another early edict makes public his personal transformation:

> Thus speaks the Beloved of the Gods, Ashoka: I have been a Buddhist lay-disciple for more than two and a half years, but for a year I did not make much progress. Now for more than a year I have drawn closer to the Order (*Sangha*) and have become more ardent ... This is not something obtainable only by the great; it is also open to the humble, and if earnest they can reach heaven easily. This is the reason for this announcement – that both humble and great should make progress and that neighbouring peoples also should know that the progress is lasting. (MRE I)

For the next quarter-century, until his death in 232, the Mauryan emperor will operate as Buddhism's foremost evangelist and material benefactor.

The majority of edicts are concerned with *dhamma*, and given the semantic openness of the term many scholars have argued that Ashoka's program was more generic and inclusive than any direct application of Buddhist principles. There are three difficulties with this interpretation. First, the emperor's announcement that he had become a Buddhist was featured in the initial set of edicts, a circumstance that would have "cued" the public reception of Ashoka's subsequent injunctions.

Second, while it is true that the Four Noble Truths, Eightfold Path, or nirvana find no mention in the edicts, this is scarcely surprising, given the mass audience intended. Third, Buddhist *dhamma* is effectively bimodal, with distinctive sets of expectations for monks and laity; many of the norms for the *upasakas* are precisely those of the generic sort, such as honesty, respecting parents and elders, and similar conventional virtues.

Perusal of the contents of Ashoka's *dhamma* instructions confirms the emperor's own testimony as to their spiritual inspiration. Three overlapping Buddhist themes can be identified: *ahimsa* or non-violence, compassion for all beings, and universal ethics.

Following his conversion, Ashoka promptly issues a decree banning the killing of animals; a second speaks more realistically about "promoting restraint in the killing and harming of living beings" (RE I, IV). In another edict the emperor announces that the slaughterous custom of royal hunting expeditions will be replaced by charitable pilgrimage tours to honour sacred sites in the Buddha's life (RE VII). The impracticalities of a total ban on butchery for meat were eventually realized, as a later edict from 243 presents an assorted list of animals "to be protected," ranging from geese, bats, and turtles to wild asses, deer, and pigeons. Also included are prohibitions against killing farm animals nursing their young, burning forests or husks that contain living beings, and feeding animals to other animals (PE V). As for violence against humans, we have already seen how Ashoka's reign was transformed in consequence of the psychological torments and remorse he experienced over the Kalinga conquest, to the point of abjuring military adventurism and replacing "the drums of war" with "the sounds of *Dhamma*" (RE XIII, IV). Security concerns, however, preclude disbanding of the army, and in one edict forest tribes are threatened with punishment should they abuse his merciful forbearance. But *ahimsa* now clearly shapes Mauryan foreign policy, as ambassadors are dispatched to various Greek-ruled states in the west – the Seleucid empire and Ptolemaic Egypt most notably – to convey and promote the principles of *dhamma*. Indeed, in a bilingual Greek-Aramaic edict posted on the Afghan frontier, the emperor expresses his ambition for "peace throughout the whole world."

Another Buddhist precept – compassion for all living beings – receives repeated affirmation in the edicts. Particularly noteworthy are the extensive public works sponsored "for the benefit of humans and animals." These include medical facilities stationed along the main roads (even beyond the borders!), the planting of fruit and shade trees, wells dug and watering-holes placed at regular intervals, and establishment of rest houses (RE II; PE VII). Ashoka also orders major penal reforms, insisting that officials henceforth refrain from assigning punishments according to caste and "act with impartiality," so that the people under them "suffer no unjust imprisonment or harsh treatment" (1st Separate Edict). Even those condemned to death merit compassion, and must henceforth be granted a three-day stay of execution to allow clemency appeals from kin. Prisoners will also be encouraged to fast or offer charitable donations to improve their rebirth chances, "for it is my wish they should gain in the next world" (PE IV). Whenever administrative matters are expressly considered, Ashoka espouses a benevolent paternalism: "All men are my children," he declares, and his overriding desire is to secure "their welfare and happiness, both in this world and the next" (1st and 2nd Separate Edicts; RE V, X; PE VI). In another edict the emperor informs his "children" that all his waking time is devoted to furthering their welfare, for by doing so he is "repaying the debt" he owes "to all beings to assure their happiness in this life and attain heaven in the next." May *dhamma* endure, he petitions, and may all his descendants follow it "for the welfare of the world" (RE VI).

Buddhist principles likewise provide the inspiration for the ethical exhortations conveyed in the edicts. As noted above, the Buddha "relativized" caste-bound rules and norms by subordinating them to ethical criteria, such that purity and virtue, pollution and vice, are determined not by birth status but by the moral quality of actions. Ashoka affirms this view by calling upon "the humble and the great" to exert themselves equally on behalf of *dhamma,* which requires cultivating "mercy, charity, truthfulness, and modesty" while abstaining from "cruelty, harshness, anger, pride, and envy" (PE II, III, VII). The emperor is especially keen to specify the relational side of *dhamma* ethics, reiterating across several edicts that parents should be obeyed; relatives, neighbours, and teachers respected; slaves and servants treated kindly; Brahmins and ascetics generously supported; and the poor and distressed comforted (RE III, IV, XI; MRE II). A particularly important edict, promulgated in 256, registers the Buddhist devaluation of Vedic ritualism: "the fetter of clinging to rites and rituals" that erroneously attributes karmic efficacy to sacrificial offerings and magical-ritualistic procedures. Ashoka notes the ubiquitous recourse to such practices, but discounts their effectiveness in comparison to "the ceremony of *Dhamma,*" which is enacted ethically through considerate treatment of slaves and servants, reverence for teachers, restraint in killing animals, and charitable support of ascetics and Brahmins – meritorious acts all that will yield the "great fruit" of "attaining heaven" (RE IX).

Despite the evident zeal of Ashoka's devotion to *dhamma*, many eminent scholars – beginning with Max Weber – have assigned rather more weight to instrumentalist considerations in explicating his turn to Buddhism. For Weber, Buddhism's capacity to function as "a means of *Massen-Domestikation*" within a centralizing patrimonial state will have held strong appeal, as its universalizing norms and "circumvention of status barriers" coincided with imperial objectives of unification and internal pacification (1958, 235–44). Thapar similarly draws attention to the role of Ashoka's *dhamma* in fostering "cultural homogeneity" within a diverse and dynamic empire of spreading urbanism and increasing commercial and craft development (2004, 175). Inclining the same way, Tambiah characterizes the emperor's policy as "an efficacious ideology of pacification, political stability, and security" (1976, 56). These are, to be sure, sociologically plausible interpretations, but do they perhaps slight the agency and causal significance of the royal conversion? For if Buddhism or an inclusively generic *dhamma* carried such obvious imperial advantages, why did it take more than a decade of rule before Ashoka hit upon the winning formula? Nothing similar, it needs noting, had been attempted by his two predecessors, his grandfather Chandragupta Maurya (r. 322–298) having favoured the hyper-ascetic Jains while his father Bindusara (r. 297–72) patronized the predeterminist-ascetic Ajivikas. Is it any less telling that Ashoka's unstinting support for Buddhism was promptly discontinued by his dynastic successors?

At the time of Ashoka's ascension, Buddhism was one among several dozen or more heterodox sects and schools competing for patronage and followers, its presence still concentrated in the Gangetic heartland. And if the down-dating chronologies of the Buddha's life are accepted, the history of the movement must be compressed by a century or more, cutting in half the time available for membership growth and organizational development. It was Ashoka's patronage, in other words, that propelled Buddhism into the very centre of life on the subcontinent, through both his ideological campaigning and the lavish material benefactions bestowed. The Rock and Pillar Edicts were not simply royal proclamations inscribed on stone; they were "live" conduits in an ongoing system of communication, hallowed sites to which local populations were regularly summoned to receive instruction in *dhamma* and to learn of their ruler's paternal benevolence.

To oversee and implement these massively intrusive measures, the emperor created a new stratum of officials known as *Dhamma-Mahamatras* (RE V). These "Ministers of Morality" exercised supervisory authority over regional and district officials and were chiefly tasked with ensuring the acceptance of *dhamma* among the diverse constituencies of the empire, ranging from the destitute, elderly, and imprisoned on up to soldiers, ascetics, and even the imperial household. Officials at various levels were also required to conduct periodic "inspection tours" in their jurisdictions for purposes of holding *dhamma* sessions and to address the needs of the inhabitants (RE III). Complementing these determined efforts to transform hearts and minds was a large-scale imperial undertaking to transform the physical landscape, through extensive construction of stupa shrines, monasteries, worship halls, and the burnished pillars capped by Buddhist symbolic imagery (lion, wheel, etc.). Though precise dating for many of the discovered ruins and relics remains difficult, archaeologists are in agreement that the transition from timber and mud to stone and brick monumentality was initiated under Ashoka (Fogelin 2015).

There was one further contribution the emperor made to the advance of Buddhism: the sending of state-sponsored missionary delegations to lands beyond the empire. Mentioned briefly in several edicts (RE II, V, XIII), this activity receives significantly more attention in later Buddhist texts, which recount the dispatch of nine monk-led "conversion missions" to places such as Kashmir, Gandhara, and Mysore, up into Central Asia, and eastwards to Myanmar – setting in motion diffusion processes that would eventually carry the religion throughout East Asia. The most famous of these missions, however, was to Sri Lanka, as it was jointly led by a monk and nun of royal blood, the progeny of Ashoka Maurya.

In light of the emperor's extraordinary efforts on behalf of Buddhism – not only within his kingdom but beyond – the question arises as to why he did not venture to complete the process by incorporating the Sangha within the apparatus of the state? Here we must again take into consideration the pluralistic nature of the religious field that regulated the thoughts and actions of all participants. Several edicts make it abundantly clear that Ashoka not only accepted sect diversity, he also provided material support to all groups; indeed, even the most adversarial of rivals, "Brahmins and ascetics," are repeatedly coupled in his calls for charitable lay support (RE IV, IX). Discriminatory practices would certainly have undercut the broader message of imperial paternalism, but Ashoka's commitment to inclusive tolerance oversteps any calculating prudence in its inspired affirmation. In two of the earliest edicts, the emperor actually lectures the religious sects directly, urging them to exercise "purity of mind" and "controlled speech" in their disputations, and to refrain from bringing disgrace upon their own sects through partisan divisiveness (RE VII, XII). A monopolizing ascendancy for any preferred sect under these circumstances could scarcely have been imagined, let alone implemented, and certainly not for a movement committed to non-violence.

The emperor did, however, intervene in the affairs of the Sangha in ways that carried the potential for significantly deeper interrelations. In the midst of his reign (c. 250), the Third Buddhist Council was held in the imperial capital to deal with doctrinal controversies and schismatic disturbances. Tradition records that Ashoka not only convened the council, but also interrogated and defrocked the factions charged with heresies: "all these adherents of false doctrine did the king cause to be expelled from the Sangha" (*Mahavamsa* V). The aftershocks of this affair are clearly registered in two separate edicts that seek to promote greater consensus and discipline among monastics and laity alike. Declaring his devotion to the teachings of Lord Buddha and reverence for the Sangha, the emperor presents his own selective list of preferred sermon texts that should be "listened to and meditated upon frequently" to assure "long survival of the true *Dhamma*" (MRE III). The other edict orders his officials to defrock and banish "any monk or nun who divides the Sangha" through deviant beliefs or practices. To safeguard unity and arrest incipient deviancy, wide postings of the decree are insisted upon, and monastics, *upasakas*, and officials are all required to gather on fortnightly fasting days to reaffirm this command (MPE II).

By thus taking on responsibility for doctrinal as well as disciplinary concerns within the Sangha, the emperor has moved appreciably beyond his role as royal patron of Buddhism. A pathway had seemingly been opened towards some form of Caesaro-papism, a normative model for which already existed in the notion of a Buddhist king, a "wheel-turning" *Dhamma-Raja* who would govern righteously in accordance with the Buddha's teachings (Chakravarti 1996, 150–76). But that step, of institutionally converting the Mauryan monarchy into an openly Buddhist kingship, was never taken. From the edicts it appears that Ashoka's confidence in the progress of *dhamma* was based on expectations that his successors would continue with his policies. He was mistaken. Upon his death in 232 he was succeeded by a grandson who favoured Jainism; and no other descendant till the time of the dynasty's overthrow in 185 is known to have shared Ashoka's preference for the Sangha. Regional polities replaced the vast empire, and Buddhism, benefitting from the momentum imparted by Ashoka's patronage, would flourish for several more centuries within India before its gradual eclipse through assimilation within a syncretistic Brahmanical Hinduism (Bronkhorst 2011; Hazra 1995).

Conclusion: The Mega-Actor Question and the Logic of Historical-Comparative Sociology

The destinies of two of the world's major religions were decisively influenced by the patronage interventions of two of the world's most renowned imperial rulers. In both cases, royal conversions functioned as powerful catalysts in (a) altering the *directionality* of sociocultural change and (b) significantly accelerating the *temporal pace* of ongoing historical processes. The transformative actions of Ashoka and Constantine thus raise once again the hoary old question regarding "the role of the individual in history," and its bearing on the logic of inquiry in historical-comparative analysis. Before addressing those issues, let us recapitulate our principal findings, as presented in Table 11.1.

From this inventory of similarities and differences, it can be inferred that the "structure of the religious field" is the *differentia specifica* of greatest causal impact, both directly and through its secondary shaping of "ruler interests," "opportunity frames," and "modes of patronage." The broadly syncretic, pluralistic nature of Indian religiosity inclined towards accommodative tolerance and provided no inner rationale for the elimination of competing beliefs and practices – a disposition greatly strengthened by Buddhist and Jain elevation of non-violence as a sacred principle. In contrast, Christianity's exclusionary monotheism – the "gods" of others are malevolent demons – encouraged a sacred militancy, its activation conditional upon existing balances of power. Hence the ease with which Ashoka combined preferential benefactions for the Sangha with appeals for mutual tolerance and continuing charitable support for Brahmins and ascetics. Constantine's choices reflect the field logic of an irreconcilable opposition between Christians and polytheists; successive advances in his quest for absolute sovereignty are duly accompanied by yet greater backing for the Church and increasing hostility towards traditional cults. As to "social contexts / trend lines," Ashoka's program of grand imperial largesse was necessarily dependent upon the material prosperity generated by an expanding

Table 11.1 Royal Conversion Factorial Matrix

	Ashoka & Buddhism	Constantine & Christianity
Social Contexts & Trend Lines	New expansionary empire; economic dynamism; changing class structure attributable to agricultural, craft, and commercial growth; rising population and urbanization boom	Longstanding empire in protracted decline, beset by ongoing economic, political, and military crises; polarized elite-mass class structure; rural-urban divide; eroding confidence in traditional beliefs and customs
Structure of the Religious Field	Highly pluralistic; multiple spiritual paths credited; a non-hierarchical, competitive religious environment; non-violence central to several sects; Buddhism organized monastically	Polytheistic inclusiveness vs monotheistic exclusiveness and militancy; ancestral cults repudiated as demonic, Christianity denounced as treasonous superstition; Christianity organized congregationally
Ruler Interests	Conversion genuine, rooted in personal existential distress; strong missionary ambitions; Buddhism provides universal norms for integration of the masses in a multi-ethnic empire	Crusader mentality after mystical conversion; zealous advocate for the "true religion" revealed by God's Son and His Church; proper worship of the Divine will bring peace and prosperity to empire and world
Opportunity Frame	Maximal leeway for royal intervention, owing to imperial triumphs and enhanced state capacities; macro-societal changes necessitate new norms and practices	Christianity a high-risk option for royal conversion: illegal status, widely reviled, persecuted; demographically and socially marginal; during period of divided imperial sovereignty, freedom of action constrained
Patronage Modes & Institutionalization	Zealous advocacy and copious material support for the Buddhist Sangha, but tolerant and supportive of all sects; royal patronage arrangements remain discretionary rather than institutionally incorporated within the state	Lavish material endowments and committed ideological support for Christianity; coercive measures against pagan cults intensify; deepening functional integration of Church and State at the legal-juridical and administrative levels

agro-commercial economy, which also produced the merchants, artisans, and landed householders who were drawn to the new ethical universalism and status recognition on offer in Buddhism. Constantine's problem situation was an empire reeling from economic regression, political instabilities, and military reversals, all of which induced waning confidence in the ancestral deities and growing appeal for an eschatological message of imminent world-destruction and eternal paradise for those baptized in Christ's name.

If all five components of our analytical matrix are thus causally implicated in the differing historical trajectories of Buddhism and Christianity, how might we assess the mega-actor contribution? Here it is necessary to venture onto to the shifting sands of the counterfactual, by positing alternative but objectively plausible scenarios of royal intervention.

For Ashoka and Buddhism, it does not strain credibility that the emperor could have favoured a different sect, as did father and grandfather. Equitable beneficence for Brahminism and all ascetic movements was another viable option. In the event of either, how might Buddhism have fared in the absence of Ashoka's preferential, massively scaled patronage? Without the monumental building projects and substantial monetary donations, the incessant advocacy of *dhamma* by imperial officials across the length and breadth of empire, and state sponsorship of conversion missions beyond the borders, it is all but certain that Buddhism's cultural influence would have been limited, its growth significantly smaller and slower than actually occurred. Longer-term prospects would have diminished accordingly. Alternatively, what might have followed had Ashoka embraced Caesaro-papism or otherwise incorporated the Sangha within the governing operations of the state? This counterfactual is altogether more intriguing, since institutionalized collaboration would presumably have accelerated normative integration, thereby dampening the separatist tendencies that expedited the dynasty's downfall. A stable, unified subcontinental empire – free from or less burdened by the constrictions of caste – might have progressed rapidly along the path of urban expansion and commercialized economic development, with agricultural output and craft production synergistically linked through expanding domestic markets and overseas trading opportunities. Mauryan imperial collapse and ensuing political fragmentation foreclosed those possibilities, and their global implications.

For Constantine and Christianity, two counterfactual scenarios merit consideration: a history "without" Constantine; another with a "later" Constantine. At the time of his conversion, Christianity was an illegal and persecuted cult movement, its membership ranks comprising at most some 15 per cent of the empire's population; representation within the institutions of power – the army and high officialdom – was smaller still. As emperor, Constantine not only arrested the course of the "Great Persecution," he promptly set about repealing anti-Christian legislation and endowing the Church with immense subsidies from state coffers. Grand basilicas and martyr shrines are constructed, special immunities and legal powers are granted to clerics, Christians receive preferential appointment to court positions and military commands, laws begin to codify Christian values and place restrictions on polytheistic cult practices, a new Christian imperial capital is established on the banks of the Bosporus. All this – a world-changing reversal from persecution to patronage, and thence to anti-paganism – could not have been initiated by anyone other than Constantine, whose commanding talents and unbroken string of military triumphs secured the loyalty of his troops and the reluctant acquiescence of the vast pagan majority, elites and commoners alike. Remove Constantine from that historical equation and Christianity remains an illicit, socially marginal, and widely reviled *superstitio*, attracting converts in times of calamity and crisis but also drawing persecutorial wrath as the offending cause of the lost favour of the ancestral deities. As for our second counterfactual, the arrival of a "later" Constantine, this would certainly have exposed Christians to continued persecutions in the interim, either precluding or delaying by decades the surge in conversion that followed upon imperial patronage. Conversion of the Germanic tribes, already underway under Constantine, might never have occurred, with the consequence that the fall of the Roman empire in the West would not have been succeeded by Christianized barbarian kingdoms, a precondition for the consolidation of Christendom in the European Middle Ages.

Our comparative analysis thus furnishes considerable empirical warrant for the counterfactualist's credo: "it might have been otherwise, and radically so." Absent the interventions of Ashoka and Constantine, the histories of Buddhism and Christianity would have taken dramatically different form, thus altering in ramifying ways the developmental trajectories of the societies in which they were involved. But with that proposition, are we not surreptitiously resuscitating the long discarded "great men of history" theory, using as cover the more generic concept of "mega-actors"? To establish the crucial sociological difference, let us briefly review the contending positions in that memorable debate.

Though the "kings-and-battles" historiography that prevailed until the modern turn towards social history is obviously relevant, the most apt point of entry is Hegel, whose concept of "world-historical individuals" was introduced to account for the great social transformations in universal history. The conflict-ridden passages from old worlds to new, Hegel argued, summon forth those exceptional individuals capable of discerning the "requirements of the time" and realizing within their own projects the objective necessities of their epoch – necessities ultimately determined by the progressively "rational" workings of the World-Spirit. More prosaically, Thomas Carlyle insisted that "the History of the world is but the Biography of great men," by which he meant all the many leaders and creators "of whatsoever the general mass of men contrived to do or to attain" (1841, 17). While this memorable aphorism has oft been faulted for its implied reductionism, Carlyle himself took pains to situate his representative heroes – Mahomet, Dante, Luther, Shakespeare, Cromwell, Napoleon – within their formative milieus, if only to establish their uniqueness and surpassing talents. Herbert Spencer, in his *The Study of Sociology*, offers a full-blown critique of the "biographical view of human affairs," which he decries as "utterly incoherent" (1873, 33–5). The entire "great man theory" crumbles, he insists, on a single, simple question: "whence comes the great man?" For is it not incontrovertible that "before he can remake his society, his society must make him"? Finally, there is Plekhanov's (2003) well-known Marxist disquisition on the issue, in which he attempts to dialectically mediate and transcend the impasse. His argument rests on an ontological distinction between "the individual features" and "general trends" in historical processes. Historic individuals, "talented or incompetent," can exercise considerable influence on the former, but are incapable of altering the latter. This is largely due to the fact that such actors are themselves "the products" of those determinant trends that carried them to their heights of opportunity and power. Special talents or traits of character are of historical consequence only to the extent permitted by the social forces and needs of a given epoch.

On close examination, it is clear that each side in this debate concedes a combined causal relevance to "individual traits" and "social conditions," while differing over the proportional weight assigned to each. Explanations highlighting the role of "great men" are criticized for grossly inflating the causal powers of historic individuals; explanations emphasizing the social constitution and empowerment of such agents are charged with slighting the distributional singularities of capability and character. Overcoming this circular deadlock will accordingly require some form of bridging mechanism, an analytical category that can flexibly identify and accommodate situations wherein the exceptional qualities, talents, and traits of select individuals do exert decisive influence on historical processes, while also registering the social basis of their extraordinary empowerment.

As I have tried to document empirically through case comparison, those requirements are optimally fulfilled in the "mega-actor" concept, the grounding sociological premise of which is that *powers of agency are a combined function of unequally distributed individual capabilities and the differential resource endowments derived from stratified placement within roles, institutions, and organizations*. The analytical utility of such a category for historical-sociological inquiry cannot, I submit, be overstated.[9]

REFERENCES

Allchin, F.R. 1995. *The Archaeology of Early Historic South Asia*. Cambridge: Cambridge University Press.

Bailey, Greg, and Ian Mabbett. 2003. *The Sociology of Early Buddhism*. Cambridge: Cambridge University Press. https://doi.org/10.1017/CBO9780511488283.

Barnes, Timothy. 1981. *Constantine and Eusebius*. Cambridge, MA: Harvard University Press.

Bechert, Heinz, ed. 1995. *When Did the Buddha Live?* Delhi: Sri Satguru.

Bourdieu, Pierre. 1971. "Genèse et structure du champ religieux." *Revue Francaise de Sociologie* 12 (3): 295–334. https://doi.org/10.2307/3320234.

Bronkhorst, Johannes. 2011. *Buddhism in the Shadow of Brahmanism*. Leiden: Brill. https://doi.org/10.1163/ej.9789004201408.i-294.

Bryant, Joseph M. 2010. "The Sociology of Early Christianity." In *The New Blackwell Companion to the Sociology of Religion*, edited by Bryan Turner, 311–39. London: Wiley-Blackwell. https://doi.org/10.1002/9781444320787.ch14.

9 I was emboldened to undertake this exploration by the example of John Hall, whose voluminous contributions to historical-comparative sociology are much enlivened by frequent discussion of named politicians, conquerors, sages, prophets, scientists, and poets.

Burckhardt, Jacob. 1949. *The Age of Constantine the Great*. New York: Pantheon.
Carlyle, Thomas. 1841. *On Heroes, Hero-Worship, and The Heroic in History*. London: James Fraser.
Chakravarti, Uma. 1996. *The Social Dimensions of Early Buddhism*. Delhi: Oxford University Press.
Collins, Randall. 1998. *The Sociology of Philosophies*. Cambridge: Harvard University Press.
de Ste Croix, G.E.M. 2006. *Christian Persecution, Martyrdom & Orthodoxy*. Edited by Michael Whitby and Joseph Streete. Oxford: Oxford University Press.
Fogelin, Lars. 2015. *An Archaeological History of Indian Buddhism*. Oxford: Oxford University Press. https://doi.org/10.1093/acprof:oso/9780199948215.001.0001.
Gellner, Ernest. 1988. *Plough, Sword, and Book*. New York: Collins.
Gibbon, Edward. 1776. *The History of the Decline and Fall of the Roman Empire*. Vols. I and II. London: Strahan and T. Cadell.
Gombrich, Richard. 1988. *Theravada Buddhism*. London: Routledge. https://doi.org/10.4324/9780203310878.
Hall, John. 1985. *Powers and Liberties*. Berkeley: University of California Press.
Hazra, Kanai. 1995. *Rise and Decline of Buddhism in India*. Delhi: Munshiram Ltd.
Hopkins, Keith. 1999. *A World Full of Gods*. London: Phoenix.
Kosambi, D.D. 1965. *The Culture and Civilization of Ancient India*. London: Routledge.
Lahiri, Nayanjot. 2015. *Ashoka in Ancient India*. Cambridge, MA: Harvard University Press. https://doi.org/10.4159/9780674915237.
Lane Fox, Robin. 1987. *Pagans and Christians*. New York: Knopf.
Lenski, Noel. 2016. *Constantine and the Cities*. Philadelphia: University of Pennsylvania Press. https://doi.org/10.9783/9780812292237.
MacMullen, Ramsay. 1984. *Christianizing the Roman Empire*. New Haven: Yale University Press.
Mann, Michael. 1986. *The Sources of Social Power*. Vol. 1, *A History of Power from the Beginning to AD 1760*. Cambridge: Cambridge University Press. https://doi.org/10.1017/CBO9780511570896.
Mouzelis, Nicos. 1991. *Back to Sociological Theory*. London: Macmillan.
Plekhanov, Giorgi. 2003. *The Role of the Individual in History*. Honolulu: University Press of the Pacific.
Spencer, Herbert. 1873. *The Study of Sociology*. London: King and Co.
Stark, Rodney. 1996. *The Rise of Christianity*. Princeton: Princeton University Press.

Tambiah, Stanley. 1976. *World Conqueror and World Renouncer*. Cambridge: Cambridge University Press. https://doi.org/10.1017/CBO9780511558184.

Thapar, Romila. 1997. *Asoka and the Decline of the Mauryas*. Delhi: Oxford University Press.

– 2004. *Early India*. Berkeley: University of California Press.

The Theodosian Code and Novels and the Sirmondian Constitutions: A Translation with Commentary, Glossary, and Bibliography. 1952. Glossary and Bibliography by Clyde Pharr. Princeton: Princeton University Press.

Weber, Max. 1958. *The Religion of India*. Glencoe: Free Press.

Conclusion: Reflections and Replies

JOHN A. HALL

The contributors to this volume have critiqued and extended the ideas found in my work with great care and sophistication. In this chapter I add my own thoughts by explaining the nature of the contribution I have sought to make over the years. I then turn my attention to particular groupings among the authors. Let me say that responding has not been easy: criticism and the course of events have made me aware of complacency in my position. At the end of his life Leonard Cohen mentioned "a better way" before noting that "it's not the truth today." That is how I feel at the moment, as this conclusion makes clear.

The "Hallsian" Perspective

Francesco Duina's account of the principles of and tensions within what he has captured as the "Hallsian" view is almost entirely accurate – indeed, it has a level of clarity I might not have been able to produce myself. Still, it may be useful to underline what he has said by describing the concern with nations and states, power and civility in a different way, by means of the genealogy of what was involved.[1]

I had been frustrated studying history as an undergraduate at Oxford because of the conservative tenor of the discipline at that time. Barrington Moore's ability to combine explanations in history with normative advocacy came as a revelation, turning me to comparative historical sociology. It was almost natural, then, to turn to Max Weber

1 I concentrate on intellectual matters, but offer more personal details elsewhere (Hall 2005).

given his historical range, but I did so as well for two other reasons. First, Althusser's structuralist Marxism, so popular at the time, almost forced me to a Weberian stance because of the utter rigour – admirable in its way – of its insistence that everything could be explained in economic terms. I have never been able to believe this: human beings face a political problem at all times, in which some seek dominance over others. The second reason was purely personal, namely the impact of Ernest Gellner – Weberian to the core in both sociological and philosophical terms, longing at that time to write his own philosophic history. The years that followed were enormously pleasurable. For one thing, I used to wander around the British Museum most days for an hour or so when writing my doctoral thesis in its Reading Room, unconsciously absorbing knowledge about the world civilizations, a delight that I have since often shared with Joe Bryant, one of the contributors to this volume. For another, this was followed by a seminar titled "Patterns of History" at the London School of Economics that I co-organized with Gellner and Michael Mann. Week after week specialists on aspects of the world civilizations would come to talk, often to a tiny audience, whilst the seminar convenors took notes and gained bibliographies. All three of us then wrote philosophic histories.

What is most immediately notable about mine, *Powers and Liberties* (Hall 1985), is its acceptance of *the* Weberian question, namely the need to explain the rise of the West. I remain true to the question, and am indebted to Joe Bryant for insisting that something must explain the difference with other civilizations – even if the difference needs to be dated later as the result of arguments put forward by the Californian School (Bryant 2006). To stress the rise of the West can lead one to be accused of "Eurocentrism," that is, the imputation that the West was more dynamic or rational, or otherwise morally more advanced. I refute that charge, always now making use of a brilliant intervention from Patricia Crone. The great Danish historian of early Islam exploded in frustration at the end of a conference titled "The European Miracle." All that stuff about dynamism and restlessness, she insisted, should be reclassified as immaturity, mere juvenile delinquency when compared to the settled way of life provided by the great imperial civilizations. Behind this lay a powerful view of social evolution that immediately entered into my mental framework. Evolution demands adaptation to circumstances. The great imperial systems successfully managed this, in marked contrast to the messier situation in northwestern Europe. But evolutionary advance comes from failures, from the ill-adapted. One element within

Europe was the creation of states – and eventually national states and nation-states – that proved to be great power containers as competition forced them to interact closely with their societies so as to gain the fiscal means necessary to survive in a world of fierce competition. I continue to believe that multipolar state competition does much to explain the rise of the West, and that the characteristic workings of this model have since spread to the world polity.

But there is something more important to say about the book. There is much truth to the view that the earliest intellectual work of any type contains the seeds of everything that is to follow. It was very hard to find the title of the book (it took a week to do so, sitting in the library of the Ecole des Hautes Etudes in Paris!), and a good deal hangs upon it. I was well aware of power seen as coercion but had quite as much in mind the alternative view of power, present both in Hannah Arendt and in Talcott Parsons, stressing the generative capacity that could be created when people worked together. Marriages were often exercises in male coercion, but a couple that agreed could power to something stronger and larger. The level of coordination in eighteenth-century Britain – a world in which the "liberties" of the aristocracy worked together with the state – struck me forcefully. So too did the capacity of states blessed with internal consensus to swim successfully in the larger sea of capitalism: social cohesion inside seemed the best way to live in the external world described by Adam Smith. That view is at the heart of my recent book on small states in the face of the financial crisis, written with John Campbell (Campbell and Hall 2017). The classic contrast was obvious: France was larger and richer than Britain but it lost most wars with its rival in the long eighteenth century because the stalemate between aristocracy and state meant that its fiscal take was less than that of the island state. The comment of Tocqueville (1955, 64) about the old regime of eighteenth-century France seemed apposite, that its rule was negative and limited, preferring control over groups to allowing them autonomy. Equally revealing is the reply of the Emperor Trajan to Pliny (when he was the governor of Bithynia-Pontus) as to whether to allow local organization of a fire brigade in Nicomedia: such organization should not even be contemplated, the emperor insisted, for once gathered together minds would drift from fires to politics (Pliny 1969, letters 33 and 34).

The concern with civility that developed is an expansion of the notion of liberties, most obviously by moving beyond the historic rights that make up "liberties" so as to consider popular politics. The concept comes from insisting that a particular attitude is necessary within civil society, that most popular term of recent years, if political decency is to be assured: mere societal self-organization guarantees nothing – what matters is the recognition of difference, or, in a simpler formulation, a diminution of those ideological convictions that make mass slaughter seem desirable and moral. But the deeper notion at work concerns political life in a different sense. Bluntly, do softer politics have the capacity to tame extremism, and thereby to provide decency and stability? Would reform, to put it differently, make people move away from the barricades? A general view supporting this was the stability of the advanced societies of the West compared to those of East and Central Europe, to which I had devoted much attention. I was deeply impressed by Solidarity's contribution to the ending of communism in the socialist bloc: the demand for a trade union, coming from a declining shipbuilding city, played a considerable part in the collapse of a whole regime. Those who sought a union had to take on their state because it would not allow such self-organization. The imposition of martial law to control this movement from below thereby did much to destroy the very core of socialist legitimacy. In contrast, union activities in liberal capitalist societies mostly diffused conflict through society, rarely being – or, rather, having to be – directly set in opposition to the state. Sociological research has made it possible to see that political openings systematically defang political extremism. In late Tsarist Russia extremism was closely linked to political oppression, with reformist attitudes coming to the fore immediately political openings were on offer (McDaniel 1988). Exactly the same is true of nationalist movements: secessionist demands have little chance when facing liberal regimes that allow entry and cultural rights. Hence entrepreneurs try constantly to create grievances that would make it possible to move forward. This was true recently in Quebec when the Parti Québécois proposed a xenophobic "charter of values" in the expectation – had they had the chance to put it into effect instead of losing an election – that it would have been rejected by the Supreme Court, thereby allowing them to call a referendum on the grounds that Quebec was being humiliated, ruled from the outside. Still it is harder to appease nations than social classes. Gellner (1983) was correct to say that particular dynamite results when social class inequalities *combine* with a cultural marker; Matthew Lange (2013) added to this the discovery that sudden educational expansion of a majority population is likely to lead to conflict in societies dominated by an ethnically different minority. So nationalism can all too easily demand so much homogeneity as to rule out civility altogether.

This leads to two final thoughts. The first concerns the enemies of civility in relation to both class and nation. In this matter I follow Tocqueville (1955, 136), the French aristocrat who came to realize that the inability of classes to cooperate in France was not caused by the popular drive for equality, as he had expected, but rather by the behaviour of the kings of France, dividing one group from another so as better to rule over them. But just as important as spreading distrust within society is the complete opposite already noted: ideological convictions determined to homogenize whole societies into a single frame. The second point concerns brutality. Countries that enter the modern age with a good deal of national homogeneity – as the result of losing wars in the case of Denmark, or of processes of centralization that took place over centuries in the case of England – are lucky. Such civility as there has been in Europe since 1945 is the result of horror, of the solving of the national question through ethnic cleansing, mass murder, and population transfer. It ill behoves Europeans to offer moral advice to the rest of the world: what matters is that the South does its best to avoid Europe's pattern of development.

All of that is to take civility in factual terms, to show that it works when it is present. But civility can also be considered in normative terms. I admit that this was something of a development for me. I had initially followed theorists who argued that civility worked without social planning, as it were behind the scenes. Adam Smith had made this case for capitalist society, arguing that keeping up with the Joneses was a positive illusion that replaced the harder politics of redistribution, a point echoed later by Gellner (1979) when insisting both that the "Danegeld" provided by economic growth served the same function and that the growth of technical expertise would slowly but surely liberalize communist societies. The work of Albert Hirschman (1978) suggested the possible impact of an altogether more active political approach. If you give voice, then it is possible to gain loyalty; in contrast, the denial of voice will encourage exit in the case of nations, and violence more generally from those who are excluded. It is as well to admit that this is advice for rulers, suggesting that political opening can ensure stability – even perhaps thereby allowing rulers to remain in power, or at least to exit it without facing reprisals.[2] Several

2 I concur with Ziblatt (2017) in thinking that the actions of elites have great importance, and am very much at one with his account of structural features, above all economic growth, that ensure that politics is not a zero-sum game that would otherwise rule out decompression.

authoritarian regimes have taken this route, perhaps most strikingly South Korea since the 1980s. The mechanics involved can be seen just as clearly within liberal democracies: internment without trial in the midst of "the troubles" of Northern Ireland, for example, led to an escalation of violence, whilst the political opening created by the Easter Peace Accords has led to a fundamentally settled condition. There are of course great intellectual difficulties here. One concerns definition: there is a marked contrast between openings leading to assimilation to a single ideal and those allowing integration of continuing diversity within a single frame. The Swiss in a sense managed both in a world of multiple identities, cantonal, ethnic, and national. A second difficulty concerns evidence: dogs that don't bark – countries in which different ethnicities find ways to live together – often do not generate the data on which social scientists concentrate. But we need to do better here, for the question of ethnic diversity within states is one of the central issues of our time.

Let me end with two final considerations that structure much of what follows. First, there is a sting in the tail in the normative recommendation to include: depoliticization can lead to passivity, as seems to have happened in much of the advanced world of liberal capitalism in recent years. Second, the fact that the politics of inclusion and reform was at least possible raises perhaps the central question that faces comparative historical sociologists: why did social progress in European history result in disaster? Why did civility prove to be so vulnerable?

Readers should note that I will discuss the various contributions to this volume by grouping them around five key themes; I thus follow a different order than the one found in this volume.

Religion in Pre-Industrial Empires

Interest in the world civilizations led me to study the imperial rule that often but not always dominated their existence in pre-modern circumstances. I am of course aware of weaknesses in my accounts of pre-modern empires, most notably in taking Max Weber's view of imperial bureaucracy preventing capitalist advance too seriously, thereby failing to properly recognize the character of imperial economies and so underestimating their power (Bang 2008). Nonetheless, to term these polities as "puny" Leviathans still makes sense. They lacked capacity to organize most social relations, letting – to adapt Robert Walpole's phrase – dogs lie as long as they remained asleep. These worlds were not the societies that we have now: elites characteristically sat on top of variegated communities with their own beliefs and practices (Crone 1989; Gellner 1983). This is not to say that culture could never be shared between people and elite. Something like this did occur in Byzantium, and the resulting strength helps explain the longevity of that empire.

The chapters by Joe Bryant and by Yansei Sun and Dingxin Zhao significantly advance my ideal-typical view of empire. For one thing, they bring in a proper awareness of variety; for another they advance my understanding of the link between empire and religion, doing so in a related and cognitively powerful manner.

Bryant's essay on Ashoka and Constantine is a wonderful piece of comparative historical sociology based on deep and sustained scholarship. He provides a new five-point conceptual apparatus to explain the impact of mega-actors that combines structural and cultural elements in a way that will be immensely useful for other scholars. His analysis of Constantine does show that a key historical figure can change the shape of history. He makes his case in a way that is wholly sensible, as he is well aware of structural factors, seeking merely to locate the moments when an actor with power can then make a decisive difference in the historical record. It is at this point that he is most original. What was at issue was not the amount of immediate political or economic power possessed by the two emperors in question. Instead it is the structure of the religious field – the extent to which it is diverse – that mattered most, limiting the long-term impact of Ashoka in contrast to that of Constantine. The structure in question, to put it in different words, is cultural. This is to emphasize somewhat more than I had done the autonomous impact of religious doctrine, its capacity to lay down the tracks of historical development.

It is here that there is a strong link to the second chapter concerned with religion and empire. The focus of Sun and Zhao on toleration leads to a splendid categorization of most pre-modern empires in terms of the extent to which they tolerated difference. Their view is of course wholly sophisticated: most of what they are discussing is the inability to impose any homogeneous view rather than the acceptance of difference. But they go beyond this to explain the variation in tolerance by means of two variables, the possession of a singular truth and the desire to propagate the message it contains. Their view of Buddhism neatly fits with Bryant's analysis of Ashoka, and they stress even more strongly the autonomous impact of the religious field. This is a marvellous contribution, and it ends with a thought – that evangelical monotheisms have within them the capacity for intolerance and, in opposition to that, the possibility of learning how to live with difference – that draws attention to my concern with civility.

Imperialism and Nationalism

Siniša Malešević experienced the third Balkan wars, but has somehow managed to turn the insights gained from horror into high-powered sociology – becoming our leading expert on war and nationalism. His work has at all times stressed the need for the presence of ideological coherence and bureaucratic force as the basis of societal effectiveness. This lies behind his marvellous demonstration that the gaining of independence by states in the Balkans in the nineteenth century had little to do with national sentiment from below, being rather the product of great power politics. In this he is a modernist, and convincingly so when dealing with material over which he has unmatched mastery. There is an amusing point to be made about this. He was briefly a student of Gellner, whose late work proposed ad hoc explanations for the rise of Balkan nationalism that pre-dated the rise of industrialism at the core of his theory (Gellner 1997). Malešević provides the explanation that Gellner needed to save his basic position, namely that there was no nationalism to be explained away! I largely agree with him on all these points, and welcome the interesting contribution he makes here. Nationalism and imperialism did coexist in modern times, and in complex ways, and he shows here that the history of imperial achievements was used by newly independent nineteenth-century states as ideological support. Malešević is especially enlightening on the difference between the world of "Foxy Ferdinand" in Bulgaria, dreaming of becoming emperor of renewed Byzantium, and that of Serbia, where imperial ideas were used to promote the national cause.

Malešević is right to say that combinations of nationalism and imperialism caused chaos. But it is not quite clear why this should be so – at least to me, for this is the subject that is currently at the centre of my attention (Hall 2017). There may be a difference between us when it comes to explaining the origins of the First World War. He notes the claim of many scholars, including Hiers and Wimmer (2013), that the rise of nationalism explains the onset of war. The fear that Serbia might become a Balkan Piedmont is often seen as causing the harsh reaction from Vienna in 1914. Malešević would agree that Serbian nationalism had strengthened in the years immediately prior to 1914, as can be seen in the switch in loyalty from Vienna to St Petersburg. But he wishes to dispute this general view that nationalism caused war, suggesting that no real danger existed for Vienna given the political immaturity of the Serbs within Bosnia-Herzegovina. This might seem to suggest irrationality on the part of Vienna – a term that I much dislike in general, although the editor of this volume thinks I subscribe to it. The matter is so important that it deserves a digression.

"Rationality" is complex; distinctions must be drawn. I tend not to follow rational choice theory in any complete sense because its capacity to predict is so limited. Jeremy Bentham was once asked how his theoretical schema could explain self-mortification, vicious or otherwise: he replied that pain could be a form of pleasure. But if everything is pleasure, we have no guide to the future. The same is true of the concept of "national interest"; whatever happens can be described after the event in terms of this concept, but the fact that interest can mean honour, pride, and prestige as much as material self-interest means that the concept has little power to predict. This point can be put in a different way. The purpose of sociology is to rationally reconstruct the reasons for action held by individuals and groups; it is always important in this context to remember that what is believed to be real is real in its consequences. Of course, the beliefs held by a group of people in some form of social interaction can lead to an outcome that we – blessed with our own sense of morality – feel to be "irrational." These distinctions will be put to use in a moment when we return to the world before 1914. But before we do so a problem in the philosophy of social science and in moral philosophy needs to be raised. Bluntly, if everything is explained, if all actions make sense to the actors involved, is there sense to any notion stressing political responsibility? Does explanation mean that everything is forgiven? I certainly cannot go that far, but the dilemma remains. All that can be said is that distinctions can be drawn between reasons for action that seem soundly based and those that are irresponsible, wholly unnecessary, and opportunistic.

It is true that statesmen took immense risks in the years before 1914, but it is not hard to see why. For one thing, war might well be a way for elites to cement their own status in the face of radical social change (Judson 2016). For another, they were focused on the future. Nationalism might not be a danger now, but it soon would be – making it feel rational to nip it in the bud when occasion arose (Levene 2005). After all, many states consciously sought to build up nationalities within the territories of their rivals so as to weaken them (Reynolds 2011). Maybe elites reacted too harshly, but these great states were obsessed by questions of honour, prone to behave like tigers (Lieven 2015, 311–12). So perceptions of secessionist nationalism by empires had some role in the onset of war. That this is so needs to be set against the moral condemnation of elite behaviour that one is itching to make. I had not expected that understanding would diminish my condemnation of the elites, and still cannot stop myself from thinking that they ought to have done better.

It is important not to leave the causal story of the onset of war at this point, for other factors were at work. Great power rivalry certainly mattered, and archival research may support Malešević's hunch that Vienna was as worried by Russian interference in 1914 as by Serbia. Then there is the fact that secessionist nationalist movements were partly created by attempts of the great powers to homogenize their own territories. Equally important and very often neglected was nationalist pressure within great states, from middle-class actors such as Max Weber, keen for a rising power to play a greater role on the world stage. Finally, one must remember that the key Anglo-German rivalry had little to do with nationalism. All this is to say that the onset of war had many causes. The consequence was collapse, in whose aftermath many nations were "set free" – as Wimmer (2013, chap. 3) somewhat inconsistently recognizes elsewhere.

Luyang Zhou's brilliant comparative historical sociology of the two great twentieth-century communist revolutions challenges Wimmer's (2013, chap. 4) general view of a sustained move from empire to nation-state. On the one hand, the collapse of empires in 1914 did not mean that the nation-state form immediately became hegemonic. Hitler is the appalling and obvious exception, although his ultimate goal may well have been that of a homogenous Aryan entity. Tsarist rule was followed by the more straightforward continuance of a multinational empire under different management. Of course, a good deal of the explanation for this comes from the national factor, as Zhou, following Riga (2012), makes clear. The awakened nationalism of the peripheries was an obstacle to the continuation of the state: a universal ideal was needed to contain it. But Zhou's great expertise is in the Chinese case. He shows and then explains that here it was the absence of nationalism that drew the communist elite to universal ideals – although ironically they then sought with success to build a nation-state.

I have learnt a great deal from his work and can only make two points. First, the comments he makes about civility and its absence allow me to clarify my position. Only a sustained political opening has the ability to integrate and depoliticize: the situation of the Bolsheviks was in a sense the worst possible – able to survive but continually radicalized by the actions of the regime. The Chinese situation adds another nuance: absolute repression can create order, although this may have disastrous long-term consequences. Second, his concentration on the military clearly gives us insight into the future of the regime – another issue that must be at the centre of our current political concerns.

Nation-Building after Empire

My interest in the South has deepened over the years. I remain convinced of the structural power of the North within the world political economy – such that the South depends on the North rather than, as dependency theory had it, the other way around. But I have become more and more aware of the deleterious legacies of imperial rule for the South. I had initially followed Gellner in believing that nation-building would be relatively easy, thereby allowing development to take place. Sustained reflection has made me realize that the presence of national homogeneity is key to successful development. Hence it has become natural to turn to the legacy of imperial rule for nation-building. No scholar has done better work nor has a richer future agenda in this matter than Matthew Lange, and he is blessed with an ability to work in a sophisticated manner with varied mixed methods. His chapter joins his earlier work on colonialism with newer work on missionaries to produce a convincing comparison between Burma and Thailand. Divide-and-rule politics of the colonial power in combination with penetrative missionary activity among minorities have led to Burma facing vicious ethnic violence; in contrast, the presence of an independent national state in Thailand allowed for assimilation of minorities in the way that had been true of France or England in early modern Europe.

One criticism of Lange's work does come to the fore, and it is an amusing one. The chapter seeks to show the difficulties of nation-building in parts of the South by contrast with the smoother process characteristic of European history – albeit, as noted, with Thailand resembling some of the more successful European cases. But one might wish to reverse this method, to look at European history in light of the South! Many European states were composite in character, with divide-and-rule tactics being relatively common – as was true, for example, of British rule in Ireland. Furthermore, nationalist missionaries were altogether present inside the great powers, often causing problems at the margins of empires (Judson 2007). And great powers sought to create "nations" abroad, thereby creating the toxic brew of imperialism and nationalism that has just been discussed.

I have had enormous pleasure teaching in Turkey as well as in visiting the fieldwork sites of my graduate students there, and have the Ottomans and their successor states currently at the centre of my attention. Yesim Bayar's work has been of particular importance. She is an expert on different conceptions of the nation in the late years of the Ottomans and the early years of the Republic (Bayar 2014). During the war the fateful choice was made to save the state at the expense of the empire, with the state shortly afterwards surviving dismemberment by foreign powers (Reynolds 2011). One contribution of her work has been to show that behind Kemalism's secular façade lay a measure of accommodation with Islam. In this sense, there is a measure of continuity with the AKP party led by Recep Tayyip Erdogan. The picture she presents of the stages of national formation, and of the difficulties at the heart of the state, is crystal clear. It occasions further reflection on political responsibility. The early years under Erdogan promised a great deal: a softening towards the Kurds, in part prompted by a desire, backed by business, for entry into the European Union, looked as if the split at the heart of the state might be healed. The failure of this opening owed a good deal to the recalcitrance of Sarkozy and the reluctance of other Europeans, but much must be laid at the door of Erdogan himself. His determination to stay in power was so great that he was prepared to end the opening to the Kurds, even to start a civil war against them. One can understand the choice but still insist that it was not necessary, and certainly not in the interests of Turkey. Divide-and-rule policies destroyed the better way open to the elite; the lust for power triumphed over civility, a pure example of political irresponsibility. Turkey has gone up and down politically, with democracy interrupted on several occasions by military intervention. One fears that Turkish politics will now be conducted in a single vein, at once popular and authoritarian.

Berna Turam is well aware of this history of political division, and she makes much of its legacy of distrust, seeing this rather than Islam as an excuse for the authoritarian instincts of the current regime. She is appalled by current developments, whose effects she traces within urban settings. As a tremendously sensitive ethnographer, she identifies trends going in the opposite, more positive direction. For one thing, she notes the entry of pious Muslims of middle-class background into secular areas of the city, keen to enjoy the consumer benefits that are available. For another, she describes the activities of young people seeking to protect public spaces within the city. Her own heart is here! But her research has expanded beyond the Islamic world so as to take in sanctuary cities, not least those in the United States. One suspects that we have here the start of a sociology that will take urbanism seriously. It is well to remember in this context that authoritarianism feeds more off fear than from reality, and that fear often comes from those without any experience of the other. London voted against Brexit, and Montreal was clearly against the nasty charter of values proposed by the Parti Québécois. So Turam's work ends on an optimistic note that sets it apart from that of most of the other contributors.

The United States

These last comments bring me to the two chapters that concentrate on the United States, with special reference to *Is America Breaking Apart?*, co-authored with Charles Lindholm (Hall and Lindholm 1999). Both tend to question what they take to be a measure of optimism in our treatise. Their negative critique is justified; I had not expected dissension to rise so high. Nonetheless, there were two elements of our argument that were very far from being optimistic, as Lilli Riga recognizes. First, the unity of the United States came from civil war: there was no civility in a conflict so savage that is so unlikely to happen ever again. Second, we were always aware that the most positive point made, that of outmarriage from different ethnic groups, had an exception: rates were extremely low for black men, and still lower for black women. In that context, we noted the important argument of Orlando Patterson (1982), that the idea of freedom that was so important for poor whites had its basis in a sense of racial superiority. Nonetheless, they make strong cases, and I will resist them only in part.

Before doing so it is important to note something more general. I have felt for some time that nationalism was changing its character, becoming less an elite project than one for those threatened by the speed of social change, ill equipped to compete in a more globalized world (Hall 2011). This was very noticeable to me in the Danish vote against adopting the euro: all elements of the political elite were in favour of joining, but males outside Copenhagen, with lower educational standards and poorer employment prospects, prevailed for a "Denmark first" policy.

The best way to interpret this seemed to be to recall Karl Polanyi's *The Great Transformation* (1944) – as important a book to emerge from Vienna as those of Popper and Hayek. The interpretation offered therein of the European catastrophe of the twentieth century was perhaps not empirically correct, but the notion that capitalism made people so uneasy because of its relentless push for social change that they would demand to be protected was enormously suggestive. This is surely the background condition that does much to explain the current rise of populism. But that rise is still poorly understood. There was a huge difference between populism in Tsarist Russia and that in the United States before 1914 – the one seeing intellectuals going to the people to participate in their purity, the other *being* the people up in arms, fully possessed of their own culture, deeply contemptuous of intellectuals. There are touches of that division even today, not least in the behaviour of those elements of the British upper class toadying to popular xenophobia.

John Campbell is certainly right to point to significant changes that have taken place in the two decades since the book first appeared. Polarization has increased, government has become dysfunctional, inequality has soared, and racial tensions are all too evident – all factors that he explains with an impressive array of empirical detail. He insists that the United States is on a course of decline, sure to lose international standing under President Trump. It is possible – and to some degree necessary – to accept what he says, thereby taking the easy route of claiming that our book was once right but has been overtaken by events! But I would like to push back a little. For one thing, many social movements still want to get into the American social contract. Remember that the last twenty years has seen the entry of gay people into the mainstream of American life. For another, the basic mechanism of inclusion is still present. Marriage rates between ethnic groups remain high, fabulously high in fact compared to the situation in Europe. But there is something more important. Campbell tends to see class in economic terms. But there are American cultural peculiarities here that need to be taken fully into account if we are to understand, as Campbell wishes, the rise of Donald Trump. An immediate point is that the poor blame themselves for not being successful, and have no aversion to the rich. Many are poor but patriotic, proud of their country (Duina 2018; cf. Hochschild 2016; Isenberg 2016; Vance 2016). What seems to irritate them most is the professional classes consequent on the rise of a service-oriented economy. This class seems to float above their humbler condition, all too inclined to scorn their concerns – to consider them, to use Hilary Clinton's awful but revealing expression, as "deplorable" (Frank 2016; Reeves 2017). And one should remember that Trump's supporters are not always the poorest: particular bite seems to have been lent to lower-middle-class elements suffused with fear that downward mobility is likely in the near future – a particularly shocking fear given that the promise of American (but not European) life is that of self-improvement. All of this goes beyond simple monetary reward. To it one should add on occasion the brutal anti-intellectualism and paranoid style that does have its place within a genuinely popular culture (Hofstader 1963, 1966).

Riga gives us a deeper and nastier part of the explanation. She too notes Patterson's view of the status privilege of whites, but treats it much more systematically. Her brilliant new work on Americanization has discovered that white nationalist ideology was created much later than had been believed, and she makes us realize that it was both more powerful and systematic. Her discoveries are frightening, but in a way not surprising: race remains the crime of American life, as Tocqueville realized long ago. In this regard she is surely right to say that the hope expressed at the end of *Is America Breaking Apart?* – that trans-ethnic lower-class unity might produce political reform – has proved illusory. It was Nixon who began divide-and-rule politics in the postwar period by saying that affirmative action for African Americans was at the expense of white Americans. Trump has done the same, attacking Obamacare on the grounds that it transfers money to blacks. Nonetheless, I am reluctant to accept the complete pessimism implied by her position. For one thing, one should remember that Obama recently gained two substantial electoral victories despite the dreadful effects of the financial crisis. For another, it is too easy to say that poor whites are simply racist and sexist (Williams 2017).

Conceptual Innovations

One of the great privileges of my life has been to see Michael Mann's (2013) *Sources of Social Power* develop and come to completion. I have always thought of him as our Max Weber, and remain in awe of what he has achieved. His concept of infrastructural power has been most influential, though I have a weakness for his concern with caging – and see both as representing the main contribution of his work as a whole, namely its incredible fertility, its ability to help us approach society in novel ways. He offers here a fundamental rethinking of his conceptualization of state power. There is something of an overlap with Lange's opening pages in this volume – both are concerned with techniques of rule, with different social situations at the forefront of their minds.

Mann makes two fundamental points against me. I am inclined to accept the first, that I have been more concerned to see the dangers of state than of capitalist power. There are two reasons for my failure in this regard. The first is that the great disasters of the twentieth century seem to me to be the result of geopolitical conflict, often going to extremes as the result of revolutionary elites driven by ideological convictions. The world wars do not seem to me to have been caused by capitalist actors, few having geopolitical visions of any sort. Second, I had naively thought that the lessons of the Second World War were permanent, that a measure of class compromise was likely to become a permanent part of liberal democracy. Walter Scheidel's exhaustive treatment of inequality has reminded us that moments of equalization have come in the immediate aftermath of mass conscription warfare (Scheidel 2017). Such warfare is no longer present in the most advanced societies. Memories seem to be all too short; much that had been learnt is forgotten. People often forget that Kant's famous essay on peace did not rule out war everywhere, but welcomed its presence outside his liberal league on the grounds that it would remind them of the horror of war. One can note that the costs of Brexit may well give the European Union a new lease on life, a positive development but one that is hard to swallow for a British subject. But neither point can hide my failure to have capitalist power at the centre of my attention – although I have clearly noted how it can destroy life chances, diminish civility, and lead, as already described, to the dangerous desire of society to protect itself against the market (Hall 2015, 247–54).

The second point concerns the nature of state power. I have already admitted to believing that regimes that draw on the energies of the people gain in strength; constitutional regimes in the modern industrial world characterized by high levels of infrastructural penetration were likely, as noted, to be stronger than their despotic rivals. Of course Mann is right to point to particular moments when authoritarian regimes have demonstrated huge capacities. States can be good at different things, and few can rival Nazi Germany in terms of the capacity to kill or the Soviet Union in terms of a brutal drive for victory. Nonetheless, two rather different points deserve to be made about his claim that highly despotic regimes in the modern world can be very powerful.

First, one must add to the defeat of the Nazis, which he notes, that of the Soviet Union. It is hard to maintain mass enthusiasm over time; certainly the Soviet Union's last years were those of stagnation. Much of life seemed to take place against or apart from the state, something that memorably led to Gorbachov pounding the table ordering civil society to come into being! There are, second, further complexities here. Gellner (1967) once claimed that industrialization was likely to rule out democracy, as it had to be forced upon reluctant populations – and accordingly he had a measure of sympathy for figures such as Ataturk who were able to transform their societies, hoping, however, for liberalization after the great jump to the modern world had been made. Barrington Moore veered in this direction when claiming that the human costs of revolution in China might prove to be less than those of the social inaction characteristic of democratic India. It is very hard to make judgments here, but necessary all the same. Scepticism towards the view that revolutions from above are necessary and successful is needed. Senem Aslan (2015) has suggested that the draconian policies of Turkey towards its Kurds have been a failure in comparison to the softer policies Morocco adopted towards the Berbers; it may yet be that the failure to solve the nationalities question in the former affects its long-term economic performance negatively. Then there is the case of Russia. Might it not have industrialized without revolution? Is there not something to be said for the view that centralized power allows enormous mistakes to be made, as Amartya Sen (1981) argued for India and as is surely apparent when reflecting on collectivization? In this context, one must remember the huge numbers of deaths caused by the tragedy of that revolution. The greatest twentieth-century killer was Mao – although here there is a stronger case for arguing that only revolution could have forcibly modernized that society. Mann hates killing as much as I do, so I wonder if he might have qualms about his endorsement of the effectiveness of high despotic power in the modern era. But we should put all this to one side in order to ask whether state power has changed in the last years in a way that strengthens his claim that authoritarian regimes are highly effective. The last chapter of the first volume of *Sources of Social Power* noted continual movement between state and society in regard to the means of power: what was invented in one area could then be used by the other. Most scholars have seen the rise of the internet as a means for society to diminish state power; he sees modern techniques as having the capacity to increase state power, perhaps in this matter being influenced by Kandil (2016).

He may be right, in which case my hopes diminish – though the problem is a political one, not one to do with social class.

Frank Trentmann has long been one of the most original voices writing about civil society and nationalism, as can be seen in his great *The Empire of Things* (2016). To begin with, he problematizes the notion of national identity, showing that feelings of this sort by no means predominate at all times. To the contrary, the refugees entering Germany from the east encountered hostility because their religious and social backgrounds were often very different from those of their host communities. He then goes on to explain the different levels: relatively unscathed and rural Schleswig-Holstein and Bavaria faced the largest influx of refugees, found those refugees very unlike themselves, and felt threatened by the possibility that their property rights might be curtailed. The relative lack of civility shown in these regions is contrasted with the warmer welcome shown in the great German cities that had faced horrific destruction. But his case is a mixed one. Shared language was a background factor that allowed for assimilation over time; intermarriage mattered too, although the precise way in which this worked is interpreted by Trentmann with great subtlety. But the most important point that he makes, derived from his new work on moral change, concerns social action. In this context, he demonstrates the positive role played by religious organizations in helping refugees find their feet in West Germany. But the larger point is that civility should not be taken for granted, as simply the absence of conflict. To the contrary, it has to be established, and fought for actively. He is right to criticize my far too passive view here; and this point leads naturally to concluding reflections.

Conclusion

The editor is right to stress that I have always seen civility as fragile, vulnerable because it lacks deep sociological roots. European societies felt proud of their domestic achievements during the nineteenth century; this did not limit their brutality overseas, nor did it prevent their descent into barbarity at home. As the lessons learnt from catastrophe are fading from memory, is the civility recreated in the postwar world again becoming vulnerable to collapse? Mann's pessimism about the future of democracy poignantly raises this issue. If there is truth here, then another worry comes to the fore. Mann notes my interest in normative matters. But the trouble with normative argument is that it can replace analysis with hope. Might it be the case that the hopes that I have held have been unrealistic?

One does get the impression at present, to use Arnold Toynbee's phrase, that history is on the move again. My own fears can be expressed in two ways. Despite my move away from Gellner I had great respect for his apolitical view that the modern social contract would include science, a measure of irony towards nationalism as it became established, and relative social stability as economic growth allowed for rising living standards. The world does not seem like that now: facts can be trumpeted as "false," economic growth for many has ceased, and nationalism in its new form certainly lacks any sense of irony. Second, the normative point that I have made about civility – that allowing entry can depoliticize, and so ensure stability – depends upon a responsible and intelligent elite recognizing that this is the better way to rule. The empirical record here now gives considerable cause for worry. One interesting study of the American corporate elite makes it clear that the sense of responsibility was closely linked to the lessons of war, and to the need for national reconstruction – and that it has now faded (Mizruchi 2013). Erdogan, Putin, and Trump can scarcely be seen as seeking a better way; all can properly be viewed as irresponsible, condemned for foul behaviour. I did take civility slightly for granted, believing that it could be achieved both through unconscious social processes and by the likelihood of elites choosing a better way.

All of this is to say that civility is once again vulnerable. Furthermore, vulnerability may well be deep seated. Technological change does not seem likely to guarantee mass employment, with all that this means for increasing inequality. Overcoming global warming might require a measure of redistribution on a world scale, a virtual impossibility especially given the position of the United States. Still, one should not give in to complete pessimism. Most immediately, Trump lost the popular vote. Crucially, the absence of war between the greatest powers because of the presence of nuclear weapons rules out – one prays, doing so in current circumstances with some trepidation – any repeat of the situation of 1914. Raymond Aron (1978) was wont to say that hope is a duty. Whilst true, that is insufficient. Active involvement and struggle are needed to maintain and to extend a world of decency and civility.

REFERENCES

Aron, Raymond. 1978. "War and Industrial Society: A Reappraisal." *Millennium* 7 (3): 197–210. https://doi.org/10.1177/03058298780070030201.

Aslan, Senem. 2015. *Nation-Building in Turkey and Morocco: Governing Kurdish and Berber Dissent*. Cambridge: Cambridge University Press.

Bang, Peter. 2008. *The Roman Bazaar: A Comparative Study of Trade and Markets in a Tributary Empire*. Cambridge: Cambridge University Press.

Bayar, Yesim. 2014. *Formation of the Turkish Nation-State, 1920–1938*. London: Palgrave Macmillan. https://doi.org/10.1057/9781137384539.

Bryant, Joseph. 2006. "The West and the Rest Revisited: Debating Capitalist Origins, European Colonialism, and the Advent of Modernity." *Canadian Journal of Sociology* 31 (4): 403–44. https://doi.org/10.2307/20058730.

Crone, P. 1989. *Pre-Industrial Societies: Anatomy of the Pre-Modern World*. Oxford: Blackwell.

Duina, Francesco. 2018. *Poor and Patriotic: Why Poor Americans Love Their Country*. Stanford: Stanford University Press.

Frank, Thomas. 2016. *Listen, Liberal: Or, Whatever Happened to the Party of the People*? New York: Metropolitan Books.

Gellner, Ernest. 1967. "Democracy and Industrialization." *Archives Européennes de Sociologie* 8 (1): 47–70. https://doi.org/10.1017/S0003975600004720.

– 1979. "A Social Contract in Search of an Idiom: The Demise of the Danegeld State." In Gellner, *Spectacles and Predicaments: Essays in Social Theory*, 277–306. Cambridge: Cambridge University Press.

– 1983. *Nations and Nationalism*. Oxford: Blackwell.

– 1997. *Nationalism*. London: Weidenfeld.

Hall, John A. 1985. *Powers and Liberties: The Causes and Consequences of the Rise of the West*. Oxford: Basil Blackwell.

– 2005. "Life in the Cold." In *The Disobedient Generation: Social Theorists in the Sixties*, edited by Alan Sica and Stephen Turner, 129–40. Chicago: Chicago University Press.

– 2011. "Nationalism Might Change Its Character, Again." In *Nationalism and Globalisation: Conflicting or Contemporary?*, edited by Daphne Halikiopoulou and Sofia Vasilopoulou, 17–26. New York: Routledge.

– 2015. *The Importance of Being Civil: The Struggle for Political Decency*. Princeton: Princeton University Press.

– 2017. "Taking Megalomanias Seriously: Rough Notes." *Thesis Eleven* 139 (1): 30–45.

Hall, John A., and John L. Campbell. 2017. *The Paradox of Vulnerability: States, Nationalism and the Financial Crisis*. Princeton: Princeton University Press.

Hall, John A., and Charles Lindholm. 1999. *Is America Breaking Apart?* Princeton: Princeton University Press.

Hiers, Wesley, and Andreas Wimmer. 2013. "Is Nationalism the Cause or Consequence of the End of Empire?" In *Nationalism and War*, edited by John A. Hall and Siniša Malešević, 212–54. Cambridge: Cambridge University Press. https://doi.org/10.1017/CBO9781139540964.013.

Hirschman, Albert. 1978. *Exit, Voice and Loyalty: Responses to Decline in Firms, Organizations, and States*. Cambridge, MA: Harvard University Press.
Hochschild, Arlie. 2016. *Strangers in Their Own Land: Anger and Mourning on the American Right*. New York: New Press.
Hofstader, Richard. 1963. *Anti-intellectualism in American Life*. New York: Alfred A. Knopf.
– 1966. *The Paranoid Style in American Politics and Other Essays*. New York: Alfred A. Knopf.
Isenberg, Nancy. 2016. *White Trash: The 400-Year Untold History of Class in America*. New York: Viking.
Judson, Pieter. 2007. *Guardians of the Nation: Activists on the Language Frontiers of Imperial Austria*. Cambridge, MA: Harvard University Press.
Judson, Pieter. 2016. *The Habsburg Empire: A New History*. Cambridge, MA: Harvard University Press.
Kandil, Hazem. 2016. *The Power Triangle: Military, Security and Politics in Regime Change*. Oxford: Oxford University Press. https://doi.org/10.1093/acprof:oso/9780190239206.001.0001.
Lange, Matthew. 2013. *Educations in Ethnic Violence: Identity, Educational Bubbles, and Resource Mobilization*. Cambridge: Cambridge University Press.
Levene, Mark. 2005. *Genocide in the Age of the Nation-State*. Vol. 2, *The Rise of the West and the Coming of Genocide*. London: I.B. Tauris.
Lieven. Dominic. 2015. *Towards the Flame: Empire, War and the End of Tsarist Russia*. London: Allan Lane.
Mann, Michael. 2013. *The Sources of Social Power*. Vol. 4, *Globalizations*. Cambridge: Cambridge University Press.
McDaniel, Timothy. 1988. *Autocracy, Capitalism and Revolution in Russia*. Berkeley: University of California Press.
Mizruchi, Mark. 2013. *The Fracturing of the American Corporate Elite*. Cambridge, MA: Harvard University Press. https://doi.org/10.4159/harvard.9780674075368.
Patterson, Orlando. 1982. *Slavery and Social Death*. Cambridge, MA: Harvard University Press.
Pliny. 1969. *Letters: Books VIII–X*. Translated by B. Radice. Cambridge, MA: Harvard University Press.
Polanyi, Karl. 1944. *The Great Transformation*. New York: Farrar and Rinehart.
Reeves, Richard. 2017. *Dream Hoarders: How the American Upper Middle Class Is Leaving Everyone Else in the Dust, Why That Is a Problem, and What to Do About It*. Washington, DC: The Brookings Institution.

Reynolds, Michael. 2011. *Shattering Empires: The Clash and Collapse of the Ottoman and Russian Empires, 1908–1918*. Cambridge: Cambridge University Press. https://doi.org/10.1017/CBO9780511762017.

Riga, Liliana. 2012. *The Bolsheviks and the Russian Empire*. Cambridge: Cambridge University Press. https://doi.org/10.1017/CBO9781139013628.

Scheidel, Walter. 2017. *The Great Leveler: Violence and the History of Inequality from the Stone Age to the Twenty-First Century*. Princeton. Princeton University Press. https://doi.org/10.1515/9781400884605.

Sen, Amartya. 1981. *Poverty and Famines: An Essay on Entitlement and Deprivation*. Oxford: Clarendon.

Tocqueville, Alexis de. 1955. *The Old Regime and the French Revolution*. New York: Anchor.

Trentmann, Frank. 2016. *The Empire of Things: How We Became a World of Consumers, from the Fifteenth Century to the Twenty-First*. London: Allen Lane.

Vance, J.D. 2016. *Hillbilly Elegy: A Memoir of a Family and Culture in Crisis*. New York: Harper Collins.

Williams, Joan. 2017. *White Working Class: Overcoming Class Cluelessness in America*. Boston: Harvard Business Review Press.

Wimmer, Andreas. 2013. *Waves of War: Nationalism, State Formation, and Ethnic Exclusion in the Modern World*. Cambridge: Cambridge University Press.

Ziblatt, Daniel. 2017. *Conservative Parties and the Birth of Democracy*. Cambridge: Cambridge University Press. https://doi.org/10.1017/9781139030335.

Contributors

Yesim Bayar is Assistant Professor of Sociology at St Lawrence University, USA. She is the author of *Formation of the Turkish Nation-State, 1920–1938* (Palgrave 2014) and articles in journals such as *Nations and Nationalism, Nationalities Papers,* and *Comparative Studies of South Asia, Africa, and the Middle East.* Her research focuses on nationalism, nation-building in Turkey, minorities, and human rights.

Joseph M. Bryant is Professor of Sociology at the University of Toronto, Canada. He is the author of *Moral Codes and Social Structure in Ancient Greece: A Sociology of Greek Ethics from Homer to the Epicureans and Stoics* (SUNY Press 1996) and co-editor, with John Hall, of *Historical Methods in the Social Sciences,* vols. 1–4 (Sage 2005). He has published in several fields of inquiry, including the sociology of philosophy, military history, Christian origins, the philosophy of the social sciences, social theory and methodology, and comparative world history. His work has appeared in a variety of journals, including the *British Journal of Sociology, History of Political Thought, Archives Européennes de Sociologie, Method & Theory in the Study of Religion, Philosophy of the Social Sciences,* and *Canadian Journal of Sociology.*

John L. Campbell is Class of 1925 Professor of Sociology at Dartmouth University, USA. He has authored or edited numerous books, including *The National Origins of Policy Ideas: Knowledge Regimes in the United States, France, Germany, and Denmark* (Princeton University Press 2014), *The Paradox of Vulnerability: States, Nationalism, and the Financial Crisis* (Princeton University Press 2017), and *American*

Discontent: The Rise of Donald Trump and Decline of the Golden Age (Oxford University Press 2018). Campbell has also authored nearly seventy articles and book chapters and is the recipient of a US National Science Foundation grant and numerous other grants and awards. His interests span economic and political sociology, comparative political economy, and institutional theory.

Francesco Duina is Professor of Sociology at Bates College, USA. He is also Honorary Professor of Sociology at the University of British Columbia, Canada. He has authored several books, including *Broke and Patriotic: Why Poor Americans Love Their Country* (Stanford University Press 2018), *The Social Construction of Free Trade: The EU, NAFTA, and Mercosur* (Princeton University Press 2006), and *Winning: Reflections on an American Obsession* (Princeton University Press 2011). He has also published numerous articles in journals such as *New Political Economy, Social Movement Studies, Economy and Society, Review of International Political Economy*, and *Regulation & Governance*.

John A. Hall is the James McGill Professor of Sociology at McGill University, Canada. He has authored or edited nearly thirty books and one hundred articles and book chapters, and is the recipient of numerous prestigious awards (including the Prix du Québec, the highest honour bestowed by the Government of Quebec in all fields of culture and science, and the Innis Gérin Medal from the Royal Society of Canada, an honour bestowed biannually for distinguished and sustained contribution to the social sciences). He has put forth ground-breaking theories and insights about some of the deepest and most pressing problems facing the world over time and today: war, nationalism and nationalistic movements, ethnic strife, economic crises, the threat to social cohesion in the United States and other advanced countries, and the ability of nations to adapt to the rigours of the international economy.

Matthew Lange is Professor of Sociology at McGill University, Canada. His work focuses on state-building, nationalism, ethnic violence, development, colonial legacies, and comparative-historical methods. In addition to numerous articles and chapters, he has authored *Lineages of Despotism and Development: British Colonialism and State Power* (University of Chicago Press 2009), *Educations in Ethnic Violence: Identity,*

Educational Bubbles, and Resource Mobilization (Cambridge University Press 2012), and *Comparative-Historical Methods* (Sage 2013). He is a co-editor of *States and Development: Historical Antecedents of Stagnation and Advance* (Palgrave Macmillan 2005) and *The Oxford Handbook of the Transformations of the State* (Oxford University Press 2015).

Siniša Malešević is Professor of Sociology at University College Dublin, Ireland. He is an elected member of the Royal Irish Academy and of Academia Europae (the European Academy), and an elected associated member of the Academy of Sciences and Arts of Bosnia and Herzegovina. His recent books include *The Rise of Organised Brutality: A Historical Sociology of Violence* (Cambridge University Press 2017), *Nation-States and Nationalisms: Organisation, Ideology and Solidarity* (Polity 2013), *The Sociology of War and Violence* (Cambridge University Press 2010), *Identity as Ideology* (Palgrave 2006), and *The Sociology of Ethnicity* (Sage 2004). He co-edited *Nationalism and War* (Cambridge University Press 2013) and *Ernest Gellner and Contemporary Social Thought* (Cambridge University Press 2007) and has authored over eighty peer-reviewed journal articles and book chapters.

Michael Mann is Distinguished Research Professor of Sociology at the University of California, Los Angeles, USA. He is an elected member of the American Academy and an elected fellow of the British Academy. He is the author of the four-volume work *The Sources of Social Power* (Cambridge University Press 1986, 1993, 2012, and 2013), nearly fifty articles and book chapters, and several additional books and edited volumes. The recipient of numerous prestigious awards and honours, his work has been the subject of two books: John A. Hall and Ralph Schroder, eds., *The Anatomy of Power: Social Theory of Michael Mann* (Cambridge University Press 2006) and Ralph Schroder, ed., *Global Powers: Michael Mann's Anatomy of the 20th Century and Beyond* (Cambridge University Press 2016).

Liliana Riga is Lecturer in Sociology and Program Director of the MSc in Sociology and Global Change at the University of Edinburgh, Scotland. Her interests are in comparative historical and political sociology, and in particular ethnicity, nationalism, and empire. She is the author of *The Bolsheviks and the Russian Empire* (Cambridge University Press 2012), and articles in *American Journal of Sociology, Nations and Nationalism,* and other leading journals. Her current research is on assimilation, immigration, race, and social inequalities in American nation-building.

Yanfei Sun is Associate Professor of Sociology at Zhejiang University, China. Her work, which focuses on state and religion in China, social movements, and historical sociology, has appeared in *American Journal of Sociology, Pacific Affairs, Modern China,* and other journals. In spring 2106, she was Visiting Associate Professor in the Department of East Asian Languages and Civilizations at Harvard University, USA.

Frank Trentmann is Professor of History at Birbeck, University of London, England. He is the author of *Free Trade Nation: Consumption, Civil Society, and Commerce in Modern Britain* (Oxford University Press 2008), which won the Whitfield Prize from the Royal Historical Society, and of *Empire of Things: How We Became a World of Consumers, 15th Century to the Present* (Penguin/HarperCollins 2016). He has edited fifteen volumes, has authored dozens of journal articles and book chapters, and has been director of the five-million-pound research program Cultures of Consumption, co-funded by the Economic and Social Research Council and the Arts and Humanities Research Council in the UK.

Berna Turam is Professor of Sociology and International Affairs at Northeastern University, USA. She is the author of *Gaining Freedoms: Claiming Space in Istanbul and Berlin* (Stanford University Press 2015) and *Between Islam and the State: The Politics of Engagement* (Stanford University Press 2007), and was editor of *Secular State and Religious Society: Two Forces at Play in Turkey* (Macmillan 2012). She has published articles in journals including *British Journal of Sociology, Nations and Nationalism, International Feminist Journal of Politics, Journal of Democracy,* and *International Journal of Urban and Regional Studies.*

Dingxin Zhao is Professor of Sociology at the University of Chicago, USA. He is also Thousand Talents Professor of Sociology at Zhejiang University, China. He is the author of several books, including *The Confucian-Legalist State: A New Theory for Chinese History* (Oxford University Press 2015) and *The Power of Tiananmen: State-Society Relations and the 1989 Beijing Student Movement* (University of Chicago Press 2001), the latter of which won the American Sociological Association's 2001 Asia and Asian America Section Outstanding Book Award and the American Sociological Association's 2002 Collective Action/Social Movements Section Outstanding Book Award. His articles have appeared in *American Sociological Review, American Journal of Sociology, Social Forces,* and other leading journals.

Luyang Zhou is a PhD candidate in sociology at McGill University, Canada. His dissertation compares the Bolshevik and Chinese Communist revolutionary elites, examining how the old political and social systems were translated into communism. His research interests include empire and nationalism, war and army, and repression and civil society. Some of his findings appear in the journal *Nations and Nationalism*. He is now developing a project analysing the continuities of the Bolsheviks and Chinese communists with their historical precedents.

Index

www.ingramcontent.com/pod-product-compliance
Lightning Source LLC
La Vergne TN
LVHW090149080826
844660LV00013B/738/J

* 9 7 8 1 4 8 7 5 0 2 3 7 9 *